SOCIOLOGY AND SCIENTISM

Sociology
and
Scientism

THE AMERICAN QUEST FOR OBJECTIVITY,

1880–1940

Robert C. Bannister

The University of North Carolina Press

Chapel Hill and London

© 1987 by the University of North Carolina Press

All rights reserved

Manufactured in the United States of America

Library of Congress Cataloging-in-Publication Data

Bannister, Robert C.

Sociology and scientism.

Bibliography: p.

Includes index.

1. Sociology—United States—History. 2. Scientism—

History. I. Title.

HM22.U5B34   1987   301'.0973   86-24985

ISBN 0-8078-1733-3

ISBN 0-8078-4327-X (pbk.)

Dorothy Parker, "Indian Summer,"

The Portable Dorothy Parker. Copyright 1926, renewed © 1954

by Dorothy Parker.

Reprinted by permission of

Viking Penguin, Inc.

95 94 93 92 91   6 5 4 3 2

FOR JOAN

CONTENTS

ACKNOWLEDGMENTS

The research for this study was begun and then substantially completed under two grants from the National Endowment for the Humanities—the first under the Younger Humanists program for 1970–71, and the second under the program for College Teachers for 1979–80 (Category B, grant # 079-7). Swarthmore College has also provided generous support in the form of research grants, marvelous word-processing facilities, and a liberal sabbatical policy. I am especially indebted to William Ryan, Jody Ann Malsbury, and their associates at the Swarthmore Computing Center, whose assistance saved me countless hours in preparing and revising the manuscript.

Because the study took several different directions before assuming its present form, I had ample occasion to visit most of my favorite libraries here and abroad. The incomparable resources of the Bodleian at Oxford, the British Library in London, and the Sterling Library at Yale provided access to the bulk of the published materials, only a portion of which are finally cited. Curators of manuscripts at the university libraries of Brown, Chicago, Columbia, Duke, Johns Hopkins, Michigan, Minnesota, North Carolina, Penn State, and Yale, and at the Historical Society of Wisconsin, bore my endless requests for service and photocopying with unfailing good cheer. I want to offer special thanks to Peter Gottlieb and his staff at the Pennsylvania State University for facilitating my research in the Luther Lee Bernard Papers, and to Jessie Bernard for permission to quote from letters and other materials in this rich collection. Without the earlier work of Luther Bernard, who collected materials for an unpublished history of sociology for more than a decade, this study could never have been completed.

Finally, I am indebted to several scholars who read and commented upon portions of the manuscript: William Dusinberre of the University of Warwick, England; Ross Paulson of Augustana College; and David A. Hollinger of the University of Michigan. If I still haven't got it right, it is not their fault.

SOCIOLOGY AND SCIENTISM

INTRODUCTION

*We, as scientific workers in sociology, are so definitely
launched upon [the] trend toward objectivism and
definiteness of method . . . that it is needless to argue
in its defense.*

Luther L. Bernard, 1919

1

During the 1920s, American sociology found new life in the old idea that the natural and social sciences were (or should be) governed by similar concepts and methods. In one form or another, of course, this idea went back at least a century to Auguste Comte's proposal for a "positive" science of society. Objectivity had been a professional norm since the establishment of sociology as an academic discipline in the 1880s. But a "scientific" sociology was now to be objective in three quite special senses.

First, a scientific sociology must confine itself to the observable externals of human behavior, thus carrying to a logical conclusion the strict inductionism of sensationalist psychology. This goal meant an end to the cataloguing of feelings, interests, or wishes, a principal activity of prewar sociologists. Epistemologically, it rested on the conviction that experience is the sole source of knowledge; ontologically, on a distinction between objects accessible to observation (about which knowledge is possible) and those not accessible (about which there can be no knowledge).[1]

Secondly, sociologists must apply rigorous methods in the production of social scientific knowledge. During the twenties, this injunction occasioned vigorous debate over the *case study*, the *participant observer*, and the *comparative* methods, although by 1930 statistics was the method of choice.[2] And finally, sociologists should observe strict neutrality in matters of ethics and public policy. "Sociology itself passes no moral judgment," the argument went, "and sets up no ethical standards for human conduct."[3]

From these premises, certain predilections followed naturally, if not inevitably. Among them was a focus on individual behavior rather than on the formation and transformation of social structures; an emphasis on an inductive and incremental model of science; and, in the long run, a bureaucratic vision of team research and social science institutes.[4]

This "objectivism," as it was termed, took various forms in the different academic disciplines: in philosophy, the referent linguistics of Charles A. Ogden and I. A. Richards, and later logical positivism; in jurisprudence, the legal realism of Karl Llewellyn and Jerome Frank; in psychology, the behaviorism of John B. Watson, and the craze for educational testing; in political science, the public opinion surveys and other empirical work of Harold Lasswell and Charles E. Merriam; in economics, the institutionalism of Wesley Mitchell.[5] In sociology, it appeared in different forms in the work of William F. Ogburn, F. Stuart Chapin, and Luther Lee Bernard.

Because most social scientists profess a belief in objectivity in some sense, it is useful at the start to distinguish this interwar version of the value-free ideal from earlier and later statements of a similar creed. Prewar sociologists, in fact, thought of objectivity in several ways: first, as deriving from the nature of the subject matter, as in Lester Ward's notion that "pure" sociology dealt exclusively with the consequences of nonpurposive human behavior; second, as the methods used by trained observers, as in Franklin Giddings's increasing emphasis on statistics; and finally, as the attitude of the unbiased observer— the most common use of the term. At the same time, the prewar founders typically qualified these definitions so as to put sociology at the service of society, as for example in Ward's "applied" sociology, or Albion Small's insistence that, in studying human values in an unbiased fashion, the sociologist nonetheless fostered reform. What distinguished the interwar objectivists was the extreme to which they took one or several of these propositions, and in particular, the extreme to which they took the premise that human volition and the subjective consciousness have no place in social science. Objectivity, that is, lay not simply in the lack of bias, but in the elimination of the psychological dimensions of experience and, finally, of the willing, feeling self.[6]

Nor was the positivist conception of value-neutrality the only possible one, as later developments showed. When "value-free" became a controversial term in the 1960s, Max Weber and his American followers were as often the target of criticism as were their positivist predecessors.[7] But the Weberian conception did not rest on the identity of the natural and social sciences. Rather, the gulf between "nature" and "man" mandated different methodologies for studying each, the method of *Verstehen* in the case of human society.

Nor did value-neutrality mean a passion for quantification: from Robert MacIver to Reinhard Bendix, proponents of the first have led battles against the second.[8]

As a distinct episode in the history of American sociology, the interwar objectivists deserve study for several reasons. Their narrow and often rigid definition of science—their "scientism"—was part of a major reorientation of American thought that centered in the years between 1907 and the outbreak of the First World War, when a language of "efficiency" and "social control" gradually eclipsed the humanitarian, moralistic rhetoric of earlier reformers.[9] Objectivism, it will be argued, was a response to a fear of social fragmentation and disintegration that deepened in the years immediately before the war. This fear was especially acute for certain socially marginal individuals for whom the future was troubling and the past irrelevant.

The emergence of objectivism within the matrix of prewar sociology, in addition, provides an important case study of the role of institutions, politics, and personalities in the transformation of the so-called "pragmatic" or "anti-formalist" revolt of the 1880s. In creating their own version of social science, Lester Ward and the other antiformalists had to deal with the central problem of eighteenth-century thought: the attempt to translate the rationalist quest for a unified understanding of experience into an empirical program, and thus to fuse reason and experience, knowledge and utility.[10] Operating within the empirical tradition, they wished to recapture the reformism and incipient holism of the Enlightenment program, *without* the metaphysics that had vitiated empiricism from John Locke to Herbert Spencer. The restatement of positivism in objectivism marked the failure of this program.

Objectivism was also an important chapter in the history of American sociology. Although the names of the leading objectivists soon faded from the professional journals, they exercised considerable influence within the profession in their day and represented an impulse that shaped the discipline long after they had passed from the scene.[11] In Ogburn's case, this legacy included the pathbreaking work of his student Samuel Stouffer in *The American Soldier* (1949), as well as the less well known "social forecasting" of S. C. Gilfillan, and later of O. D. Duncan.[12] For the movement as a whole it also included the propagandizing of George Lundberg, a onetime student of both Bernard and Chapin, whose "operationalism" was a final attenuation of interwar positivism.

Historians generally have ignored this strain in American sociology in favor of the urban sociology of Robert Park and his students, the case studies of W. I. Thomas, and the tradition of social interactionism from Charles Horton Cooley onwards. To right the balance, this study traces the emergence of objectivism in prewar American sociology, specifically in the work of Lester Ward, Albion Small, Franklin Giddings, and William Graham Sumner (chapters 1–7); examines its development in the careers of Luther Lee Bernard, F. Stuart Chapin, and William Fielding Ogburn, three prominent members of sociology's second generation (chapters 8–12); and looks at the disputes their program occasioned within the American Sociological Society during the 1930s (chapters 13–15). My focus is less on the substance or content of sociological analysis (treatments of class or race, for example) than on competing conceptions of the nature and public role of the discipline itself—that is, what sociologists thought social science was in the first place.

2

Within sociology, objectivism appeared in what may loosely be termed "nominalist" and "realist" variants.[13] For William Fielding Ogburn, F. Stuart Chapin, and their allies, a scientific sociology was nominalist, statistical, and advisory; that is, it was concerned with means rather than ends. Because "society" was essentially a name for the collective responses of individuals, sociology should confine itself to the measurement and tabulation of environmental change and of responses to change. Social class, in one of Chapin's better-known studies, could be reduced to a point system for different items of home furnishing, rather than being a matter of self-cum-community perception *or* of power relationships. Studying trends rather than causes, the sociologist qua scientist was limited to the *how* rather than the *why* of public policy.[14] For Luther Bernard, in contrast, scientific sociology was realist and presumptively radical in that it provided an "objective standard of social control" and, hence, absolute standards for social reconstruction. Although Bernard shared the fashionable enthusiasm for quantification, he insisted that true science required a "projective logic," akin to imagination, whereby an ideal state is posited as a basis for further analysis.

In the broad sweep of western sociology, these two versions of objectivism in effect split the legacy of Comtean positivism: the one adopting the emphasis on quantification as the route to positive knowledge, and the other, Comte's utopian program, without the mumbo jumbo of the Religion of Humanity. Closer to home, the objectivists brought into the postwar years the perspectives (and rivalries) of their prewar mentors: Franklin Giddings of Columbia, in the case of Ogburn and Chapin, and Albion Small of Chicago, in that of Bernard—with the important difference that objectivity, for most of the prewar generation, had ruled out neither the study of intentions and desires, nor political and ethical commitment.[15]

During the twenties, the "scientific" sociologists gained power and influence: Chapin at the University of Minnesota, where he became chairman in 1922, and Ogburn at the University of Chicago, to which he migrated from Columbia in 1927. From time to time, the two collaborated in work for the Social Science Research Council (S.S.R.C.) and the Laura Spelman Rockefeller Memorial. Ogburn represented sociology on President Hoover's Committee on Social Trends, while Chapin edited *Social Science Abstracts*, both projects being funded by the S.S.R.C. Luther Bernard, meanwhile—although less close to these centers of power, and increasingly alienated by developments within the profession—championed his version of objectivism, first in the relative obscurity of the universities of Florida and Missouri, then for a decade at Minnesota under Chapin, and then in a series of posts that led finally to Washington University in St. Louis.

During the 1930s, the two versions of "scientific" sociology met head-on in a series of battles within the American Sociological Society (A.S.S.), although the split was one of many and the alliances, accordingly, complicated. In the end, however, neither Bernard nor Ogburn and his allies could claim to have won a significant proportion of the profession to either objectivist program. By the late 1930s the Bernard rebels were in disagreement and disarray, and Bernard himself was increasingly bitter. When Chapin, Ogburn, and others formed a by-invitation-only Sociological Research Association (S.R.A.) to realize their old dream of an exclusive body of truly "scientific" sociologists, Bernard found himself excluded. By 1940 he had declared war on virtually the entire profession in a newsletter called *The American Sociologist*.

Although Ogburn and Chapin continued to enjoy a measure of prestige and influence into the 1950s, their contributions to quantitative sociology were soon eclipsed by those of Paul Lazarsfeld and his associates at Columbia. In the same postwar years, the "grand theory" of Talcott Parsons and the "middle range" work of Robert Merton and his students posed a challenge to positivism more fundamental than any during the early thirties. In light of later developments, the battles of that decade, in fact, had their own irony, because these earlier struggles within the A.S.S. helped break the monopoly of twenties-style "Chicago sociology" only unintentionally to pave the way for an informal Columbia-Harvard alliance that combined the theoretical work of Talcott Parsons and the technical proficiency of a new generation of quantifiers, with the latter in a distinctly subordinate position.[16]

3

To study one of the many strains within a discipline as diverse as American sociology raises three immediate questions: what to call it? how to explain it? and whom to include or to omit? The first is by no means trivial. The terms "empiricist" and "positivist" (or "neopositivist") identify traditions that embrace the entire movement for the more scientific study of society. But "empiricist," in a general untechnical meaning, equally describes almost all interwar American sociologists (including especially Robert Park and his students), if not most American sociology from its beginning. "Positivist" and "neopositivist" are arguably more precise, but have so often been used as derogatory epithets in the past few decades as to lack any meaning they may once have had.[17]

Other labels bear the scars of the battles that spawned them. "Objectivist," the pejorative used by hostile contemporaries, implies a major role for Durkheim, who was at most marginally influential on the figures considered. "Behaviorist" captures the general mood but wrongly suggests a direct tie to J. B. Watson and behavioral psychology, and it ignores the fact that the label itself was polemical. The objectivists themselves spoke blandly of a "natural science" or "scientific" sociology, terms that make up in neutrality what they lack in precision. "Scientism," although also a term of abuse since Friedrich von Hayek first popularized it in the 1940s, better captures the movement's mood—in particular, an often naive faith in the neutrality of scientific method, and a confidence bordering on arrogance that the "modern" American millennium was just around the corner.[18] Bearing these caveats in mind, the present study uses these several terms more or less interchangeably.

The issue of interpretation is more difficult. A catalogue of the many roots of objectivism alone would indicate how complex and deep-seated the impulse was, both in European thought and in contemporary American developments: a partial list includes Comte's sociology, the work of the German Cameralists who inspired Albion Small, the Rankean dictum of history "wie es eigentlich gewesen," the triumph of objective over personal journalism in such papers as the *New York Times*, and even the late-Progressive Era craze for scientific management and I.Q. testing. Its emergence within American sociology, however, has given rise to several more general questions that inform the present study. Does science inevitably and necessarily tend toward greater precision and methodological sophistication?[19] Or were the key factors a social-psychological status crisis associated with the rural or small town, and the predominantly Protestant backgrounds of most early sociologists?[20] Or were they the professionalization and bureaucratization of scholarship?[21] Or the needs and imperatives of corporate capitalism?[22]

Although histories of the discipline abound with answers to these questions, most of them, unfortunately, explain too much or too little concerning objectivism: too much, in that these several explanations apply in a general way to virtually every school within American sociology; too little, in that the questions themselves are not focused sharply enough. In the emergence of objectivism the crucial issue was *not* the development of a ubiquitous "science," but the changing definitions of the term from mid-nineteenth-century Baconianism to the nominalism of the 1920s; *not* simply Protestant moralizing, but a profound disjuncture between present and past that rendered traditional values especially meaningless for key members of the post-Progressive generation who came of age in the years immediately before the war; *not* a ubiquitous process of professionalization or institutionalization, but these processes tempered by individual personalities and institutional histories that differed in significant ways—notably at Columbia and Chicago, the two major centers of early sociology; *not* uncritical or even willing service of an emerging corporatist order, but a gradual, unconscious, and finally ironic transformation of the potentially radical subjectivism of Ward's *Dynamic Sociology* (1883) into programs of social control and a creed of the service-intellectual.

This book is organized around individual careers in the belief that this is the manner in which the interrelation of the above-listed factors can be best understood. The strategy doubtless has risks. Some historians may complain at yet another example of "great man" sociology, especially when the leading actors, with the possible exception of William Graham Sumner, were not really that "great" after all. Others may fault the absence of systematic sampling, content analysis, and the like, and may even resist the notion that objectivity *has* a history. In answer to the first, this study will attempt to show that, when all the institutional and other shaping factors are considered, the creation of American sociology was a highly personal and often passion-filled affair. As to the second criticism, it is precisely the assumptions behind it that are under scrutiny.

A final issue concerns the cast of characters. This study does not pretend to be a complete history of American sociology from the 1880s through the 1930s, or even of all facets of the careers of the individuals considered. Prewar "founders" (Ward, Small, Giddings, and Sumner) are treated primarily as their careers illuminate the roots of objectivism. Among the first generation the most serious omissions are probably Edward A. Ross and Thorstein Veblen, each of whom was arguably closer in outlook to objectivism than any of the founders save Sumner; but neither possessed the organizational force of a Small or a Giddings, or left enough graduate students to constitute a "school" in the sense that these academic empire-builders did.

Among the second generation, Bernard, Ogburn, and Chapin are treated because they were prominent and prolific spokesmen for particularly controversial versions of scientific sociology, and they were active professionally. Others might well have been included. Robert Park and his students, as already noted, doubtless helped set American sociology on the road to a narrower empiricism, as described in two excellent studies of the past decade.[23] Considerations of space alone must be pleaded in the case of two other second-generation leaders: Emory Bogardus, whose "social distance scales" were another example of the 1920s craze for measurement; and Howard Odum, whose Institute for Research in Social Science at Chapel Hill was a prototype of the social science institute. Because both fit the profile of the other objectivists more than has been recognized, this study may indirectly shed new light on their careers.

Also missing, or treated only tangentially, are representatives of a third generation who carried the objectivist spirit into the post-1945 period, notably Read Bain, a Bernard ally who later edited the *American Sociological Review*; Stuart Rice of the University of Pennsylvania, who worked closely with Ogburn within the A.S.S.; Hornell Hart, a professor at Duke; and such younger men as George Lundberg, Samuel Stouffer, and Stuart Dodd, who together deserve a study of their own.

It is worth noting that the quest for objectivity was only half the story, the other half being the notion that personal values and emotions constitute a vast, unchartable realm. Because they were human—and often passionate—beings, the leaders in the fight for a more scientific sociology reflected in their own lives the growing separation of work and leisure, public and private, objective and subjective that was coming to characterize American life and thought. Denying emotion a role in the public self, the most hard-boiled devotees of scientific sociology sought a variety of private outlets for feeling, whether in a special fondness for children (Sumner), in writing poetry or in painting (Giddings, Bernard, and Chapin), or in a quest for exotic travel (Ogburn). Less happily, the pose of disinterested activity in several instances barely masked chaotic inner lives and a penchant for professional infighting that, as one observer remarked, seemed to betray the professional's pretense of superior rationality.

Although to conclude on a personal note is to affirm the pervasiveness of this modern bifurcation of self and profession, a brief statement of my own assumptions may add perspective to what follows. Throughout this study, I have proceeded with mixed feelings concerning the sociologists' quest for objectivity. My early saturation in the idealist epistemologies so popular in New Haven in the fifties, and my later training as a historian, made me from the start suspicious of the objectivists' blatant rejection of custom and tradition, and suspicious also of definitions of inquiry that ruled out passion and commitment in the discovery of truth. At the same time, like most products of American education in the post-World War II era, I was taught repeatedly the virtues of "being objective" in some form or other. During the sixties, I instinctively resisted the charge that objectivity is inherently a mask for the interests of class, gender, race, or modern corporate capitalism. My work on this study has confirmed some of my assumptions, but modified others. Although I remain sympathetic to the desire to define standards for public policy and private behavior that transcend the push and pull of narrow group interests or the self-indulgence of individual gratification, and although I continue to believe that the much-maligned "meritocracy" is superior to possible alternatives, it seems to me undeniable that the glitter of scientism had unfortunate consequences for American sociology, no less than for the careers of its major proponents. Further, scientism expressed the personal needs, while serving the class and professional interests, of some Americans more distinctly than of others, whether this was intentional or not. An awareness of the distinctly historical character of one phase of the movement may be a first step toward reassessing the assumptions that inspired it. A second lesson, unhappily, may be that the founders of American sociology also wanted something different, but that for some reason they failed to achieve it.

1

AN AMBIGUOUS LEGACY

*The fact is that [Ward] makes on almost everybody the
impression that his sociology is essentially archeologic and
static, whereas in his own mind it is essentially dynamic.*

Albion Small, 1903

1

Although Lester Ward is the acknowledged founder of American sociology,
he set the discipline two different agendas. In the first agenda, the starting
point for sociological inquiry is "feeling," because this alone produces social
change. Society being a product of the interplay of social forces, sociology is
more than "fact-gathering": its goal is a radical "sociocracy," not the pallia-
tives that pass for social reform.[1] In the second agenda, feeling is inseparable
from the functions (structures) to which it gives rise. And because dynamic
laws can "only be expounded from empirical data of a statical nature," social
science, after all, consists in the collection and classification of "statistical
facts." By the turn of the century, Ward's dynamic sociology had given way to
a division of labor between pure and applied branches of the discipline—the
first totally unconcerned with "what society ought to be," and the second more
appropriately the province of social technicians than of sociologists.[2]

Lester Ward has had several historical lives, and most accounts have fas-
tened on the first rather than the second of his sociologies. During the 1930s he
emerged as the hero of a tradition that was both humanist and reformist. In the
1950s, he was both criticized for being too speculative and praised for anticipating the hypothetico-deductive method in science. During the 1960s, he was
celebrated for reviving the Enlightenment program of a "man-centered" social
science. Although some sixties critics indeed condemned his calls for "expertise" and "social control," no one has explored the relationship between his two
apparently contradictory views of the nature and goals of the discipline.[3]

A reexamination of Ward's career with reference to the emergence of objectivism focuses precisely on the antipathies in his thought. Was sociology to study feelings and activities (functions), or institutions and customs (structures)? Was Ward's sociology "dynamic," as he himself claimed, or "static," as Albion Small and others finally saw it? Did "scientific method" mandate classification, statistical analysis, or something else?

An attempt to answer these questions requires a close look at the development of Ward's thought from the 1860s until his death in 1913, with special reference to his conceptions of "science" and "social science." From the start, Ward was torn between a radical vision of desire unimpeded by social restraint *and* a deep—if half-conscious—recognition of the destructive potential of such impulses in the absence of order, organization, and authority. In *Dynamic Sociology* (1883), the first dominated: individuals crave pleasure for its own sake, and rightly so; feeling, although directed by intellect and checked by nature, is finally subordinate to neither; sociology is dynamic because it is concerned with this creative force. Ward thus opposed positivism, as he understood the term, and defined science in ways that anticipated similar efforts eight decades later.

But *Dynamic Sociology* was a special product of time and place, in effect combining the Common Sense realism of Sir William Hamilton and British sensationalist psychology with Comte and Spencer, Kantianism, and Lamarckian evolutionism—all with a garnish of German *Naturphilosophie*. So viewed, Ward's early career constitutes a pivotal chapter in the breakdown of the Scottish realism and related Baconian view of science that had dominated American intellectual life since the 1830s.

Despite the majesty of the effort, however, troubling questions would not go away. How did mind evolve from nonmind? Would not anarchic "feeling" make society impossible? Was this doctrine an open invitation to the untutored impulses of agitators? By the 1890s, these questions were impossible to ignore. In his later work, accordingly, Ward stressed social structure and social control. He then found himself, willy-nilly, examining the "statical" aspects of society, while at the same time prescribing a "pure" sociology that cared for neither human intentions nor satisfactions.

Because Ward was primarily remembered for *Dynamic Sociology*, these later developments in his thought had little direct influence on younger objectivists. But his distinction between "pure" and "applied" sociology was nonetheless significant: the first was an early version of the value-free ideal; the second, an anticipation of the methods and assumptions behind the objectivists' call for statistical studies. So viewed, Ward's career provides a necessary starting point for the study of the social, institutional, and ideological factors that shaped American sociology in its earliest decades.

2

Born in Joliet, Illinois, Lester Frank Ward (1839–1913) never forgot his humble origins. Since the arrival of the first Wards in Boston in the 1630s, the family had pushed westward in search of riches that never quite materialized. Ward's father, Justus, was an itinerant mechanic and millwright who moved from New Hampshire to western New York and finally to the Midwest, where he built locks for the ill-fated Illinois and Michigan canal until the coming of the railroad doomed the venture in 1855. Ward's mother, Silence Rolph, the daughter of a New York clergyman of modest literary attainments, was sensitive, cultivated, and intensely religious. Each left young Ward a quite different legacy. From his father, he inherited a vision of nature tamed to human purpose: the end of sociology was the constructive channeling of potentially destructive social forces.[4] From his mother, he received an emotional nature, and a belief in the primacy of feeling. "I love so intensely," he once confessed, "I am like a woman."[5]

Neither parent, however, left him much in the way of family affection. When Justus Ward died in 1857, Lester apparently broke with his mother, and he rarely mentioned her again. When he later petitioned for a job in Washington, he described himself as an orphan, despite the fact that she was still living. "Pride of ancestry," he observed on one occasion, "is a mark of degeneracy." With no past worth mentioning, he sought a future in science, where family background, a classical education, and the right schools were only marginally important.[6]

But what was "science"? Ward's earliest thoughts on the subject came not in a laboratory, but less directly: in school teaching, in a torrid romance, and in reading a philosophical text—experiences that together brought him face to face with the problems of impulse and reason, freedom and order, that were to occupy him for the remainder of his career.

The teaching was first. During 1860–61 Ward taught school to finance his education at Susquehanna Institute in rural Pennsylvania. There he had his first taste of the Common School creed, now three decades old and showing signs of age. In theory, common school reform combined high idealism, scientific pedagogy, and state controls: teacher training and state accreditation were means to the ideal of universal education. In practice, however, it introduced its own stultifying rituals.[7]

Ward knew both the ideal and the reality. "What great end can a small school of common pupils in an obscure country place bring about?" he once asked his students. The answer was not to gain status or fame, but to be a part of the "grand theme" of universal education, and ultimately to achieve a oneness with all humanity.[8] But things looked different when he sat for his accreditation examination, or tried to introduce the latest innovations into the classroom. The "people" and the reformers were hopelessly at odds, he told his classmates in one of several sardonic essays on the subject in the college newspaper. In the popular view, the Common School "literati," armed with their "catalogue of scientific innovations," were figures of mirth. The "ideal" teacher was one who stuck to the textbook, and wasted no time giving explanations or introducing collateral material. If students preferred lengthier explanations, so much the worse for them. "Learn to think. Pshaw." "Successful" teachers must have strong rods, a powerful physical frame, and a capacity for anger "to overcome their chickenhearted sympathies during the process of flagellation."[9]

Although Ward intended this irony as a defense of "scientific innovations," his tone suggested that he was aware that science and popular opinion could well be at odds. Universal education remained the bedrock of his thought; but the Common School creed clearly needed a sounder basis in theory. This basis his sociology would eventually provide.

Ward's courtship of Lizzie Vought, the daughter of a local shoemaker, taught lessons less cerebral but no less important. This time the tension was not between democracy and science, but between feeling and reason. His feeling knew no bounds. Chronicling their romance in his diary, Ward strained for words to express his joy. "O bliss! O love! O passion pure, sweet and profound." But emotion was not enough. Feeling was feminine: like woman, it needed control. The quickening of "mental machinery," he wrote in one diary entry, raised Victor Hugo's Marius "from an effeminate and listless youth" to an "enthusiast for principle." "The manly authority of science," he explained in a different context, was the antidote to the "effeminate incredulity" that accepts ideas merely on authority.[10]

Passion was also risky at a time when birth control was still in the handicraft stage. Consumed by his love, Ward turned for guidance to Hollick's *Physiology*, a birth-control manual of the day. After a night together that produced new intimacy ("all that we did, I shall not tell here, but it was all very sweet and loving and nothing infamous," he wrote), he decided to show Lizzie the Hollick. "How much of it she read I do not know, but she liked it," he confessed. "After that we became more familiar." So also, throughout his life, he preached that intellect and passion together increase happiness.[11]

The Common Sense realism of Sir William Hamilton structured these half-formed conceptions.[12] From Hamilton's *Lectures on Metaphysics* Ward learned that the human mind consisted of intellect, will, and the emotions. He especially liked Hamilton's concept of will, and his image of the human mind as active and striving. From Hamilton he later borrowed the term "conation" (from the Latin *conare*, to endeavor) to describe "the efforts which organisms put forth in seeking the satisfaction of their desires." "By this [faculty, man] is enabled to comprehend the truth of Nature and by this he is compelled to admire the sublime, investigate the unknown and wonder at the marvellous," he wrote in one college essay.[13]

Ward revealed a potential conflict when he referred to nature as both "law" and "unknown." In one sense, nature displayed "a symmetry, a consistency, and a perfection upon which man may as securely rely as upon the successions of day and night." But in a second sense, nature and man ultimately were shrouded in mystery: "The three great Kingdoms of Nature [Man, Earth, Heavens] . . . fill the contemplative soul with awe and astonishment," he wrote. In face of this mystery, humanity would "willingly submit the question [of the nature of things] to the ruler of Eternity." Nature as perfect symmetry and predictable law; nature as unchartable mystery. The first led to a mechanistic positivism, the second to the quest for "deeper and more general truths" of nature and society. Although this contradiction had profound implications for Ward's later view of social science, for the moment he ignored the problem.[14]

3

The Civil War began a new stage in Ward's intellectual apprenticeship. After serving in the Union army, and being seriously wounded at Chancellorsville, he joined the many veterans seeking jobs in Washington. Out of work, with a wife and young child to support, he petitioned Lincoln for a clerkship, and was finally rewarded with a position in the auditor's office of the treasury, the beginning of his career in the federal science bureaucracy. In 1867 he received a B.A. from Columbian University (later George Washington), and four years later a law degree. In 1870, he helped launch the *Iconoclast*, a Freethought paper he edited for the next two years. In these years he also first encountered positivism, and in the process he began to develop his own ideas of what social science was and was not.

For Ward, and for his associates at the *Iconoclast*, "positivism" was initially and primarily a weapon against traditional Christianity. Applying the term ubiquitously to thinkers from Comte to Huxley, he lauded this "rising school," while blasting away at the rock of ages. But Ward's attitude toward religion was actually more complicated than these attacks suggest. In his early teens, he had apparently undergone a conversion experience. In his college essays he referred freely to "the Creator." In Washington Ward and his wife attended church regularly, shopping among denominations as suited their fancy. In the end they settled, not for an atheistic positivism, but for Unitarianism—as a compromise between sentiment and reason, tradition and science, similar to that which Ward would seek in his sociology.[15]

Philosophically, positivism forced the issue between idealism and empiricism, an issue that Hamilton conveniently blurred. Hamilton claimed that we somehow have direct awareness of the underlying "noumena," despite the fact that knowledge is relative to phenomena. In maintaining this position, the Scot (like Herbert Spencer after him) had apparently managed to take both sides in the battle between idealism and empiricism: experience was the source of all knowledge, but one could "sense" something beyond it.[16]

For Ward, as for many of his contemporaries, John Stuart Mill upset this comfortable compromise. In *An Examination of Sir William Hamilton's Philosophy*, and in other essays that Ward read in the late 1860s, Mill insisted that Hamilton's relativism led straight to the very positivism he pretended to eschew. Ward wanted to believe Mill for reasons that had little to do with metaphysics, notably his views on women's rights. He also shared Mill's view that happiness was the rightful end of human activity, and, more importantly, the qualification that this end could be achieved only indirectly.[17] But he also feared and distrusted the skeptical implications of Mill's empiricism. Contrary to the Hamilton he remembered, Mill's Hamilton seemed to him unfortunately to limit knowledge to "facts" narrowly conceived, and so to deny the active mind.[18]

Ward, also like many of his contemporaries, found a way out of this impasse in Kant's *Critique of Pure Reason*. In statements such as "Every effect has a cause," Kant argued, mind imposes order (the "categories") upon experience, but is itself dependent upon that experience. Without categories such as causation, experience is literally impossible, because our conception of experience implies causality. These statements Kant termed "synthetic *a priori*."[19] Although Ward ducked the technical issues, he embraced the Kantian position. "Consciousness . . . is not only all that Sir William Hamilton claimed for it, but it is more," he wrote. "It underlies sensation itself." He also followed Kant in criticizing the current passion for fact-gathering. The "mere fact-gatherers" have their role, he wrote, stressing the need of hypothesis. But more important are the "great systematizers, theorizers, and organizers of the world."[20]

Ward's Common Sense training also shaped his reaction to Comte's positivism, in its way as corrosive as Mill's rendering of Hamilton. As with Mill,

Ward liked Comte for his politics if not for his philosophy, notably his support of universal education and his opposition to laissez-faire. No utopian, despite the activities of some of his disciples, Comte insisted that social progress required order, just as organic life demanded organization. He put sociology squarely in the service of this melioristic vision. But the Frenchman also embarrassed Ward. Ignorant of evolutionary theory, he continued to believe in "fixity of forms." He omitted psychology from his hierarchy of the sciences, and his scientific priesthood was a "chimera."

In the end, Ward handled Comte much as did his fellow Unitarians, accepting his positivism only after conflating it with the British natural-law tradition as represented by Spencer.[21] In the process, he rejected Comte's view of scientific method on at least three grounds: his failure to distinguish final from efficient causes; his view that scientists need not believe in the "reality" of matter but should instead treat it as "merely *phenomena*"; and his discounting of the role of hypothesis. To identify uniformities rather than to search for ultimate causes was, in Ward's view, to remove "all power of explanation." To abandon hypothesis was to ignore "the great principle, which even Bacon recognized, that the most important phenomena of Nature lie deep-hidden within her and are not seen by the average observer."[22]

On this point, Spencer was an improvement, if only slightly, because he at least allowed for efficient cause and hence for rational explanation. But his definition of "force" as a point of resistance was a "pseudo-idea," because it denied the common-sense notion that reality ("the ultimate atom") consisted of bits of stuff that were *really* there. Our "early vulgar impressions are usually erroneous," Ward conceded; but this was not the case with "man's intuitive ideas of the nature of matter." From this "new wild flight of reason," he predicted, there would soon be a return to realism similar to that of " 'Common Sense' [after] the erratic ravings of the idealists and nihilists."[23]

Although Ward attacked religion in the *Iconoclast*, and had already moved beyond the Baconians philosophically, these references to Bacon were significant in that his strategy for legitimating science within the confines of American Protestant culture resembled the Baconian one in an important respect. Science, in promising to uncover nature's "deep hidden secrets," rested on certainty of knowledge rather than, as for positivism, certainty of method (the position a majority of objectivists would later adopt).

Ward's qualifications of positivism also explain the nature and limits of his interest in statistics during his fourteen years at the Bureau of Statistics (1867–81). Although the experience was not a happy one personally, it put him in contact with some leading social scientists, including Francis Amasa Walker, the political economist, and Alexander DelMar ("the miserable DelMar," Ward called him), a bimetallist who had recently edited the Spencerian *New York Social Science Review*.[24] Ward's major responsibility was an annual compilation of immigration statistics, which he later modestly judged "undoubtedly . . . the most important information on the subject . . . that has ever been published in this country." This same pride resurfaced in his view of sociology and its public role. Scientific method *was* statistics, he wrote at one point: the Bureau was the model for all "scientific lawmaking."[25]

Why, then, was *Dynamic Sociology* not the source of later interest in the use of statistics in sociology? The answer lay again in Ward's belief in the reality of natural law. He conceived of statistics, not in terms of correlations and distributions, but as proof of the regularity of law and the reality of causation in human affairs no less than in the cosmos. He thus had little interest in what positivists since Hume had termed "constant conjunction." His serial compilations of immigration figures were barely "statistical" in any modern sense.[26]

Nor had Ward any interest in probability theory or the law of chances. When actual events seemed to defy expectations based on normal laws of cause and effect, they were "coincidences." This concept fascinated him throughout his life, conveying, as it did, a sense of the complexity of the universe without abandoning the certainty of law.[27] Despite his temporary romance with statistics in the late 1860s, Ward continued to believe that classification was the key to scientific method. Such was the method he employed as his work in the government shifted to botany and paleontology. And such was to be his approach to social forces in his sociology.[28]

4

During the 1870s, Ward's life took another important turn. In 1872 his wife Lizzie died suddenly of appendicitis. "This sad event threw a gloom over his life," he later wrote, as if of a third person, "and left a blank never again completely filled."[29] Compulsively, almost inexplicably, he proposed marriage that same summer to a New York widow after a single chance meeting and was married the following spring. Already disillusioned with the law, he was meanwhile at work on a master's degree in botany and zoology. Sustained by loans, by money from his new wife, and by her ambitions for his career, he joined a growing body of Washington naturalists, including John Wesley Powell, under whom he served at the Smithsonian.

Against this background Ward at last discovered Darwinism. Despite his praise of Huxley and Darwin in the *Iconoclast*, his world view remained remarkably pre-Darwinian until 1873. Then, in a flurry, he plunged into the work of Darwin, Huxley, Spencer, Bagehot, and even Ernst Haeckel, whom he pronounced "more Darwinistic than Darwin himself."[30] Given the enormous literature on the subject, however, it is important to state clearly what Darwin's lesson for Ward was and was not: it was *not* a simple belief in "evolution," because Ward had insisted on the reality of change since his college days; nor, at the other extreme, was it a selectionist vision of social struggle, a view he later developed from sources quite independent of Darwin.

Rather, Darwin forced Ward to think more deeply about science and scientific method. Although often ignored, Darwin's challenge to nineteenth-century ideas of science was scarcely less basic than his challenge to traditional concepts of the nature of man, or to the doctrine of Providential design. To many mid-Victorians, natural selection seemed to abandon a mechanistic view of law in favor of what one critic termed a law of "higgledy piggledy," that is, no law at all. Selectionism also failed to provide a "true cause," as the term was understood—substantially the charge Ward leveled at Comte. Finally, in abandoning the vitalism of Lamarckian biology, the *Origin* appeared to make the environment all-important, a road, some said, that led directly to behaviorism.[31]

Contemporary debate on the issue offered Ward three choices. In the first, Darwin-the-humble-investigator was the model Baconian. In the second, popularly identified with Asa Gray of Harvard, evolution replaced "creation wholesale" with "creation retail," a position that salvaged both the Creator and a mechanistic natural law. And in the third, and most extreme, natural selection depicted law in probabilistic rather than mechanical terms.

For different reasons, Ward rejected all three. Given his view of "fact-gatherers," the first was hardly attractive. The second, in effect, denied natural selection, which Ward saw to be the heart of Darwin's contribution. The third, which he encountered in the writings of Alexander Winchell and C. S. Peirce, ruled out his search for "true causes," which in social terms were willing, feeling individuals.[32]

Fortunately, however, at least two other theories of the day suggested strategies whereby natural selection might be translated into a theory at once mechanistic *and* voluntaristic. One was Lamarckianism as filtered through Spencer's *Principles of Biology*. Unlike Darwin himself, Ward accepted not only Lamarck's view that environmentally-produced modifications are passed to offspring, but also the corollary that organisms are able to will such changes to the extent of being in the right place at the right time.[33] Applying this theory to human evolution, and attempting to reconcile Lamarck and Darwin, Spencer outlined a two-tiered process whereby natural selection ("indirect equilibra-

tion") operates among animals and in primitive human society, while Lamarckian modifications ("direct equilibration") play an ever-greater role at
higher levels, being "mainly direct" among "civilized human races."[34]

In *Dynamic Sociology*, this distinction answered the question of how "subjective desires" (feelings) serve the "objective" needs of survival. Individuals
act solely to satisfy desire. Nature *selects* those acts that serve its own ends, the
preservation of the race. Subjective desire thus gives rise to objective social
forces that act in two ways: indirectly, in serving the needs of nature; directly,
in altering the environment immediately to serve the needs of humanity. Still
following Spencer, Ward assigned far greater value to the latter: direct action
(as in reform) was a true cause, while the indirect operations of nature were
not.

Ward made similar use of Ernst Haeckel's doctrine of the vital force or
nisus. Synthesizing Germanic *Naturphilosophie*, materialism, and finally
Darwinism, Haeckel fashioned a radically naturalistic monism, tempered by
the apparently contradictory view that atoms have souls.[35] In a review of
Haeckel's *Genesis of Man* in 1877, Ward accordingly drew two lessons. The
first was a materialistic monism. Haeckel's theory that "ontogeny recapitulates
phylogeny" (the view for which he was best known) proved that a single
process operates throughout the universe. A second lesson was that a *nisus* or
life force suffused the entire evolutionary process, an elaboration of Lamarck's
view that organisms willed their biological destinies.[36] A backdoor traffic with
German idealism continued to be an important factor in Ward's sociology. Just
as he had turned to Kant and now Haeckel, so he later found similar ideas in
Schopenhauer's concept of "will" and in Hegel's "self-activity."

The achievement of *Dynamic Sociology* lay precisely in Ward's success in
avoiding extremes. Human freedom was to be realized through organization
and control: a scientific social policy was to be devised to take account of the
irrationality and unpredictability of human behavior, and a sociology created
that was at once reformist and scientific. At the heart of this vision lay the
conviction that the subjective and creative impulses of humanity are no less
amenable to scientific study and understanding than are their external manifestations.

5

During the 1890s, the assumptions that supported this synthesis came under
attack both from the "new psychology" of Wilhelm Wundt and the later
functionalists *and* from the neo-Darwinism of August Weismann and his

disciples. Meanwhile, social unrest, mounting disorder, and the institutional-ization of sociology weighed against the entire notion that a radical subjectiv-ism would produce the ideal society. The decade thus marked the turning point from Ward's "first" to his "second" sociology.

The "new psychology" dealt the first blow. As psychology enjoyed a vogue similar to that of biology two decades before, Ward realized that his view of "mind" as highly organized matter was inadequate.[37] Whereas Wundt's theory of introspection (*Selbstbeobachtung*) allowed the trained scientist to observe directly the modes and laws of perception, Ward had instead brought subjec-tivity into the realm of science by reducing consciousness to its physical components. Wundt promised scientific laws while treating consciousness qua consciousness, that is, without reducing it to nonmental phenomena.[38]

Measured against the functionalism of William James and John Dewey, Ward looked even worse. Attacking the mind-body dualism at its roots, James rejected the reductionism of British psychology *and* the mentalism of the German tradition.[39] Turning the attack on James himself, Dewey in "The Reflex Arc Concept" (1896) criticized the conventional notion that stimulus begets ideas that in turn beget responses. This sort of analysis made an ongoing process into a "patchwork of disjointed parts," Dewey argued. Rather, stimulus and response describe temporary events within an overall act of "coordination" between organism and environment.[40]

Hoping to update his own psychology, Ward in *The Psychic Factors in Civilization* (1891) turned again to the German idealist tradition, this time in the person of Arthur Schopenhauer, whose *The World as Will and Idea* (1813) he had read in a literary club two years before. Schopenhauer's *Wille*, he now insisted, was the driving force at the root of all life, similar to Haeckel's *nisus* but more clearly mental.

The reviewers, however, were not persuaded. From an essentially Wundtian perspective, the economist Simon Patten argued for a franker dualism between psychic and physical, and a recognition of the "subjective environment" (cus-toms, traditions, and values) as a source of progress.[41] John Dewey, in con-trast, faulted Ward for clinging to traditional dualities: between sensation and idea; between desire (as remembered sensation) and the object that satisfies it; and between feeling (whether pleasure or pain) and the action to which it gives rise. Ward's psychology was an unhappy marriage of Locke's sensationalism and Schopenhauer's theory of the will, Dewey charged. Unable to transcend these dualities, Ward failed to see a third benefit in the satisfaction of desire: *psychologically* for the individual, in pleasure (for example, in eating); *func-tionally*—or really structurally, because this was what Ward meant—in meet-ing the needs of nature (for example, in building the body); and *totally* for

society, in that individual action to satisfy desire results in material transforma-
tions that benefit neither the individual, nor nature, but society as a whole (for
example, in the creation of a network for food production and distribution).[42]

Despite their own differences, both critics presented an alternative to the
individual-nature opposition: Patten, in the idea of "subjective environment,"
akin to later notions of "culture"; Dewey, in the evolution of a truly social
intelligence. For the economist, the payoff was the importance of invention
and the abundance it provided; for the philosopher, the socializing functions of
education. Ward's picture of the permanent antagonism of man and nature, as
Dewey observed, led instead to the conclusion that an increase of intelligence
would only "bring the conflict into clearer relief," forcing a choice between the
ends of the individual and of society—a choice later behaviorists and social
controllers eventually made.[43]

Although Ward responded to the two reviews, he learned from neither.
Already squabbling with Patten over the review policies of the *Annals* of the
American Academy, he took comfort in reports that others agreed Patten's
position was "absurd."[44] Although he had already made a brief foray into
James's *Principles of Psychology*, he confined his comments to "Bosh" scrib-
bled in the margin. To Edward Ross he lamented that his own point of view
was "so different from everyone else's that I rarely find anything I can use." He
vowed to study psychology more systematically once *Psychic Factors* was
finished; however, although he culled a few quotations from James and others,
that hope was unfulfilled.[45]

The neo-Darwinists meanwhile challenged Ward's scientific assumptions.
Positing an inviolable germ plasm, and rejecting Lamarckian use-inheritance,
August Weismann and his disciples presented would-be reformers a Hobson's
choice: either work directly to improve the human "stock," as in eugenics; or
adopt a conception of culture and personality totally independent of biology.
Ward's reactions to the new psychology had already made it clear that the latter
was beyond his grasp, while eugenics seemed to him to deny the basic premises of his program of reform through education.[46] Spiritually and professionally, Ward's sentiments were with the neo-Lamarckians, as they were now
called.[47] But unlike many reformers, he could not reject neo-Darwinism out of
hand. He had, after all, identified selectionism as the essence of Darwinism,
and he knew that many prominent British scientists supported neo-Darwinism,
including Alfred Russel Wallace.

As a result, he equivocated. In a speech before the Biological Society of
Washington in 1891, he praised neo-Darwinian selectionism as an argument

for the intelligent control of evolution, and even toyed briefly with eugenics. But if the neo-Darwinians were right, "education has no value for the future of man," he wrote in the *Forum*. Lacking conviction, he turned finally to whimsy. Posing as the neutral observer at a quarrel of experts, he concluded that, until the "doctors of science" could agree, mankind might just as well "hug the delusion" of hereditability. Although struggle and selection played an increasing role in his sociology, due largely to his discovery of the work of Ratzenhofer and Gumplowicz at the turn of the century, he remained ambivalent toward neo-Darwinism. In mid-1894, after listing "Weismann's Concessions," he dropped the scientific debate entirely.[48]

The full impact of neo-Darwinism on Ward's sociology, however, came as he wrestled with Thomas Henry Huxley's *Evolution and Ethics* (1894) and Benjamin Kidd's *Social Evolution* (1894), two attempts to apply Weismann's insights to society. Attacking Spencer (although not by name), Huxley argued that cosmic evolution and human ethics were permanently at odds. Ethical progress depended "not on imitating the cosmic process, still less in running away from it, but in combatting it." Although restraining individual self-assertion, ethics ultimately weakened society in its struggle for existence. As a solution, Huxley offered only a "larger hope" that "intelligence and will, quickened by sound principles of investigation," might somehow improve the conditions of existence for the present generation.[49] Playing David to Huxley's Goliath, Benjamin Kidd insisted that progress of any kind demanded the operation of unmitigated competition, selection, and survival. For those individuals thus eliminated, the process was senseless: religion offered the mass of mankind the only sanction for progress, enjoining the faithful to subordinate personal interests to an otherwise unfathomable good.[50]

Of the two, Kidd the popularizer ironically had the greater effect on Ward. After ignoring *Evolution and Ethics* for several years, Ward finally decided that Huxley said nothing that he himself had not said first, conveniently overlooking the fact that the Englishman was at best skeptical of the sort of reform Ward proposed.[51] In contrast, he gave a sympathetic lecture on *Social Evolution*, sent Kidd offprints of his work, and as late as 1898 termed the "tone" of the book "generally healthy."[52]

Two different considerations underlay this enthusiasm. One was the mounting fear of social disorder. Ward instinctively liked Kidd's insistence that a narrowly egoistic intellect could be as socially destructive as was unchecked feeling or will at early stages of human development. In the America of the mid-1890s the point was more than academic: utilitarianism fed a corrosive struggle among individuals and groups; socialism promised to stop it at society's peril. Despite Kidd's talk of an *ultrarational* sanction in religion, he looked to some higher efficiency (which he later termed "the struggle for the life of the future") that was neither individualist nor socialist.[53] The second consideration was tactical. Before public opinion soured on Kidd, *Social Evolution* seemed not only a prop to Christianity, but a proof against the charge that sociology was irreligious, handy at a time when Albion Small (by now Ward's chief patron within the university world) was assuring his students that *Dynamic Sociology* was not harmful to their faith.[54]

Ward revealed his new debt in 1898. Although he continued to deny that religion was an "instinct" ("religion is rational through and through"), he now admitted that it was *analogous* to instinct in that it checked the destructive urges of the egoistic intellect, just as mind had checked feeling and instinct had countered will at earlier stages in the evolution of the human faculties. The sexual impulse, for example, if pursued egoistically, would result in a socially destructive promiscuity. By organizing "marriage systems," religion established and sanctioned "the family relation upon which society so largely rests." For rational beings, religion was the substitute for instinct among irrational beings. Like instinct, religion looked to function (i.e., structure), the objective end of nature; its purpose was to secure order.[55]

Aside from pleasing Small, this concession had two important implications for Ward's sociology. First, in identifying yet another mechanism of restraint, he gave greater attention to "social control," a term then entering the sociological lexicon thanks to Edward Ross.[56] In *Pure Sociology*, Ward added law and government to his list of necessary social constraints, according them a permanency he had been reluctant to admit in his more radical days.[57] Secondly, he admitted that even dynamic sociologists must study social structures and institutions. Human achievement remained the subject matter of sociology— but his use of the term "achievement" vacillated between achievement-as-activity and achievements as the products of activity; achievement as function, and as the resulting structures.[58] Although this line was easy to cross, the result at the extreme was significant. In the first meaning, the subjective self is the moving force in history; in the second, individual activities are conditioned by objective social structures external to the self.

6

Thus was the stage set for Ward's final two books: *Pure Sociology* (1903) and *Applied Sociology* (1906). With a characteristic sense of occasion, he announced the project at a gathering of prominent Washingtonians at his home on January 1, 1901 (the "first day of the Twentieth Century"). The guests included leading government scientists and bureaucrats, among them, John Wesley Powell, Assistant Secretary of State David Jayne Hill, and Carroll D. Wright, United States commissioner of labor. Ward announced that he planned first to write a "pure" sociology, followed by a study of the applied aspects of the field. The first would appeal to scientists already attuned to the pure-science ideal in their own disciplines; the latter, to those such as Hill and Wright who were more concerned with practical applications.[59]

In his first volume Ward went immediately to this distinction. Pure sociology dealt with genetic or "non-telic" phenomena "unaffected by the purposeful effort of man and society itself." Applied sociology treated "telic" and "artificial" products. Pure was thus theoretical, while applied was practical; pure was ethically and politically neutral, applied was concerned with the means of changing society.[60]

Although Ward's definitions were rooted in the pure-science ideal of the 1870s and 1880s,[61] they also reflected his experiences of the previous decade. Philosophically, the idea of a genetic or non-telic realm had overtones of Huxley's universe unconcerned with human values.[62] At the policy level, pure sociology combined the bureaucratic ideal of disinterested service with a developing distinction between theory and practice within academic sociology. Whereas in Ward's early work, "static" and "dynamic" were two dimensions of *theory*, this conflation implied that theorists (that is, sociologists, as opposed to whoever would apply their findings) had no concern with social well-being. Together, they implied that objectivity derived from both the nature of the subject matter *and* the attitude of the observer, a conclusion that anticipated the position of some of the leading objectivists two decades later.[63]

The pure-applied distinction also betrayed the fundamental ambiguity in Ward's concept of "achievement"—as activity (function), and as institutions or custom (structures). While it was one thing to see the first as giving rise to the second, it was quite another, as one critic later commented, to identify the activity with the things it produces. To do so was akin to a grammarian's expanding the definition of "noun" to include all verbs because action results in objects. This confusion cut across the others in that it sometimes seemed that pure sociology was concerned with structures (nouns), applied sociology with functions (verbs).[64]

Pure Sociology thus left more questions than it answered. If pure sociology was value-neutral in the nature of its subject matter, and in its approach, how to explain Ward's endorsement of "collectivism" at the book's close?—a "delicious lapse," as Small observed, from his pretended objectivity. And what should be made of his apparent encouragement of freer sexual expression, a portion of the book that seemed to invite trouble? ("[The] frank treatment of the subject of 'natural love' . . . exposes the teacher who would place the book in the hands of a mixed class of immature people to criticism which would be nonetheless damaging because undeserved," counseled Ross.)[65] The fact was that *Pure Sociology* dealt with both telic and non-telic phenomena, and was scarcely neutral in its treatment of them. The problem was compounded when it came to applied sociology. Was it to be confined to study of human psychology, and social forces in the Wardian sense? And if so, as one younger sociologist wondered, would it provide "the best results in the way of social control and direction" in the absence of an understanding of the non-telic customs and institutions that govern human behavior?[66]

These questions surfaced almost immediately in a tiff with Small that followed the publication of *Pure Sociology* and almost ended their relationship. The trouble began with the assignment of the review of *Pure Sociology* in the *American Journal of Sociology* (*AJS*) to a young psychologist who attacked the book soundly, particularly Ward's conception of science. "Magical phrases" such as synergy and creative synthesis were not enough to demonstrate that spiritual phenomena are as natural as physical ones, the reviewer insisted.[67] Ward in turn concluded that there was a plot to "freeze out" the book. "My own opinion is that the owners of the University of Chicago have issued their instructions to give it the cold shoulder, and Small has not the courage to disobey it."[68]

Although Small assured Ward that he was not responsible for the review assignment, he responded with a series of "Notes" in the *AJS* that made things even worse. Resurrecting the charge of unresolved dualisms, Small noted that Ward's terminology itself betrayed him. Although the emphasis on achievement suggested the existence of free will, Ward repeatedly spoke of function (structure) in a mechanical way that denied it. More seriously, he confused phenomena *and* the study of them, subject matter *and* the attitude of the observer. Small himself believed that the social scientist should be a neutral observer, but should study the purposeful activities of individuals in society. The discipline would thus serve the cause of ethics and social reform, without losing its scientific character.[69]

The upshot was a curious exchange in which Small and Ward accused each other of abandoning reform. When Ross, in an attempt to placate Ward, suggested that it was a trifle unlikely that the entire University of Chicago viewed his work as a "menace to property or the Standard oil monopoly," Ward replied that Small's "four snivelling attacks" were "the sort one might expect a penny a line newspaper reporter to make against a book."[70] Small in return charged that Ward's sociology was not only reactionary but old-fashioned: "Indeed, the query may be raised whether he is not to be classed as a philosopher rather than a sociologist." Years later, when some of the scars had healed, Ward remembered that Small had attempted to read him out of the profession.[71]

What was the truth behind these mutual accusations? In a sense, Ward's ambiguities had come home to roost: his defense of feeling and fear of its consequences, his social (even sexual) radicalism and civil service neutrality, his pietism and his positivism. The radical subjectivism of *Dynamic Sociology* was potentially more threatening to the status quo than was Small's use of "interests" as an explanatory tool. But the value-neutral protobehaviorism of Ward's later work seemed to put sociologists out of the reform business altogether. Although the Standard Oil Company was probably *not* trying to get Ward on any blacklist, progressives of Roosevelt's stripe were more likely to find in Small's "interests" a blueprint for their pragmatic pluralism than in Ward's portrait of the radical disjuncture between man and nature.

Although *Applied Sociology* was to be the proof of the pudding for those who questioned Ward's commitment to reform, the book turned out to be surprisingly narrow in scope. Defending universal education against the hereditarianism of Francis Galton and others, and relying heavily on a work by an obscure French professor named Odin,[72] Ward argued that the relatively great concentration of genius in certain French provinces from the fourteenth through the nineteenth centuries could not be explained by such external factors as climate or population density, but was the result of a superior "educational environment." Where factors such as urban life made a difference, it was because they served an educational function. Ward confessed that his own philosophy of education had at first been "a sort of intuition." But Odin's statistics showed "how such strictly social questions may be reduced to a rigidly scientific treatment."[73]

Concerning the nature and role of a scientific sociology, however, Ward remained in a quandary. To critics of his "non-valuing attitude," he stressed the "ethical character of all science." Citing Bacon and Comte, he attacked sociologists such as Durkheim who "affected to see in sociology a science without a purpose."[74] But privately he had some second thoughts. "To judge from the number of reminders of that promise that have come from all sources," he wrote in a preface he finally omitted, "it might be inferred that nobody cares for science in and of itself, and all that is wanted is some sociological panacea that promises to cure all the ills of society."[75]

Some reviewers hailed *Applied Sociology* as a contribution to the literature of educational reform,[76] but the more perceptive noted that its message and method were curiously at odds. The message was the importance of human achievement; the method was one that proved the efficacy of education by showing statistically that no other factor would explain relative concentrations of genius. Although education was duly defended, this placing of schooling on a par with population density or climate opened the door to precisely the behaviorist pedagogy that Edward Lee Thorndike and others were pioneering at Columbia. Significantly, a protobehaviorist critic of the "social forces error" a few years later noted that in *Applied Sociology* Ward effectively dropped his emphasis on social forces in order to focus on the "conditioning environment" and how it could be modified. If *Pure Sociology* had betrayed its own distinction between non-telic and telic, *Applied Sociology* compounded the difficulty by reducing both to conditioning factors.[77]

Ward's defenders rightly claimed that there was a good deal more to his sociological legacy. His conception of evolution as "sympodial" rather than linear anticipated a similar conclusion then emerging in anthropology. His view that free will is not incompatible with social determinism looked to later "action theory," however much his system differed from the Parsonian one. His attack on the empiricist-positivist tradition resurfaced in discussions of the philosophy of science four decades later.

But this legacy was at best ambiguous. When Ward died in 1913, Albion Small praised his early work lavishly, but characterized the later studies as "scientific anticlimax." Ross noted that the Nestor of their discipline had mellowed in his views and become "very gentle with the honest holders of ancient beliefs."[78] In fact, this shift in emphasis was more profound than Ross suggested. A sociology that had begun with subjective desire now admitted the pure study of non-telic forces. A program of individual liberation somehow became a call for greater social control. A quest for a scientific method that might probe dimensions of reality closed to mere empiricism yielded to an apparent celebration of statistics.

In retrospect, it appears that various aspects of Ward's life and career together help explain the gradual emergence of what has here been termed his "second" sociology: a social marginality that left him with little sense of tradition or community; exposure to the positivism of Mill and Comte at the high tide of its influence; his own work in statistics; and the intellectual and social upheavals of the 1890s that finally rendered his radical subjectivism intellectually indefensible and politically suspect. Yet related factors also explain why the objectivist side of his thought developed so belatedly and incompletely: the strength and vitality of Common Sense realism and the natural-law tradition; an openness of intellectual life that allowed a still-amateur sociologist to shop freely in philosophy and literature; and, of course, his unflagging faith that education could and must make the world a better place. In the world of academic sociology, the world of Small and Giddings, the situation would be significantly different.

2

THE SOCIAL ORGANISM

I hereby utter my antemortem *statement that I have nothing
to regret in my connection with the biological analogy.*

Albion Small, 1910

1

Objectivity was one of Albion Small's favorite words, but he used it in several different ways. Used in one way, a legacy of his German training, it meant a substantive grasp of experience in its totality, a holistic understanding that transcended the limited perspectives of any one individual or group. In a second, it derived from the techniques that scientists used as they went about their work, as in the Rankean dictum that the scientific historian must verify by original documents, preferably official ones. In a third, it meant raw observation without bias; thus, Chicago professors could study the trusts "just as objectively as our botanists study flowers," despite the bequests of John D. Rockefeller to the university. For the first Small, sociology was the philosophical master of the social sciences; for the second and third, it was the disciplined empiricism that characterized "Chicago sociology" long after he had passed from the scene.[1]

Politically, Small also equivocated, resolutely seeking a middle ground. In the mid-nineties he rejected "radicalism" of all varieties in favor of the Chicago Civic Federation, an organization that some later historians have pictured as embodying the corporatist ideal of Rooseveltian progressivism. On the eve of the First World War, he flirted with socialist ideas while denying the label. At the start of the postwar Red Scare, he inveighed against the ruthlessness of Bolshevism and "fantasies of Lenin," while warning that class conflict threatened American society unless the churches took constructive action.[2]

These twists and turns did not diminish Small's influence within the profession. Although scarcely an original thinker, and great only by the standards academics apply to their own kind, he was unofficial dean of the profession from the mid-nineties until the outbreak of the war. Appointed at the University of Chicago in 1892, he chaired the sociology department for three decades. In 1894 he coauthored the first American textbook in the field, and later published prodigiously. After the establishment of the *American Journal of Sociology* in 1896, he was its editor during a period in which it had a virtual monopoly. Active in the formation of the American Sociological Society, he served as its fourth president.

Small's reputation, then and later, nonetheless reflected the tensions and ambiguities in his thought. Giddings of Columbia warned his students against the philosophical pretensions of a sociology that claimed to coordinate all other social sciences. Former students and younger colleagues at Chicago faulted Small for not being sufficiently empirical, while Small himself, in repudiating his early use of the "organic analogy," half agreed. By the time of his death in 1926, many saw his armchair theorizing as an anachronistic survival of a benighted sociological age. By the 1940s, however, yet another generation saw him as the progenitor of pragmatic realism who left the Chicago school a solid legacy in the idea of the "group as a tool of research"; in the concept of the social "process"; and in stressing "facts as they are."[3]

Small's politics likewise spawned conflicting interpretations. Albert Keller at Yale thought him to be the worst example of western windiness and social mush-headedness. Luther Bernard, in his own quest for an objective standard of social control, considered him not radical enough. During the 1930s, Harry Elmer Barnes pictured him as a "relentless" critic of "unmitigated capitalism." During the 1960s, he emerged as both a model for a genuinely radical sociology *and* a model of "liberal syndicalism."[4]

On one point, however, most recent commentators have agreed: Small, to an unusual degree, experienced in his own career the shaping forces of late-nineteenth-century intellectual life: the move from small town to metropolis, from old-time college to university, from seminarian to academic, from Common Sense philosophy to German historicism. In so doing, he met head-on the central dilemmas of his age: science versus moralism, professionalism versus reformism, specialization versus a comprehensive view of man and society. In the attempt to create a sociology at once empirical and idealist, Small effectively domesticated Ward's doctrine of "feelings," bringing sociology into line with the moderate perspectives of progressive reform. Whereas Ward's universe was one of irreconcilable opposites (feeling and function, individual and society, applied and pure sociology), Small's was a place in which all dichotomies dissolved—or so he hoped. The result was something less than a success. To the radical sociologist Ernest Becker he was finally a tragic figure, caught between a radical vision of his discipline and the demands of the profession. To Vernon K. Dibble, he was simply a victim of his own success. In either view, the outcome was the same: the profession he helped to create abandoned his program for sociology.[5]

Nevertheless, for this very reason Small's efforts at synthesis constitute a critical link in the transition from Ward's social evolutionism to the anti-theoretical positivism of the interwar period. These efforts, as will appear, mark four rather distinct stages in his career: first, his use of the "organic analogy" in *An Introduction to the Study of Society* (with George Vincent, 1894); second, his adumbration of "process" theory in *General Sociology* (1905); thirdly, a last attempt to restate his vision for a unified social science *and* a socialist society in *The Meaning of Social Science* (1910) and *Between Eras* (1913); and finally, a mounting disillusion that ended with the conclusion that, since much of what passed for "science" was only a fragment of the truth and a cloak for self-interest, sociology should confine itself to "techniques." The first of these stages is the subject of the present chapter.

2

Born in Buckfield, Maine, Albion Woodbury Small (1854–1926) grew up in a region his ancestors had settled more than two centuries earlier.[6] Although neither wealthy nor famous, the Smalls were comfortable by nineteenth-century standards. In 1872 young Albion entered Colby College, where his father had also studied prior to entering the Baptist ministry, and of which he was later the first alumnus or son of an alumnus to become president. This nest of comfortable associations left its mark on his sociology. Unlike Ward or the later objectivists, Small instinctively believed that society was a natural and relatively unproblematic state, a thing to be observed rather than dissected through arcane methodology. "I am known to everybody in Maine," he wrote the University of Chicago in 1891, explaining his reluctance to leave his native state, "& to nobody in Illinois."[7]

At Colby (B.A. 1876) and at the Newton Theological Seminary (1876–79), Small remained relatively immune to the scientific debates that were reshaping the world of Ward and Giddings. Baptist ministers held authority, not by virtue of superior training or priestly prerogative, but by their ability to evoke practical, observable responses. The Baptist creed, however paradoxically, disposed many parishioners to assume that because experience was the best test of truth, science and religion could not be opposed. Theologically, Small thus accepted "science" without first rejecting Calvinism. The result was a theological liberalism that assumed, without much worrying, that evolution altered the traditional accounts of Creation in no fundamental way. Just as the Baptist test of faith was empirical, so Small's sociology began with the assumption that subjective desire and objective behavior are united in observable "interests."[8]

These convictions found support in the Common Sense moral philosophy and the Baconian ideal of science. As a student, and later as president at Colby, Small absorbed and dispensed liberal doses of this philosophy in the senior-year course in "Mental and Moral Philosophy," the capstone of nineteenth-century American collegiate education. This course, in turn, served as model for his view that sociology, in addition to being empirical, was the master, or coordinating, social science. Modern universities, he later complained, "are putting students off with a list of uncorrelated courses instead of giving them a unified view of life," a function earlier served by the senior course. The only "thinkable substitute," he observed, "must be some version of sociology."[9]

Like most educated Americans of his generation, Small traced modern science to Bacon, even though in his early textbook he appeared to conflate Roger and Sir Francis. "Objective knowledge of society was impossible until the sciences that dealt with simple combinations had developed the objective method," he told students. Comte built on this method, but was seriously flawed. Sociology's ultimate goal was to identify, not simply the facts of society, but a social unity that for the moment lay beyond direct perception.[10]

At Leipzig and Berlin (1879–81), and later at Johns Hopkins (1888–89), Small encountered the German ideas that were proving so exciting and unsettling to many of his contemporaries. Politically, the sweeping reforms of Bismarckian socialism inspired various radical visions. Intellectually, the historicist tradition in history and philosophy raised the spectre, on the one hand, of limitless speculation concerning an unfolding world spirit, and, on the other, of the worship of particularistic research, a rendering of the Rankean program especially popular at Johns Hopkins.[11] Although Small was apparently unfamiliar in these years with the work of the historical economist Gustav Schmoller, who arrived at Berlin soon after he left, Schmoller's battle with Carl Menger in 1883 anticipated later debates between the historical school and the marginalists in the United States, and, by extension, Small's still-later disputes with Franklin Giddings. At issue was social science methodology. For Schmoller, theory required a basis in history, supplied by the collection of experiential and historical facts; for Menger, theoretical research that aimed at a knowledge of the universal was equally valid.[12]

During the Hopkins years, Small again met the twin perils of German historicism in the work of the constitutionalist Hermann von Holst (later a colleague at Chicago). He faulted von Holst's work on two grounds: first, for his attempt to impose a monolithic spirit of nationalism derived from the German experience upon the events of the American Revolution; and second, for his particularistic conception of research. Von Holst was, "after all, only a German scholar of the type so nearly constant in the present generation that variations are conspicuous," Small wrote in 1888. As a result, the discipline of history was becoming "microscopic at the expense of the power of judgement."[13]

In the end, Small weathered his first exposure to the German storm. Personally, his German stay gave him a wife (the daughter of a general), a Bismarckian dignity that bordered on pomposity, and a taste for imperial efficiency that found ample scope in university affairs. Intellectually, it prompted him to restate the case for a middle ground between speculation and fact-gathering, the thrust of both his early teaching at Colby and his Hopkins doctoral thesis, *The Beginnings of American Nationality* (1890). Challenging the "folklore" that American nationality appeared full-blown with the Constitution, he argued that this feeling developed gradually, starting in the mid-1770s, from "interests" that were social as well as economic, the "thought and feeling without which written constitutions are simply words." Small's method involved the painstaking collection of data—but his resulting view of the American past was hardly less inspiring than most popular histories of the day, not an "economic interpretation" such as Charles Beard would later present.[14]

At Johns Hopkins, Small also saw that academic specialization posed its own threat to his vision of the unity of knowledge. Nominally, the social sciences were organized under a single department, headed by the historian Herbert Baxter Adams, and the social scientists shared their work in a monthly "Historical Seminar." But the institutional reality was different. Although Hopkins authorities made numerous overtures to "social science," as they understood it, sociology got short shrift. A proposed alliance with the American Social Science Association in 1879 never materialized. Monthly seminars rarely dealt with purely social topics. When *Dynamic Sociology* was reviewed at one meeting of the Historical Seminar, Small later remembered that Richard Ely was the only faculty member who had heard of Ward's book. After 1885, instruction was dominated by Amos G. Warner, a charity expert who proposed to make the field "scientific" through the collection of statistics and other data.[15]

"Ideally, the Hopkins arrangement . . . corresponds most nearly to the unities of the situation," Small later wrote to Ely. "Practically we all know the disadvantages of that organization, from the viewpoint of all but the head of the department." Chicago, by comparison, would turn out to be even worse: it "divides departments so that many students never see that the departments are still actually concerned with one and the same subject matter," he wrote to Herbert Baxter Adams from the perspective of a decade. Although Hopkins remained a model for his conception of the unifying role of sociology among the social sciences, Small clung to the ideal in face of mounting evidence of its unworkability.[16]

By the time Small finished his formal education, he had encountered conflicts that concerned him one way or another throughout his career: between religion and science, speculation and fact-gathering, a unified world view and academic specialization. Among intellectuals of the 1880s he was hardly alone in facing these issues. What distinguished Small was his apparent equanimity: by a happy coincidence of birth and circumstance he approached each issue with the sure conviction that a middle ground could always be found.

3

When Small was appointed professor of sociology at Chicago in January 1892, the university was less than two years old and not yet open to students. A bold dream, it rested on a legacy of Baptist piety and the Rockefeller oil fortune. Although a chair in sociology was already in the works at Columbia, Small's professorship was the first in the United States. His annual salary of $7000, the norm at Chicago, broke records in a market where the most distinguished professors made several thousand less. The position seemed to be everything Small wanted: a Baptist institution dedicated to the highest standards of scholarship; a potpourri of extension activities that put sociology at the service of society; and an empire of "affiliated courses" to feed his ambition to be a coordinator of the social sciences.[17]

Chicago's President William Rainey Harper and Small were made for each other. Born in New Concord, Ohio, in 1856, Harper was almost exactly Small's age. He was a graduate of Muskingum College, with a Yale Ph.D. in Hebrew and Biblical studies acquired at age eighteen, and had had little contact with the social sciences; but his training and career disposed him to moderation on the controversial issues of religion and science, liberal education and professionalism. While no relativist, he supported the new Biblical criticism. He was a member of the faculty at Denison in the late 1870s and converted to the Baptist faith. During the eighties he worked actively for

Chautauqua, an adult education movement that served to link scholars and laymen until the turn of the century. In 1886 he joined the faculty at Yale, the most conservative of the new universities.[18]

Although Harper's reasons for choosing Small remain murky, the decision to found a separate department of sociology was half an accident. In economics, Harper wanted a Hopkins man in the historical tradition; he thus angled for Richard Ely to offset the classicism of J. Laurence Laughlin, the Harvard economist who was appointed in December 1891. In history, Harper tried to tempt H. B. Adams of Hopkins; the post eventually went to Hermann von Holst, with whom Small had already disagreed, but Adams meanwhile suggested Small for the history position. Harper judged Small not qualified in history; however, he clearly liked him. But for what position? Small had issued a syllabus in sociology for his Colby students, but he was scarcely a sociologist, even as then defined. Nevertheless, that was the position he was offered. In accepting his appointment, he suggested facetiously that he hoped to hire Francis Wayland, Francis A. Walker, Samuel Dike, and Ward—two economists, a reformer, and one sociologist—a hint that he had no clear idea of his mandate. The field, in short, was wide open for whatever definition of sociology Small wished to devise.[19]

As former president of Colby, Small also had the administrative experience to coordinate a polyglot empire that included ministers and social workers, students of "sanitary science," and the affiliated work. His department was actually four sections in one: (a) Anthropology, under Frederick A. Starr (later assisted by George Amos Dorsey, a Sumner student from Yale); (b) Sanitary Science, directed by Marion Talbot, combining personal and public health, urban housing, and home economics; (c) the training of ministers through the Divinity School, where Charles Richmond Henderson offered work in the "3 D's"—delinquents, defectives, and dependents; and (d) Sociology proper, where Small was assisted in the early years by George Vincent and William Isaac Thomas.

Moreover, Small was a Baptist. Although the subject never explicitly entered the negotiations, Small's faith was a decided plus. A Colby-made-good, the new university was reared on the foundations of an older Baptist college (also called the University of Chicago). Its principal patron and its early supporters were Baptists, and its site committee included the head of the Newton Theological Seminary. In early dealings with Harper, Small subtly leaned on the religious connection. Strong work in social science would make Chicago a better Baptist school, he wrote in late 1891.[20]

The position promised an ideal marriage of theory and practice, scholarship and social activity. "The City of Chicago," boasted an early catalogue, "is one of the most complete social laboratories in the world." The university's links with the outside world included an extension program of off-campus lectures, evening and correspondence courses for workers, and library extension; the formal support of settlement work, including Hull House; and informal participation in the work of Chautauqua, which continued to provide Chicago professors with summer jobs. The extension staff featured Edward Bemis, an already-controversial economist, and Charles Zueblin, a socialist who became one of the program's most popular lecturers. After several years, Small urged even closer cooperation with the University Settlement, and opened the pages of the *American Journal of Sociology* to social workers.[21]

In most regards, Chicago was thus the perfect place for someone of Small's intellectual disposition. Relatively young, and recently rebuilt, the city wore its problems on its sleeve to an extent that most older ones did not, an open invitation to the sort of empirical work that early became a Chicago trademark. The practical needs of social and settlement workers confirmed this tendency. At the same time, Small's polyglot empire and a curricular openness at the university encouraged a broader, interdisciplinary conception, if only as a matter of survival.[22] Yet in the early nineties, several problems lay just over the horizon: interdepartmental bickering; social turmoil and a protracted academic freedom battle; and a new round in the debate over evolution that even Small could not ignore. Against this background, he turned to the "social organism" and "biological analogies."

The result was *An Introduction to the Study of Society* (1894), which Small coauthored with George E. Vincent. Designed for university students, the text was also intended for popular use in Chautauqua, of which Vincent was then vice-chancellor. After crediting Comte with founding sociology, and praising the Baconian method of induction, the authors turned to the elaboration of Spencer's theory of the social organism, as developed in Albert Schäffle's *Bau und Leben* (1875–78). Posing as a "laboratory guide," the work attempted above all to convince students that a social unity lay beyond their powers of observation. Ostensibly reformist, it also warned against the dangers of radicalism.[23]

At the book's heart was the analogy between organisms and society. On this point, however, the authors walked a tightrope. To the strict Baconian, analogy was fraught with danger. But analogy was necessary as "hypothesis" (anathema to the strict Baconian) to reveal facts and relations otherwise hidden. Biological analogies were really symbols of a higher reality, the authors insisted, quoting Spencer. "They are devices of speech hit upon to suggest a truth at first dimly perceived, but which grows clearer the more carefully evidence is examined." They thus repudiated a "literalism which identifies the social body with physical organisms." But they agreed with Spencer that somehow there was "a real analogy between an individual organism and a social organism."[24]

For several reasons, Small's version of the biological analogy was an ideal strategy for the time and place. First, it answered mounting criticism of the university from left and right. Critics to the left charged that "Rockefeller's University" was a bastion of reaction. G. Stanley Hall of Clark later ascribed Harper's difficulties in recruiting faculty to the university's reputation as "a 'Standard Oil' institution." On the right, potential donors feared professorial radicalism. Extension lectures to nonuniversity audiences, such as those offered by Bemis and Zueblin, were special nightmares to administrators who internalized the fears of patrons with a fervor exceeding the original.[25] A vision of social unity, grasped prematurely by intuition or deduction, led to utopianism. The organic analogy, if applied literally and strictly, would stifle all change—but a unity dimly perceived through the welter of daily events was a spur to cautious activism.[26]

Secondly, biological analogies provided a trademark to distinguish sociology from nervous competitors, economics in particular. A squabble over the appointment of Edward Bemis was the first of several incidents to strain Small's relations with the economist Laughlin. In late 1894, another broke out concerning the teaching of statistics, Small's embrace of which might have set Chicago sociology on quite a different path. But biology proved the way out: "[Because] of the attempt to separate biology here from economics," Bemis wrote to an associate in 1894, "[Small] must bend his greatest energy to developing biological & other not strictly or even indirectly economic phases of social science."[27]

Finally, Small's particular version of the biological analogy allowed him to reconcile the different concepts of science and objectivity that coexisted in his thought. Analogies, on the one hand, were "methods"—the organic conception was simply "a working tool, a useful instrument" through which the social scientist could understand the "social facts." But on the other hand, they provided a glimpse of the social unity.[28]

The reviewers, unfortunately, complained on all three counts. Politically, organic analogies led straight to socialism, suggested the economist Simon Patten. Pedagogically, another charged, they were unsuited to university instruction, however colorful. "The attempt to make one book for the college classroom and for Chautauqua is a mistake," chided Giddings; "it inevitably results in a book for Chautauqua." Finally, analogies, no matter how vivid, were not science. Small's method was precisely the opposite of that employed in a genuine social science, wrote a reviewer for the *Nation*. A science of law or political economy was possible only through *abstraction*: the consideration of activity by viewing humans solely as "law-obeying" or "wealth-producing animals." "A synthesis of the whole would not be science," the reviewer concluded; "it could be the work only of omniscience."[29]

4

During the next few years, three separate developments drove these lessons home. The first was the case of Edward W. Bemis, an Ely student from Hopkins whom Harper hired to teach economics soon after he appointed Small. Harper engaged Bemis to teach extension courses over the objection of J. Laurence Laughlin, who grudgingly allowed the younger man a single course in his department each year. Small became involved in the case in August 1893 when Laughlin asked Harper to remove Bemis entirely, or at least to transfer him to sociology. The next January, Harper attempted to ease Bemis out entirely, offering as reason the poor enrollments in his extension classes. After Bemis refused, and further offended the authorities by championing the striking Pullman workers, Small was gradually drawn into the fray.[30]

Although every aspect of the case had two sides, it would appear, after all hairs are split, that a quieter Bemis might have survived. Despite denials from the university, his opinions *were* at issue. Harper acknowledged pressure from potential donors, and feared that Bemis might cost the university much-needed funds in a critical period of development. In a joint statement that effectively sealed Bemis's fate, Small and the extension dean based their case on a distinction between statements made in university and extension classes *and* before the "promiscuous audience" at the time of the Pullman strike. They thus argued that "freedom of teaching" was not at issue—rather, they condemned Bemis's "untimely and immature" (that is, politically unacceptable) public statements.[31]

For present purposes, the interest of the Bemis case lies, not in the rights and wrongs, but in the conflicting conceptions of social science that surfaced during the debate. Bemis and Laughlin had in fact begun this debate during an hour-long discussion in 1891, when the older man was still at Harvard. The subject was the merits of the "English" and "historical" schools, then in bitter contention. Although Laughlin admitted that the English economists had sometimes been "pigheaded" in their defense of laissez-faire, he charged the newer school with mindless induction. "[Laughlin's] own method," Bemis later wrote to Ely, "was to start with premises & use facts & history & statistics copiously for verification, but not as the chief groundwork of a composite collection of material or something which he seemed very much in doubt about." Laughlin's devotion to "science," so defined, ruled out membership in the American Economic Association or any organization with a constitution "save love of truth."[32]

At Chicago, Laughlin translated his objections to Bemis's politics into a question of scientific method. "I do not see how we can escape saving ourselves," he wrote to Harper as the affair reached its conclusion, "except by letting the public know that [Bemis] goes because we do not regard him as up to the standard of the University in ability and scientific methods."[33] Anticipating this sort of argument, Bemis had earlier ridiculed Laughlin's view of science in a letter to Harper of February 1892. "His remarks 'axiomatic' on necessity of 'scholarship,' the desire for truth for its own sake, etc. are either meaningless or impertinent," Bemis charged. "They sound exactly like the attitude he has always assumed toward Ely, and must have been used with meaning." (In fact, Laughlin's concern was not entirely "truth for its own sake." At the time of Bemis's Pullman remarks, he was trying to interest the railroads in the university.)[34]

Until Bemis went public, Small supported him within the bounds of tact and diplomacy.[35] But by early 1895 there were signs that this support was crumbling. Although still claiming Small's support, Bemis wrote Ely that Small had wondered why the extension teacher was "before the public" more than Harper or "even myself," a remark they both interpreted as evidence of Small's "jealousy." When Small finally turned against him, Bemis dated his opposition to a conversation in which Ely told Small that the university "would suffer" if Bemis were dismissed. By August 1895, Small was unequivocally in Harper's corner. In the joint statement with the extension dean, Small endorsed Harper's view that Bemis was not "strong enough" for a university post.[36]

Small by this time feared that Bemis's "mythical martyrdom," as he now termed it, was the focus of efforts to destroy the university. But his turnabout also reflected his emerging view of what should and should not constitute academic sociology. Describing the issue, Bemis had earlier writtten to Ely: "Small held that the fundamental courses had been provided for [in sociology] & such courses as I mentioned—viz. trades unions, cooperative building and loan associations, profit sharing, life insurance, population, factory legislation, immigration—were too special to be fitted for University instruction, but I could write splendid scientific books on them." At issue was the same distinction between theoretical and applied sociology that influenced Ward. For the time being Small evaded the issue, and identified as "bad teaching" work that was probably fine for its purpose. He continued to boast that Chicago was an ideal "laboratory" for social science. But he retreated to a more transcendental view of social theory that consigned the raw materials of everyday life to instructors unfitted to teach real "sociology." Thus, the Bemis case pushed Small further toward "theory," and toward a transcendental conception of "science" that he had initially rejected in his German student days.[37]

Small articulated this position in a revealing discussion with Bemis in the midst of the fray. Sociologists had two choices, he argued, given prevailing prejudices against the discipline: they could become narrow specialists, or grand theorists. "[In] these days a man is not considered scientific who claims to speak on more than one small corner of a subject," he insisted. Here "scientific" meant narrow, the sort of work he later told Bemis was "too special" for the University of Chicago, but "splendid" for "scientific books." The use of the word "small" suggested his negative view of such work. To avoid specialization, and yet to allay popular "misapprehension of sociology as a series of reforms," Small said he himself was "now going off in [his] lectures into transcendental philosophy so as to be as far as possible from these reform movements and thus establish the scientific character of my department"—scientific, that is, in the second and more universal meaning. The divorce of theory and practice, of transcendental understanding and fact-gathering, was in no sense complete by the turn of the century. But once opened, this gap would be difficult to close.[38]

The formation of the Chicago Civic Federation in 1895, against a background of increasing social tension, led Small further to reassess the nature of his discipline and the scholar's public role. In the opening issue of the *AJS* in January 1896, he praised the Civic Federation as a model, not only of reform, but of scholarship. As a vehicle for constructive reform, the federation represented "a most important advance along natural lines of progress in our city." As a model for "transcendental" science, it also suggested an answer to Bemis and to the university's critics. The division of labor, in making economic life territorial and international, diminished the individual's sense of "dependence upon physical conditions." As a result, more emphasis was placed on "subjection to human devices" and "advantages to be won by personal combinations," that is, on technology and organization. Socially, the unfortunate consequences of this were the clash of groups "promiscuously perplexed by each other's presence" and, even worse, a fragmented vision in dealing with these conflicting interests. Likewise, the enemy within sociology was also fragmentation, the "splendid specialism" Small saw as the bane of the profession. "Analytic and microscopic scholarship is abortive without the complementary work of the synthetic scholar who builds minute details into comprehensive structures." The need was a "federation of scholarship," which, like its civic counterpart, would promote the common welfare. The *AJS* perforce would be "technical," but it would not deal with "fossil facts" *or* reforms as such. Rather, facts *and* reforms would be set within the context of "a just and adequate social philosophy."[39]

The modern university was the institutional embodiment of this transcendental perspective; the professional scholar, its agent. Discussing "Scholarship and Social Agitation," Small stressed that the scholar was somehow able to substitute the "interests of men" for his personal interests.[40] Discussing "Academic Freedom" in the *Arena*, he applied this analysis to the Bemis case: "The university professor is so placed that he cannot easily see facts that tend to confirm the social claims of one interest without at the same time seeing the facts that present the counterclaims of other interests. He is consequently not free to be fractional in his judgements." Private universities, endowed by beneficent capitalists, were uniquely suited to this mission. Businessmen who gave money to universities were unlikely to "muzzle" professors, Small reasoned. "If they were bigoted and intolerant, and unwilling that the truth should come out, they would use their money in other ways." In fact, they opposed only "partialism posing as science."[41]

If Small's facts were debatable, his search for a "super-perspectival social science" (to use Vernon Dibble's phrase) was a special product of time and place. Seeing Bemis and others punished for sympathizing with the interests of a particular class, social scientists such as Small shifted their loyalties to a class-above-class, claiming that their interests were those of "all men."[42]

The neo-Darwinist debate of the mid-nineties provided a final reason to jettison the "biological analogies" of the *Study of Society*. Until the Fundamentalists revived the issue in the twenties, Small rarely mentioned Darwin or his work. In his Hopkins thesis, he had charged in passing that "great man" theorists ignored evolution, for in his understanding the latter theory ruled out cataclysmic change. Otherwise, he appeared to make the rather extraordinary assumption that the *Origin of Species* made no difference. Development theory in biology merely extended the insights of German historicism. "In their own way, historians have arrived at a perception of fact which they might have given the name evolution," he wrote. On the eve of the battle between neo-Darwinians and neo-Lamarckians in the early nineties he confessed to Ward that he was "poverty-stricken in the rudiments of Biology."[43]

By forcing the issue of natural selection, however, Kidd and Huxley presented the issue in ways that even Small could not ignore, and his reaction was predictably cooler than Ward's. Huxley's concept of "evolutionary ethics" was being used to deny an ultimate standard of morality, and any authority beyond our individual wills, Small charged. Restating a basic premise of the Common Sense philosophy, he urged all Christians "to answer that the moral order of the universe is no more a product of man's reflection upon that order than is the physical order of the universe."[44]

Small also distinguished "evolution" from Darwin's particular version of it, a popular strategy among those who shared his outlook. "For myself, I don't believe the evolutionary hypothesis is anywhere near its final form in details, but I have no question about the substantial correctness of its essential idea," he wrote Ward. "The Darwinian categories 'struggle for existence,' 'survival of the fittest,' [and] 'natural selection,'" he added later, were "guesses about details" and not "oracles of the substance of nature itself."[45]

In later years, Small refined this distinction into two readings of Darwin, and of science itself. In effect, there was a bad and a good Darwin: the bad one made "guesses" that Huxley and others elevated into a cosmology; the good one demonstrated continuity and constancy in nature. Science also had two meanings: the "methods" (i.e., theories) that produced the "specialisms" Small condemned; and, "in its utmost perfection," a means of grasping "all reality as it is reflected in the omniscient mind."[46]

Small's obvious uneasiness nonetheless colored his attitude toward all biological analogies. Although he initially ridiculed Simon Patten's charge that the organic analogies led to socialism, he capitulated to a mounting consensus that "biological sociology" had unfortunate ethical and social consequences. In 1897 he charged that Spencer's alleged "principles of sociology" were really "supposed principles of biology prematurely extended to cover social relations." At the turn of the century, he wrote defensively to Richard Ely: "We place no stress on the biological analogies which most of our critics have found so offensive in our book, but we use them for all we ever intended to maintain they are worth." But it was clearly time to get out of the biology business.[47]

By 1905, Small was ready for a "confession." Although still defending the "symbolic" use of analogies, he measured progress in the discipline "by gradual shifting of effort from analogical representation of social structures to real analysis of social processes." Taken "symbolically" they might still express an underlying social unity. But without their aid, the unity of things seemed somehow more a matter of faith, a position the Common Sense moralist could accept only with difficulty.[48]

Whatever its shortcomings, the organic analogy had expressed Small's convictions that there was a wholeness in society no less than in the cosmos, *and* that evidence of this unity was given in experience. "Self-serving" in that it legitimated a new priesthood of professional sociologists,[49] it also had roots deep in his Baptist faith and his early training in the Common Sense philosophy. "Conservative" by some standards, it represented an attempt to steer between a series of extremes that Small had been trying to avoid since the late 1870s: on the one hand, Rankean particularism, curricular fragmentation, and Bemis's promiscuous empiricism; on the other, von Holst's Germanic world spirit, the mere piety of many "Christian sociologists," and the socialists' pie-in-the-sky utopianism. In the new century, he would miss it more than he realized.

3

FROM TELOS TO TECHNIQUE

It is a terrible scandal in the scientific household to have too much vision at once.

Albion Small to Hugo Munsterberg, 1909

As matter of fact, Small now speaks more frequently about objective standards and objective point of view, and other objectives than he used to speak about Sabbath Day's journeys.

Edwin Sutherland to Bernard, 1912

1

During the first decade of the new century, Small was at the height of his power and prestige. His close relationship with William Rainey Harper made him a force to contend with at the university. In 1904, he became dean of the Graduate Division, a position he kept until 1924. His status in the profession also grew steadily. In 1904 he was a key organizer of the Sociological Section of the St. Louis Exposition, the occasion of Max Weber's only visit to the United States. In 1905, he published his theory of "interests" and the "group process" in *General Sociology*, a book that for a time promised to provide the discipline a new paradigm.

But things gradually soured. After Harper's death in 1906, Small's power within the university was never quite what it had been. A concerted effort to reestablish unity in the social sciences on the basis of his distinction between "Science" and "science" ran afoul of growing attacks from within and without the discipline. A rebellion among graduate students on the eve of the war, the war itself, and radical changes in the personnel of the department contributed to a growing doubt as to whether "science," after all, was more than whatever techniques scientists employed.

General Sociology grew from a seminar Small first offered in 1898 when the synthesis of his *Introduction to the Study of Society* was coming unraveled. After criticizing his early mentors Spencer and Schäffle, he provided a synopsis of the views of Gustav Ratzenhofer, whose theory he pronounced almost identical to his own.

At its heart were three related concepts that henceforth were to be *the* subject matter for all sociology: "interests," "association," and the "social process."[1] "Interests" were the building blocks of society. Six in number, they comprised nothing less than the cause of "all the acts which human beings have ever been known to perform": health, wealth, sociability, knowledge, beauty, and righteousness. Like the atoms of physical science, interests were not immediately observable. Rather, they were a convenient starting place for investigation. They were at once subjective and objective, the wanting of something ("an unsatisfied capacity") and the thing wanted. The term was thus used in two ways: to describe human desire (similar in this regard to instinct); and to refer to the complex of objects desired (for example, as in popular reference to the "business interest"). In combining a psychological and a material component, Small again took the middle road, sidestepping the battles of mind and matter, dualism and monism, that had divided sociologists for a decade or more.[2]

In seeking to satisfy different interests, individuals come in contact with others, first in "collisions," but eventually in ever more comprehensive "association." Each separate interest is in itself insatiable—but within the individual, and then within groups, interests check one another. Thus, "individuals enter into more or less persistent structural relationships" called institutions, which in turn channel activity "into certain more or less permanent directions of effort, which we may call social functions." These structure-functions then lead to new conceptions of interest (for example, in family, clan, or nation). Increasingly complex permutations and the cross-checking of interest by interest produce more comprehensive forms of association. Small called this activity "the social process." Groups rather than individuals are the fundamental units of sociology, he concluded, stating what was to become the central tenet of Chicago sociology in the prewar years.[3]

Just as the concept of "interests" combined the subjective and the objective, so Small's formulation of the "social process" hid an important ambiguity. At times, the term referred solely to the *form* of the activity, without content or purpose. This usage echoed the work of Georg Simmel, and was a view of social interaction that led directly to behavioristic definitions of the social process (although at other times, Small was less rigorous and equated process with a temporal "becoming" or growth, a definition that readmitted the idea of progress and related values).[4] His formulation was not without a price. Henceforth, the focus would be on *how* things occurred, rather than *why*. Description of relation and interaction replaced the search for causation and meaning. Process theory, in stressing how over why, thus marked a step on the road to transactional analysis and political behaviorism.[5]

Politically, these formulations suited the more moderate mood of post-1900 progressivism. The idea of process provided a metaphor to express the unity of society without the negative connotations of the now-discredited organic analogy.[6] The theory of interests likewise supplied a theoretical basis for the image of university scholars as a class-above-class: the quest for knowledge was alone self-transcending in that it might be "without reference to any ulterior end."[7] In practice, this formulation effectively removed the sociologist from the public arena. The most valuable contribution to "concrete questions" could be made "by provisionally not working on them at all."[8]

These sentiments, not surprisingly, brought into the open the feud between Ward and Small that had been simmering for some time. Unlike Ward, Small saw no sharp break between subjective desire and the external order. Although recognizing conflict, he remained closer to Locke than to Hobbes. Interests, unlike the social forces, were something more than desire: they were to desire as "substance to attribute" or "genus to species," that is, a more comprehensive and fundamental category. Interests were thus in no way accurately reflected in the demands of the mob or the slogans of the agitator. "Our interests may be beyond or beneath our ken," Small wrote; "our desires are strong and clear."[9]

To Ward, Small's attack on *Pure Sociology* seemed nothing less than personal and political apostasy: Small was taking orders from Chicago reactionaries. In reality, however, their quarrel finally brought into the open the differences between Ward's evolutionism and Small's emerging pluralist, pragmatic analysis. The first was potentially radical, the second more attuned to the piecemeal initiatives of Progressivism. In Small's view, sociologists could be objective without denying the hopes and desires (the "interests," as he now termed them) of human beings in society. Because the sociologist studied these interests, which ultimately constituted the moral order, the objective social scientist was at the same time a reformer.

2

Despite Ward's reaction, *General Sociology* was part of a campaign to restore unity within sociology, and among the social sciences. In the sociological community, the work offered an olive branch to Franklin Giddings at a time when their earlier quarrels already showed signs of abating. "I hope that this means more fruitful cooperation among the sociologists, and the benefit of more systematic exchange of criticism," Small wrote Ross after a productive evening with his Columbia rival in 1903. In *General Sociology*, and in several public statements in the same period, he seemed willing to put their philosophic differences aside. Giddings was "a monist and a dualist in precisely the same sense in which all modern thinkers are both or neither."[10]

General Sociology also straddled a growing split between "social psychology" and "sociology." Chicago graduate students were increasingly finding John Dewey's and George Herbert Mead's conceptions of mind and of the self more sophisticated and satisfying than the formulations of Small or Henderson. Some of the best students, such as Charles Ellwood, built their doctoral theses squarely on Dewey's psychology. Others debated whether the "social unity" was basically psychical or material. Ratzenhofer's great merit was his emphasis on "the objective stimuli of associated action," Small wrote Ross in 1901. "This doesn't prophesy sidetracking of individual and 'interindividual' psychology by any means, but it calls a halt on the tendency to assume that human subjectivity has operated in a vacuum."[11]

In being both psychic and physical, the theory of interests allowed Small to proclaim an affinity with Dewey and Mead, while maintaining his autonomy. "Our formula," he wrote in one of several tortured footnotes on the issue, "attempts to express a conception of something back of consciousness, and operating more generally than in the facts of consciousness." Cataloging "Points of Agreement Among Sociologists" in 1906, Small made further overtures to the social psychologists, while at the same time proposing that each faction carry its own insights as far as possible.[12]

Developments within sociology, however, soon proclaimed these efforts a failure. A survey of the varieties of European sociology that Ward prepared in 1902 for inclusion in *Pure Sociology* grew so long that he published it separately.[13] Distinctive schools of sociology were developing at Chicago, Columbia, Wisconsin, Penn, Michigan, and Yale. Even social psychologists couldn't agree. In *Human Nature and the Social Order* (1902), and later in *Social Organization* (1909), Charles Horton Cooley proposed an interactionist social psychology that went beyond Dewey, and finally convinced even E. A. Ross that he was on the wrong track. In *Folkways* (1906), Yale's Sumner gave new force to the physical interpretation of society.

At one point, Small himself wondered momentarily whether any understanding of an ultimate unity were possible. The quest of sociology, he lamented, "flies so uncontrollably from one aspect of humanity to another; we not only waver in our faith that the problem may be solved, but, if the truth must be told, we sometimes wonder whether, after all, a real problem exists." Seizing upon this statement, a reviewer in the *Atlantic Monthly* noted its depressing effect. "The truth is, I believe, that no such real problem as the author proposes does exist; and if it did, no finite mind could grasp it."[14]

By making sociology the capstone of the social sciences, Small also hoped to restore unity among fields now increasingly divided within themselves and from one another: history, torn by battles between "new" and traditional historians; economics, now severed from sociology after the establishment of the American Sociological Society at the American Economic Association meeting in 1903; and political science, which was also now separate following the formation of the American Political Science Association in 1905. With these developments doubtless in mind, Small in 1906 resumed his attack on the "whole petty claptrap of academic divisions." Again he insisted that there was science and Science, the first particularistic, the second universalistic in the understanding it provided. On the basis of the second, unity could be restored.[15]

But representatives of these several disciplines unfortunately could not be brought to accept Small's view. Sociology's relations with history, despite the "new history," did not improve. At a joint meeting of 1903, Small criticized historians as newsmen whose items were out of date. Five years later, the president of the American Historical Association in his annual address replied that sociology had resurrected the ancient enemy, the "philosophy of history": historians, caught between the cult of science and the specter of speculation, should fall back on the unsophisticated faith that facts are facts. Small learned the price of these continuing disagreements when the *American Historical Review* refused to notice his study of *The Cameralists* (1909), his first return to history since his Hopkins days.[16]

Economists, as represented by Robert Franklin Hoxie, a colleague at Chicago, were also not persuaded. Noted for his studies of labor and scientific management, and for his tough-mindedness, Hoxie disliked the image of the economist as social philosopher. If the economist sometimes played the role, "he does so unwillingly." The social sciences were to be differentiated, not because each dealt with separate bundles of facts, but because each defined the problem to be solved in a different way, and hence assumed a distinct perspective. Each science takes all reality as its subject, but approaches it from "the standpoint of some distinct and legitimate human interest." No crude empiricist, Hoxie also insisted that science begins with an act of volition and is necessarily selective. "We go to science because we wish to control the forces at hand so as to realize better some human purpose."[17]

But the perspectives remained distinct for each discipline. Responding to Small's "Relation between Sociology and the Other Social Sciences," Hoxie attacked the idea that there was a hierarchy among the sciences, or that any one social science could comprehend human experience in its totality. This idea was a throwback to the medieval notion that there was some ideal, the work of a "Divine Architect," beyond the experience of any individual. By Hoxie's standards, Small was either a theologian, or the poetic dreamer of Dante's *Paradise*.[18]

Hoxie's attack galled Small for several reasons. The claim that science begins with a desire to realize a purpose, assumed "for the time being" to be the goal of human activity, seemed to him to reintroduce a dangerous arbitrariness. With the social situation heating up after 1907, this approach, as evidenced by Hoxie's labor studies, seemed to invite unacceptable activism. Finally, and more personally, Hoxie's classes were becoming a mecca for graduate students in sociology, who were already tiring of Small's measured excursions into social philosophy.[19]

In political science, Arthur Bentley attacked Small from a more frankly behaviorist perspective. Half a generation younger than Small, Bentley also came from a prosperous, small-town background, although his father was a banker rather than a clergyman. After earning a Ph.D. under Ely at Johns Hopkins, Bentley had taught briefly with Small in 1896 before entering a career in journalism. Like Small, he drew heavily on the German historical school. In his doctoral thesis, he argued that social science must focus on intelligent, goal-directed activity. However, during the next decade, Bentley's outlook altered dramatically. The result was *The Process of Government* (1908), which was to become a minor classic of the transactionist, pluralist analysis of American politics that gained prominence half a century later.[20]

Bentley proposed a radical concept of interests in terms of the overt behavior of "interest groups" that converge in government, each represented in proportion to the pressure it exerts. As preface, he launched a blistering attack on older theorists, including his former professor. Small, Bentley charged, sometimes referred to interests in an objective sense, but at others fell back on the "soul stuff" (as he termed it) of subjective desire. He then gratuitously assumed a connection between desire and behavior. His painstaking enumeration of individual desires, correlated with external associations that cater to them, was unnecessarily elaborate. To explain the transition from the killing of enemies to the taking of slaves, for example, Small would presumably "introduce a wealth desire (making the prisoner work) in place of a health desire (self-protection by slaughter)." "But how artificial a procedure it is!" Bentley continued, because one would then have to explain the new desire. Despite a dozen years of writing on the subject, Small had not isolated or proved the existence of a single interest "apart from the social phenomena they are intended to explain." His "soul stuff"—the six interests in their subjective aspect—was actually derived from "popular psychology," "the practical terminology of everyday speech," and "a cursory inspection of social facts themselves." The "railroad interest" was a "social fact," not a congeries of individual desires, Bentley insisted, echoing Durkheim. Better drop the "soul stuff" entirely, and examine interests as they perform within the social structure.[21]

Bentley's attack irked Small even more than did Hoxie's. "If similar petulance were observed in a child, the diagnosis would be not science but worms," he wrote. Ducking the substantive issue, he defended his use of "soul stuff" on pedagogical grounds. The business of sociology for three decades had been "less to explain social situations than to create a constituency capable of perceiving that there are social situations to be explained." The appeal to "sympathy" to explain an action, for example, was justified on these practical grounds, for to develop a new vocabulary was a lengthy and complex business.[22]

Yet this defense was essentially an evasion. Bentley's major point was that one should not talk about things one way, and think about them in another. Small admitted that there was work to be done if the distortions of "popular speech" were to be avoided. But he appeared to think of this task, not in terms of the elimination of the "soul stuff," but as a "radical analysis of the psychic elements presupposed in explanation of social processes," a proposal that seemed to lead to the social psychology of Cooley or Mead. Bentley's behavioral analysis, in contrast, substituted "group boulders" for the individual entities that others allegedly used to explain social dynamics. "His account leaves no more place for psychic factors, than we can discover in the masses of rock that make up an avalanche," Small concluded.[23]

In a final attempt to reverse the tide of specialization and to reaffirm his conception of sociology, Small in 1908 sent a questionnaire to twenty-six prominent social scientists concerning the nature of their fields. Nineteen individuals responded, thirteen of them with "courteous acknowledgments" and "reasons for not answering the questions." The questions, given the trend toward specialization, were, in fact, embarrassingly archaic. "Do you believe that reality is fixed in its ultimate nature and constitution? If not . . . ." "Not in my province," shot back the Columbia economist John Bates Clark. "Metaphysical, not sociological," added a historian at the University of Nebraska. Although Small tried to make the best of it, he could not veil his bitterness toward what he now termed the "pedantry that pursues isolated curiosity-hunting without caring whether it is related to anything else than individual whim." Somewhat later, he referred with regret to the questionnaire "incident."[24]

3

Politics during the Progressive Era also undermined Small's faith in "Science." In several respects *General Sociology* reflected the mood and assumptions of Theodore Roosevelt's first term. For T. R., the industrial and financial giants, if properly restrained, held the key to social stability; Small likewise viewed the trusts as a model for the ever-widening forms of association. Like Roosevelt, Small believed that social fragmentation and the division of labor demanded a frank recognition of interest groups, whether ethnic, regional, or economic. But also like the president, he assumed that the political process ultimately served a common public interest. Politicians catered to interest groups; statesmen were more than power-brokers. Sociologists, in recognizing interests, helped reestablish a social unity.[25]

But as Roosevelt himself discovered in his second term, rhetoric and reality can be two different things. Throughout the Progressive Era, politics teetered between the moralism of T. R. and Wilson, and the pluralist model that emerged during and after the New Deal. An increasing clamor for special-interest legislation after 1905 distressed old-line liberals and younger Progressives alike. In the spring of 1906 Roosevelt publicly censured the muckrakers for their excessive zeal in attacking the political and business system. The Wall Street Panic of 1907, although short-lived, frightened the business community, and polarized opinion on left and right. Socialism attracted more Americans than ever before or since, while the Wobblies' talk of sabotage sent shudders through the middle class. As war approached, industrial strife and violence reached new heights.

Against this background, Small continued to defend his ideal of social unity, or "vision of social efficiency," as he now called it, adopting the jargon of the day. In 1907 he confessed a certain "warming" toward the socialists. In public, he grew more outspoken concerning the evils of capitalism and the selfishness of businessmen. In the murky rhetoric that had become his trademark, he assured a Conference of Legal and Social Philosophy on the eve of the war that social policy in the future would be something more than a mosaic of individual or group interests—a transcendent, absolute standard of the public good.[26] But, predictions aside, Small was increasingly upset by the situation in American society. Like Emerson, whom he often quoted, his optimistic predictions also contained a grim picture of contemporary society: of "poor wretches who would stoop to any infamy for money," and of magnates who would plunge the world into war "rather than sacrifice the interests of capital."[27]

Could science usher in a new era? Small still insisted that Science, in its larger meaning, could alone create a consciousness of interrelationship, and substitute a sense of public good for private interest. But the line between science and imagination grew unclear. In 1913, he told members of the A.S.S. that he would "take the liberty this evening of throwing science to the winds and instilling imagination in its place." A year later, in an article titled "Shall Science be Sterilized?" he distinguished "science" from a "more-than-science" that "loyalty to life demands," thus making explicit for the first time a distinction previously buried in his arabesque prose.[28]

An immediate result of this retreat to imagination was *Between Eras* (1913), Small's single venture into fiction. The novel described the successful resolution of a protracted industrial conflict when the son of the company's president agreed to a tentative profit-sharing arrangement with the workers. The hero proclaimed that the plan was frankly an "experiment," but asked: "Isn't the Golden Rule an instance of this sort?" Small had always said that science and morality were one, and *Between Eras* in one sense merely carried the logic of his sociological analysis to its conclusion. But if moralism and imagination were needed to pave the way to the new order, what became of the special claims of "science" and sociology? And why could the novelist describe an outcome that the sociologist was unable to find in the real world? By 1914, Small had no real answers to these questions.[29]

4

Events in Small's department after 1910 added to his woes. By this time, the outlines of a Chicago sociological empire were becoming visible. Although half of the two dozen Ph.D.s before 1910 had taken jobs outside academia, Chicago graduates already held positions in sociology departments at the leading western state universities: Charles A. Ellwood (Ph.D. 1899), at Missouri; John M. Gillette (Ph.D. 1901), North Dakota; Edward C. Hayes (Ph.D. 1902), Illinois; Romanzo Adams (Ph.D. 1904), Nevada; Eben Mumford (Ph.D. 1906), Michigan State; and Cecil North (Ph.D. 1908), Ohio State (after 1916). In the years before the war, the list of Chicagoans holding major academic positions grew to include Luther L. Bernard (Ph.D. 1910), whose wandering ways took him from Florida to Minnesota and finally to Washington University; Emory Bogardus (Ph.D. 1911), who established an outpost at U.C.L.A., where he edited *Sociology and Social Research*; and Ernest Burgess (Ph.D. 1913), a prominent figure in the "Chicago School" of the twenties.[30]

The core of the Chicago sociology faculty in 1910 remained Small, W. I. Thomas, George Vincent, and Charles Henderson. But in their minors, sociology students took advantage of a variety of newer approaches: with Robert Hoxie in economics, George Herbert Mead in philosophy, and James R. Angell and Harvey Carr in experimental psychology. Bogardus later recalled that each taught a different lesson: Small, that sociology was a study of "the process of human association"; Thomas, the importance of gathering "life histories"; Mead, the theory of "role playing"; and Angell and Carr, the "behavior approach." Anticipating later battles between subjectivists and objectivists, these lessons also ranged from the conceptual to the methodological: from Mead's "synthetic self" to the construction of a model of the Hampton Court maze to study the learning processes of a hundred white rats.[31]

Among these students, Small had a mixed reputation. Some of the prewar graduates fondly remembered the grand old man, now a giant in the field, and of these Bogardus was probably the most generous: "Often attacked vigorously by graduate students, and sometimes made fun of by his colleagues, Professor Small always maintained a pleasing, poiseful serenity, and frequently 'came back' with a warm shaft of humor." Others were less kind. Bored with grand theory and historical surveys, a new breed of practical-minded students demanded relevance. Privately, they complained that Small could not find them jobs, even when they existed. As Columbia came to produce almost twice as many Ph.D.s in sociology as Chicago, the word spread that the New York institution was a better bet for training in the field.[32]

Luther Bernard gave the first signs of trouble in a letter to Small in October 1910, but the tempest broke between 1912 and 1914 after the irascible Bernard had already left. The "objectors," as one of the group termed the dissidents, at one point numbered at least seven. The principal agitators were apparently Edwin H. Sutherland, a student of the unemployment problem, and later an expert in criminology; Stuart Queen, a professor at the University of Kansas in the 1920s, and later a colleague of Bernard at Washington University; and Norman J. Ware, a distinguished labor economist and historian. Others mentioned in Sutherland's vivid accounts of the affair were the son of W. I. Thomas (although the elder Thomas was himself on leave when the storm broke), and Max Handman, a Roumanian-born Jew who later had a colorful career in economics and academic administration.

Political and social convictions, although only part of the issue, colored the entire debate. Edwin H. Sutherland (1883–1950), born and raised in populist Nebraska, the son of a college president, came initially to sociology with a "missionary interest" in curing the world's ills. His first exposure to the subject was a University of Chicago correspondence course, using one of Charles Henderson's texts on social problems. As a graduate student he wrote his thesis under Henderson while working for the Chicago Unemployment Commission. A self-professed "socialist," Sutherland used the term less to describe a concrete program than as a symbol for the inadequacy of all other reform efforts ("I never studied [it] and . . . I did not understand [it] in a constructive way," he later confessed). Overwhelmed by the seeming impossibility of changing the world, he turned in his second year to Thomas's course in ethnology where, as he later told it, he could at least "be dealing with a situation that was specific and concrete."[33]

Although Sutherland rejected Bernard's behaviorist dream of an "objective" standard for society, he shared the same taste for what they both termed "reality." Taking a lead from Hoxie, who supervised his thesis while Henderson was on leave, Sutherland demanded realistic social analysis. "I could not find theory that amounted to anything," he recalled. "I could not find a justification for sociology, except as it was a means of solving practical problems." Only after the war did he regain interest in sociology as a "general theory of behavior," and then it was in the work of Thomas, Park, and Burgess, rather than that of Small. Despite his self-proclaimed radicalism, Sutherland was also realistic in a more general sense. When offered a job teaching economics at William Jewell College in Liberty, Missouri, in 1912, he reported to Bernard that he was "going there to do work which the founder of the chair wants to make socialistic, which the President wants to make practical evangelism, and which I wish to use as a source of income and promotion."[34]

The other dissidents shared these reform interests. Stuart Queen (b. 1890) had entered the field through a route similar to Sutherland's: a course at the University of Nebraska under George E. Howard, a reading of Ward's *Applied Sociology*, and a "radical" persuasion that thought itself superior to Henderson's "social uplift." Max Handman (1885–1939) was soon at the center of a radical-cum-bohemian circle at the University of Missouri. Norman Ware (1886–1949) served briefly as director of the University Settlement in Toronto, and later combined careers as an economist and a labor arbitrator.

Sutherland launched the "onslaught," as he called it, by asking in seminar in May 1912 why the American Sociological Society should not, like the German *Verein für Sozialpolitik*, explore "concrete problems" such as employers' associations, wage agreements, and housing conditions. To his surprise, Small replied that he had recommended just this policy to the directors of the organization. "Would that not mean that method would be omitted from the discussions?" Sutherland wondered. Small replied that there must be some method to structure miscellaneous facts. Although the argument was similar to the one Small had used against Bemis two decades earlier, Sutherland nonetheless was "immensely pleased."[35]

Pedagogy joined politics when the battle resumed during the academic year 1912–13. A major source of discontent was a course in the history of sociology taught by an instructor named Scott Bedford. His approach, so the dissidents alleged, consisted of superficial comparisons of one theory with another, coupled with statements that "Spencer overemphasized the biological, De-Greef overemphasized classification, etc. etc. . . ." In October, Queen, Sutherland, and Ware seized the occasion of a quiz to "jump the course," and wrote their objections in detail. Sutherland, who made his case badly, was inadvertently taken for a supporter and given an A plus, he later told Bernard. Describing the mix-up, Sutherland continued: "Because Ware and Queen stated more clearly what their objections to the course were he gave Ware 'E' and Queen 'C' . . . . But as a matter of fact [we] were all trying to say the same thing." When, a month later, Queen criticized the metaphysical cast of most sociology, Bedford remarked sarcastically: "I suppose Queen is passing through the same state that I was in the first year I did college work; I thought it was necessary only to pitch in and solve the problems, and that philosophy was not of any value."[36]

In January, the focus shifted to the introductory course. Sutherland complained that Small was not giving the graduate students sufficient help in teaching the course. Seizing the initiative, the Sociology Club then proposed a model more to its own liking, one built around a single problem or social movement "such as socialism, feminism, trade unionism, i.e. a problem which the people generally are trying to solve, rather than a problem which interests the academic mind only."[37]

By May 1913, if Sutherland is to be believed, Small's animus toward the "objectors" began to show. When Ware failed his first doctoral exam, Small reportedly took "great glee in telling his seminar" of the failure. Ware claimed that he had misunderstood Small's questions, which caused the professor to misinterpret his answers. "But the important fact about it," Sutherland observed, "is that Small told the whole thing to Burgess privately and then to his seminar and then gloated over Ware's confusion."[38]

Small's alleged failure to place graduate students completed the list of grievances. Bernard was bitter after being sent off to Florida, even though he remained a supplicant of Small for more than a decade. Sutherland claimed that he, Queen, and a third student named Clark got their first positions through personal friends, only to discover later that Small was unaware the jobs existed. Ware received "news of one rather puny job through Small," Sutherland conceded, but he otherwise relied on the historians. "So you see," he concluded, sympathizing with Bernard's plight, "Small must be ignored in the efforts to get jobs."[39]

To Sutherland's disappointment, morale among the graduate students improved considerably by the spring of 1915, thanks largely to the boosting activities of one popular student whom he described as the "book agent" for *Between Eras*. Yet the improvement, in his view, rather than being a victory for theory over relevance, reflected a conscious decision by all concerned to treat Small as a "great man" but to ignore his work. "They care very little for theory in the Smallian sense," Sutherland wrote of the booster and another prominent student, "but are strong for Democracy and The People and Control and Group Tolerance,—all of them with capitals. Both of them are fighters, are non-theological and don't give a damn about absolute standards." Sutherland meant this to be a warning against Bernard's attempt to devise a positivistic "objective standard" and to support his own view (derived from Hoxie) that science must begin with an act of conviction. If Sutherland's portrait of the pro-Small faction as activists who cared little for theory is true, they can have been of little more comfort to Small than was Bemis in the nineties.[40]

Although this teapot tempest can largely be ascribed to the usual student griping, these particular complaints are significant because they further challenged Small's contention that the sociologist must search for the underlying unity of things and stress theory over practical involvement. Already in a running debate with Bernard, Small fought back against the dissidents. But in Sutherland's judgment, he was also trimming his sails: "Small is changing very rapidly," he reported as early as the fall of 1912; "he advised two people here to take economics rather than psychology," whereas a few years earlier he was predicting that the discipline would be psychologized. Whether the cause was the persuasiveness of Bernard's arguments for the "objective standard," or Small's awareness that something like behaviorism lay down the road, Sutherland did not know.[41]

When in 1915 Bernard wrote his mentor that he was thinking of jettisoning theory for practical work, Small himself hinted how profoundly and personally these departmental struggles had affected him. "I have often envied the practical workers in the field of social uplift when the different sorts of scorn and ridicule have been pointed at the mere theoretical people," he wrote his former student. "It is sometimes pretty hard to keep pegging away with the consciousness that scarcely anybody regards one's work as much better than a parasitic affair."[42]

5

The First World War was a particular tragedy for Small. Since his student days, ties of family and profession had bound him closely to the German people. Under his editorship, the *AJS* became an outlet for the latest German social thought. In 1904 Small helped bring Ratzenhofer, Werner Sombart, and Max Weber to the St. Louis Exposition. In his study of *The Cameralists* he rooted modern sociology in the German tradition.[43] Although not blind to the rising threat of German militarism, he was nonetheless shocked by the boldness of Paul Rohrback's *German Idea in the World*, and the writings of Treitschke and Bernhardi. When in 1915 Georg Simmel charged that the American opinion of Germany was based on lies, Small threatened their long-standing friendship by replying publicly that nine out of ten American academics understood and condemned Prussian militarism.[44]

In the end, Small again reexamined the conception of science he had brought from Germany decades before. "The conduct of the German professors," he wrote in *The Origins of Sociology* (1922), ". . . seems to me to be the most startling demonstration which history has ever staged of the detachment of academic science from all sorts of practical applications, and of the uncertainty whether expert knowledge and skill . . . insures safe common sense in dealings with current social affairs." The lesson finally was one of "humility," of lowering one's sights and not expecting too much certainty from science.[45]

The situation in Small's department contributed to his malaise. By 1919 the original Chicago department was scarcely recognizable. In 1911 George Vincent left to become president of the University of Minnesota (and eventually head of the Rockefeller Foundation). Four years later, Charles Henderson died. In 1918 Thomas was dismissed after being charged with violating the Mann Act, a decision that reportedly reduced Small to tears.[46] Meanwhile, a new regime took shape with the appointments of Robert Park (1914), Ernest Burgess (1916), and Ellsworth Faris (1919). When in 1923 Faris replaced the retiring Small as department head, the transition was complete.

Although they differed over the merits of quantification, and the best methods for sociology, these new Chicago sociologists insisted that scientific methodology, not social reform, had top priority within their discipline. In *The Polish Peasant* (1918–20), W. I. Thomas and Florian Znaniecki brought new precision to the study of the subjective life and dealt armchair sociology a blow from which it never recovered. In their pathbreaking *Introduction to the Science of Sociology* (1921), Robert Park and Ernest Burgess set a new standard for systematic, empirical research. "Sociology seems now," they wrote, ". . . in a way to become, in some fashion or other, an experimental science."[47] The lesson was not lost on graduate students. "Park is a 'pure scientist' or tries to be," Sutherland wrote Bernard in 1915. "He studies people just as the chemist studies his materials." As a result, Small was "certainly losing ground here as a sociologist," he added, "and from the reports of the students, I judge that he is beginning to realize it."[48]

Together, these developments drove a final wedge between Science as comprehending "all reality," and science as a set of procedures for studying limited portions of this reality. "Science in its utmost perfection is a completely objective representation of the totality of phenomena in all their relations," Small wrote in 1922. The practice, however, was less inspiring: "All that we call 'social science' in any of its divisions . . . is relatively inchoate, relatively fragmentary, relatively insulated." Although he continued to pay homage to the ideal until his death, he urged for the time being a devotion to "technique" that made no cosmic claims.[49]

In *The Origins of Sociology* and several late articles, Small accordingly redefined "social process" and "interests" so as to eliminate the essentialism of his initial formulations. Concerning "process," he now distinguished an "operative" (objective) and "content" (subjective) aspect of the social process; the latter, he termed "the human process." The distinction was analogous to the meanings of the term "railroading" as used by a specialist and by a layperson: to the former, it meant the technical processes of finance, maintenance, or auditing; to the latter, the services performed and their value to consumers.[50] Objectivists, as it turned out, adopted the first of Small's definitions, subjectivists the second.

Small also made it clear that the "values resident in people" (the content aspect) were not quite the same as his earlier "interests." That doctrine, he now confessed, stood for "a hypothetical something back of wishes or wants" (Thomas's terms) that could now be ignored. To understand human "wants," that is, one need not know their essence.[51]

The concession had immense implications, because this "essence" was precisely the glue that held apparently conflicting interests together in a promise of social harmony, and kept conflict from being an endless push and pull of discrete interest groups. Small now conceded that the satisfaction of wants was only a "quasi-absolute" standard. The human process, in its most general formulation, was the "conservation of compatibles," that is, the preservation of only those wants that proved mutually compatible, not the realization of an ever-larger unity.[52]

Small clung to the belief that this formulation rested on a "conscious and unblushing acceptance of experience as a coherent reality," but he now acknowledged that this was a matter of faith rather than Science, even when capitalized. Sociology must be frankly "relativistic." Personally he believed that the values of the few were being democratized through the dissemination of technology and scientific knowledge, and he even thought "progress" a useful term to describe these advances. But the old certainty was gone. Whereas he once saw the category of process as an oracle, it now seemed only a "searchlight." In studying group phenomena scientifically, sociology must perforce give up its ambition to be queen of the social sciences. Just as history and economics had become the servants of statecraft, so "the sociologist may be typically a bureaucratic routinist, . . . a surveyor of the world for the world." No longer a point of view *within* the social sciences, sociology was an assortment of techniques among others.[53]

This conversion from telos to technique was not without consequence. In the early twenties, the University of Chicago was buzzing with plans for a cooperative research institute, established the next year as the Local Community Research Committee. In late 1922, at the same time that his statements on science-as-technique were appearing in the *AJS*, Small urged a reluctant President Judson to back the plan. During early 1923, Small himself led the battle for it among the senior faculty in social science. Although a "federation" grounded in "technique" was not the unity he had once envisioned, it was the next best thing—an echo, in fact, of the organization he had early admired at Johns Hopkins. Such federation was also the key to foundation funding. "Unless we can show the people with money that we have the will and the competence to be and to do something of a higher order," he told his colleagues, "only driblets of unsophisticated money will respond to our appeals." The age of corporate scholarship had begun.[54]

Despite this success, Small was never quite happy with current definitions of "research." Speaking before the A.S.S., he bade his colleagues to "return from their dissipations among impersonal husks and harlots, and . . . resume their duty of developing their proper patrimony—the personal possibilities of people." In 1925, a year before his death, he viewed with dismay the "pack of mongrels" fighting over scraps of information.[55]

In one sense, Small had not changed: naive empiricism was to be avoided, whether in Bemis's pronouncements, graduate student demands for "relevance," or trivial research. The organic analogy, his definition of "interests," and his call for more sophisticated technique were similar in that each was based on the view that things are not what they at first appear. But in another sense, things had changed. Whereas earlier his concern was "premature" radicalism, his reference to the "possibilities of people" hinted that some sociological researchers had abandoned the discipline's historic reform mission. Had Small lived to participate in the debates over objectivism in the early thirties, he most likely would have opposed Ogburn and others, just as he had already criticized Bernard. But, if so, his latter-day recognition of the "objective" side of the social process, his view of the sociologist as bureaucrat, and his definition of science as technique would have considerably weakened his position.

4

FIRST PRINCIPLES

*I think [Giddings's] book as a whole is dominated by
the spirit of pre-Cartesian philosophy, instead of
marching . . . as G. supposes, in the train of post-
Darwinian science.*

Albion Small to Lester Ward, 1896

1

During the 1890s, the rivalry between Franklin Giddings and Albion Small
was the talk of the profession. After reading Giddings's *Principles of Sociology* (1896), Small wrote Ward that it was "the most hopeless confusion of
undigested learning and arrogant sciolism that long-suffering sociology has
had to father." Its central concept was trivial, its method utterly unscientific. "I
feel depressed," Small continued, "that it is possible for that sort of work to
deceive its own author into the illusion that it proceeds upon the positive
method."[1]

Their feud smouldered for a decade. When in 1895 *Popular Science* praised
Columbia as the "first American university" to establish a sociology department "officially called by that name," Small told Ward that the chances were
"1000 to 1 that Giddings wrote it." That same year, Giddings remarked that
Small's textbook was best suited for Chautauqua. Small in turn gave a cold
shoulder to *The Principles of Sociology*. Giddings later wrote Ward that when
he sent Small a copy, the Chicagoan acknowledged it with a "nasty" note "in
which he did [not] so much as say thank you."[2]

Their differences, of course, were more than personal. Small thought
Giddings's conception of mind to be static and mechanical: "consciousness of
kind" and "imitation" boiled down to nothing more than "like response to
stimulus." He charged that Giddings violated the "positive method"—that is,
the Baconian view that science collects and categorizes the "facts" of experience. Giddings insisted instead that logic, deduction, and even "speculation"

were the essence of scientific method. Revising Spencerian evolutionism in light of neo-Darwinian selectionism, he moved haltingly toward a nominalist and statistical concept of order that he termed "pluralistic behaviorism."[3] Whereas Ward viewed objectivity as deriving from the non-telic nature of the subject matter, and Small primarily in terms of the attitude of the observer, Giddings finally accepted the dictum that the essence of science lay in method, not material.

Although the rivalry mellowed after the turn of the century, historians kept it alive, usually to Giddings's disadvantage. Thus, the German-trained Small rejected Herbert Spencer and "biological sociology," whereas Giddings was a "social Darwinist," if a moderate one. Small was a "collectivist," while Giddings remained an "individualist" who revised Spencer only to suit his convenience. Small stressed the reality of the "group," while Giddings moved from an untenable theory of "imitation" to a faith in statistics unmatched by his ability in mathematics. Small was a skillful administrator whose department became the envy of the profession, Giddings a petty tyrant who "surrounded himself with satellites."[4]

These differences seem at first puzzling, given the many similarities in the background and career of the two men. Exact contemporaries (Giddings was born a year after Small), they both traced their American ancestry to the seventeenth century, both were sons of New England clergymen, both entered sociology almost by accident, and both stressed the "psychological" over the "biological" nature of society. If Giddings repudiated socialism, while Small was nominally sympathetic, both fell politically into the broad spectrum of "progressive" reformers. Both were finally intellectual casualties of the First World War. Yet minor differences often make major disagreements, and these two sociologists were no exception. How these differences contributed to the shaping of a distinctive "Columbia sociology," will be the subject of this and the next chapter.

2

Franklin Henry Giddings (1855–1929) inherited distinguished ancestors, comfortable surroundings, and a Calvinism that he found stifling. His mother's family had arrived on the *Mayflower* and claimed to be descended from the first speaker of the House of Commons. Other American forebears included four captains, two majors, and a colonel in the Revolution. Giddings's paternal grandfather owned considerable land in western Massachusetts. In the small town of Sherman, his boyhood home in western Connecticut, the Giddings family had considerable prestige. Enjoying the benefits of community, Giddings accepted the realities of deference. Initially, at least, he viewed the problem of social order with less urgency than did such uprooted westerners as Ward or Ross. Social progress seemed a natural process, not an artificial one. Social selection guaranteed development at once orderly and moderate. Extremes, whether radical or conservative, were eliminated in society no less than in nature.

A Congregational clergyman, Giddings's father was "orthodox and Puritanical" by one account. Rejecting this faith, Giddings sought escape in the practical details of farming and mechanics, and in 1873 he entered Union College to study surveying and engineering. Although he abandoned his engineering course after two years, his interest in science grew. He read Spencer's *Study of Sociology* in monthly installments in *Popular Science*, and by graduation had worked his way through a reading list that virtually duplicated Lester Ward's of the same years: J. S. Mill's *Principles of Logic*, Spencer's *First Principles*, and the major works of Darwin, Tyndall, and Huxley.[5]

Giddings's Calvinist background inclined him to take Darwinism more seriously than did many of his contemporaries, including Small.[6] As with Jonathan Edwards, whom he admired, free will was the central problem. How could one have free will in a universe ruled by an omnipotent God? In Giddings's secular version: What effect had human volition within a natural order that seemed oblivious to the wishes and activities of mankind? Against the determinists, he insisted that human will is free: individuals freely will what they will. But nature alone decides which of these volitions will contribute to survival.

Although Giddings stressed the importance of deduction in science, his reading of Darwin ultimately took him beyond either "induction" or "deduction" as these terms were then used. Selectionism eliminated the lingering remnants of the "direct" effects of human activity in the works of Spencer and Ward. Darwin, for Giddings, redefined "natural order" in terms of probabilities. As in nature, the result of social selection was not chaos but order. But, as for earlier Calvinists, this order remained problematic. Unlike the Common Sense moralists, Giddings found in nature no Paleyite clockworks, no certain assurance of a clockmaker. Unlike natural theologians, the Calvinist had no direct knowledge of God, whether through deduction from first principles or direct observation.

In the fifteen years between Giddings's graduation from Union in 1877 and his appointment at Columbia, the elements of his later sociology gradually took shape. After a brief fling at teaching school, he became a reporter for the *Springfield Republican* and other papers of the region. In the early eighties he investigated the cooperative and profit-sharing movements for the Massachusetts Department of Labor, and he later earned a reputation among younger economists of the "marginalist" and "historical" schools. In 1888 he received an appointment at Bryn Mawr in economics, where he remained for five years. Each job left its mark on his sociology.

Giddings became interested in the cooperative movement in the aftermath of the railway strikes of 1877. Although this movement was supported almost exclusively by skilled workers in the antebellum years, after the Civil War it captured the imagination of middle-class liberals like E. L. Godkin of the *Nation*, no less than of labor leaders. By the mid-seventies, Massachusetts was a stronghold: one observer counted twenty-three cooperative workshops in the state in 1875. No threat to property rights, and independent of state aid, cooperation provided an answer to the labor problem congruent with the leading tenets of laissez-faire. More importantly, it served as a vehicle for the respectable middle class to express dislike of both the new industrial magnates *and* their discontented factory operatives.[7]

For Giddings, the cooperative movement was a bridge from economics to sociology. In probing worker motivation, the profit-sharing and cooperative movements appeared to challenge the basic premise of "all deductive economics," namely the view "that self-interest is the chief motive in the creation of wealth." "The wage system enlists the self-interest of the wage earner but partially," Giddings reasoned. "The great moral forces of his personality are not called into creative action." From concern with the larger self, and the assumption that institutions shape personality, it was a short step to the idea that one could not understand the economic system without seeing individuals in a larger social context.[8]

The marginalist revolution in economics meanwhile provided a middle ground between the historical school and the laissez-faire theorists. Giddings was not among the founders of the American Economic Association (A.E.A.) in 1884, but he was in informal contact with several of its members and soon joined the organization. In a general way, Giddings agreed with the historical school that the "famous economic man" violated history and evolution, and that classical economics bore little relation to the realities of industrial America. At one point, he wrote Ely that waste in railroad construction proved the folly of pure competition. At another, he complimented Ely's *Outlines of Economics* (1889) for its "treatment of property," adding that the book approached economics from "the right standpoint, the sociological." In 1888, Ely helped arrange Giddings's job at Bryn Mawr.[9]

At other times, however, Giddings could be devastatingly critical of Ely and the historical school. In October 1886 he wrote to John Bates Clark, later a colleague at Columbia and the closest of the A.E.A. founders to classicism: "There are a dozen pages in one of your chapters that are worth more than all the padded books and monographs that Ely has produced put together." Several years later, without naming names, he alluded to "that extreme left wing of the historical school which takes a curious pride in advertising its ratiocinative limitation."[10]

These economic debates, in turn, raised questions concerning the meaning of "natural law" and of "science" with which Giddings had yet to come to grips. Were natural laws "real"? Or were they simply perceived regularities, or even codifications of past practice? In either case there was nothing "inexorable" about them. Classical economists of "severely deductive habits and somewhat reactionary tendencies" endowed natural law with a reality that Giddings found unacceptable. Other thinkers ("if we may call them such") denied natural law in the social realm and likened competition to a social disease—a view he also rejected. A "scientific" assessment held that "the self-conscious forces sustain some relation to the physical and automatic forces by way of limitation and supplement."[11]

Within economics the problem was to determine the impact of "moral forces" upon the "natural" or "competitive" rate of wages. This concern led Giddings to marginalism and the mathematical economics of W. Stanley Jevons, Alfred Marshall, and the Austrian School. It was subjective judgment of utility, not the labor expended in production, that determined value, these economists argued. Although each additional unit of a good increased overall satisfaction (total utility), the contribution per unit became progressively less (marginal utility). Because satisfaction depended ultimately on the values, customs, and traditions of society, political economy had a "sociological character," Giddings added.[12]

Marginalism thus shaped Giddings's sociology in several ways. First, in sharpening the classicists' distinction between the "is" and the "ought" of the economic system—its essential functioning and its public policy—marginalism provided an example of value-free analysis. Secondly, Jevons in particular suggested that economic value could be given mathematical expression as a relation among variables through use of the differential calculus. Finally,

Jevons and the others confirmed Giddings's belief that deduction held the key to scientific method.[13]

Marginalism, in rooting value in utility, also presented a problem similar to a central one that Giddings later faced—namely, how to distinguish subjective consciousness from its behavioral manifestations. Could one measure utility apart from value? "Value depends entirely upon utility," wrote Jevons. But as the verb "depends" indicated, the two were not identical. Jevons doubted that utility (feeling) could be measured directly, but must rather be seen in buying and selling. Total utility was an unknowable abstraction; economists could know only the relative significance of changes. Jevons sometimes equivocated on this point, treating utility *as if* it could be measured directly. But the gap remained.[14]

For Giddings this was not satisfactory. Utility *was* value, he insisted; exchange merely transformed "potential" into "actual" utility. In measuring value in exchange, economists measured utility. The issue persisted in his sociology. Were subjective consciousness and its objective manifestations so directly related that in charting *how* individuals behaved, one learned *why* they did so? From the aggregate behavior of individuals in groups could one detect a "consciousness of kind"? Or, as Small charged, did his sociology *really* dispense with consciousness altogether in favor of "like response to stimulus," a mechanical interpretation of human behavior that Small found abhorrent? Giddings resisted this construction, but he gradually abandoned reference to "consciousness of kind," in effect agreeing with Jevons that feeling was elusive and finally irrelevant.

Although Giddings met Ward only once in the eighties and had not yet come to terms with *Dynamic Sociology*, his interest in marginalism led to a question roughly similar to the one Ward faced: how can subjective "feeling" (in Giddings's case, "utility") be related to an objective "natural" realm that is indifferent if not hostile to human purpose? In answering this question, the two agreed on a number of points: that the "psychic factor" was central for sociology; that social problems could not be left to the workings of a "natural" order; and that understanding of this process required more than naive empiricism. But differences were also apparent. "Utility" and "feeling" were alike only in representing the subjective aspect of experience. Compared with Ward's passionate natural man, Giddings's utility maximizer was closer to the *homo economicus* of classical theory. Giddings distrusted the radical subjectivism in Ward's theory, and cared less for the fulfillment of desire than for the correlation between the subjective intention and the objective outcomes. He also disliked the bureaucrat's penchant for organization and state control. A ubiquitous "consciousness of kind," voluntary and painless, seemed to him the best guarantee of a progressive social order.

3

Giddings's appointment as professor of sociology at Columbia offered the chance to develop this theory. As with Small at Chicago, the opening owed a great deal to chance and good fortune. In 1891 the Columbia statistician Richmond Mayo-Smith invited Giddings to fill in for one year while he went on leave. For the next two years, Giddings continued to teach one course per term, until in 1894 President Seth Low finally created a chair of sociology. Two years later Giddings published *Principles of Sociology*.[15]

The sociology of Giddings differed dramatically from that of Small and Vincent in its frank embrace of evolution, and its explicit selectionism. Building on Spencer, he pictured social evolution as a threefold process. The first stage is aggregation: the formation of social groups by external conditions such as food support and temperature. The second is association: the development of "consciousness of kind" and subsequent efforts to extend social relations through "imitation," concepts he borrowed from the French sociologist Gabriel Tarde. At a third stage, the "physical process" reappears as natural selection weeds out "ignorant, foolish, and harmful" choices from those "enlightened, wise, and beneficial."[16]

Giddings's view of science also differed from the Chicago brand. His method was "avowedly and without apology deductive as well as inductive," he wrote. Science demanded "speculation." In fact, "all true induction" was actually "guessing"—"a swift, intuitive glance at a mass of facts to see if they mean anything." Instead of defining a basic principle from which consequences could be deduced, most sociologists were engaged in the "tiresome endeavor" of listing the many motives that drive individuals. A prime example was the Small and Vincent textbook, but the remark applied to all previous efforts to explain society in terms of volition, including Ward's.[17]

For this conception of scientific method, Giddings drew on George Henry Lewes's *Problems of Life and Mind* (1874), and John Stuart Mill's *System of Logic* (1843). From Lewes he derived a conception of natural law as the relation of "antecedents" and "consequences," a view closer to positivism than Ward or Small would accept.[18] From Mill, he adopted the Methods of Difference and of Agreement, a major source of the "social experiments" that later became the trademark of students such as F. Stuart Chapin.[19]

In the *Principles*, Giddings had not yet arrived at the statistical conception of the natural and social order that he later termed "ballistic." Nor had he entirely abandoned the realist or essentialist assumptions that sustained older definitions of "cause" and "natural law." These equivocations allowed Small and others to charge that he waffled hopelessly between Baconian induction and a scholastic deductionism. By 1896 he nonetheless had moved much closer to the "new statistics" than had any of his sociological contemporaries.

The academic situation at Columbia meanwhile reinforced this narrowly scientistic conception of the discipline. As professor of sociology, Giddings joined the Faculty of Political Science, a relatively recent division of the university, although one with a formidable tradition in politics and law.[20] His colleagues, who were professional and highly specialized for the time, included Richmond Mayo-Smith (appointed 1876), author of the widely-used *Statistics and Sociology* (1894); Henry L. Moore, a Johns Hopkins Ph.D. (1896), who succeeded Mayo-Smith following his untimely death in 1901; Monroe Smith, in comparative jurisprudence; E. R. A. Seligman, in economics; and William A. Dunning and Herbert L. Osgood, in history. The overall production of doctorates was impressive: between 1883 and 1892 the faculty trained a total of thirty-four Ph.D.s, making it one of the most productive in the country.[21]

Although both Giddings and Mayo-Smith contributed to social investigations for the Charity Organization Society (one of President Low's special interests), there was no panoply of "affiliated work" under the sociological umbrella, and generally little contact between the sociologists and the "practical" workers. While sociology and social work gradually differentiated at both Chicago and Columbia, the division was sharper at the latter. As the two divisions went their ways, social workers increasingly sought their own special training, leaving Giddings even freer to impose his conception of the "science" of sociology upon his students.[22]

Giddings had a shrewd sense of the demands and opportunities the university presented. The indifferent success of European universities in establishing departments of sociology convinced him that the "leftovers" notion of the discipline was fatal. Equally impractical were conceptions of sociology as all-inclusive (Comte and Ward) or as "broad outlines of abstract truth" (Spencer). The critical questions were "Can it be taught in the classroom?" and "Will it lend itself to the modern methods of the seminarium?" Defined as deduction from basic principles, sociology would become the "definite and concrete thing" the university demanded.[23]

Small would have none of this. "Prudential considerations about sociology as a university study have no place in a system of scientific methodology," he lectured in a review of Giddings's *Principles*. "Giddings does not properly distinguish between considerations calculated to win academic tolerance for the new science, and arguments with collaborators about the scope and method of science." "This is a veritable parody of science," Small continued. It was like charting a scientific route to the North Pole with an eye to its popularity with tourists! But in his anger, Small missed the central point that the university setting *was* a major influence in shaping the discipline, if not at the North Pole, at least in Chicago and New York.[24]

Neo-Darwinism provided a final element in Giddings's sociology. Although Giddings had proclaimed himself a Darwinian, and had spoken loosely of "natural selection" through the eighties, he initially accepted the Spencerian-Lamarckian view wherein some acquired characteristics were inheritable (in the case of man, the most important ones).[25] The doctrine of the "consciousness of kind" coupled with his social selectionism was in effect an attempt to restate the Spencerian doctrine of altruism within the neo-Darwinian framework. Social "choices," no less than individual organisms, struggled for survival. "Those subjective values will survive," Giddings wrote in the *Principles*, "which are component parts in a total, or whole, of subjective values that is becoming ever more complex through the inclusion of new interests, and at the same time, more thoroughly harmonious and coherent." Because extremism was fatal, evolution guaranteed the "middle view" that Giddings continued to seek.[26]

In stating his theory of social selection, Giddings walked a tightrope. He knew that in reform circles "natural selection" (and, soon after, "social Darwinism") was a code phrase for everything society must avoid. At the same time, neo-Darwinian selectionism instinctively appealed to his elitist sense. To resolve this conflict, Giddings effectively widened the gap between nature and nurture, between man's physical makeup and what he now termed the "social medium." He then applied selectionism to the latter with the abandon of the most convinced neo-Darwinist.[27]

By 1898, this cultural selectionism had moved Giddings a step closer to the probabilistic or "ballistic" conception of causation that emerged fully in his later work. His guide again was some recent work in the philosophy of science, this time Ernst Mach's "On the Practice of Comparison in Physics" (1894), which he discovered in the late nineties. Scientific laws, according to Mach, enable us to describe and anticipate phenomena—but he refused to posit a "reality" behind the appearance of these phenomena, whether primary qualities, atoms, or other "essences."[28] Coupled with his own previous conclusion that conscious action could not reach its goals directly, Mach's theory moved Giddings closer to the idea that individual activity was a scattershot, the overall pattern of which was determined by a process of selection beyond conscious control. So persuaded, he was more than ever convinced that the minute dissection of "desires" (Ward) or "interests" (Small) promised little understanding of society.

Inevitably, institutional and personal rivalries complicated the reception of the *Principles*,[29] but the reviewers converged on three points. First, they found the psychology behind the "consciousness of kind" to be at once too much and too little. Ross felt that the psychological phraseology was excessive, while Small charged that "consciousness of kind" was merely the "commonplace that *like causes under like conditions* produce like effects."[30]

Secondly, they faulted Giddings's conception of science. Citing the venerable Bacon, the *Nation* insisted that the aim of science was to trace phenomena to a true cause. Giddings's account of conditions, volition, and selection posited a "plurality of causes," which made it necessary at the start to eliminate some in favor of others, a process of elimination that opened a "Pandora's box" of subjectivism. Small likewise objected that the *Principles of Sociology* vacillated between a method that was "essentially the Baconian," and another that stressed deduction from "first principles." Giddings provided "a picturesque yoking together of the scientific ox and the speculative ass." In a subsequent exchange he added that Giddings's method was "pre-Cartesian" rather than "post-Darwinian."[31]

Thirdly, the critics attacked Giddings's alleged failure to stress the dynamic character of feeling. Ward himself led the charge: Giddings had gone "too far in denying that the individual mind working for the individual's ends, entirely apart from any *consensus*, is attended with social consequences." The lone dissenter, that is, often effected great social changes. Ross similarly objected to the notion that natural selection homogenized social choices, and defended Ward's theory that purposeful human action substituted "artifice" for "nature."[32]

In the heat of debate, Giddings unfortunately interpreted one of Small's remarks as a personal attack and responded, not on the merits, but in kind. "My methods may be wrong, my argument may be illogical, but I have not intentionally deceived or misrepresented," he wrote indignantly.[33] However, their now-divergent sociologies were, in fact, deeply rooted in minor differences that finally outweighed their similarities: Giddings's more distinguished ancestry, his Calvinist Congregationalism, his training in marginalist economics rather than history, his reading of Darwinism, and subtle differences in the university setting. Both were indebted to Spencer, but each in effect had drawn a different lesson from his work: Small, the organic analogy; Giddings, the evolutionism.

For Giddings, the issue now was to answer the several questions his reviewers had posed. Did "imitation" gratuitously assume a "natural" sociability? Was "consciousness of kind" merely "like response to stimulus?" Was his view of science hopeless speculation, and his system as "metaphysical" as those he criticized? In one way or another, these questions set his agenda for the new century.

5

PLURALISTIC BEHAVIORISM

*A sociology which follows society back to quanta and
electrons and projects telesis into a new heaven and earth,
cannot hope to escape satirical description as a science of
organized smatter.*

Franklin Giddings, 1929

1

From 1900 until his retirement in 1928, Franklin Giddings *was* Columbia sociology. Combining the careers of scholar and journalist, he published half a dozen books, numerous articles, and countless pieces in such magazines as *Harper's Weekly*, the *Century*, and the *Independent*. In 1910 he was elected to a two-year term as president of the American Sociological Society.

In these years, Giddings's thought developed in two quite different directions. Inspired by the "new statistics," he called for a more rigorous, quantitative sociology, first in *Inductive Sociology* (1901) and later in rather technical articles in the *Journal of the American Statistical Association*. At the same time, he provided increasingly shrill assessments of national and world affairs for a popular audience. For a time scientist and publicist worked in uneasy harmony—but following a nervous collapse in 1911, and the approach of war, the two parted company. While the scientific sociologist contributed crisp, dry, and sometimes unreadable statistical analyses to the scholarly journals, a second Giddings published a highly unscientific volume of *Pagan Poems* (1914). After the war, Giddings pressed his demand for what he now called "pluralistic behavior" in *Studies in the Theory of Human Society* (1922) and *The Scientific Study of Human Society* (1924), while his students developed their own versions of his scientism.

2

Giddings's conversion to pluralistic behaviorism began with his discovery of the "new statistics" soon after the *Principles* was completed. Although statistics, in the sense of numerical tabulation, were already the rage,[1] the new statistics was another matter. An offshoot of the Darwinian revolution, this latest British import was rooted in the work of Francis Galton, and had been popularized by the London University mathematician Karl Pearson. Pearson's "new statistics" nicely complemented his study *The Grammar of Science* (1892), in which he warned scientists not to probe the "real world"—Kant's *Ding an sich*—or to conceptualize experience under the category of causation. Statistics was a way to obtain measurement and description *without theory*. "Correlation," as the historian Bernard Norton has noted, offered a "looser" form of "cause." This formulation, as it turned out, also provided a defense of natural selection against foes such as Lord Salisbury who charged that Darwinism was "unscientific" because unprovable within the canons of Baconianism.[2]

Given Giddings's interest in selectionism, and his still-evolving views on scientific method, he found this thinking immensely appealing. Small, after all, had leveled substantially the same charge against the *Principles* that Salisbury had against Pearson. Why not focus on correlations alone, without attempting to explain social behavior in any deeper sense? In *Inductive Sociology* (1901), Giddings took a tentative step toward this conclusion. The major elements in the new statistics, as he identified them, were (a) the ranging of figures to establish averages, medians, maximums, and minimums; (b) the calculation of the "standard deviation" from the mean; and (c) the use of the "coefficient of correlation." He barely explained these terms, much less their uses in sociology, but his enthusiasm was unbounded. "The Correlation Coefficient," he wrote, "is always equivalent to a generalization or a law." Although Giddings never formally repudiated the concepts of "imitation" and "consciousness of kind," these terms gradually faded from his writing, and with them, all concern with the subjective elements in social behavior.[3]

Giddings's new departure met with a mixed response. Charles Ellwood, a recent Chicago graduate, was uneasy with the suggestion that statistics would henceforth measure only "more" and "less"; but he was willing to give the new method a chance, an ironic concession given his bitter opposition to "scientific" sociology in later years. The philosopher Peirce, who had seen the statistical implications of Darwinism two decades before, was less charitable: Giddings, like Gabriel Tarde, copied "the phraseology of mathematics, as if that possessed, in itself, a secret virtue of rendering vague ideas precise," he wrote in the *Nation*. Why, he wondered, did sociologists insist on saying that "tradition is authoritative and coercive in proportion to its antiquity," when they meant only that the older the tradition, the more likely people are to be in awe of it?[4]

Columbia continued to provide an ideal setting for this approach. Between the turn of the century and the outbreak of war in 1914, the university was the nation's most productive graduate institution. From 1898 to 1907 it ranked third in the total production of doctorates, behind Chicago and Harvard. During the next seven years it surpassed both institutions, granting an average of sixty-three Ph.D.s annually, with approximately two-thirds in areas outside the natural sciences. Sociology made a small but growing contribution to these totals. Although the half-dozen doctorates nominally in the field before 1904 were scarcely recognizable as being in sociology, the thirty-four candidates who received degrees in the next eleven years included a number of future leaders in the profession. Between 1908 and 1914, the department granted twenty-five of the fifty-six doctorates in sociology given by all American universities, the Chicago sociology department running a distinct second with eleven.

With or without Giddings, the drive toward behavioral and statistical approaches was well under way at Columbia. Among the many new appointments in social science and related departments were the psychologists James McKeen Cattell (1891) and Edward L. Thorndike (1899), the latter soon to be famous for his behavioristic cat-in-the-box experiments in educational psychology; and the institutional economist Wesley Mitchell (1913). Henry L. Moore, a leading statistician, gradually took over this latter area, although Giddings offered work in it for several years after Mayo-Smith's death.

Sociology remained largely a one-man show. Aside from Edward Devine and Samuel Lindsay in social work, and Moore and the other statisticians, the one permanent addition in sociology was Alvan A. Tenney (1876–1937), who became assistant in statistics in 1905 and later a full member of the sociology department. A social theorist with interests in population, public opinion, and international peace, Tenney came to sociology via the New York School of Philanthropy, where he studied in 1898–99, and the Dependent Children's Bureau of the New York Charity Organization Society, for which he worked intermittently from 1900 to 1905. From this work he developed a lifelong interest in what he termed "the biological phases of social causation." In a thesis entitled *Social Democracy and Population* (1908) he attacked "anthropo-sociologists" and other biological determinists, arguing instead that intelligent knowledge of biology allowed increased "social democracy" through policies such as immigration restriction.[5]

Giddings's "diminutive associate," as one fellow sociologist remembered Tenney, remained literally and figuratively in the great man's shadow. Like Keller at Yale, he was better known for loyalty than for originality. Devoted to his family, to his community, and to Giddings, he also gave countless hours to his graduate students. Like Giddings, Tenney believed that "reform" and "science" were compatible—but unlike his mentor, the "splendid mental conflict" between the two, as another associate described it, produced a writing block that kept his published work to a minimum. But his teaching was not without impact. In one of his advanced seminars he developed techniques for the quantitative measurement of public opinion that later inspired Malcolm Willey's *Country Newspaper* (1926), the work of a leading quantifier at the University of Minnesota.[6]

As a result of the Giddings monopoly, and perhaps of his unwillingness to brook competition, Columbia sociology was more distinguished at the periphery than in the home department. At the center of this sphere of influence were the University of Pennsylvania, with James P. Lichtenberger (Ph.D. 1910) and later Stuart Rice (1924); Clark University, with Frank Hankins (1908); and New York University, with Rudolph Binder (1903). Columbia sociologists also established themselves in some of the more prestigious institutions in the western New York-Ohio hinterland, from Hamilton (Frederick M. Davenport, 1905) to Miami University in Ohio (Edwin S. Todd, 1904).[7] Whether through lack of personal contacts, or because a shadow of "materialism" hung over Giddings's sociology, the Columbia network did not extend to most of the older New England colleges and universities, nor to the midwestern state universities, with the exception of Wisconsin, where John Gillin (1906) assumed a lifelong post in 1912. In later years, as will appear, Columbia graduates moved further afield, notably Howard Odum to North Carolina in 1919; F. Stuart Chapin to Minnesota in 1922; and William F. Ogburn to Chicago in 1927.

Without Giddings, as many later testified, this network might never have been as it was. In their choice of thesis topics, no less than in their method of development, most were self-consciously "Giddings men." Of these, the best were anointed members of the "F.H.G. Club," an informal group that met regularly at Giddings's home.[8]

3

The changing political situation also underlay Giddings's developing interest in statistics. Politically, the new statistics appealed to Giddings initially because its methods seemed to prove that social selection produced the ideal society: a balance between individual liberty and social control, and of homogeneity and heterogeneity in social groupings. By 1908, as social fragmentation threatened this vision, statistical analysis provided a way to measure the amount of social control needed to hold society together.

Despite his later reputation as a reactionary, Giddings shared the views of many advanced liberals in the late nineties, including their support for imperialism. Although a standard patrician liberalism (civil service reform, a universal gold standard, and free trade) marked his politics in 1900, he gradually, if cautiously, expressed sympathy for a variety of progressive reforms, including the control of trusts, child labor laws, compulsory schooling, conservation, and banking and currency reform. Traditionally a Democrat, he charged Bryan in 1906 with ignoring the realities of exploitation, and with attempting to extend to "artificial persons" such as corporations the liberties due only to "natural persons." Instead, he proposed a division of labor between socialism and individualism: "Socialism for things socialistic, state regulation for things state created, individualism, natural liberty, for things naturally individualistic." When a Columbia alumnus complained that a book by the socialist John Spargo was being used at the university, Giddings responded that there would be "no harm done if it were. It is a thoroughly good book."[9]

For Giddings, the heart of the social problem was not poverty so much as social fragmentation, a development he characterized in Spencerian terms as one from "homogeneity" to "heterogeneity." Like many native-born, middle-class whites, he was worried about the impact of the "new immigration," changing manners and lifestyles, and the apparent breakdown of law and order, made worse by a punishing inflation. Concerning immigration, his model of social selection restated the liberal faith in free immigration and the "melting pot," although in statistical rather than physiological terms. In *The Principles of Sociology* he argued that social vitality demanded a mean between rural and urban, poor and rich. In *The Theory of Socialization* (1897) he developed "index numbers" to measure degrees of social homogeneity, expressed as the ratio of different immigrant groups to native population. Thus, excessive Americanism, as expressed by the American Protective Association, correlates with extreme homogeneity, whereas "progress and social leadership" come from communities where the leadership is "neither perfectly homogeneous nor excessively heterogeneous."[10]

In *Inductive Sociology* Giddings developed a schema for graduate students to use in testing these hypotheses, the result being a series of community studies designed to test his theory that social selection worked to eliminate harmful extremes: Thomas J. Jones, *Sociology of a New York City Block* (1904); Edwin S. Todd, *A Sociological Study of Clark Co., Ohio* (1904); John L. Gillin, *The Dunkers* (1906); James M. Williams, *An American Town* (1906); Warren H. Wilson, *Quaker Hill* (1907); Howard B. Woolston, *A Study of the Population of Manhattanville* (1909); and Frederick J. Soule, *An American Village Community* (1911).

By and large, the theory seemed to hold. One student reported that "Blankton," a Great Lakes community of three hundred, had developed a "natural" democracy rather than an "artificial aristocracy" —that is, one that produced "the rule of the fit at the willing recognition and voluntary choice of the majority." Others reported that destructive individualism of the nineteenth-century variety was giving way to solidarism. Only one confessed that he found it futile to measure the "morality" and "vitality" of classes in this fashion.[11]

Some of these theses, however, revealed how thin was the line that separated faith in reasonable heterogeneity from fears of disintegration and the demand for greater controls. Edwin Smith Todd concluded that heterogeneity was not resulting in a golden mean between freedom and control despite the fact that "the process of social selection is rapidly going on." Thomas J. Jones, a native of Wales and later executive secretary of the Phelps-Stokes Fund, deplored social fragmentation with a passion that anticipated Giddings's wartime tirades: "The impulsiveness of the Italian must be curbed. The extreme individualism of the Jew must be modified."[12]

National events toward the end of Roosevelt's second term dramatized these fears. If the rise of socialism and labor militancy were not enough, American society itself appeared to be unraveling. The Atlanta riot in the fall of 1906, and racial disturbances in Springfield, Ohio, two years later, signalled new concern over what the journalist Ray Stannard Baker called "the color line." During the theater season of 1907–08 New York audiences wept nightly over Israel Zangwill's "The Melting Pot," a drama of New World romance blighted by Old World animosities. Gradually, appeals to humanity and charity gave way to calls for "efficiency" and "social control."

Giddings accordingly shifted his emphasis, starting about 1908. The aim of sociology was now the measurement of the "social pressure" necessary to effect change, rather than the chronicling of the progress of evolution through selection, as in the community studies. One factor in this shift was Giddings's growing doubt that reform of any sort could achieve its goals. A "social marking system" to index "subhomogeneity" was necessary, he wrote in 1910, "if mankind is warranted in believing that by an expenditure of educational and reformatory effort, it can standardize knowledge and conduct, and can assimilate alien habits and ideals to prevailing or national types." No longer an inevitability, reform had become a problem.[13]

As Giddings continued, it became clear that "science" was finally a way of dealing with a situation one did not like, but would not remedy—specifically, a fear that society was coming apart *and* a dislike of the controls necessary to curb the dissolution. In 1912 Giddings cited the "terrible figures on homicide" as proof that the "normal functioning of society has broken down." Some Americans, as a result, ran "in haste" to impose new controls. Quantitative studies of criminality and controls provided "scientific measures of the price we must pay for our idealistic attempt to mingle [antagonistic races and nationalities] in one political aggregate."[14]

A stricter "science" was also a way of coping with the growing demand among graduate students for "relevance," a development similar to that at Chicago in the same years. As insurgency bubbled in Congress, and socialists daily gained strength, Columbia graduate students turned for thesis topics to areas in which "progressive" legislation was most hotly debated: sexual relations (eugenics and divorce); labor laws, especially for women and children; compulsory education; sumptuary laws; the condition of the working class and blacks; and immigration restriction. Most wished quite straightforwardly to further the reform in question. But Giddings's insistence that they take a statistical approach channeled this enthusiasm in more respectable, scientific directions.

A partial list of doctoral theses written at Columbia between 1908 and 1913 tells much of this story: G .B. L. Arner, *Consanguineous Marriages* (1908); James P. Lichtenberger, *Divorce* (1909); Bertha H. Putnam, *Enforcement of the Statutes of Laborers* (1909); Philip A. Parsons, *Responsibility for Crime* (1909); Maurice F. Parmelee, *Inebriety in Boston* (1909); Robert C. Chapin, *Standard of Living Among Workingmen's Families* (1909); F. Stuart Chapin, *Education and The Mores* (1911); George E. Haynes, *The Negro at Work in New York City* (1912); William F. Ogburn, *Progress and Uniformity in Child Labor Legislation* (1912); L. S. Blakey, *The Sale of Liquor in the South* (1912).

Descriptive in the old social-work tradition, most of these studies gave only a nod to Giddings's schema. Others praised statistics ("the inductive method *par excellence*"), but only Lichtenberger and Ogburn attempted anything more than elementary numerical tabulations. Mayo-Smith's *Statistics and Sociology* remained a favorite. The correlation coefficient waited another decade before appearing in any Columbia thesis. The list nonetheless contained the names of many leaders in the drive toward quantification during the interwar years.[15]

At the height of his influence, Giddings realized that he had seriously overextended himself. During 1910–11 he served his first term as president of the American Sociological Society while continuing to teach and write. In the spring of 1911 he wrote Columbia President Nicholas Murray Butler to thank him for a substantial salary increase that would permit him "to drop a lot of pot boiling work which I have detested, and devote my full strength to my department and my scientific work." But the next year he was back with an "urgent" request for an assistant to help Tenney and himself, now deluged with 320 registrations, and a total of 215 individual students and 90 majors for the M.A. and Ph.D. During the academic year 1912–13 these pressures resulted in a near breakdown that coincided with, and possibly triggered, the separation of head and heart that had been in the making for almost a decade.[16]

"I have been almost in a bad way," Giddings confided to a colleague once the crisis had passed. "For years I have been working too hard. I did not admit to myself that I was suffering any ill effects, but it is plain enough now that I had been. The first thing I noticed as wrong was a complete failure of will-power in respect to one specific thing. I could keep up my lecturing, and my desk work as far as university matters went, but I could not attend to my own affairs." Initially he had found himself unable to accept or to refuse invitations for outside lecturing; eventually, he could not answer personal correspondence. Meanwhile, his brother in Connecticut fell extremely ill with tuberculosis, requiring Giddings to make frequent trips back and forth. "I was pretty nearly at the breaking point," he continued, "and one day while lecturing, a table of statistics I was using went 'batty.' They read to my eye and perception in a way that my surviving common sense told me was wrong." The incident convinced him to sleep and exercise more, and to smoke less. By early 1914 this regimen put him on the road to recovery.[17]

The incident left its mark in a sort of intellectual schizophrenia that characterized Giddings's work for the remainder of the decade. In a remarkably dreary collection of *Pagan Poems* (1914), he attempted to express his "inextinguishable faith" in the limitless possibilities of the human experience. In *The Principles of Sociology* and his other earlier works, science and values had communed in the warm embrace of an evolution that bound morality and progress in a unified vision. By mid-1914, however, he was less confident. Pietism divorced from science wandered in a wilderness of poor poetry:

To what end?
We know not why our own life,
    Our smilings and our tears,
Why Nature's power works grimly on,
    Through the eternal years.

Yet dour or glad we strive,
    Loathe from the task to cease,
Content, if thus we learn to tell
    The Blue Bird from the Geese.

Giddings knew that this stuff was out of character. "Why should he who has given his best years to science and discussion . . . turn aside to make a book of verse?" he asked in the preface. "I made this book because it bade me make it!"[18]

Political disillusionment during the war years completed Giddings's conversion to a narrowly scientistic behaviorism. Standards of common decency had entirely collapsed, he wrote in one of a series of editorials in the *Independent* between 1913 and 1921. The cause was the nation's social diversity. "Everything goes because our mixt population offers to every sort of human being a group within which his particular kind of conduct actually flourishes as a folk way of that group." In the "Mannerless Age" nothing prevailed against "our egoistic impertinence and our democratic determination to be common." In jeremiads worthy of his puritan ancestors, Giddings pounded away at the "craze for dancing, . . . the vulgarity and lewdness of the stage, the speed mania of the automobilists, [and] . . . the wanton extravagance in dress and entertainment."[19]

National politics alternately raised and dashed his hopes. Wilson's message to Congress in December 1913 delighted him: during the next year he supported legislation to control the trusts, and even went beyond the president in demanding that the railways be made a national monopoly. But by January 1915, Wilson's appointments to the United States Industrial Commission, and to other agencies, lowered Giddings's estimation of the administration. Called to testify before the Industrial Commission, he referred to the appearance as a "waste of time."[20]

The sinking of the *Lusitania* in the spring of 1916 destroyed what remained of Giddings's intellectual sobriety. Although he had previously praised "public socialism" in Germany, he now saw the war as a battle of good and evil, and he demanded America's immediate entry. When Henry W. L. Dana and J. M.

Cattell were dismissed from Columbia for antiwar statements in 1917, Giddings defended the university's action on the ground that the two had overstepped the bounds of legitimate free speech. In *The Responsible State* (1918) he demanded the total destruction of the German state. "The book," commented a disappointed critic, "is thoroughly Theodorian, and carries with it very little of the liberalism that was once associated with Professor Giddings's name." The Russian Revolution was the final straw. "Bolshevism is a massing and turmoil of the criminal elements of society let out of jail and on the loose," he wrote in January 1919, as the national Red Scare gained momentum.[21]

Specific issues aside, the outcome of Giddings's postwar tirades was not reasoned reaction but a resigned cynicism that found outlet in Menckenesque satire. The "Ohio Idea" and normalcy were occasions for ridicule rather than recrimination. "Camouflanguage," the official tongue of President Warren Harding, was cause for sarcasm. Although Giddings himself had once railed against "lewd women," attempts to regulate the scanty dress of the flapper now seemed only amusing. In answer to those who condemned nakedness, he now suggested that "Eve invented clothing not to save the human race by concealing nudity, but by giving it something to be interested in." As with Mencken, these statements represented a nineteenth-century liberalism gone sour. In this mood, Giddings gave up his career in journalism in 1921 to devote his energies once again to the more sober business of "scientific" sociology.[22]

4

In *The Scientific Study of Human Society* (1924) Giddings redefined consciousness as "a mechanistic state of things," virtually conceding everything that Small and others had said about his materialism. "Likemindedness" now seemed to be "the sum of like reactions, instinctive, habitistic, and rational." Accordingly, he now described himself as "a behaviourist" within "scientific limits," by which he meant that he would not follow extremists who denied consciousness altogether—but he would abandon the attempt to know mind directly. Mental and social energies could be measured only "in terms of what they do."[23]

He also formally distinguished "mechanistic" from "ballistic" causation (a term, as a former student described it, that "calls to mind the scattergram of shots at a bull's eye"). Given the almost limitless number of variables determining any outcome, it was impossible to isolate two or three leading ones, or to speak of such mutually exclusive abstractions as "heredity" and "environment." Correlations were at best "approximations," that is, statements about how variables were likely to consort with one another. "These are by no means perfect substitutes for constants," he conceded with a trace of nostalgia, "but they are the next best thing."[24]

Meanwhile, in revisions of earlier articles, Giddings unveiled the altered world view that sustained this theory. In "The Costs of Progress," now a chapter in *Studies in the Theory of Human Society* (1922) but earlier a chapter in *Democracy and Empire*, a reference to "progressive evolution" was changed to read "continuing selection." Intelligence, earlier viewed "as a product of social conditions," was now the result of "selection and discipline under social conditions." In making these and similar revisions, Giddings unknowingly followed in the path of his mentor Herbert Spencer, who in the mid-1890s had revised his own early essays so as to root out all vestiges of theology, metaphysics, and a faith in progress.[25]

Giddings made no attempt to hide the political implications of his conversion. The variability of experience, as demonstrated by statistics, gave the lie to socialism and all other leveling philosophies. Modern society required the talents of the "engineer," not "untrained and unchastened uplifters" or the "phosphorescent ignorati of revolt and revolution." The engineer, in contrast, "knows that feasibility is limited and is grimly conditioned by human constitutions, nerves, and energies, and by the costs which must be met out of finite incomes." Implicit in this image was the notion—soon to be developed by Ogburn and others—that the social scientist as engineer was concerned with the *how*, not the *why*, of social change.[26]

During the twenties, Giddings also declared open war on Ward's "ill-informed disciples" who appropriated the least-true parts of his teachings for their own purposes. He had little patience with "the many list makers following Ward [who] name appetites and desires among primordial social energies." Of "social forces" he now wrote: "For quacks and amateurs, the phrase is charged with mana." In one of his final articles, he twisted the knife with his comment about the "science of organized smatter."[27]

Although some reviewers welcomed Giddings's latest works as a tonic for the general reader,[28] younger objectivists felt that he had not gone far enough. Luther Bernard regretted the unfortunate assumption that sociology should confine itself to taboos, social selection, and the like, while economics considered cost of living and family interests. George Lundberg, later chief architect of "operationalism," applauded the stress on statistics as *the* scientific method for sociology, but found the historical and anthropological sections of the

Studies somewhat old-fashioned.[29] Reviewing *The Scientific Study*, F. Stuart Chapin criticized the inadequate discussion of sampling, and faulted Giddings for ignoring a growing literature on specific techniques of social measurement. Malcolm Willey urged him to extend his theory to include the doctrine of the "conditioned response," discovered by Pavlov and described by J. B. Watson. Frank Hankins, in an otherwise lavish obituary tribute, wondered if lingering vestiges of "consciousness" really added anything to the theory.[30]

These criticisms, however, could not diminish the fact that Columbia was developing its own style of sociology. The doctoral theses of the 1920s fit no single mold, but the more distinguished ones continued to advance the frontiers of quantification. In a study of *Negro Migration* (1920), Thomas J. Woofter used the correlation coefficient to demonstrate that migration from the South was associated with lack of agricultural opportunity. Frank A. Ross's *School Attendance in 1920* (published as Volume 2 of the Census Report of 1924) pushed statistical analysis even further. In *Diagnosing the Rural Church* (1924), C. Luther Fry invented a quantitative measure for gauging the vitality of various forms of religious activity. In *Farmers and Workers in American Politics* (1924), Stuart A. Rice, soon to be a professor at Penn, attempted to determine statistically whether sufficient agreement existed between the two groups to predict success for a Farmer Labor Party. Malcolm Willey's *Country Newspaper* (1926), although indebted to Tenney as much as to Giddings, applied statistics to the study of public opinion.[31]

For this, Giddings deserved a large measure of credit, for better or worse. Although he could "hardly add" in arithmetic, William F. Ogburn recalled, his enthusiasm for statistics had affected his students. Whatever his errors and inconsistencies, Giddings made Columbia the center of the demand for more rigorous quantitative sociology in the interwar years.[32]

6

UP FROM METAPHYSICS

I should not be bold eno to say that all *metaphysics,
filosofy, etc. are fantasies, but they all should be viewed
with suspicion.*

William Graham Sumner, ca. 1880s

1

William Graham Sumner loved "facts." In describing the "facts and information" of social existence, sociology could obtain the "accurate, positive shape"
of an exact science. "I want to have the notion of science built on this thirst for
reality," he told members of Sigma Xi in 1905. Consequences rather than
purposes were the sociologist's main concern. "Motives and purposes are in
the brain and heart of man. Consequences are in the world of fact." The
distinguishing characteristic of his *Folkways* (1906), as several reviewers
commented, was its almost overwhelming assemblage of facts.[1]

Sumner assumed this position after sampling the full range of nineteenth-
century opinion concerning the nature of science. As an undergraduate at Yale
in the 1860s, he imbibed the prevailing Baconianism. At Göttingen he toyed
briefly with the speculative methods of the Higher Criticism, and at Oxford
with the positivism of Henry Thomas Buckle. During his years as an Anglican
clergyman (1867–72), he attempted a compromise between potentially threatening theories in science and his inherited Baconianism. During the seventies,
he drifted gradually to the deductionism of the classical economists, and of
Spencer, as antidote to the "empiricism" (as he termed it) of do-gooders in the
Historical School of economics. In the eighties, however, he learned again, as
he already knew, that speculative reasoning had its own perils. The result was a
gradual retreat to the apparent Baconianism of *Folkways* and the increasing
celebration of fact in his final years.

This is not to say that Sumner's understanding of scientific method was
either profound or consistent. Most of the time he seemed an unreconstructed

realist, but he occasionally sounded more nominalistic in urging that "method" was the key to science. Hence, in the same Sigma Xi talk of 1905, he cited Pearson's *Grammar of Science* to the point that the "highest test of truth" lay in the "opinions and methods" of the community of trained observers.[2] For this very reason, *Folkways* became a beacon for younger objectivists in both camps. For the Columbia nominalists, its reification of custom as "mores" invited the quantification of social change. The "mores," as F. Stuart Chapin put it, "are the objective products of interstimulation and response." For the realist Luther Bernard, they were the starting point for the creation of an "objective standard of social control."[3]

This portrait of Sumner as a progenitor of objectivism differs markedly from the conventional one of the "leading Spencerian" and "social Darwinist" who dealt fast and loose with analogies drawn from biology.[4] In science, Sumner sought, not a justification for the jungle-like struggle, but a more certain basis for order and authority than that provided by existing institutions and beliefs. Nor was he a Spencerian in any significant sense: his debt to the Englishman was minimal and short-lived, their differences were considerable, and their spiritual affinities virtually nil.[5] Nor was he a "Darwinian" as usually pictured. Forced finally to read Darwin's works late in life, he resisted all evolutionary explanations of social change—to the lasting regret of his chief disciple, Albert Keller.[6]

A reexamination of Sumner in this light also brings into sharper focus the factors that propelled him and others toward a value-neutral conception of sociology: social marginality, resulting in a radical disjuncture between past and present; an interest in science combined with an uneasy sense that a misinterpreted science threatened cosmic and social disorder; increasing disillusion, even cynicism, over the course of politics and society; and an institutional setting that encouraged an especially narrow view of social science. Sumner's worship of "facts," not a "social Darwinism" woven of bogus analogies, was the end product of an earlier liberalism turned sour.

2

William Graham Sumner (1840–1910), born in Paterson, New Jersey, was heir to a tradition of English working-class radicalism. Sumner's father, Thomas, a northcountry Englishman like his contemporary Spencer, had left the low wages and unemployment of Lancashire just in time to feel the sting of the American depression of 1837, and he was soon chafing at the injustices of the "company store." By marriage he was distantly related to a prominent free-trader and temperance advocate, causes he also made his own. However, a stubborn practicality and gruff common sense shielded the elder Sumner from the temptation to set the sterner realities of life in a Spencerian setting of cosmic progress. This trait he passed on to William. In 1881 he died almost as poor as on his arrival in America, and was remembered only as the "forgotten man" of his son's best-known essay.[7]

Young Sumner enjoyed neither security of place nor the comforts of the emotional life. During their first decade in Hartford, the family moved frequently. The death of William's mother when he was eight placed him in the custody of a stepmother whose concern with economy at the expense of affection grieved even her taciturn husband. Although Sumner never referred to the deprivation, it left the legacy of a keen sense of the inner and outer life, and of the separation of the private and public spheres—the realms, in turn, of sentiment and fact. As an adult, "Billy" Sumner's sternness was legendary. "Root, hog, or die" was his motto. But a tenderness also surfaced with surprising intensity—in the love letters he wrote to his fiancée, for example, and in his celebrated fondness for children, an indulgence once desired but never received.[8]

Honoring a debt to his father, and to several generations of Lancashire Sumners, William in his early years championed tradition against the age's passion for "progress." "The traditions of centuries have a true *moral* authority," he told his parishioners on one occasion. "We must begin with the world as we find it, that is, as it is handed down to us from the past." As a caution, he warned only that the "true use of tradition" should be distinguished from "traditionalism," the blind acceptance of "old errors" and "worn-out falsehoods." In the hurly-burly of Gilded Age America, however, this position seemed less and less tenable. Gradually, Sumner turned to "science," not in praise of progress, but as a substitute for traditions that would not hold.[9]

At Yale, where Sumner matriculated in 1859, science meant Baconianism: in the moral philosophy classes of Noah Porter, a leading representative of the Scottish realism, and in the laboratories where the influence of the elder Benjamin Silliman remained strong.[10] Inductionism also suited the just-the-facts mood of the young democracy, and of audiences with little time for theory. Political economy traditionally had consisted of formal, abstract, and regrettably "cold dry principles," Harriet Martineau wrote in *Illustrations of Political Economy* (1834), a work that Sumner read in his early teens. Like most "new sciences" it was a monopoly of a learned few. Martineau instead presented its teachings "in a familiar, practical form" through concrete examples. As a clergyman, Sumner later received similar counsel from his friend and patron, William C. Whitney: an "effective" sermon must illustrate its salient points. Even later, when Sumner had moved from preaching to partisanship, the publisher Henry Holt advised of his forthcoming book on free trade: "Make it an arsenal of facts, and illustrations against the Philistines."[11]

At Göttingen, where he studied from 1863 to 1865, Sumner encountered a more radical and rationalistic conception of science in the Higher Criticism.[12] Although he later equated "German thought" with almost everything that was wrong with the world, he felt otherwise at the time. "I can scarcely find words for the tremendous interest it has for me," he wrote an American friend after beginning his study of the new Biblical criticism. "It makes me sad now to think that our ministers at home give us so little real satisfaction in their sermons, when they might give us so much." Compared to the Germans, the English theologians seemed "low and groveling." "Thoroughly Teutonized," he returned home via Oxford, where eight months' study brought him to the safer ground of his childhood Anglicanism. Whatever their faults, the English at least treated the Bible "as a religious book." Thanks to Oxford, he underwent "the toning down process which is necessary to bring a young man back to common sense."[13]

Meanwhile, Oxford introduced Sumner to a third conception of science that proved almost as challenging as the corrosive rationalism of the Higher Critics. A true social science, wrote Henry Thomas Buckle in the *History of Civilization in England* (1865–66), was an "induction from history." Historians traditionally gathered masses of facts, but "hardly anyone has attempted to combine them into a whole." For Buckle this "whole" was not the German's God (or reason) in history. Nor was it the empiricists' "necessary connection" wherein natural laws were considered "causes." Rather, following Comte, Buckle maintained that law was essentially a perceived regularity or constant conjunction that allowed accurate prediction. The key was statistics, which demonstrated that even so personal and apparently irrational an act as suicide, when taken in the aggregate, occurred with lawlike regularity.[14] For Buckle, the choice of scientific method had important socio-political implications. In countries where deduction predominated, "knowledge, though often increased and accumulated, has never been widely diffused." Induction appealed to the masses; a prime instance was the spread of the "Baconian philosophy" in the seventeenth century.[15]

In appealing to Bacon, Buckle in one sense reaffirmed lessons Sumner had already learned at Yale. But in grafting positivism onto the older empiricism, he went further than Sumner was prepared to follow. Although the young American and his Oxford friends agreed that Buckle was "on the right track," they "did not see how the mass of matter to be collected and arranged could ever be so mastered that the induction could actually be performed," especially if the idea of an "induction from history" were strictly construed.[16]

After serving for three years as a classics tutor at Yale (1866–68), Sumner spent the years between 1869 and 1873 struggling with these conflicting lessons while attempting to find the best outlet for his talents. He plunged into the cauldron of Anglican church politics, first as editor of *The Living Church* and utility pastor in New York and New Haven, and then, from 1870 to 1872, as minister of The Church of the Redeemer in Morristown, New Jersey. At the time, the Anglicans were torn between High and Low Church groups, the one stressing dogma and tradition, the other science and progress. Identifying with a moderate Broad Church faction, Sumner sought the compromise that still eluded him.[17]

His weekly sermons told the story. His starting point remained the Baconian dictum that "every scientific investigation is a prayer to the God of nature." He thus initially refused to recognize the existence of any "warfare" between science and religion. Properly understood, science was a friend of true religion. "Caesarism and popery," he wrote his fiancé in 1870, were "going down before civilization and science." Yet, as the warfare heated up, he was forced to concede that writers such as Huxley and Spencer posed a threat to faith. "Modern speculation and science," he warned in his farewell sermon, raised the possibility that "all religion may be lost."[18]

Sumner's solution was to distinguish science as "method" from the "speculations," as he described them, of individual scientists. He found "no great fault" with Darwin, Huxley, or Spencer in "their original works," he told his New Jersey congregation. "They may be right or wrong in their speculations and theories," but they were "honest, sincere, and industrious" in method. But what was this method? Many Baconians at this point simply retreated to a celebration of facts over hypothesis. Sumner instead noted "a mischievous ambiguity" between science and natural science, as the terms were usually employed. "Science is the source of rules by which the human mind is guided in investigating truth. These rules are given in the structure and methods of the action of the human mind. They are universal." When pressed, that is, Sumner fell back on the deductive method with its "universal" rules of the human mind.[19]

Sumner characterized this position as moderate rationalism, which for a time sustained his middle position among the contending church factions.[20] By the autumn of 1871, however, he found this middle ground uncomfortable, if not untenable—one reason, perhaps, why at that point he decided to leave the clergy. With his own view of science still in limbo, he accepted a call to Yale as professor of political economy the following spring.

3

In the decade following his 1872 appointment to Yale, Sumner established a formidable reputation as scholar, publicist, and one of the university's most popular teachers. On campus, he supported the "Young Yale" movement, championed academic freedom against President Noah Porter, and helped liberalize the curriculum. He also launched a short-lived political career in October 1873 when he won election as Republican alderman, a post he held for three years. His written work included historical studies and popular defenses of free trade, hard currency, and laissez-faire in the *Nation*, *Harper's*, the *Independent*, and other leading journals.

Meanwhile, Sumner vacillated between his new-found fondness for deduction and the narrower empiricism upon which he had been raised. In an "Introductory Lecture" to his classes in 1873, he took as his text John Tyndall's "Scientific Use of Imagination," an address of three years earlier. Still seeking a middle ground, Sumner now made room for both observation *and* generalization. He was glad to see that Tyndall had "vindicated the deductive method even for the physical sciences." But there was a limit: "The inductive method, though slower and more commonplace, is far more sure and convincing."[21]

At the same time he discovered that a just-the-facts inductionism could be a dangerous weapon in the hands of reformers who capriciously catalogued social "ills" without understanding the principles behind them (a discovery similar to that which Albion Small made during the Bemis case two decades later). At the annual meeting of the American Social Science Association (A.S.S.A.) in 1874, Sumner blamed "empiricism" for unintelligent social experimentation and the resort to chance remedies, his specific target being a group of social workers within the A.S.S.A. who were locked in a struggle with academics for control of the organization. A call for "first principles," with the implication that extensive training and arcane knowledge were required in order to understand society, conveniently served the purposes of incipient professionalism. It also had political implications. Turning Buckle on his head, Sumner argued that empiricism gave the masses the erroneous impression that one person's opinion was as good as another's.[22]

The rise of the German historical school in economics during the late 1870s confirmed this bias. As younger economists returned from Germany, Sumner viewed the growing debate with alarm. "Anyone who follows the current literature about economic subjects," he wrote in 1879, "will perceive that it is so full of contradictions as to create a doubt whether there are any economic laws." The fault was not with the historical method, properly practiced. Reviewing William Roscher's *Principle of Political Economy*, Sumner noted that its approach was "the deductive method common to all the economists," despite its presentation of historical and statistical material. Roscher's followers discredited the historical school by rearing socialist schemes on scraps of past information.[23]

Continuing the discussion, Sumner hinted, however, that his heart was still with empiricism. "The rise of a school of historical economists is itself a sign of a struggle towards a positive and scientific study of political economy," he wrote in 1881, ". . . and this sign loses none of its significance in spite of the crudeness and extravagance of the opinions of the historical economists." In attempting to meet the enemy halfway, he was ready to retrace his steps from deductionism to a narrower empiricism.[24]

4

During the 1880s, three separate episodes sped Sumner on the path to empiricism: his controversy with Yale President Noah Porter in 1880–81; the reception of *What Social Classes Owe to Each Other* (1883); and the rise of new social specters in the form of giant monopolies, on the one hand, and Marxism, on the other.

At issue in the Porter affair was Sumner's use of Spencer's *The Study of Sociology* (1874) in a senior social science class in 1878. When Porter learned that Sumner planned to offer the course again the next year, he wrote to object to this choice of textbook. Although the two men attempted to settle the matter privately, a report in the *New York Times* in 1880 caused both to go public. Sumner challenged Porter's right to dictate texts, and finally threatened resignation in an open letter to the Yale Corporation and the faculty in 1881. In the end, both men could claim victory: Sumner, because he refused to concede the issue of principle; Porter, because Sumner stopped assigning the book.

Given Sumner's earlier feelings toward Spencer, the affair had a certain irony. Although he had been unimpressed by *First Principles* when he read it a decade earlier, Sumner took a new interest in Spencer with the appearance of the *Study* in the *Contemporary Review* in 1871–72. This discovery, in turn, reinforced his new-found fondness for deduction. Sumner's rhetoric told much of the story. "We must seek [the] regeneration [of our political system] by returning to first principles and applying them with scientific vigor," he intoned. Other Spencerisms gradually crept into his prose: "progress . . . from the simple towards the complex"; "social force"; and the effects of "action and reaction." Until the Porter affair made an issue of it, however, Sumner was scarcely a Spencerian. The odd phrase aside, he avoided Spencer's metaphysics entirely, seldom cited his name, and called his own course in the area "social science" rather than "sociology."[25]

Then and since the Sumner-Porter affair has been subject to sundry interpretations: as a skirmish in the ongoing warfare of religion and science; an early episode in the struggle for academic freedom; or the confrontation of an academic discipline in a "pre-paradigmatic" stage seeking "identity and security" within an educational institution in a period of curricular adjustment.[26] None of these interpretations, however, sufficiently highlights the fact that the central issue was not Christianity *versus* science, but science itself. Science could be theistic or antitheistic, Porter had written earlier in *The American Colleges and the American Public* (1870). "The question is not whether the college shall, or shall not, teach theology," he continued, "but what theology it shall teach—theology according to Comte and Spencer, or according to Bacon and Christ." In the Sumner case, the issue likewise was not science but Spencer's view of it: "the cool and yet sarcastic effrontery with which he assumes that material elements and laws are the only forces which any scientific man can recognize."[27]

Sumner himself recognized that definitions could make or break him. Writing to the Yale Corporation, he defended the scientific character of Spencer's work, while insisting that he taught "sociology as a science, from second causes only"—a distinction scientists themselves had employed for a century or more to make their work acceptable to churchmen. He also made a point of his own ignorance as to how science should be applied to society: "All that we can affirm with certainty is that social phenomena are subject to law, and that the natural laws of the social order are in their entire character like the laws of physics."[28]

Sumner's tentativeness and self-deprecation were partly battle tactics: how could anyone criticize an enterprise as yet undeveloped? "To deride or condemn a science in this state," he wrote in the *Princeton Review*, "would certainly be a most unscientific proceeding." But they also reflected a genuine uncertainty concerning his foray into the realms of speculation. What, after all, were "natural laws"? or "the laws of physics"? Were Spencer's cosmic laws merely "splendid generalizations for the weak-minded," as Porter alleged? In a revealing footnote to the *Princeton Review* article, Sumner acknowledged that no proof of the existence of "social laws" was possible other than the observation of the "sequences, relations, and recurrences" that the scientist "has learned to note as signs of the action of law." With this nod to positivism, the episode closed.[29]

But the Porter incident left its mark. Soon after, Sumner changed his assigned readings in the sociology course, and with them, the focus of his teaching. In 1883–84 he cautiously reintroduced sociology for graduate students (but not for undergraduates), but he described the course modestly as "text-book lessons, explanations, etc." Although a reading course in social science was continued on an alternate-year basis, he gave top billing to anthropology. He also added a year-long elective in anthropology for senior undergraduates, with readings in E. B. Tylor's *Anthropology* and in other texts longer on historical fact than on cosmic speculation.[30]

The reception of *What Social Classes Owe to Each Other* (1883) taught Sumner a similar lesson. In structure and in tone, the work combined pulpit oratory and deductive logic, both legacies of his past. Sermon-style chapter titles summoned the faithful to weekly meeting: "That It Is Not Wicked To Be Rich; Nay, Even, That It Is Not Wicked to Be Richer than One's Neighbor." Schoolbook logic captured the essence of all humanitarian schemes: "that A and B decide what C shall do for D."[31] Formulations of the "if-then" and "therefore" variety dotted its pages. For this reason, the work soon appeared anachronistic to a younger generation grown accustomed to facts and specifics. "Good logic," scrawled an anonymous reader in the margin of his copy of *Social Classes* in 1916, "but exactly what does this mean?" "Facts!???" this reader demanded at another point.[32]

But *Social Classes* also looked to the narrower inductionism of Sumner's later work, notably in its definitions of the terms "liberty" and "equality." On this point, Sumner was clearly in difficulties. He was reluctant to abandon the certainties of the natural-law tradition, but he regretted the metaphysical connotations of terms such as "natural rights." His solution was to propose a crudely empirical translation of "nature" into the soil, rocks, and trees from which humanity must gain a living in a struggle for existence. In this translation, natural rights meant nothing more than a chance to dig, to quarry stone, or to fell timber on equal terms with one's neighbors.[33]

In thus stressing the struggle for existence, Sumner did not intend to graft a Spencerian or Darwinian metaphysic onto natural-law theory. Rather, he sought to find in the "facts" of nature a more certain basis for the policies he favored. The appearance of *Social Classes* nevertheless fueled charges that he was misusing biology to justify a dog-eat-dog social order, the essence of the later accusations that he was a "social Darwinist." Without reiterating the details of the ensuing debate, suffice it to say that it reinforced the lesson that Spencer was dangerous company. "The 'economic harmonies' are a great subject," Sumner wrote in June 1884 in the last of several apologies on the subject, denying that he held to Darwinian doctrine as charged. Although he promised to "publish [his] notion in proper detail," he effectively dropped all use of analogical language, Spencerian or otherwise.[34]

Sumner's strategy was, in fact, virtually the opposite of that which the critics suggested, although nonetheless "conservative" by their standards. Historically, there is an enormous difference between metaphysical definitions of "rights" and "liberties" and narrowly empirical ones: the first look toward restraint and limits to the powers-that-be, and liberation from the burden of the past; the second, toward acceptance of the established order and traditions. In redefining "nature" and "natural rights," rather than rejecting the natural-law approach outright, *Social Classes* obscured this distinction.

In distinguishing "is" from "ought" Sumner also anticipated a distinction between scientist and citizen that would later become a basic tenet of objectivism. Political economy, as he put it, "does not assume to tell man what he ought to do. . . . It only gives one element necessary to an intelligent decision." As citizen, the scientist would have "sympathies and sentiments" upon which he was obliged to act, and for which he bore final responsibility. But as scientist he could merely predict the outcomes of this or that course of action. For Sumner this distinction corresponded to that between private and public action, in accord with his belief in laissez-faire; for later objectivists, it described the relation of government to "experts." In both cases, however, the gap between "is" and "ought" was glaring, and the basis for "sentiments and sympathies" ultimately vague.[35]

Sumner's work in the mid-eighties also reflected the intrusion of new issues. Whereas free trade and the land issue (especially Henry George) had been the focus of much of his writing through *Social Classes*, he turned now to strikes, monopoly, and Marxism.[36] Escalating his assault on metaphysics, he redefined abstract conceptions in terms of hard, irrefutable, material facts. A term such as "proletariat," thus reduced, had virtually no meaning: the real social contest was between the "House of Have and the House of Want." "Monopoly" referred to the natural monopoly inherent in the technology of railway and telegraph, and was in no way a product of "capitalist society." "Capital" was not, as Marx maintained, a product of an exploitative system, but was rather the banked reserves of past effort.[37]

"Facts" became a fetish. The issue of socialism, Sumner wrote toward the end of the decade, turned ultimately on "The Challenge of Facts." Questions concerning the well-being or progress of humanity required comparison of present and past societies. In his teaching and scholarship, Sumner accordingly turned from political economy to history, the result being biographies of Jackson, Hamilton, and Robert Morris, and a two-volume work on the finances of the Revolutionary period. From the conviction that monopoly was natural, and from mounting anthropological evidence that group solidarity was the key to survival, he fashioned his own version of solidarism, now termed "antagonistic cooperation."[38]

This reorientation culminated in "The Absurd Effort to Make Over the World" (1894), probably his best-known essay, and one quite different in tone and argument from *Social Classes*. Sumner wrote the piece in the midst of one of the nation's worst depressions, two years after overwork and a near-breakdown had persuaded him to accept private support for a sabbatical stay in Germany. Unlike his earlier appeals to logic or to the "laws of nature," he now answered social reformers with an "appeal to the facts"—specifically, historical facts. Stressing objective study over "philosophical doctrine," he demanded "particulars and specifics" from those who would change things. Among these facts, he now frankly recognized the increase of "social power" through greater organization, an emphasis on both power and organization that contrasted with his earlier stress on individual rights and liberties.[39]

Sumner's antagonist was now ostensibly Edward Bellamy, whose *Looking Backward* was then attracting considerable attention. But he tacitly admitted that in his own way he himself had been guilty of "the vain fancy that we can make or guide the movement." In this deeper sense, as the historian Donald Bellomy has noted, "The Absurd Effort to Make Over the World" was Sumner's farewell to reform. Its implications for his later work would become evident as he turned to write *Folkways*.[40]

7

THE AUTHORITY OF FACT

I long to see a "Darwinian" sociology, in the sense of an array of significant and solid facts.

A. G. Keller to Sumner, 1903

The mores have the authority of facts.

Sumner, *Folkways*, 1906

1

In the nineties, Sumner's private woes compounded his public traumas. He was over fifty and had been teaching uninterruptedly for two decades. His health had never been good, and in 1890 he fell victim to what was termed a "nervous illness," the result of a punishing work schedule that had yielded sixty articles and two books in the previous three years. In December he set sail for an extended stay in Europe, financed in part by donations from forty-two loyal supporters, among them Yale graduates Henry Holt, Chauncey Depew, and Sumner's close friend William C. Whitney.[1]

Sumner resumed his duties at Yale in the fall of 1892, but the collapse took a permanent toll on his energies and output.[2] Between 1876 and 1890 he had published some 108 articles in addition to seven books; in the five years following his breakdown, he wrote "only" four articles and two books. Although in 1896 he added another dozen articles and a book, he averaged only two articles per year during the rest of his career and left uncompleted his projected "science of society," save for the substantial fragment that appeared as *Folkways* (1906).[3]

Sumner's ill health alone does not explain the tone and mood of his later work. But whether the issue was domestic policy, overseas expansion, or Yale politics, he judged the world from a bed of pain. Completing his voyage from economics to sociology, *Folkways* was the personal, no less than intellectual, testament of a mid-Victorian liberal strayed into a world he found acutely uncomfortable.

2

Politics was at the center of this growing disillusionment. After breaking with Hayes and the Republicans in 1876, Sumner had made an uncomfortable peace with the Democrats, who promptly nominated him for a third term as New Haven alderman. When he failed to win election, he gave up politics, never to return. In 1880 he discarded his ballot rather than vote for either major party candidate, or for the opprobrious Greenbacker James B. Weaver. Joining the Mugwumps, he supported Cleveland in 1884 and 1888. But during the 1890s he found little to choose between the protectionist McKinley and the silverite Bryan, and in any case he left no record of his vote. American jingoism from the Venezuelan crisis of 1895 through the war with Spain three years later strengthened his despair.[4]

This disillusionment, in turn, had important implications for his intellectual development. Firstly, the gap between American ideals and current realities pushed him toward both a thoroughgoing relativism *and* the reification of national folly in terms of "folkways" and "mores," words he coined to describe the unconscious and the more formalized patterns of behavior manifested in a society. The United States historically had one set of principles, but in 1898 it found some of these inconvenient and dropped them; "There are no dogmatic propositions of political philosophy which are universally and always true," he wrote with new-found resignation.[5] Secondly, the war dramatized the difference between "purposes" and "consequences," a distinction that led directly to the behavioristic orientation of his later work. Preaching "liberty," American statesmen in 1898 embarked on a policy that was certain to have consequences that would make it "exceedingly difficult, or impossible for us to exercise any liberty at all." Purposes actually had nothing to do with consequences. Nor should the latter be studied in the light of ethics: "Since consequences are entirely independent of motives and purposes, ethics have no application to consequences."[6]

During these years, Sumner found support for his views in the work of several other theorists. Like Small and Ward, he was especially attracted to the work of Ludwig Gumplowicz and Gustav Ratzenhofer, representatives of the "struggle school" of Austrian sociology. From both he learned the importance of warfare in the early stages of society. But unlike Small, Sumner preferred

Gumplowicz's *Realpolitik* to Ratzenhofer's ethical idealism. "Ideals are necessarily phantasms," Sumner later wrote, citing Gumplowicz. "They have no basis in fact."[7]

The blustering Theodore Roosevelt, and the "fads" and "delusions" of the Progressive Era, completed this descent into political cynicism. With T.R. at the helm, Sumner feared that America was entering its dangerous "glory days." (The feeling was apparently mutual: "They both lie," T.R. allegedly remarked of Yale's Sumner and Harvard's Charles Eliot Norton, adding that he liked everyone else on the faculty of both institutions.) But to Sumner the alternative of Bryan seemed even worse. "We shall have to vote for Teddy in 1908 in order to Ward off Bryan and Hades," he commented. But in doing so, he would be "disgraced forever."[8]

Accordingly, Sumner came to view politics as a game whose players he watched with amused contempt. "I found out that I was likely to do more harm in politics than almost any other kind of man, because I did not know the rules of the game and did not want to learn them," he wrote of his earlier political career. "Therefore, the adepts at it could play with me in more senses than one." The experience enabled him to "gauge the value of the talk we hear about 'civics' and 'citizenship.' " Thus alienated, he judged even Bryan's proposals, not as passing folly, but as significant indicators of changes in the national "mores," a term he first adopted in 1899 when he began to work seriously on his proposed science of society.[9]

In distinguishing purposes from consequences, Sumner, strictly speaking, was saying only that consequences can be observed without being judged, because they are beyond individual control and choice. The "objective" status of the mores *as knowledge* (epistemologically) did not necessarily establish or entail the neutrality of Sumner the observer (practically)—another sociologist might have studied the mores to discover what reforms were most feasible. Nor did his reification of the mores as social "facts" necessarily commit him to a narrowly scientistic methodology (procedurally); he might, for example, have explored the question of how mores are internalized by individuals. In the end, however, *Folkways* exhibited all three tenets of the emerging objectivism: in defining customs as "facts" apart from individual intention or desire; in positing the emergence *within* the mores of the objective frame of mind; and in collecting and classifying the mores in the best tradition of Baconian science.

3

While political cynicism provided the context for Sumner's reification of human values and activities as mores, Albert Keller lectured him on the meaning of Darwin and science. Born in Springfield, Ohio, on April 10, 1874, Keller entered Yale College in 1892, just as Sumner returned from his stay abroad. Unhappy with his early college experience, young Keller found in Sumner and Sumnerology both cause and career. He completed a doctoral thesis on Homeric society under Sumner in 1899 (published 1902); he then joined the department, and was ultimately Sumner's successor. After Sumner's death in 1909, Keller devoted himself to the completion of the projected *Science of Society* (1927), against the advice of Yale's President Hadley among others. In memory, as in life, his affection for Sumner was unbounded. "I loved and admired the man very deeply," he once confessed to E. A. Ross. "There was nothing small about him."[10]

Keller began his campaign to convert his mentor to Darwinism in the spring of 1903. Keller's own views at that point were in something of a tangle. Discovering Darwin during the neo-Darwinian controversy of his undergraduate years, he had been persuaded that Lamarckianism was inadequate. But he distrusted Weismann's exclusive reliance on the "dogma of the non-transmissibility of Acquired Characters," and the attendant emphasis on struggle and selection. He felt that this stark biological determinism ruled out the cultural elements that are the hallmarks of human association.[11]

To resolve this dilemma, Keller eventually adopted two not entirely consistent strategies. To counter Weismann's biological determinism, he developed his own theory of "societal selection" in which cultural rather than biological selectionism played a major role, a bold and frankly speculative use of selectionist analogies. But he also insisted that true Darwinian method was strictly inductive. "[Since] Darwin's time there has been merely deductive reasoning on the great principle of Natural Selection," he wrote Sumner in 1901, citing a recent study of evolution; "now the younger naturalists insist on returning to the inductive methods of the founder."[12]

Keller, as a result, was in the curious position of trying to convert Sumner to an evolutionist view of the mores, while at the same time arguing that Darwin was the Baconian of Baconians. A truly "Darwinian sociology" would contain an "array of significant and *solid* facts," he wrote in an early letter on the subject. Although he then discovered to his dismay that Darwin in *The Descent of Man* was himself not immune to metaphysics, he continued to urge Sumner to adhere to the *true* Darwinian method. "Now in my judgment, your 'mores' are going to fill out that part of it which D. fell down on, to say nothing of a great deal more."[13]

Writing after Sumner's death, Keller elaborated this argument. Again he insisted that Darwin's fact-gathering, not Spencerian speculation, provided the basis for a "general belief in organic evolution." In this version, Darwin was almost a comic-book Baconian: "It was the solid, brute force of Darwin's 'shovelfuls of facts,' together with his reputation for dispassionateness and scrupulous candor, that carried 'Darwinism' forward to its destiny." By this standard, most of what currently passed for "sociology" deserved all the criticism it got.[14]

By this time, however, Keller had also gone public with his social selectionism, the other half of his reading of Darwin. He now insisted that Darwin's theory of evolution—adaptation through variation, selection, and transmission—could be applied to social developments. In *Societal Evolution* (1915) he argued that folkways and mores were both evolutionary products, brought into adjustment through the combined action of variation, selection, and transmission within the cultural realm. If correctly interpreted, this Darwinian view of society did not rule out a belief in progress to be achieved through patient study. "No writer of sanity, let alone ability, ever scoffed at progress," he continued, downplaying the fact that his mentor had come close to doing so on a number of occasions.[15]

Unfortunately, Keller's dual strategy raised some awkward questions. Was social evolutionism at odds with the Baconian view of science? By employing the concepts of variation and selection, was Keller himself not guilty of invoking a "biological analogy"? Further, was this reading of evolution not a backdoor attempt to get just a *little* progress? Although he faced these questions in several tortured passages in *The Science of Society*, he proved only that he had no answers.[16]

On the premise that social theory should be somehow "Darwinian," Sumner could have gone in any of several directions. First, he could have adopted a probabilistic view of natural and social development, wherein folkways and mores could be analyzed statistically—essentially the route of Giddings and his students. Secondly, he could have accepted Keller's social selectionism,— a moderate version of the Giddings approach. Or thirdly, as finally happened, he could accept the Baconian rendering of Darwinism to the exclusion of all evolutionary models of society.

Sumner toyed with the first. Interested in what he termed the "aleatory element," he probed the role of chance in human affairs in his classroom lectures. "I am glad you are interested in 'chance,'" wrote the economist

Irving Fisher in 1903, during an exchange on the subject. In *Folkways* Sumner discussed briefly the Galtonian conception of a genetic group as a variety of traits distributed about a mean. To earlier observers, the "coherence, unity, and solidarity" of the group appeared "to conceal a play of mystic forces"—but propositions about it were ultimately like those about a run of dice.[17] Were the mores simply probability predictions concerning the way individuals in fact responded under such and such conditions? Were they capable of "statistical specification"? In an unpublished essay entitled "Mores and Statistics and Mathematics," Sumner finally put these questions directly: "The answer is that the pure mores are not capable of such treatment at all." Luck remained a term to describe occurrences where the "facts" were not known, not an occasion for redefining natural law as a statement of probabilities.[18]

On the issue of social selection, Sumner apparently accepted Keller's criticisms of analogical reasoning, and even of Spencer, whom Keller often used as a whipping boy. In an unpublished piece written shortly before the appearance of *Folkways*, Sumner argued (with apparent reference to Spencer) that it was impossible to arrange the mores "in a logical scale of advance, even if time and place were disregarded." "I agree with your opinion of Spencer," he wrote to Keller shortly before his death. "I will cut out the biolog[ical] parallels and shorten the lessons. I was half a mind to do it a year ago. Now I have decided."[19] But for this very reason, he would not buy Keller's evolutionary view of the mores, let alone his social selectionism. Speaking to the Anthropology Club at Yale shortly before *Folkways* appeared, he flatly rejected an evolutionary view of the mores, although in deference to Keller he did not include the address in *Folkways*, as he had initially intended.[20]

Sumner thus finally took the third route, rejecting both statistics and social selectionism. In a speech on "The Scientific Attitude of Mind" in 1905, he turned for the first time formally to the subject of scientific method. Science must be defined in terms of its end product, he insisted, as "knowledge of reality," not merely the settled opinion of a community of the competent. This reality was not "rationalism," because "that is only a philosophy." Nor was it "natural or realistic in the philosophical sense [i.e., idealistic], because that would imply a selection of things, in operation all the time, before the things were offered to us." Instead, it consisted of the brute and undeniable givens of experience, Baconianism without the religious aura. His "thirst" for this reality amounted to a passion.[21]

Judged in the light of the intellectual battles of the 1880s, Sumner's embrace of a stripped-down Baconianism involved something of a paradox. The conservatives of the time were popularly perceived as defending the "deductive" approach while their opponents in the historical school stressed induction.

Now the situation was reversed, or so it seemed to Henry Farnam, a Yale economist and colleague of Sumner. "While the lines seemed in the beginning to be drawn on the whole between the deductive school . . . as represented by Sumner, and the inductive or historical on the other," Farnum wrote to Richard Ely the year after Sumner's death, "the literature of the period shows that Sumner's work has been almost entirely historical, and that his treatment of sociology . . . is largely descriptive."[22]

4

The situation at Yale also shaped Sumner's (and Keller's) perception of science and sociology. In New Haven, distrust of science remained endemic. Whereas science was fine in its place, that place was separate from the rest of the curriculum. After the old guard lost the battle for the classics, Yale College became a bastion of "liberal culture," an ideal that preserved the prevailing scepticism toward anything scientific. The establishment of the Sheffield Scientific School, ostensibly a concession to useful and scientific knowledge, institutionalized the two cultures. Anyone who wanted such learning, the College said in effect, could go to Sheff.[23]

Although the appointment of Arthur Twining Hadley as president in 1899 ostensibly promised to change all this, it soon seemed a disaster to Sumner and Keller. Once in office, Hadley moved in two different directions, both equally troubling: first, he made concessions to the Yale College tradition, and the antiscientific liberal cultural ideal; secondly, he attempted to modernize the faculty by stressing publications over teaching (Keller pictured himself and his mentor preeminently as teachers), by instituting an "up or out" policy for appointments, and by setting a mandatory retirement age of sixty-eight, which gave Sumner less than a decade.[24]

Even worse, Hadley was unwilling or unable to integrate the scientific outlook, and with it the social sciences, more squarely into the curriculum. "We are in for trouble at Yale in the next years," Sumner wrote Keller in 1904. "Woolsey put 'science' off in a corner where it could not contaminate Greek and Filos. We are about to reap the consequences." Sumner's feelings toward Hadley were "deep and powerful," Keller later confided to a friend, "and profane." Keller shared this animus. "Sumner told someone then that Yale was sure to go to hell now," Keller later recalled of those years, "and we have meandered a long way toward that place."[25]

Yale orthodoxy and a lingering distrust of Darwinism converged in the charge, then popular in liberal-culture circles,[26] that science was, after all, just another faith. "But of course now people say 'you see, Darwin had to have a metaphysic like everybody else!' " Keller wrote, concerning *The Descent of Man.* "That enrages me." He was further outraged to learn that "even the (English) instructors claim to believe that Darwinism has been overthrown and tell the students that . . . . It infuriates me to hear such stuff." In this climate, a Baconian Darwin was in any case safer than a "speculative" one.[27]

The realities of classroom teaching also worked against Spencer and ana-logical reasoning. Although Yale never adopted totally free electives, the absence of prerequisites had become a problem by the first decade of the new century. For Spencer's "synthetic philosophy" this fragmentation was fatal. "I have been reading Spencer and with great relish," Keller wrote Sumner in 1908, temporarily overcoming his distaste for speculation. "But I must say the part on the analogy between a society and an organism palled on me. I am convinced that this is the part the students don't like." In proposing to cut out the biological parallels in his projected study, Sumner apparently agreed.[28]

A rigorous distinction between facts and speculation suited prevailing no-tions of the ideal Yale man. Attention to the facts provided "mental discipline," an attenuation of the classical ideal that enjoyed something of a renaissance in the Hadley years. "It seems to me well to give them a big dose of Darwin," Keller wrote Sumner of his teaching, "if for no other purpose than to cultivate careful thinking and scientific method." If no longer a response to God's Creation, fact-gathering was character building. "There was in Darwin no whining about hostility," Keller wrote, "rather was there an avidity for all criticism and an absence of sensitiveness about personal glory."[29]

Above all, fact-gathering was manly. "I was glad to hear . . . that you are projecting a 'He-Book,' on Sociology," Keller wrote to Ross several years later, forgetting some earlier doubts concerning the westerner. "Lord knows there are enough 'It-Books,' not to mention the 'She-Books.' If some scientific virility can be injected into this sadly emasculated subject, the sociologists will not need to climb a tree every time a real scientist heaves into sight." On this scale, Sumner again outranked Spencer. "Spencer was something of an old maid and perhaps a little feline now and then," Keller later reminisced. "But Sumner, with all his hard hitting . . . ought to appeal to anyone who, in these times, prays: 'O God, give us a Man!' "[30]

The inductive imprint also distinguished Yale sociology from other schools then emerging, although Keller was more sensitive to this fact than was the ill and aging Sumner. Part ideology, part regional snobbery, Keller's opinions of the competition were characteristically pointed. "The wild attempts of Ross to show he has read Faust etc. etc. are very absurd," he wrote Sumner of *Social Control*, before his opinion had mellowed; a penchant for "theories" affected "many of the teachers of small western colleges." Albion Small was almost beyond contempt: "He is a professor at Chicago and is an extremely windy man," Keller wrote an acquaintance some years later. "He likes to balance other people's ideas and give smart evaluations of them." Warning against an even greater sin, he added: "make allowances for an emotional writer." Given this opinion, Keller could not resist punning Small's name. "Very likely they pose as great frogs in the 'small puddle,'" he wrote of Ross and other western sociologists. Discussing "small" to Sumner on another occasion, he reduced his handwriting in size, but finally confessed that he could not write the name "smaller."[31]

5

In *Folkways*, Sumner shaped these lessons into one of the two or three most important books in sociology published in the United States in the prewar years. Its thesis was beguilingly straightforward: Humanity is driven by the four basic instincts of hunger, love, vanity, and fear—a naturalism that reflected Sumner's pessimistic assessment of the human condition. In all societies, individuals attempt to satisfy these needs as best they can. Through trial and error, one method of satisfying demand becomes customary for all or a significant part of a society; these methods Sumner termed "folkways." Initially experimental, folkways gain a moral sanction through a process of comparison and reflection. The "mores" are folkways grown moral and reflective. Once established, they become "fixed and coercive." Sumner's choice of terms expressed this difference: the Anglo-Saxon "folk" for the unconscious ways; the Latin "mores" for the tangle of custom and morality that rules all societies.[32]

The inductive spirit infused both method and message. The method was Baconian with a vengeance: in preparation, Sumner collected thousands of notes on human customs and traditions, past and present—a collection that finally filled more than fifty file boxes. Between its opening and closing chapters, *Folkways* was a veritable warehouse of information on topics ranging from incest to sports. The mores similarly were themselves "social facts," to be collated and compared *as if* still on notecards. "The mores contain embodied in them notions, doctrines, and maxims," he intoned, "but they are facts. They are in the present tense."[33]

There was, of course, a trick in all this determined empiricism. The mores, insofar as they embraced beliefs as well as behavior, were not "facts" in quite the same sense as are tables and chairs. As Charles Ellwood later asked, "Who ever saw a tradition?" Rather, the notion of the mores represented a new way of *conceptualizing* social reality. The term was an imaginative construct no less than "Gemeinschaft" or "primary group." Mores were "facts," not literally, but by analogy: they had the "authority of facts."[34]

To complicate things, Sumner went on to say that, although the mores define "right" and "good," they are sometimes wrong and even mischievous. Accidents, irrationality, and "pseudo-knowledge" sometimes enter into their formation. Some folkways are "positively harmful." The results were things he most disliked: "advertisers who exaggerate," "the ways of journalism," "electioneering devices," "oratorical and dithyrambic extravagances in politics." These contemporary horrors were "not properly part of the mores," but they were "symptoms of them."[35]

There appeared to be another trick in that judgments of "bad" and "good" mores seemed to imply an external standard that, by Sumner's own accounting, existed only *within* the mores. This standard, however, was not a patchwork of youthful convictions (concerning individualism and the like), as some historians have claimed, but rather the "scientific" outlook itself. Although in the modern democratic era the masses had deprived the classes of their power, the classes introduced a variation in the mores of potentially even greater importance, namely, the scientific outlook. This matter-of-factness (as Sumner's former student Veblen termed it) allowed the social scientist, by examining the mores historically, to determine which had proved conducive to societal survival. The mores thus contained a self-correcting element.[36]

Science, in this view, was both relative and absolute. As theory or speculation, it was no less subject to "fashion" than were other human endeavors: witness the historical progression from "realism" to "nominalism," from "deism" to "rationalism." So viewed, even evolution, "now accepted as a final fact," might well turn out to be "only a fashion." But science, defined as apprehension of facts-as-they-are, was not ephemeral, and it was the scientific outlook in this narrow sense that was gradually entering the mores of the "classes."[37]

Did the incorporation of the scientific outlook within the mores provide a basis for conscious social policy directed by a scientific elite? Sumner sometimes seemed to imply as much: "the historical classes have . . . selected purposes, and have increased ways of fulfilling them." Whether for good or ill, the classes introduced "variation" that produced change. In a most un-Sumnerian statement he saw the goal of the "science of society" to be the development of "an art of societal administration" that was "intelligent, effective, and scientific." In the manuscript version of one of his final essays, he insisted further that the "masses" acknowledge "the authority of the specialist and expert."[38]

At the same time, his portrait of the mores as "facts," and his narrowly Baconian definition of science, distanced his proposals from those of progressives who called for "sociocracy" and "creative intelligence." Although not "natural laws" in the older sense, the mores as "facts" were automatic and inexorable in operation. In their ubiquitous inevitability, the mores ruled out most social engineering almost as surely as did the "laws of physics" to which Sumner had appealed in the 1880s. But only almost. If *Folkways* resounded with warnings against precipitous reform, it was only to insist that proposed changes conform to the mores. Whereas the mores of the "classes" (including the scientific outlook) were historically less basic than those of the "masses," this latest "variation" promised a better if fragile future.[39]

In this context, one can see why Sumner's epistemological characterization of the mores as facts led, however tentatively and cautiously, to a celebration of the matter-of-fact neutrality of social science. Although Sumner was out of sympathy with most progressive reforms, he faced a dilemma similar to that which troubled fellow sociologists, whatever their political persuasion. For his generation, the rapid pace of change, and a growing awareness of the varieties of human custom and practice, bred a troubling ethical and cultural relativism. For mid-Victorian liberals such as Spencer, the concept of modernization was one way of coping with this specter: a bipolar view of past and present— whether militarism and industrialism, *Gemeinschaft* and *Gesellschaft*, or status and contract—obliterated the troubling variety of cultures (now lumped together as "preindustrial"), while looking to the emergence of a single ethically and socially superior industrial order. Modernization, that is, promised freedom from relativism.[40]

Because Sumner rejected the theory of progress, and finally all evolutionary models of social change, this route was closed to him. Yet his hope for the emergence of a scientific outlook, however narrowly defined, revealed that he was unable to resist entirely the appeal of the modernization model. The ideal of the "neutral" observer was in this sense a functional equivalent of a progressive future in which he could not or would not believe. *Folkways* effectively proposed a radical relativism coupled with the hope that a scientific outlook would replace the forces that had produced it. By placing science within the mores, Sumner attempted to resolve the dilemma without totally accepting either relativism or modernization.

6

What, then, of Sumner's legacy to American sociology? Although the terms "folkways" and "mores" soon made their way into the literature, *Folkways* was less than a total success in the limited arena in which professional reputations are measured. Contemporary reviewers faulted its methodology no less than its political implications. As George Vincent of Chicago put it: ethnological data "seem at times to overweigh the book by their sheer bulk and multiplicity."[41] Sumner's incipient social realism challenged the perennial nominalism of most American sociology, but most work in the field, as Roscoe Hinkle has noted, remained nominalist and voluntaristic. Charles Ellwood saw an affinity between Sumner and Durkheim, but he made the point only to damn both as "objectivists."[42] When a later generation became interested in the notion that social usages had the coercive power of "facts," they turned to Durkheim's *Rules of Sociological Method*, not to *Folkways*.

The relative crudeness of Sumner's formulation explains some of this neglect, but intellectual merit was only part of the story. Another was Yale itself. Although a legend in his time, Sumner spent his career at an institution that still considered undergraduate education to be as important as graduate or professional training. Compared to Giddings or Small, he left no "school" or even disciples, save for the all-too-faithful Keller. In the prewar years, Sumner trained only six doctoral students: Kate Halliday Claghorn (1896), James E. Cutler (1903), Henry Pratt Fairchild (1909), Arthur James Todd (1911), Frederick E. Lumley (1912), and Charles W. Coulter (1914). Of these, all occupied positions at academic institutions of the second rank, and at least four were primarily concerned with social work. Fairchild published a text entitled *General Sociology* (1934), but he was better known for *The Melting Pot Mistake* (1926) and polemical pieces supporting eugenics, birth control, and immigration restriction. Lumley's *Means of Social Control* (1925) was closest to the *Folkways* tradition, but owed equally much to Park and Burgess, and to Ross, and in any case it made no claim to originality.[43]

Sumner's influence was further diminished by the fact that the best-known of these students disagreed with his politics. Fairchild, an avowed socialist and a vigorous critic of big business, proposed governmental action on a scale that would have made Sumner shudder—a factor that probably contributed to his dismissal from Yale in 1918 ("his continuance here would seriously hamper a development laid down by Sumner, followed by me, and approved by the faculty," Keller wrote circumspectly to a friend).[44] Todd also offended local conservatives during his tenure at Minnesota. And Lumley, in *The Means of*

Social Control, offered instruction to any who "find it necessary or desirable to take a hand in the work of control."[45]

The breadth of Sumner's interests also lessened his impact in an age of increasing specialization. In his review of *Folkways*, George Vincent wrote that the work "establishes Professor Sumner as a folk psychologist, however modestly—or indignantly—he may disdain the title." Albion Small later confessed that he had never thought of the Yale professor as a sociologist until, quite to his surprise, Sumner was elected president of the American Sociological Society.[46] To later observers, Sumner's writings seemed closer to anthropology or to philosophical history, two fields whose practitioners took over the issues that most interested him. His apparent lack of methodology compounded the problem. "What strikes me most strongly," wrote Charles Horton Cooley, ". . . is that *Folkways* does not conform to any of the current canons of methodology." "The Method—if it can be called a method," added Robert Park, consisted essentially of collection and description.[47]

Yet in a general way Sumner had left an important legacy. Park himself conceded as much in remarking (in 1931) that the "effect of his researches was to lay a foundation for more realistic, more objective, and more systematic studies in the field of human nature and society than had existed up to that time."[48] In their doctoral theses the leading interwar objectivists had already made the same point. Of all American sociologists, wrote Bernard at Chicago, Sumner came closest to the idea of society as a "self-existent, and organic and self-perpetuating unity."[49] At Columbia, F. Stuart Chapin and William F. Ogburn drew directly on *Folkways* in their studies of education and of child-labor legislation, even though their nominalism led to quite a different version of objectivism than was implicit in Sumner's work. For all three of the younger sociologists, social activities previously studied for their contributions to human happiness and social well-being became the impersonal "data" of science.

8

AN OBJECTIVE STANDARD

*[My doctoral] thesis was a protest against instinctive
control, pointing out its inadequacy and its essentially
subjective and individualistic reference.*

Luther Bernard to Charles Ellwood, 1911

1

A born maverick, Luther Bernard had a special talent for making trouble.
While still a graduate student at Chicago, he lectured Albion Small on the
department's shortcomings to the outrage of most of his professors. During his
academic career he moved restlessly from place to place, teaching finally at
half a dozen universities. Although a colleague once termed him "America's
favorite peripatetic professor of sociology,"[1] these moves reflected a hyper-
sensitive and often prickly personality, coupled with a penchant for sexual
adventure that clouded his professional reputation and almost destroyed his
marriage. A prodigious correspondent, Bernard created a network of gossip and intrigue probably unparalleled in the history of academia. "L.L.B.'s
onionskins"—the multiple carbons he rained upon fellow sociologists—became a trademark. During the 1930s, he led a rebellion that divided the
American Sociological Society into bitter factions.

Bernard's difficulties did not result from want of promise or accomplish-
ment. He was one of the most talented of the prewar crop of graduate students
at Chicago; in fact, Small once ranked him with Vincent and Thomas as
the best of his students.[2] His study of *Instinct* (1924) weaned a generation
of sociologists from the crude biologizing and naive reductionism of most
prewar work. Active abroad, especially in Latin America, he was probably as
well known internationally as any native-born American sociologist of his
generation.

Intellectually, Bernard was a study in contrasts. Combining behaviorism
and social realism, he viewed social acts as responses to stimuli, but he reacted

against the "pluralistic behaviorism" of Giddings and his students by insisting that society was more than the collective responses of individuals to environmental stimuli. Because "ideas" were merely a preparation for action, sociology could ignore individual feelings and interests and, indeed, would become "objective" only when it did so. Methodologically, Bernard joined those who demanded a more quantitative, research-oriented sociology, but he then insisted that "science" looked to an "absolute standard" that was neither simple description nor probability prediction.[3] During the thirties, these differences led to open conflict with quantifiers whom Bernard charged with treating methodology and research as ends in themselves.

Bernard's politics were correspondingly complicated, and easily misunderstood. His doctoral thesis (1911) was essentially an attack on the individualistic and utilitarian assumptions of earlier Progressivism for having failed to provide an absolute social standard. During the 1930s, he blasted the New Deal for not being radical enough. In an important sense, Bernard attempted to restate both the "scientific" *and* the "utopian" program of Comtean positivism, a tradition he examined in one of his final books—but, as with Comte, the result was "conservative" or "radical" depending upon one's perspective. For this reason some contemporaries, including Small, had trouble placing him on the political spectrum. Was he "radical," as he claimed, or "conservative," as he seemed to his mentor?

Because in Bernard's case the personal and the intellectual were often indistinguishable, his background and early career provide an unusual and sometimes brutally clear picture of the forces that were shaping objectivism in American sociology. In his awkward, and often painful, transition from provincial to professional, young Bernard experienced not a status crisis, as that term is conventionally used, but a radical disjuncture between past and present, value and fact, that dwarfed anything comparable in the experience of Small, Giddings, or even Sumner. The result was a pervasive distrust of self, of tradition, and of feeling. This disjuncture was manifested in ways that ranged from a constant concern with appearance and clothing (a concern that became almost obsessive in later years) to matters as basic as the redefinition of sex roles in modern society. In social policy, no less than in personal life, sentiment was a dubious guide. Seeking a new standard, Bernard distrusted the do-good humanitarianism of the more comfortable and established middle classes, and turned instead to embrace efficiency and social control.

Bernard left no school, nor a radical tradition worthy of the name, but his attempt to fashion a behaviorist sociology at once radical and realist, although a minority position, was not to be the last such attempt in American social thought. For this reason, no less than for his tempestuous role in the profession, he deserves a central chapter in the history of interwar objectivism.

2

Luther Lee Bernard (1881–1951) was born in Russell County, Kentucky, and lived most of his youth in the bleak obscurity of west Texas. Although the family name was said to mean "an inhabitant of Berne," the first Bernards had come to Kentucky from Ireland in the mid-eighteenth century. His father, Hiram Hamilton, had fought on the Union side during the Civil War, an act that took some courage in a border state, whatever his later failings turned out to be. Life after the war was not easy. Of the first three Bernard children, two died in an epidemic of diphtheria that swept Kentucky in the late 1870s. About 1878, the family headed for the first of several new homes on the Texas frontier.[4]

Bernard family life was a study in rancor. The senior Bernard was a farmer more interested in real estate than in the joys of husbandry, who bought and sold land, dragging the family from one part of the southwestern frontier to another. He was a petty tyrant whose mistreatment of Luther's mother increased as the years went on. On one occasion Luther suspected his father of depriving Luther's aged mother of money for food and medical care, as well as of attempting to swindle him out of some land. "Why do you keep up your dishonest, deceitful ruses?" Luther demanded in an astonishing letter written later in life. "Don't you think I can see thru your attempts to flim-flam me?" On another occasion he added: "Why don't you deal frankly about things? You are too old for that sort of thing." In these letters he addressed his father "Dear Sir." Privately, he suspected that the old man was on drugs.[5]

The experience left Bernard few illusions concerning yeoman virtue, inoculating him against the populist agitation that swept portions of the west during his teenage years. There was "little dispute" concerning the attitudes of the typical farmer, he later wrote in a passage that described his father no less than the provincial attitudes he battled throughout his career: "Conservatism, more or less disregard of the scientific method, religious and political orthodoxy, emotional intensity with consequent high suggestibility along the lines of his conventional interests . . . and a frugality and thrift which sometimes border upon parsimony." The root of the problem was "adjustment." No longer the yeoman of legend, the American farmer produced for a world market, and must adapt to the realities of this situation.[6]

Other family members offered young Bernard little emotional compensation. His mother reportedly took abuse obediently, and in later years she sat quietly in the kitchen even during the rare family get-togethers. When she died in the early 1930s Bernard had not seen her for two years, although he lived in the same state and was begged to visit by a younger sister. His older brother was by all accounts a worthless conniver, given to drink and betting, who perennially attempted to deprive Luther and other family members of land and income that were rightfully theirs. "He is no better than a dog, of the cur variety at that," Bernard once remarked. Soon after Luther left home for college, his father begged him to avoid his brother entirely because a dream had revealed to him the impending murder of the good brother by the no-account one, a Cain-Abel scenario that happily never occurred. For his part, young Luther openly charged that his father loved his no-account brother more.[7]

Luther dreamed of rescuing his younger sister from these tawdry surroundings, until her emotional breakdown blighted the hope. Their relations in later life vacillated between rancor and recrimination. "Your entire attitude toward the family is so bitter, so defensive, so antagonistic that an answer to any discussion concerning it is useless," his sister wrote during one partial truce. "Of course, you have suffered terribly before you became so bitter and hurt," she conceded.[8]

The single bright spot in Bernard's youth was provided by two charismatic young teachers, named Walter S. Hale and E. E. Edmondson, who served as the joint principals of "Gordon College," the ungraded high school that Bernard attended in his midteens. Together they made a profound impression on the awkward farmer's son. Intellectually, they introduced him to the theories of Darwin, Spencer, Huxley, and other giants of British and German science. "They were unflinching partisans of the Darwinian theory of evolution even in a community where church members abhorred the idea of evolution as a product of Satan himself," Bernard recalled.[9] Personally, and against all the conventions of Victorian propriety, they also taught less-elevated lessons. Edmondson, when not immersed in Blackstone's *Commentaries*, was entranced by a multivolume subscription series on "Great Lovers of History," and on one occasion he practiced on one of his students. Hale's amorous exploits also caught Bernard's notice when one day the young principal decked a companion who suggested that an impropriety had occurred between Hale and a local grade school mistress.[10]

Bernard, commenting later on Ross's autobiography, sensed an affinity between the cultural isolation, emotional poverty, and religious orthodoxy of his own youth and the background of others who shared a "revulsion against subjectivity." Ross ascribed this revulsion in his own case to close contact with two cases of delusional insanity, a situation not unlike Bernard's dealings with his family. "Perhaps too, it was a reaction against the Calvinist discipline of his Presbyterian background, with its emphasis on original sin, soul searching and motivational scrutiny," he speculated. This affinity also explained why Bernard found Ross's social psychology more congenial than that of C. H. Cooley. "To the sheltered Cooley the family was the primary group," he wrote. "To the orphan Ross, it was primarily a demographic unit." These similarities aside, Bernard tacitly acknowledged that Ross differed from him in an important regard: the Wisconsin sociologist was blessed with a "singular freedom from conflicts"; Bernard remained a tortured soul.[11]

3

In 1901 Bernard left home for Pierce Baptist College in St. Louis. His higher education was hard won. His parents, to judge from their letters, were poorly schooled and unlikely to promote college for their children. When Luther decided to attend Pierce, his father provided $18 for a new suit—but only after Luther had plowed fields for a month. (His brother "had a suit at the same time from the same source, although he had not plowed," Luther later complained.) At Pierce, he supported himself with a series of low-level teaching jobs, while he studied Latin, Greek, chemistry, and higher mathematics. In 1904 he took a B.S. degree.[12]

Bernard first encountered sociology at the University of Missouri, which he entered the following fall. His mentor was Charles A. Ellwood, a recent Chicago graduate then on the threshold of a career that was to win him professional esteem if not universal admiration. A social psychologist who proudly wore his heart on his sleeve, Ellwood in 1901 had already published several articles on charity and an attack on Giddings's concept of imitation, when he left a post as charity organizer in Nebraska to go to Missouri. When Bernard arrived at Missouri in 1904, the older man was embroiled in a battle with one of Small's students over the issue of whether society had a "real" or merely a "psychic" unity, the latter the subject of Ellwood's doctoral dissertation.[13]

Ellwood instinctively appealed to Bernard, in part because of the very eccentricities that annoyed other students. The professor shrugged his shoulders involuntarily, he recalled, "sometimes as if he would worm himself out of his clothes and especially his collar, which was always too large for him"; he also had "an annoying habit of sucking air or saliva through his teeth with a characteristic sound, possibly because his lips were too big for his Irish type mouth." The undergraduates regularly made sport of Ellwood in college publications and theatricals, and called him "Little Charlie" behind his back. But Bernard, already sensitive to appearance, saw quality behind the facade. Ellwood's dress was after all "quite conventional and perhaps more expensive than that of most of his colleagues," he observed. Those students who ridiculed their professor "were not the more industrious or better adjusted" ones.[14]

However, ambivalence and even hostility also colored this relationship. Bernard later claimed that he owed Ellwood an everlasting debt of gratitude. "I found your lectures and classes so interesting that I decided to make sociology my own career, in spite of the fact that I had strong inducements elsewhere," he later confided. (The reference was to an invitation to apply for a fellowship in psychology, and a definite offer of one in English at Harvard.) Yet, in his student days, he delighted in cutting Ellwood to pieces behind his back, a fact that other Missouri students diligently reported to their teacher.[15] Two decades later, as Ellwood led the charge against objectivism, these taunts would come home to roost.

After taking the M.A., Bernard left Missouri for Chicago, staked by a loan of $250 for which his father this time exacted 6 percent interest. Chicago's President Harper had died the previous year, but a brilliant faculty remained as his legacy. In sociology, the Small regime was at its zenith, with George Vincent, Charles Henderson, and W. I. Thomas as the departmental mainstays. Although John Dewey had departed the previous June, Bernard also profited from work in philosophy, notably with George Herbert Mead.

Bernard's graduate peers included several sociologists later prominent in the profession: Emory Bogardus, professor at the University of Southern California and editor of *Sociology and Social Research*; Cecil Clare North, who became professor of sociology and statistics at Ohio State; Max Handman, whose career eventually took him to the universities of Texas and Michigan; and Edwin H. Sutherland, an authority on unemployment and crime. Another was Frances Fenton, formerly an English instructor at Mt. Holyoke, who in 1911 became the first Mrs. Luther Bernard.

Bernard, as he later remembered it, was distinguished in this group for being worst dressed. Handman, a Romanian Jew with flowing bow tie, long hair, and a passion for opera, especially earned his attention and envy; popular with everyone, and especially with the ladies, Handman had little time for the son of the Texas farmer. "Rating me by my clothes and my recessive appearance," Bernard remembered, "I was the easiest of all his contemporaries and competitors to classify and dispose of." The fact that Handman appeared to use his knowledge of opera to impress professors, and was for a time a rival for Frances Fenton's affections, made matters worse. Although Bernard's attitude changed once he had bested Handman—first for a fellowship, and later in love—his insecurity, and constant sensitivity to slight, did not abate.[16]

At Chicago, Bernard also found, or imagined, evidence of a moral decay that at once excited and repelled him. In an analysis of the then-fashionable cult of aestheticism, apparently written for one of Small's classes, he lamented that the "moral motif" was virtually absent from modern letters. As an example, he cited "a certain well-known play" in which the heroine, after willingly being seduced by a "rake," becomes a prostitute and a "dope fiend" when her husband refuses to take her back. The intended moral was that the husband was to blame, whereas in Bernard's view the woman was entirely at fault. To make matters worse, some academic colleagues with whom he discussed the play saw it only in terms of style and technique, the lone exception being a fellow sociologist who saw its moral viciousness for what it was. Whereas the rest found only humor in questions of "present social morality," Bernard and his sociological confrere understood the "functional importance [of traditional standards] for the moral welfare of society."[17]

Bernard's conversion to behaviorism was rooted in these experiences. For the awkward provincial, the Chicago "environment" was a stark reality rather than an extension of the socially interacting self. The goal was "adjustment," as he made his way painfully from ill-clothed farm boy to successful academic. As the behaviorist later put it: "the integration of personality depends primarily upon . . . adjustment to . . . environment." Among the many responses conducive to adjustment, none ranked higher than those that were "themselves conditioned by the behavior of others serving as stimuli."[18]

So viewed, Bernard's behaviorism reflected a cultural as well as a personal crisis. In the big city, "consciousness" no less than "conscience" seemed ultimately a hindrance. By explaining human activity in terms of stimulus and response, behaviorism subtly relieved urban newcomers of moral responsibility, while at the same time allowing mastery of an otherwise threatening situation.[19] Sex was the crucial issue. Translating spirit to matter, the psychological to the physiological, one might take a neutral "scientific" approach to this tabooed area. The result, in one sense, was an escape from the Calvinist past. But more profoundly, it also marked an extension of the Calvinist's impulse to control. By policing the flesh (whether rat-pups in a maze, or the chaotic passions of humankind), the behaviorist replaced the Calvinist God who, if obeyed, promised protection of a sort from the terrors of the flesh.

Behaviorism, above all, constituted an assault on traditional ways of doing and feeling, whether embodied in instinct or in custom. "What we need is objectively tested fact to replace our venerable traditions," Bernard argued. His assault on instinct theory gave the coup de grace to a doctrine that had informed most sociological theory since Ward. "Feeling" to Bernard was "undependable," an adjective he used with revealing frequency.

The catch, of course, was that Bernard himself had more than his share of passion. But like "scientific" sociologists from Giddings to Ogburn, he early learned to segregate these feelings in private, imaginative outpourings—in his case, the countless poems that he had begun to write even before he left home for Pierce College. Tortured, usually dolorous, these poems spoke of desire unfulfilled, love unrequited, and feelings that caused only pain. Especially revealing was "My Wild Heart," written at Missouri in 1905:

> O heart I turn from thee in vain,
> Thou wilt not cease to vex me still.
> Thou hast no balm, but only pain—
> A vain regret and rankling ill.

These poems meant a great deal to Bernard. "It has been a release of my conflicts," he wrote his wife Frances, when their marriage had deteriorated beyond repair. "This poetry is the history of my life, the life that has been most intimate and unbearable to me." By this time the poems numbered more than three hundred and fifty, and in the end, over a thousand. Although he conceded that only some were good, he asked that all be published should he die prematurely.[20]

Politics also absorbed Bernard's energies during his graduate-school years. By the time he arrived in Chicago, the nation's problems seemed to many Americans to be increasingly less amenable to humanitarianism of the Hull House variety or the zesty moralism of T. R. and the muckrakers. For Albion Small, mounting evidence of class conflict underlay his formulation of the theory of "interests"; for Franklin Giddings, social fragmentation seemed to demand the more precise measurement of the "social pressures" needed to effect change. For Bernard, a fear of social and moral chaos inspired a search for social efficiency and for an "objective standard of social control."

Politically, Bernard at the time considered himself an "intelligent liberal," that is to say, one who favored a social policy based on science rather than on sentiment. During a summer on the Chautauqua circuit in 1909, he regularly debated a moss-backed individualist and a socialist who attached themselves to the tour. In these exchanges he made it clear that he opposed socialists, reactionaries, and do-good sentimentalists alike.[21] His goal was social control—a term he used often and unabashedly throughout his career, and the subject of one of his last published works.

Bernard's politics could be somewhat confusing, however. Like other social controllers, he mingled praise of democracy with calls for an "objective standard" that seemed to denigrate democratic politics, and even popular rule. Albion Small at one point, on being asked whether Bernard were a dangerous radical (a standard inquiry by prospective employers in those unenlightened times), replied that his student's tendency was "precisely in the other direction, namely to stand off in the attitude of a critic and to point out weaknesses in the position of people who are attempting to agitate the world of rights." When told of this evaluation, Bernard wrote immediately to correct Small's "mistaken impression": "I have the radical rather than the conservative cast," he assured his mentor. Assurances aside, however, Small spoke for most of his generation in the conviction that an "objective standard of social control" was not what the founding fathers of sociology meant by reform.[22]

4

In the classroom, Bernard acquired theory to structure these convictions. Among the faculty his favorite was George Vincent, who first introduced him to Durkheim, or at least to the bit that surfaced in Bernard's doctoral thesis. "The fact that Vincent taught social psychology of the French or collective type intrigued me," Bernard remembered, "and I was determined to have as many courses with him as possible." It was Vincent who in the summer of 1909 invited Bernard on the Chautauqua tour. A decade later, as president of the Rockefeller Foundation, Vincent helped Bernard obtain a grant to study in Latin America.[23]

Bernard also liked W. I. Thomas. To the appearance-conscious Texan, Thomas's demeanor was pleasantly unassuming: "a florid, almost sensual face and slightly obese body, loosely covered with a coarse gray baggy suit set off by a colorful shirt and tie, and a rounded head thinly covered with close cropped hair." "If any member of the faculty could be loved, it was surely Thomas," he reminisced. Yet this admiration did not stop Bernard from retailing student gossip concerning Thomas to Small. Revealingly, what most interested and bothered him were sexual comments that Thomas allegedly made in class. Discussing the matter with Ellwood, Bernard learned that Thomas had apparently undergone a significant change. In the early days he had held quite conventional views of marriage and the family. His more recent views on sex, Bernard concluded, were related to the generally "disorganized condition" of his teaching, and his rumpled appearance. Even more than Handman, Thomas was a lesson in modernity, a lesson underlined when in 1918 he was fired from Chicago for allegedly putting his views into practice. In the mid-twenties, when rumors of sexual scandal clouded Bernard's own career, he deftly orchestrated the election of Thomas to the presidency of the A.S.S. over the wishes of Ellwood and most of the old guard.[24]

Other Chicago faculty pleased Bernard less. "I found much to disagree with in Mead's courses," he recalled. For all Mead's brilliance, his lectures were disorganized and often incomprehensible. When on one occasion Bernard presented his own views on instinct in a course on "The Logic of the Social Sciences," Mead treated him to a "long-winded" metaphysical disquisition that "wore me out."[25]

Bernard positively disliked the ministerial Charles Henderson. "He always spoke of the church with so much apparent respect that frequently his voice dropped to a whisper," Bernard recalled. He wondered how Henderson managed not to "chuckle within." Unsure in his grasp of sociology, Henderson, in Bernard's view, accepted Small's ponderous rhetoric as proof that the chairman was a theorist. When in the third year Bernard joined Henderson's seminar, a group that met in the professor's home, the great man explicated his bric-a-brac "as if those things were as important as the subjects of the seminar."[26]

Bernard's view of Small was more complex, if only a bit more charitable. Returning from the Chautauqua summer, he was bitterly disappointed when Small offered him the honor of serving as his assistant because Vincent, whom he preferred, had made a similar offer; as chairman, Small promptly overruled Vincent, an exercise of prerogative that Bernard long resented. Crisp and precise in his own writing, Bernard ridiculed Small's "ponderous German style." "Vincent's mind," he later observed, "worked as concretely and lucidly as Small's plowed ponderously through the jungle of German metaphysical entanglement."[27]

In the extraordinary letter that Bernard wrote to Small shortly before leaving Chicago, he revealed both his hostility and his habitual way of dealing with such messy emotions. "I had intended to have a talk with you before you left in the summer regarding various matters of policy etc. in connection with the department of sociology," Bernard began. Then followed six pages of biting criticism: Faculty members were aloof; students felt that the department lacked "body or tangibility"; undergraduate instruction was a campus joke; library administration was hopelessly inadequate; the curriculum was top-heavy with theory; and the department "made little or no effort" to place graduates. Student opinion of individual faculty members ranged from condescension to derision, Bernard continued. Of George Vincent: "not a great sociologist but an after-dinner speaker"; "hopelessly clever"; "too much Chautauqua." Of W. I. Thomas: "all off on the sex question. He has read too much Bernard Shaw and not enough facts." Of Charles Henderson: "his courses are considered 'light.' " And of Small himself: "your courses do not deal with the methodology and investigation, as the students believe they should, but are concerned for the most part with a logic of mere concepts."[28]

But did Bernard share these student views? At this point, Bernard became the neutral observer, a posture he invariably adopted when dealing with feelings he could or would not otherwise handle. He simply wanted to give "a more objective viewpoint of the situation in which you, as head of the department, have been for so many years," he assured Small. He was merely a "mirror" for the comments of others.[29]

Although Small said that he wished that all students would leave such a document, ears burned and tempers flared. Thomas claimed that he took the remarks well himself, but he told Bernard that Henderson was "very angry, in spite of his Christian calm." Henderson passed the Bernard memo to Vincent with the comment that he must take his medicine with the rest. Thomas warned Bernard not to expect too much in the way of future favors from the department.[30]

In his doctoral thesis, Bernard fashioned his personal convictions and experiences into a systematic critique of the Ward tradition, including Small's reformulation in *General Sociology*. An outgrowth of utilitarianism, contemporary sociological theory shared with it the assumption that the solitary, hedonistic individual was the starting point for "all things social," an assumption that corrupted public policy no less than it did social theory. A truly "moral" social theory would focus instead on the measurable externals of social behavior, and take as its measure "the good and development of society as a whole."[31]

In one sense, Bernard was simply carrying to the extreme Small's insistence that the business of sociology was the group rather than the individual. But he also challenged several of Small's leading conceptions: The term "social process" was too "indefinite and non-descriptive" to explain the development of social interdependence. "Interests," while pretending to be objective, were "in effect abstractions or forms" beneath which lurked the old subjective impulses, a criticism similar to Bentley's in *The Process of Government*. The "interests" rested on speculation rather than on observation or experiment. "There was no conception of investigation or generalization by statistics, of weighting and selection," Bernard later commented. "It was Spencer's technique and the German industry over again, somewhat refined by a pseudo psychology."[32]

Bernard's sources were revealing. He regretted Comte's mystical Religion of Humanity, but he credited him with the first "really functional conception of the . . . social unity." Spencer's use of the organic analogy rendered this same vision concrete, although in his case it was vitiated by the individualistic assumptions of utilitarianism. Dropping the analogy, Durkheim rested his theory of the "compulsory essential unity of society" on the division of labor and social functions, a distinct improvement. American sources included Sumner's *Folkways*; G. H. Mead and C. H. Cooley, who attacked the notion of a "solipsistic self"; and the behaviorist trends within functional psychology.[33]

Theory aside, Bernard's thesis was a revealing personal document. The concern with moral decay was especially pervasive. Nietzsche, for example, represented all "frankly hedonistic theorists and agitators who regard pleasure, happiness, self-gratification as the legitimate end of all action and abhor social control accordingly." A catalogue of modern horrors caricatured the world according to Bernard: "artists and litterateurs" who "withdraw themselves into an esoteric world"; "the social whirl and dissipation" of life in modern cities; even the craze for "hobbies," the latter noted with reference to W. I. Thomas's passion for golf and opera.

Above all, the problem was sex and the modern woman. In a spirited footnote, Bernard described the "modern woman of fashion" to illustrate the "dissipation" of the current age. "Her thoughts are not arduous," he began,

but she takes utmost care—by proxy—that there shall be no discord in them. A large part of her time is given to the luxurious care of her body—by others—and the remainder is divided between her clothes and fashionable functions or personal and sensuous gratifications, involving ceaseless change and inconstancy or anarchy of social purpose. Practically all the ordinary gross stimuli, such as light and color effects, sound, touch, taste, and odor, are carefully controlled for her. Customary morality in many cases drops out, especially in the realm of sexual experience, where social conformity would make inroads upon other pleasurable adjustments.

"Such a picture has a feeble counterpart in the Greek and Roman courtesans and in the harems of the East of today," he concluded, only half in jest.[34]

Turning to the political implications of his position, Bernard wondered aloud whether his ideal of objectivity implied the "rule of an elite in any objectionable sense." The critical question was, of course, "objectionable" to whom? His reply betrayed the deep-seated distrust of democracy that later confused Small: there never had been or would be "a pure democracy of very considerable proportions in which every man is equally free and capable in forming his own opinions and in expressing his activities," Bernard insisted. His proposal demanded "the rule of an elite in no greater degree than is implied in the reasonable direction of administrative details by experts, instead of more or less irresponsible control and exploitation by professional politicians." Again, Bernard was simply carrying some of the demands of contemporary Progressivism to a logical conclusion. But freedom and dignity were nonetheless possible only by conforming to group needs, which were to be ascertained on a scientific basis.[35]

If attuned to the age, Bernard's views were anathema to his professors. Small opposed the inclusion of a lengthy discussion of neurology and physiology, and asked Bernard to delete it; it was allowed to remain only after a member of the neurology department had read and approved it. During the oral examination, Henderson demanded to know how Bernard dared disagree with views to which Small had dedicated his career, a question that triggered a bitter exchange. "Small reddened and squirmed in his seat," Bernard remembered. "I fear I looked my contempt." In the end, Henderson voted to fail him, although the effect was only to lower the grade from a summa to a magna.[36]

But more than pique was involved. In a calmer moment, Small confided to Bernard that he also believed that the attack on himself was misplaced. He too sought "objectivity" and could not detect "subjectivity" in the cases cited, that is, in his own theory of "interests." And in fact, Bernard himself was guilty of reintroducing "subjectivity" through the back door in the unstated and unprovable hypothesis that psychic elements could be excluded in explaining motor impulses: objectivity, that is, rested on an assumption that could not be proved "objectively." Small's "urgency" in opposing Bernard came from the fear that he would prove to be another case of a "good man gone wrong" in a quest for something that was not there.[37]

Edward C. Hayes, a Small protégé at the University of Illinois, joined in the attack on Bernard's hidden assumptions. Bernard's assault on psychological reductionism in a sense nicely complemented Hayes's own attack on the

" 'social forces' error"; but Hayes challenged the further assertion that social policy could ignore individual standards in favor of some hypothetical "second nature" to be achieved through conditioning. What was to be the source of the objective standard?—if the existing social order, then "no prophets should invite stones nor Christ dare the cross"; if a source other than "democratic individual satisfactions" experimentally determined, then the new order would be based on "theological or metaphysical law" that was "nothing but an apotheosis of speculative absolutizing."[38]

Underlying this debate was the perennial conflict between fact and value. Small had effectively confused the two in postulating six "interests" that were at once subjective and objective, values and things valued. Refining Small, Hayes in effect extended his implicit realism to integrate generic, ecological, and social structure in a manner that has recently earned him a reputation as an American echo of Durkheim and a precursor of social realism. But in so doing, Hayes also severely limited the scope of sociology. For the sociologist, values, no less than heredity and geography, were social facts that conditioned social behavior. But like other sciences, sociology was limited to description of the *pattern* of social relations; motives as such were irrelevant. For his ultimate values, and for the principles to guide social control, Hayes appealed frankly to traditional norms, specifically those of Christianity.[39]

Bernard found Small's closet subjectivism and Hayes's frank dualism equally unacceptable. But some uncomfortable questions remained. Was the "objective" standard either a reified status quo, or just more speculation? Was Bernard an "absolutist" after all? A lengthy exchange with his friend Edwin H. Sutherland forced these questions into the open. Bernard (as Sutherland understood his position) first attempted to prove that he was not an absolutist, or if so, that it was not a bad thing, offering as proof his support of an eight-hour law for women. Sutherland replied that he also supported such legislation, but insisted that he did so out of sentiment, not science. It was finally impossible to compare the social benefits of increased output (through longer hours) and of better health (through shorter).[40] The answer to the question of "more wealth or less health" could not be stated with reference to a standard such as "social conservation," but rather depended on "the sentiments, impulses and general experience of the persons making the decision." The "right answer" harmonized with this previous experience. Sutherland's own sentiments were such that he preferred the increment of health for the moment. "[But] I cannot prove that that is preferable if I try to . . . take an entirely impartial attitude toward the question." The "so-called scientific answer" was in any case "merely a method of persuading the uninitiated and unsophisticated."[41]

Pressing the issue, Sutherland wondered if Bernard, no less than Small, were not trapped in a closed system. Although Bernard claimed to be open to the "facts," he admitted *as fact* only such as fitted his system. Sutherland allowed that "some dogmatism must be assumed in order to get experiment started—tentative and hypothetical." But he insisted that the true social scientist must be eager to include all facts. This attitude required a frank recognition that one's personal preconceptions figure in the making of hypotheses. "Search your soul," he urged his friend, "for evidence of closedness in your system."[42]

Ever expecting that friends would desert him, Bernard misread criticism as apostasy, and dismissed Sutherland's charge. Sutherland replied that he had no intention of questioning his friend's professional competence. Bernard never conceded the point that his vaunted "objectivity" was as arbitrary and absolutist as were the values of his opponents, but he apparently began to search his soul. In April 1916 he wrote Sutherland dejectedly that he now felt he had "no system at all." Reviewing Lucius Moody's *Social Adaptation* (1916), he observed that social scientists were "better able to shake off subjectivism and individualism" than to state "tests of conduct" to be used in attaining new goals. At the same time he also confessed to Small that his thesis had addressed only half the problem: although he had cleared away obstacles, he had put nothing in their place. "I had not then worked out the matter of the nature and content of the objective and scientific substitutes sufficiently to state them in full . . . . I merely wrote a poor prospectus of them."[43]

5

Bernard's career frustrations and personal difficulties in the post-Chicago years contributed to this pessimistic assessment. Between 1911 and 1914 he taught social science and history at the University of Florida. "Exiled," as he later described it to Small, he spent "three long dreary years doing kindergarten work in four different fields, working nights and Sundays for good measure on examination papers and the like, with an average of twenty hours a week of teaching." For the three following years he taught at the University of Missouri, an appointment he ascribed to Ellwood's "political necessity," but one which put him no closer to the theoretical work he wished to do.[44]

The situation at Missouri dramatized the tension between convention and modernity that had first plagued Bernard in Chicago. At one extreme stood his mentor Ellwood, still hoping to return his "favorite student" to the path of sociological righteousness. At the other extreme was the ever-tempting world of Bohemia, which at Missouri had at its center none other than his old rival Handman, now possessed of a wealthy wife and a reputation for fabulous parties. Others in this circle included Thorstein Veblen, whose peccadilloes had earned the wrath of the Chicago authorities (although Bernard later insisted that Veblen's reputation for philandering was much exaggerated!), and a group Bernard described only as Handman's "Bohemian associates who . . . believed themselves to be brilliant and charming because they were somewhat risqué and not very profound." Bernard sensed that due to his background and temperament, this group was impenetrable. He also knew it was dangerous, because the Missouri administration had allegedly earmarked several of its members for dismissal. He remained cordial to Handman, but quietly suffered what he later termed the group's "petty slights and intrigues."[45]

A disintegrating marriage compounded Bernard's misery. His wife Frances, a Vassar graduate with social graces and a small income of her own, also embodied the life to which Bernard aspired. Almost immediately, however, their marriage fell victim to imagined slights and his still-monumental insecurity. Her very self-assuredness and independence taunted him. "I was always afraid I would not make good, and when you criticized me I felt as if you had been a traitor," he confessed to her in the final stages of their separation.[46] Resenting her affluence and the freedom it bought, Bernard believed that his wife despised the hardship of his life. When she once defended her mother against him, he was deeply wounded. While she scorned his poetry, he wondered how she could devote so much time to a scholarly project that promised no adequate monetary reward.

Just as Bernard's father represented the unregenerate, mean-spirited countryman, so his wife came gradually to symbolize the "new woman" against whom he had railed in his thesis. Among the direct causes of the disintegration of modern marriage, he wrote in a scholarly analysis soon after his divorce, were the modern woman's "assertive personality," her self-indulgence in "aesthetic and recreational interests," and her "mercenary attitudes." Worse, these traits were often encouraged by mothers who insisted that their daughters should have an easier time than they had had.[47]

In this unhappy situation, a key issue was again the tension between feelings (or "attitudes," as he eventually termed them) and their realization. Although he loved Frances, his faith in his own talent and attractiveness withered before the conventions of background and class that she embodied. "This complex began far back before we were married when you would be especially severe with me because of some awkwardness or incompetency," he confessed on one occasion.[48] Given this feeling, confirmation of self-worth came not from self-examination and inner resources, but from the adulation and affection of colleagues and especially of female students. As extensions of this attitude, Bernard's behaviorism, his professional politicking, and his philandering were, for better or worse, intimately related.

In the summer of 1916, just as he decided he had "no system at all," Bernard suffered a physical and emotional collapse. A series of operations "pretty nearly finished me nervously and physically," he wrote to his wife, while the effects of the ordeal lingered in a deep-seated depression. "I have no confidence in myself or in what I do or aim at."[49]

In 1917 Bernard received an offer from the University of Minnesota, a post that offered new and exciting possibilities. He was not yet a behaviorist, a term just then entering the social science lexicon. Nor, thanks to his heavy teaching loads, had he yet given evidence of the prodigious scholarly output that would make him a force to be reckoned with in the next two decades. But in several ways he was already an important representative of the second generation in American sociology. Just as Ogburn and Chapin from Columbia represented the development of the Giddings tradition, so Bernard extended Small's emphasis on objectivity in ways that Small himself hardly recognized, and of which he largely disapproved.

Looking back over the difficult years since he had received his degree, Bernard might well have wondered if things could have been different: had he been more diplomatic in his dealings with Henderson, or even with Small; had Vincent stayed in sociology and developed his interest in French realism; or had Thomas or Mead been more interested in cultivating and placing graduate students. As it was, he had wandered in exile for half a dozen years in jobs that everyone agreed were beneath his talents. With the appointment at Minnesota, he would now have an opportunity to complete the second, constructive portion of the work he had begun in his thesis.

9

MISBEHAVIORISM

Most of us who think or write from the [behaviorist]
viewpoint do not even trouble ourselves about the term,
but since it is not inaptly chosen, we do not resent
the appellation.

Luther Bernard, 1931

1

For Bernard, the situation at Minnesota seemed made to order. Although the university had produced only a handful of Ph.D.s, and sociology itself remained something of a stepchild, his appointment coincided with the start of a new era. In one of his final acts as the university's president, George Vincent, Bernard's mentor and now patron, created a coordinated program in sociology and civic work that led finally to an independent department and a substantial commitment to new offerings in the field. During Bernard's tenure, his colleagues included Arthur Todd, a Yale Ph.D. (1911), who took terminal leave in 1919 before departing for Northwestern three years later; Frank J. Bruno, another Yale graduate (S.T.B. 1902), who came to sociology via charity work; Manuel C. Elmer, a Chicago Ph.D. (1924), who arrived in 1919; and F. Stuart Chapin, who replaced Todd as chairman. Bernard feared that Chapin was tainted by his association with social work, but the appointment augured well for the sort of "scientific" sociology he had wanted.[1]

During these years, Bernard's scholarship flourished. Contributing regularly to the *American Journal of Sociology*, he also published a 550-page study of *Instinct* (1924), a textbook on *Social Psychology* (1926), and many incisive (and often witty) reviews in *Social Forces*. If intellectually he remained largely a counterpuncher—exposing faulty definitions, clearing away pernicious assumptions—he also attempted answers to the questions that Small and the others had raised. Could an objective standard transcend the status quo without being fanciful? If so, what were its specific implications for individual behavior and public policy? By 1930, Bernard was widely regarded as one of American sociology's leading behaviorists, a label he himself finally accepted after years of public denial.

The public record told only part of the story, however. The Minnesota years were also ones of bitter departmental squabbling and near-disastrous personal scandal. Facing dismissal from the university, and unable to obtain the Chicago post he really wanted, Bernard moved fitfully to Cornell (1925–26), to Tulane (1927–28), to the University of North Carolina (1928–29), and finally to Washington University in St. Louis. The twists and turns of this troubled career had both intellectual and professional consequences. His embrace of behaviorism, however much rooted in his earlier experiences, was in its timing an act of defiance that bespoke his growing alienation, and his discontent with the direction the discipline had taken. The conflicts of the twenties, moreover, influenced the struggles of the next decade.

2

Soon after his arrival at Minnesota, Bernard became embroiled in the first of several of the controversies that were by now his specialty. The issue was political, although almost comically so. At stake was the establishment of a "Social Science Review," approved by two deans but then scotched by the Board of Regents. "In these days of Bolshevism I don't know whether I dare state the cause even," Bernard wrote E. A. Ross, tongue-in-cheek, when the Red Scare was at its peak: "First we heard that the word 'social' was objectionable. Then we understood thru certain channels that the Review would have to be conducted off the campus if it were published." Bernard added that he felt "very strongly" about the matter, but he supposed Ross knew well the restraints on academic freedom in the United States.[2]

Other battles and slights, real and imagined, followed in rapid succession. During Todd's absence, the administration appointed Bruno rather than Bernard chairman (the "head of associated charities," Bernard sneered to Small). After three years, his salary was less than Elmer's at the same rank, and even less than that of assistant professor Ross Lee Finney, whom Bernard held in especially low regard. "Of all the men who took their degrees in sociology ten years ago," he wrote to Small after several years at Minnesota, "I am in the poorest situation financially."[3]

An effort to appoint Robert MacIver chairman in 1921 fueled the flames.

Bernard this time suspected a plot to dissolve sociology into the humanities, and he moved to block the appointment by soliciting opinions from colleagues elsewhere. Happily, most respondents confirmed his views. Small wrote that MacIver's published work merely illustrated "the chasm that separates British from American scholars in social science." Ross admitted that he knew "next to nothing" about MacIver, but he voiced a similar opinion of British sociology. All this Bernard eagerly shared with anyone at Minnesota who would listen.[4] Although MacIver was not appointed, the incident convinced Bernard that a "ruling clique" within the administration was ready to run roughshod over anyone who stood in the way. To Small a year later, he boasted of his own role in the affair.[5]

The incident left hard feelings all around. Todd, who at the time nourished hopes of returning to the department, later told Stuart Chapin that he supported MacIver but had been undercut by Bernard. Bernard, while agreeing that Todd had given pro forma support, insisted that he had not really favored the appointment. Whatever the exact truth, the resulting ill will, and the actions of the administration, convinced Bernard—or so he later maintained—that he must leave Minnesota at the first decent opportunity.[6]

The appointment of Pitirim Sorokin two years later seemed to Bernard an even greater threat, because he believed that the Russian émigré was being groomed as his permanent replacement. Unlike MacIver, Sorokin enjoyed a good reputation among American sociologists, including Ross, who had been something of a patron. Although for a time it seemed that the appointment might fail because the university's President Coffman feared Sorokin's "connection with Russian Revolutionaries" (or so Chapin wrote Bernard), it finally went through. Bernard was assured by Chapin that his position was secure, but he received the newcomer with characteristic grumbling. Rumor had it that Sorokin "assigns no readings" and was generally easy on students, he wrote Chapin; "if that is true it should be corrected at the earliest possible moment, otherwise it will demoralize the department."[7]

These incidents drew lines that would reappear in later battles within the A.S.S. Doubtless remembering Bernard's obstructive tactics in the MacIver affair, A. J. Todd was soon at loggerheads with him concerning nominations for the presidency of the society. And the apparent contradiction between Todd's and Bernard's account of the affair, whatever the truth, clearly shook Chapin's confidence in Bernard. Whether or not MacIver or Sorokin knew of Bernard's opposition (and in MacIver's case it is hard to imagine his not knowing), Bernard had failed to cultivate two potential allies. Even though both later opposed the "Chicago group" almost as strenuously as did Bernard, the three never effectively joined forces.

3

As a teacher Bernard was a great success, particularly with female students, whose frequent letters to him ranged from flirtatious to bold. Although probably few were involved with him in a sexual relationship, their adulation was elixir to Bernard, now a dapper if somewhat corpulent forty-year-old with a disintegrating marriage. "They like what I say—not boisterous, but understanding," he wrote to his wife, in one of several extraordinary letters in which he described his new-found popularity: "poised and humorous—and they like me, the sort of personality I have, refined and understanding to the last degree. One student said to me once, You ought to be a poet. I said, What makes you think so? She said, The way you say things, the color and rhythm of your language. I say that I am surprised that *all* people I have met—business and professional . . . have liked me *very* much. I can't get used to it." He also reported that another young woman, drawn to his class on a dare from a sorority sister, later told friends: "If you don't like that man you don't know what you are missing."[8]

Bernard meanwhile developed virtually a split personality between his public and private affairs. Publicly, he was the model Puritan, who never smoked or drank and condemned those who did. More curiously, given his popularity with female students, he treated his classes to misogynous attacks on the "new woman" even shriller than those of the Chicago days. After one such harangue, one woman student could take no more. "Can't you see how unfair, how unmanly, it is to take such advantage of a group of fairly intelligent women?" she demanded. "You had me so angry I was trembling and I had to get out so as not to scream."

As her seven-page indictment unfolded it became clear that Bernard had revealed a great deal of himself in these tirades, specifically with reference to his permanent separation from Frances two years earlier, and his impending divorce on grounds of her "desertion." He was "not the only one in the world who has been disappointed by those he trusted," the student lectured; not the only one "hurt" because another "did not keep the faith and has tried to ruin your life." But for all this, the student could not finally dislike Bernard. "Please don't take this as 'sassy' or 'impertinent,'" she teased. "I merely wish to get this out of my system before Thanksgiving, so as to have 'something to give Thanks for.'"[9]

The paradox was that in off-hours, Bernard had become a womanizer of almost Olympic stature, typically with much younger companions. His philandering had begun well before he arrived at Minnesota, but it was during these years that one such relationship devastated him personally, and almost ruined his career. Although the details are unimportant, and in any case difficult to decipher in the tangled web of accusation and self-justification that followed, the situation was roughly as follows: Sometime in 1922, shortly after his divorce became final, Bernard began a live-in relationship with a young woman who, as he described her to a colleague, "at the time seemed to me to have those qualities of domesticity and affection which my former wife so largely lacked." After two years of what he later termed a "common-law marriage," the two planned to wed in the summer of 1924, much against the will of the young woman's parents. When in June of that year she fell ill, Bernard was forced to go to a summer-school job at Chicago alone, only to have her break off the relationship in his absence. The young woman then refused absolutely to see him, and soon after married a physician to whom she had been previously engaged.[10]

Such liaisons, although more awkward then than today, were not in themselves remarkable. What made them so in this case was the exquisite detail in which Bernard recorded his sexual encounters. For almost a decade, in diaries large and small, fat and thin, he chronicled dates, times, and places. In the Minnesota affair he outdid himself in a volume he titled "The Journal of an Intimate Affair." In descriptions that rivaled such Victorian classics as *My Secret Life*, no detail was beneath notice. What he said, what she said. How garments were removed. The finest anatomical details from arousal to ejaculation. How it was for him, and how for her. Yet unlike most pornography, Bernard's purpose was not the arousal of passion but its reification. In his developing behaviorist logic, attitude and act were one and the same. Because an attitude was an act in the process of becoming, it was impossible to believe one thing and do another, however much one's guilt suggested otherwise. By an unstated corollary, the careful chronicling of behavior somehow legitimated guilt-producing behavior.[11]

On this point, Bernard himself bore witness of a sort. Early in their relationship, Miss X, while proclaiming her love, refused to consummate it sexually. To Bernard, such talk was nonsense. "It is your love I want," he explained in support of his entreaties. "Of course I don't think one can separate love from the expression of it. You see I'm a behaviorist!"[12]

As with his doctoral thesis, Bernard's personal trials filtered into his theoretical work. "An attitude is an uncompleted or suspected or inhibited act," he insisted. Where a conflict exists between two "behavior tendencies," or between the organism as a whole and its environment, a crisis occurs. "This is especially true if an enforced abandonment of a well-adjusted occupation or the removal of a personality upon whom one is fundamentally dependent [his wife Frances] compels a complete and rapid adjustment . . . to . . . a new or transformed environment," he continued, in terms that well described his life and loves from Chicago to Minnesota. An unstated assumption was that the truly adjusted individual has no troubling feelings, no unfulfilled acts, no burden of self-consciousness. "With complete integration, the attitude per se disappears," he concluded.[13]

For Bernard, as presumably for those who agreed with him, society seemed less a matter of shared meanings and conventions than a saga of cajoling, wheedling, and intrigue. In human society, a process of "interconditioning," through response to the "attitudes" of others, complicated the adjustment process. Across group or class lines, the result was social coercion, such as in "manners" or "certain types of moral conduct." Through interconditioning individuals also manipulated one another. Thus, the "cry baby" manages the mother with an "attitudinal onslaught," and is itself forced to modify its behavior by being labeled a "cry baby."[14] So viewed, life was indeed a lonely affair. As Bernard expressed it to his daughter much later in his life: "I learned long ago to depend on no one."[15]

A disturbing lesson in this regard came when department chairman Chapin first supported Bernard in his difficulties only finally to reverse himself. During the fall of 1924, the situation became increasingly messy. Because "common-law marriage" constituted marriage in Minnesota, Bernard's characterization of the relationship in these terms meant that his lady friend would be technically a bigamist when she married her physician fiancé. Meanwhile, several senior members of Bernard's department had been active in a campaign to make common-law marriage illegal. After the young woman and her fiancé went to President Coffman to request "protection" from Bernard, and even threatened to use family connections to make trouble for the university with the state legislature, Coffman and the dean demanded Bernard's immediate resignation.

Chapin initially favored an extended leave with full pay followed by resignation in June 1926, but at the last minute he changed his mind. The prolonged secrecy of the arrangement, and his long-standing opposition to common-law marriage, made it impossible for him to support the leave option. To the university authorities he could at best suggest a committee of inquiry. Privately, he counseled Bernard to resign at the close of the 1924–25 academic year. Despite later rumors to the contrary, Bernard technically left voluntarily in the end, rescued by an offer from Cornell. But Chapin's attitude—not to mention the lectures on morality to which he treated Bernard—permanently chilled their relationship. In future correspondence, which was infrequent, the two remained "Professor Chapin" and "Professor Bernard."[16]

Two postscripts to the Minnesota affair had a long-range impact on Bernard's career. The first, ironically, was a happy event that only made things worse. In September 1925, shortly before leaving for Cornell, Bernard was married in a secret ceremony to a brilliant young graduate student named Jessie Ravitch (Ravage), whose sociological career as Jessie Bernard eventually outstripped his own. But almost immediately, the rumor mill produced stories that Bernard, having been forced to resign, had now run off with a student "presumably in an unconventional relation."[17] Almost costing him the Cornell job, these rumors pursued him for the rest of the decade. At Iowa, where he was considered for a position, a young woman faculty member with contacts in Chicago and Minneapolis let drop remarks such as "Faris says Bernard has an inferiority complex," and "I heard a lot about Bernard's marriage. Do you suppose it can all be so?" Despite his best efforts to smother such reports, they persisted. Denied reappointment at Cornell, he suspected that "secret propaganda" emanating from the economics department was behind the decision. A few allies took up his cause, but to little avail. "He needs the support of all of us in order to overcome the unfriendly gossip that got started in Minnesota," an old Chicago associate later wrote Howard Odum; but, he added, "a rumor no matter how ill-founded is hard to live down."[18]

A second postscript concerned the election for second vice-president of the A.S.S. in December 1925, a position that led automatically to the presidency in two years. Perversely, and probably in surrogate vindication for his recent difficulties, Bernard nominated W. I. Thomas, still suffering the effects of the morals charges that had driven him from Chicago seven years earlier. The old guard rose up in arms. When he heard of the proposal, Cecil North, a graduate-school contemporary of Bernard now at Ohio State, urged him to postpone the nomination. After it was approved at the December meeting, Bernard's former chairman Arthur Todd wrote to Ross that he could "hardly put into words the sense of shame, disgust and insult which I feel as a result of that election. . . . With not the slightest desire in the world to see a man who is down still further kicked or beaten I, as responsible for a university department of sociology [at Northwestern], can not lie down tamely and accept the leadership of a man who has egregiously flouted the standards of decency and could not be elected to the faculty of any reputable college or university in the United States. I was so thoroughly sick of the business last night that my first impulse was to resign from the Society." Ellwood later implored Bernard, as a member of the nominating committee, not to go forward with the election because the public would regard it "as further evidence that sociologists as a class are not safe men."[19]

Ross, to his credit, came to Bernard's defense. Although he would oppose giving recognition to anyone "who at present is known to be flouting good morals," Thomas's offense was now seven years in the past. "The punishment for a moral offense need not be a life term," he observed. This sentiment must have comforted Bernard, but the incident did little to smooth the relations between "scientific" and more traditional sociologists.[20]

4

In his scholarly work, meanwhile, Bernard attempted to formulate a conception of "science" to satisfy earlier critics, and to provide a theoretical basis for his "objective standard of social control." Addressing the question of whether an "objective" standard could transcend the status quo, he argued that every scientific law is in a sense an *ideal* in that it describes a state of affairs not existing in experience. No object falls precisely according to the formula of the law of gravity. Just as the law of falling bodies describes the way objects fall in a vacuum under experimental conditions devised by man, so the " 'perfect' society is both an illusion and a reality." The "highest function" of all science, including sociology, was "the creation of ideal principles or laws, which are something more than the description of processes as they occur."[21]

Science thus demands generalization. An example was the work of Darwin, whom the naive empiricists wrongly cited in defense of their Baconianism. Scientific specialization and narrow fact-gathering blunted the reform impulse. Toward the end of his career Bernard went even further. Reason or intuition offered no pipeline to some "universal fund of Natural Law." Rather, the "constructive relativist," as he now fashioned himself, "invents his laws. He collects his individual specific facts and then *he looks them into perspective.*"[22]

A corollary of this "projective logic" was a frank relativism that did not entirely rule out sampling, statistical correlations, or other techniques beloved of quantitative sociologists. In the world of physics, atmospheric resistance in a vacuum is theoretically reduced to zero—but the social sciences have no comparable standard. Such abstractions as the "economic man," and even "natural law" itself, had been attempts to find "zero norms" for the "computation of normal or right conduct." Because these concepts were now discredited, sociologists must make a "temporary" return to relativity. Statistics was such a "relativity method of measurement and computation of norms." Given the nature of sampling, and the variability of social phenomena, its calculations provided a "more dependable interpretation of collective behavior" until some new "zero norm" was devised.[23]

In this way, Bernard effectively restated Comte's Religion of Humanity (minus its mysticism), wherein the social scientist finally transcends the data to present a vision of the social good. He could join the call for quantitative studies of attitudes and behavior, while at the same time claiming that science somehow defined ends as well as means. This position won him the reputation of being merely a "moderate" behaviorist (as Cooley gently described him).[24] But it also put him on a collision course with leading second-generation quantifiers no less than with founders.

In *Instinct* (1924) and related writings, Bernard examined the policy implications of his "objective standard," another issue debated earlier with Sutherland and others. Although he again attempted a middle course, he was notably short of specifics. He did not deny that "instincts" exist in some elemental form. Most theorists simply exaggerated their number and significance. Most so-called instincts were simply habit and custom so ossified that "we mistake their automatic compulsions for inheritance." A child who had reached a "rational age" was reacting in "nine-tenths or ninety-nine one-hundredths of his character directly to environment," he concluded. Social progress was possible through manipulation of this environment.[25]

This attack on habit and custom again amounted to a rejection of virtually everything Bernard disliked in contemporary America, such as wartime propaganda; advertisers and other hucksters, now armed with radio and movies; or a political blitz in Minnesota that swung the electorate to Coolidge in the final days of the 1924 campaign. These vestiges of an old order, he commented, were no different from the revival meetings of his youth. His list of bogus "instincts" was likewise a catalogue of traits he disliked in others, and more importantly, in himself: "the parental instinct, reproductive instinct, fighting instinct, instinct of self-preservation." Viewed in this way, his objective utopia of efficiency and adjustment was less an act of the radical imagination than a rejection of a past he felt to be worse than irrelevant.[26]

But had Bernard anything to put in place of the past? Passing references to contemporary efforts at social engineering gave his ideal an aura of practicality. Recent "social inventions" included the creation of new varieties of plants, resource conservation, increased efficiency in business, and eugenics (although Bernard disavowed the biological theory behind the more extreme proposals). He also spoke vaguely of "social inventions" to correct the maldistribution of wealth, but left such proposals undeveloped. "It is a mistake to suppose that a complete statement of the ends of social progress can be formulated in the present state of the development of social science," he wrote, virtually confessing the lameness of his program. "All attempts are but partial and tentative."[27]

Reviewers of *Instinct* seized immediately upon the ambiguity in Bernard's politics. Was he radical or reactionary, environmentalist or hereditarian? Critics leveled both charges, but most found his excessive environmentalism to be less radical than naive. In a *Nation* review entitled "Back to Rousseau," Frank Hankins of Smith charged that "[he] reduces human nature to a few unimportant reflexes plus a mass of nebulous and unshaped nerve tissues out of which society makes whatever personality it pleases." "It is an absurd conclusion," he continued. "It is eighteenth-century utopianism all over again."[28]

A heated exchange followed. Although Hankins claimed he had hoped only to "get a rise" from him, Bernard characteristically took the matter personally. A year later he complained to a colleague about Hankins's animosity. Still later, he wrote Harry Elmer Barnes that his book was less an attack on instinct theory per se, than on the "old Neo-Darwinian theories of inheritance," such as held by Hankins and others. As to the *Nation* review, he charged that Hankins "apparently read only the first half of [the book] and jumped to conclusions about the rest of it." So was born a grudge that resurfaced a decade later when Hankins became the first editor of the new *American Sociological Review*.[29]

Personalities aside, these criticisms *had* exposed the fatal weakness of Bernard's radical objectivism. Stripped of rhetoric and of bogus analogies concerning matter in a vacuum, his "projective logic" added up to little more than a pious hope that quantitative sophistication would amount to more than counting. Ironically, his own attempts at quantitative analysis (notably an abortive study of nationality traits in the early 1930s) came to naught, while his celebration of objectivity gave support to elements within the profession who wished to relegate theorists to the scrap heap. Politically, Bernard's extreme environmentalism—his behaviorism—also left him in a sort of limbo, emotionally to the left of all varieties of New Deal liberalism, but equally unable to embrace socialism or Marxism.

5

Between 1926 and the close of the decade, three incidents sealed Bernard's reputation as the Peck's Bad Boy of the profession, and led finally to his public embrace of the "behaviorist" label. The first was the collapse of a long-cherished hope of returning to Chicago as Small's successor. For several years before his death in March 1926, Small had invited Bernard to teach summer sessions, and on at least one occasion he had promised to recommend him as his successor. Attempting to smooth away their earlier differences, Bernard assured his mentor that he was *really* "in sympathy" with Small's system, and particularly with Small's criticism that it was a bit "esoteric" to reduce every mental operation to a "neural correlate." Apparently, however, Small was not convinced, for in a final paper before the A.S.S. in December 1925 he launched a direct attack upon sociologists who strayed at their peril into psychology or biology. Lest Bernard miss the point, he then told his former student that he had him chiefly in mind.[30]

Whatever Small's intention, others soon made it clear that they were not willing to have Bernard in the department. Soon after Small's death, Herbert Blumer, later the father of "symbolic interactionism," wrote Ellwood that he was "greatly disappointed" in Bernard's work. The crucial veto, however, came from department chairman Ellsworth Faris, a former missionary who, some said, had succeeded the erring Thomas in 1919 on the basis of his religious credentials. Faris in any case had little use for behaviorism, a movement he described to Robert Park as involving "all the metaphysical difficulties which people get into who know nothing about metaphysics." In a critical review of Bernard's *Social Psychology*, he sarcastically termed the author a "good behaviorist" whose penchant for neologism was the sort one expected from French but not American sociologists.[31]

By November 1926, Bernard knew that his chances were fast fading. "I believe that the Chicago group is still insisting that sociology is sociology and that psychology and neurology are something else," he wrote Kimball Young, a fellow social psychologist at the University of Wisconsin. When he later learned that Faris had blocked the appointment single-handedly, he attributed the action, not to their theoretical differences, but to Faris's fear that he would become an ally of Park, with whom Faris had an "intense rivalry."[32]

An appointment at Tulane (1927–28), and then one at North Carolina (1928–29) promised a new start, but they again ended in controversy and alienation. The offer at Tulane, the work of Bernard's graduate-school colleague Jesse Steiner, came at a time when he was beginning to think that his field rather than he himself was the problem: in modern America, theory was a glut on the market. After a sabbatical in Argentina, he had reapplied at Cornell, this time for an opening in agricultural sociology, only to be told that they really wanted "a man who will get right out into the field and observe the facts of group behavior at firsthand." Bernard's interests, the chairman wrote, seemed rather to be "along the line of developing general theory." Two months later, Bernard learned that he had been bested for a position at Chapel Hill by Ernest Groves, a rural sociologist also of decidedly practical bent. When he complained to Odum, baring his soul in the process, Odum replied that "a good many people who want men of your caliber, are wanting technicians in the practical field." At Tulane, the situation turned out to be roughly the same. Although in the end he could have stayed had he wanted, his reappointment was temporarily delayed because funds were allotted only for a permanent position in social work. "This seems now to be impossible," department chairman Steiner wrote of the prospects while things hung fire, "for the social workers in the city are already criticizing us for having too much theory."[33]

When the Chapel Hill post opened up, Odum extended himself to make the move a success. Worried that the Bernards would chafe against the mores of a southern town, he offered countless pages of advice and encouragement. So that they might feel their way gradually, he arranged temporary quarters for them in the picturesque Carolina Inn. The position was a prestigious one: already famous for his studies of black folkways and rural life, Odum had created one of the most distinguished research institutes in the field.

Yet differences developed within a year. Challenging the emphasis on research, Bernard insisted that the department must equally stress the training of teachers, and he was quick to take offense at any suggestion that his own work was not *really* "research." "I notice yesterday . . . you referred to research as covering the sort of thing you and Ogburn are doing," he wrote Odum two years later, after his tie with North Carolina had been severed. "This was probably but a slip, due to the force of public opinion and the mores. But it seems to me very unfortunate that almost each group of researchers we have in the country thinks of its particular form of research as THE research and of everybody else who does a different kind of research as something else."[34] In a paper delivered at the annual meeting of the A.S.S. in December 1930, he presented an only slightly veiled account of the same exchange, again revealing his increasing sensitivity on the issue. In this account a "cultural sociologist" deprecated the work of "another sociologist who had spent his own time and money" gathering data throughout the United States. The former (Odum) he termed a "narrow specialist" who regarded the work of others "contemptuously."[35]

Because Odum and Ogburn had a special relationship with the foundations, and because Bernard had indeed incurred considerable expense in the collection of materials for a proposed history of American sociology, his concern was more than academic. When in December 1932, in his presidential address to the A.S.S., he repeated the "research" story, he left no doubt on this point. "I have little sympathy with research projects that grow out of an institution's or a person's desire to get money from a foundation . . . ," he told the assembly. "In recent years I think I have seen altogether too much money wasted on research projects made to order and carried through by individuals of mediocre ability who were seeking to build for themselves and their political cronies reputations as sociologists."[36]

During 1929–30, Bernard also came in conflict with Ogburn, although less directly than with Chapin, Todd, or the others. On paper, at least, the two should have been allies. Both were small-town southerners; both began their careers as radical critics of progressivism; both sought some alternative to the extremes of Marxist economic interpretation and Freudianism. Their major works, Bernard's *Instinct* and Ogburn's *Social Change*, were nails in the coffin of "biological sociology." In other publications, they shared a common interest in such issues as living standards, the role of invention, and the family.

But, personality aside (and the two could not have been more different), major intellectual differences weighed heavily against any alliance. To oversimplify the case, Ogburn tended to the nominalist assumption that science was limited to the calculation of rates of change, while Bernard cherished the realist's dream of something more, however unable he was to define it. To Ogburn, environment in the form of technology ultimately shaped human affairs, while Bernard clung to the conviction that the sociologist could and must impose values upon experience. In studying living standards, for example, Ogburn charted actual rates of expenditure, whereas Bernard called for a "standard" to tell people what they "should" spend to achieve the ends they desired. Ogburn stressed the primacy of "material culture" in determining the pace of social change; Bernard saw "mental and method" inventions as coming first. For Ogburn, the fact that several individuals often made simultaneous discoveries proved that they were virtually "inevitable"; for Bernard, dramatic breakthroughs often altered the course of history. To the happily married Ogburn, the "problem" of the modern family was the result of a "lag" between older values (e.g., the woman's place is in the home), and the realities of modern production; to Bernard, it reflected the willful rejection of domestic ideals, by men and especially by women.[37]

Although the two never quarreled openly, their dealings during the twenties mirrored these disagreements. At the time of the MacIver incident at Minnesota, Bernard thought enough of Ogburn to include him on a list of ten "acceptable" chairmen. But in articles in which their interests overlapped,

Bernard rarely cited his rival, and then usually only to criticize him. Ogburn apparently knew enough of Bernard to be aware of his idiosyncrasies. In August 1927, with rumors about the Minnesota departure still circulating, he wrote Odum that he hoped that Bernard's "recent tribulations" would smooth the "rough edges of his personality." The next year, Bernard learned that Ogburn had blocked publication of one of his articles on scientific method in the *AJS*. In 1930, Ogburn half-heartedly recommended Bernard for a job at Smith, but added "I think he is a little hard to get along with."[38]

In 1929, the annual wrangling over the presidency of the A.S.S. brought the two directly into competition, and in Bernard's view made Ogburn a leading representative of the "Chicago crowd" he opposed during the next decade. Although the details are sketchy, Bernard apparently hoped to be the official nominee for president, an honor that he believed would give recognition to a "younger group" within the society. Shortly before the nominating committee met, however, prominent members of the old guard—including Ellwood, Ulysses Weatherly, and Frank Blackmar—agreed informally to support Emory Bogardus, a graduate-school contemporary of Bernard, and a man some younger sociologists considered no better than a popularizer. When Bernard's supporters learned of the strategy, they planned an opposing nomination from the floor. Although Bernard was furious at Ellwood (a feeling later reciprocated), he refused to let his name come forward in this fashion lest it appear that he had engineered his own election. The younger men then turned to Ogburn (whom Bernard casually mentioned was a "good man"), who later won the election.[39]

The incident opened old wounds, and created several new ones. Bernard's relationship with Ellwood reached a new low. Although Bernard's old friend E. H. Sutherland, a member of the nominating committee, assured him there were "no deep laid political plots," Bernard believed that rumors, if not the reality, of the old guard's conspiracy had worked against Bogardus. He was especially distressed to learn that Charles H. Cooley (with whom he had been corresponding cordially), along with Weatherly, had carried the day for Bogardus within the nominating committee by the fact of being senior to Sutherland and to a second Bernard supporter. He felt no better on this score when a friend speculated that Cooley *probably* acted as he did because to do otherwise would have given an appearance of professional jealousy, and that Cooley had "no great admiration" for Bogardus. The whole thing was made worse because Bernard's friend and Tulane patron Jesse Steiner was absent, and his former Minnesota colleague Manuel Elmer remained silent, along with a sixth member of the committee.[40]

Bernard said nothing directly about Ogburn's election, but he repeated to

Sutherland a rumor that Ogburn had accepted the draft from the floor in spite of the fact that Weatherly had urged him to decline. He also hinted darkly that the affair had colored his entire judgment of the man and the office. To Read Bain he reported that Ogburn had no support at all within the nominating committee.[41]

In the wake of these incidents, Bernard finally proclaimed his allegiance to "behaviorism." In one sense, the mystery is why he waited so long. Even before the war, Bernard's first wife had brought behaviorism into child-rearing in the form of careful records of their new daughter's physical and verbal behavior. During the twenties, public interest peaked with the appearance of Watson's *Behaviorism* (1925). Bernard privately, if whimsically, admitted to the label in courting his lady-love at Minnesota, while many of his colleagues assumed, as Cooley put it, that he planned "a behaviorist analysis of our field."[42]

In another sense, however, his caution on the subject derived from a shrewd intuition that the label could do him harm, especially so long as the Chicago job seemed a possibility. Despite popular interest, "behaviorism" remained suspect in academia, and even a little naughty. When Cooley referred to Bernard's "moderate" behaviorism, he was trying to be nice; but privately, he wrote to Bain that he doubted whether sociologists had any "clear ideas or techniques" concerning the study of functional groups and institutions from this perspective. To Ellwood, behaviorism was a species of the hated "objectivism." Bernard's letters to him, until their temporary break in 1929, were an extended exercise in fence-mending on this score. For most others, the term was more often pejorative than descriptive.[43]

By late 1931, however, things looked different: Small was dead, the Chicago job long gone, and Ellwood apparently lost for good. Above all, at the annual meeting of the A.S.S. Bernard finally realized his dream of being elected president. In the fall a colleague wrote him that, in a survey of social psychologists, "everyone . . . has marked you under behaviorism." In December, speaking before the A.S.S., he went public, chiding critics "who build up a straw-man behaviorist and hang on him a generous collection of their own antipathies." The allusion, in fact, was to Faris, whom he privately described as one of a group who "thrust [the term] upon me . . . when I had no particular desire to adopt the term myself." But he now adopted it proudly, while characteristically proclaiming his indifference.[44]

Because Bernard's behaviorism was rooted deeply in his background and temperament, and existed in embryo in his doctoral thesis, the quarrels, disappointments, and professional politics of the twenties do not alone explain his conversion (if so gradual a process may be thus described). But they do help explain his continuing drift toward behaviorism, and the timing of his public confession. By December 1931, with the A.S.S. presidency in his pocket and the label on his breast, Bernard was ready to transform American society and sociology in light of his vision.

10

THE PATRICIAN AS TECHNICIAN

*It seems to me that . . . a scientific sociology . . . must be
founded upon a central body of principle which involves
the concepts of societal variation, selection, transmission
and adaptation.*

F. Stuart Chapin to A. G. Keller, 1915

*Behaviorism draws the logical consequence
[of Darwinism] in its methodology.*

Talcott Parsons, 1937

1

While Bernard was the theorist of one version of behaviorist sociology, F.
Stuart Chapin was the methodologist, entrepreneur, and leading administrator
of the other. Six years after finishing his graduate studies, Chapin organized a
new school of social work at Smith College. He was appointed chairman at the
University of Minnesota in 1922 and built the sociology department into one of
the most distinguished in the country. An autocrat in the manner of Giddings,
he left his personal stamp on some thirty-two doctoral theses. As editor of the
Harper "Social Science" series for thirty-five years, he gave his imprimatur to
another seventy-five titles. In 1924 he was a moving spirit in the formation of
the Social Science Research Council and served on several of its committees;
he later edited the Council-sponsored *Social Science Abstracts*. Elected president of the American Sociological Society in 1935, he was a leading organizer
of the elitist Sociological Research Association the following year. Although
he refused to be considered for editor of the *American Sociological Review* in
1936, he served as its coeditor from 1944 to 1946.[1]

As a sociologist, Chapin rode successive waves of fashion to national
prominence: from *Social Evolution* (1913) to *Experimental Designs In Socio-*

logical Research (1947).[2] In the interwar years he popularized the idea of "social indices," including his well-known "living-room scales." Later in his career, he was a pioneer of the "social experiment," an approach that earned him footnotes through the 1950s. Although some contemporaries praised his originality, he was, like Giddings, best remembered as a proselytizer for things that others did better.

On the surface, Chapin and Bernard were a study in contrasts. Where Bernard's youth was one of family strife and cultural deprivation, Chapin's was socially secure and educationally privileged. While Bernard languished on the fringes of academia, Chapin rose to the heights. Nevertheless, despite these differences, Chapin's youth and career display elements by now familiar in the shaping of objectivism: youthful trauma and a profound sense of loss; acceptance and final rejection of the evolutionism and reformism of the founders; and an institutional setting that, in Chapin's case, encouraged an emphasis on "method" over "material" as a way of linking sociology and social work. If less original than Bernard, and doubtless less complicated a person, Chapin for this very reason offers an ideal case study of the transformation of a workaday sociologist from social evolutionist to quantifier, from patrician to technician.

2

Born in Brooklyn, and raised in comfortable surroundings on Manhattan's East Side, F. Stuart Chapin (1888–1974) enjoyed a family tradition that dated to the earliest days of New England. The first American Chapin arrived in Massachusetts in 1634, and later moved to the Springfield area, where a statue by Saint-Gaudens commemorates him. One of F. Stuart's maternal ancestors served with Washington in the Revolution, while other forebears included merchants, lawyers, judges, and, by the nineteenth century, clergymen.[3]

Chapin's grandfather moved from Yale to Princeton Theological Seminary, and then to a career as clergyman and headmaster for forty years of the Chapin Collegiate School in New York. His son, Chapin's father, held pastorates in Manhattan, upstate New York, and Pennsylvania after graduating from Princeton and Union Theological. Cast in the stern mode of Princeton theology, the family religion moderated slightly through the century. Chapin recalled that his father was only "mildly conservative, not like one of the hidebound types of Presbyterian clergymen." But Calvinism, not theological liberalism, was the matrix of his later thought.[4]

Chapin's youth was built around family. In 1895 he entered the Chapin School, as had his father and almost everyone else on the male side of the family for several decades. Chapin remembered his headmaster grandfather as "a very well balanced, just sort of person," but a family friend recalled that Chapin's schooling "included a discipline which existed prior to anything like our own present day school standard." Dominant but not domineering, his father was manly and athletic and a near-professional in tennis, although never ranked. "He taught me to play," Chapin remembered, ". . . but I was never his equal." Chapin's mother, as the Victorians held appropriate, was gentle and artistic, an amateur painter and poetess of modest distinction.[5]

Although on the surface Chapin's youth was everything that Bernard's was not, events soon shattered this comfortable existence and set the stage for his conversion to "science." In 1904, for reasons unstated, his father left his Manhattan pastorate for one in Rochester, in upstate New York. Chapin's grandfather had once lived in Rochester, and the move was thus in a sense a return to roots. But for young Stuart it meant the end of the Chapin School, and a senior year in Rochester's public high school. Commenting on the unsettled nature of Chapin's youth, a Minnesota colleague later ascribed his "detachment and coolness" to the fact that his private schooling and several moves had "separated [him] from ordinary contacts with others in some community setting." Significantly, it was at precisely this time that Chapin developed a passion for mathematics, a subject he had previously disliked. He also dabbled in inventions, the first being a photo-developing process that he tried unsuccessfully to market to the Eastman Company.[6]

In the fall of 1905, Chapin entered the University of Rochester to study engineering, a move that dashed his father's hopes that his son would follow him into the ministry. One can only guess at the anxiety that attended this decision, and the situation worsened dramatically at the end of his freshman year, when his mother died of a stroke at age forty-eight. In response—so his biographer has surmised—he veered suddenly in a new direction, painting and sketching, and enrolled in a class in oil painting at the local Mechanics Institute.[7] Although this interest did not lead to a new career, the hard-boiled quantifier, like objectivists from Giddings to Ogburn, would spend his leisure time in later years pouring emotion into art.

The family break-up brought Chapin closer to his uncle, Dr. Henry Dwight Chapin, and, through him, to a tradition of "scientific" reform. A specialist in children's diseases, H. D. Chapin (1857–1942) won a considerable reputation for social service, while serving as director of pediatrics at the New York Post-

Graduate Medical School. He was a typical "patrician" liberal who spiced proposals for reform with invectives against "communism," "socialism," and "beer-garden philosophers who would bring everybody to the lowest level." From time to time warning against attempts to repeal the "laws of nature," he offered draconian solutions to the social problems of the day, on one occasion applauding an Ohio law that provided a life sentence for any criminal convicted three times of *anything*. On another occasion, he demanded "a permanent quarantine" for "all tramps, cranks, and generally worthless human beings."[8]

But Dr. Chapin also condemned a do-nothing policy of laissez-faire. It was the function of government, he told the readers of *Popular Science* in 1887, "to prevent or mitigate any environment that all experience shows will produce not only physical and mental inefficiency, but sufficient degradation of the moral sense to make criminals." The "sociology of the future" must "devise means for a more equitable distribution of wealth." His solutions, to be sure, followed a familiar pattern: tenement-house reform, manual education, sanitary legislation, and, from the turn of the century, inoculation and other preventive medicine. Like others who looked to "science" rather than to fellow-feeling, Henry Chapin even toyed with eugenics, although this program remained too controversial through the 1890s to advocate openly.[9]

The elder Chapin also saw things through frankly Darwinian lenses. A conservative Presbyterian trained in the latest science, he saw no conflict between the two. "Darwinism and Calvinism present about an equally hopeful consideration for the unfortunates of our race," he wrote. "One says heredity and environment; the other predestination and foreordination." His stark references to the "unfit" appeared on the surface to imply that he wished to let the "struggle for existence" have its bloody way in human society, but what he meant was only that American society as presently constituted was a jungle, and that the "Darwinian" free-for-all was weakening the collective effort.[10]

Young Stuart did not accept all of his uncle's lessons, but the tutelage left him a no-nonsense, just-the-facts attitude toward reform, and a suspicion of any program based primarily on feeling. In 1915, for example, Stuart cited his uncle's calls for "modern scientific management" as a model for the direction sociology should take. At the same time, he castigated the sins and follies of the age in language that seemed to be lifted directly from H. D. Chapin's earlier harangues.[11] In the long run, more importantly, Stuart Chapin's sociology, and the cultural-lag theory he shared with Ogburn, were direct legacies of his uncle's view that the woes of the world were the result of maladaptation rather than social injustice.

3

Chapin transferred to Columbia for his senior year, and entered its graduate school in the fall of 1909. His graduate-school contemporaries, in addition to Ogburn and Odum, included James P. Lichtenberger, later of Penn, and Charles E. Gehlke, later of Western Reserve. Chapin especially liked Ogburn and Gehlke, fellow members of the so-called "F.H.G. Club" that met regularly at Giddings's home.

Pragmatism, functional psychology, and incipient behaviorism permeated the Columbia curriculum. At the University of Rochester, Chapin had already studied the work of the functional psychologist James R. Angell, a disciple of William James. He had been specifically attracted to Columbia by Edward L. Thorndike, whose cat-in-the-box experiments were a forerunner of pedagogical behaviorism, and by John Dewey, whose *School and Society* influenced his early work. Minoring in anthropology, he was also influenced by Franz Boas, whose attack on the unilinear evolutionism of Lewis Henry Morgan was then attracting notice. Boas taught him to be sceptical of all "broad and beautiful generalizations," he later recalled. The Boasians "were looking to the possibility of collecting concrete factual data. What they were after was the facts." This interest, in turn, attracted Chapin to Sumner's *Folkways*, the single greatest influence on his dissertation.[12]

In this thesis, *Education and the Mores* (1911), Chapin attacked contemporary education, perhaps remembering his own experiences at the Rochester public high school. The problem, although smothered in academic prose, was in any case, intensely personal: did the public schools "conserve obstructive tradition and mischievous prejudice?" or, in Giddingsese, did "the pressure of elementary school education as a type-forming instrument [tend] to select the timid and tradition-loving?" Chapin concluded with regret that, for 95 percent of the population, schooling preserved the customs and traditions of the "masses," whose "mores" were shot through with mystical, theological, and metaphysical assumptions.[13]

As with Sumner and Bernard, Chapin's "customs" and "superstitions" were a catalogue of beliefs he did not like. "Traditions" were inescapable, because they embraced "all the mental achievements of mankind from habits of thought and action to social institutions"; all had a "rational" justification, however slight. But customs were something else—"habits of thought and action . . . more local than tradition," and hence untrustworthy. Superstitions were traditions with "highly irrational sanctions," where the emotional element was strong. Provincialism and passion, that is to say, were the two enemies.[14]

Following Sumner, Chapin argued further that a scientific outlook allowed an elite to transcend parochialism and emotionalism. He was pessimistic concerning current education, but he hoped that social evolution was already producing a new, scientific outlook within the mores, albeit one confined to the top 5 percent of the populace. As evidence he cited the nation's great business and financial enterprises, where the tendency "toward universalism and disinterestedness" was greatest.[15]

Although Chapin lacked the self-professed "radicalism" of Bernard or the early Ogburn, he was "progressive" in the style that was increasingly fashionable in the 1910s. Analyzing the 1912 presidential election, he concluded that the rise of the independent voter since the Civil War showed that rational choice was replacing blind allegiance to the traditions of party. In *An Introduction to the Theory of Social Evolution* (1913), he argued that industry and commerce, by expanding material abundance, would bring "a more flexible structure of social relations" and would raise the "struggle for existence" once and for all "above the level of the brute" (again, shades of his uncle Henry). Writing in the *Independent* during the early Wilson years, Chapin identified specific areas where rational intelligence was being or could be applied: in the conservation of resources, in organizing the labor market, and in rationalizing old-age and sickness benefits. In these articles, and in a course on "Municipal Socialism" at Wellesley in 1911, he presented the natural scientist as the ideal. "As the chemist solves his problems by analyzing a compound into its elements, so the sociologist breaks it up into simpler rudiments," he wrote in support of accident insurance. Several years later he expanded these ideas in his *Historical Introduction to Social Economy* (1917), a book that, as it turned out, was his farewell to this particular version of prewar reform.[16]

Chapin's *Social Evolution*, although a textbook with no pretension to originality, showed him to be more thoroughly wedded to the evolutionist model than was either Ogburn or Bernard at the same time. Like Giddings, he found a model for social policy in nature's balance between stability and change. Combining Sumner and Bagehot with the insights of the "struggle school," he traced the painful process whereby custom and tradition are formed through "trial and failure." Human "instinct" rarely provides an adequate response to new demands, he argued. Rather, group pressures play an important role, by restraining, persecuting, and often outlawing departures from established usages. However, while group loyalty assures survival, it also poses the danger that "the restraint of disloyal members . . . [sometimes] fails to discriminate between helpful innovations and dangerous egotism." This warning aside, the result was a relatively optimistic social evolutionism, and a more frankly evolutionary view of the mores than that accepted by Sumner.[17]

During and immediately after the war, several related developments weaned Chapin from this overt evolutionism, setting the stage for a nominalistic and decidedly less reformist view of social science. One was the irrationality of the war itself. Hints of pessimism had clouded his earliest writings, but the war evoked jeremiads worthy of Uncle Henry at his most bitter. "Moral conduct may be secured by the compulsion of tradition," he wrote in 1915, adding: "but most of us are subject to strange and inconsistent lapses." Then followed a blistering attack on the sins of the age, from "brutally unscrupulous" business-men to the "flimsy pretext" that ignited the "holocaust of Europe." "Moral conduct," he concluded, "is often a thin veneer which covers up unsuspected depths of primitive brutishness and crude impulse."[18]

To rationalize this new pessimism, Chapin now distinguished "societal" (psychic) from "social" (physical) evolution in an appendix to the fourth edition (1919) of his *Social Evolution*. Whereas "social" evolution eliminates individuals and groups physically, the "societal" variety "spills no blood," and shows its effects relatively soon, as in the establishment of health ordinances. The problem is that reforms aimed only at habits and customs (societal) fail to "stay put" because they are not "capitalized in instincts and race habits." At issue was a point of great concern to reformers ever since the neo-Darwinians had laid waste to the Lamarckian theory concerning the inheritability of envi-ronmentally induced changes: Could reform, as traditionally conceived, *really* affect permanent improvement?[19] One answer, of course, lay in eugenics—a form of selection, whatever its drawbacks, that promised to "stay put." But after flirting with that movement for almost a decade, Chapin finally rejected it, and with it the evolutionary framework that had inspired the original interest.[20]

Chapin's work with the Red Cross and other administrative tasks in the 1910s further weaned him, not only from evolutionism, but from theory altogether. "I think that you have to recognize that these people, according to their own likes and ideologies, are very practical minded," he later said, in describing his dealings with the social workers. "If anything is abstract, they don't understand it and you can't get them to listen long enough to understand it."[21] His increasing involvement in academic administration reinforced this lesson. In 1915, already immersed in administrative duties at Smith, he lec-tured fellow academics concerning the benefits of "The Business System in the Professor's Study." By 1919, a career in business seemed an attractive alterna-tive to poorly paid teaching. "I had rather be efficient in business," he wrote to Ross, lamenting the plight of a college professor with four mouths to feed, "than efficient as a teacher and scholar."[22]

The rise of Fundamentalism suggested also that evolutionist arguments could cause trouble. Soon after arriving at Minnesota in 1922, Chapin was besieged by representatives of the Northwest Bible and Missionary Training School, an influential group of Fundamentalists. This group singled out *Social Evolution*, now in its fourth edition and still a popular text, along with works by Ross and others, as among the most "sacrilegious and scornful" books in print. Although this attack actually stimulated local sales, it brought unwanted publicity to sociology in a university where the field remained suspect.[23]

But if "science" was not evolutionism, or specific proposals such as eugenics, what was it? During his early years, Chapin ran the gamut on this question,[24] but by 1919 he had settled on the increasingly fashionable nominalism of Pearson's *Grammar of Science* (1892). "The core of science is method not material," he announced in 1919. This method consisted of four steps: the formulation of hypotheses, observation, classification, and generalization. It found its fullest expression in statistics.[25]

Pearson, of course, was not the only source of this view. As noted by commentators from Peirce to Parsons, the statistical concept of order was implicit in evolutionary theory, a point Chapin himself made in "The Elements of Scientific Method in Sociology" (1914). His contact with social workers also contributed. "Subjective reporting" was the nemesis of the profession, he told a group of social workers in 1919. A subjective approach produced the premature generalization of findings into "principles of human relations that have the universal validity of a scientific law." The hypothetico-inductive method, in contrast, placed the "statistical method of interpretation" at the top of a methodological hierarchy, above the "historical method" and "field work."[26]

This view of science-as-method in turn altered Chapin's conception of the relation of sociology and social reform. So-called reforms were really trial-and-error approximations whose success remained to be proved. In trying to determine the advantages of one proposal over another, sociologists worked at a disadvantage as compared to natural scientists, for the ideals of individual freedom and the sanctity of life usually made it impossible to perform laboratory experiments. Nor were utopian communities a substitute, as some Comteans implied, because their isolation and atypicality made the drawing of reliable conclusions difficult. Statistical analysis, by measuring the correlation between two or more variables, was in social matters the best equivalent of laboratory experiment, and was hence the main business of sociology.[27]

4

After serving as director of Smith's Training School of Social Work for three years, Chapin in 1922 became professor of sociology *and* director of social work at the University of Minnesota. During the Minnesota years, his interest continued to shift from social evolution to "cultural change," and finally to methodology, as he drifted steadily toward behavioral analysis and scientific neutrality. The results were the "living-room scales" and "social experiments" that finally won him a modest reputation as a pioneering technician of the new sociology.

At thirty-three Chapin was the youngest chairman of a major sociology department in the nation. Building on the initiatives of Vincent and Todd, who had already brought Bernard and Manuel Elmer to Minnesota, he continued to add to the department's luster. Appointments at the senior level included Pitirim Sorokin (1924–30), who had emigrated from Russia two years earlier; Edwin Sutherland (1926–29), already on his way to a distinguished career in criminology; Malcolm Willey (1928–34), another Giddings Ph.D., who later became dean and assistant to the president of the university; and George B. Vold (1928–57), a criminologist, who replaced Sutherland. Graduate students included the future head of the United States Census, Conrad Taeuber (Ph.D. 1931), and several others who were especially active within the profession during the next decade: Carle C. Zimmerman (Ph.D. 1925), a rural sociologist who later followed Sorokin to Harvard; Harold A. Phelps (Ph.D. 1925), who became a professor at the University of Pittsburgh, and first permanent secretary-treasurer of the A.S.S.; and George Lundberg (Ph.D. 1925), whose "operationalism" carried the battle over scientific sociology into the 1940s.[28]

Despite Chapin's steady drift toward a more scientistic sociology, it would be a mistake to exaggerate this tendency during his first few years at Minnesota. The merger of sociology and social work, begun before Chapin arrived, gave a practical as well as a socially oriented cast to the work in both areas. By 1929 the seminars for sociologists included Applied Sociology, Social Theory, Statistical Theory, Evolution, and Rural Sociology—with another four in various aspects of field work for the social workers. The lines between the two tended to blur, however, as the "scientific" impulse within sociology fused with the "professional" thrust of the social work.[29]

Chapin's earliest doctoral theses reflected this fusion, as well as the still eclectic and "unscientific" nature of Minnesota sociology by later standards: P. Perigord, "International Labor Organization"(1925); C. R. Hoffer, "Services of Rural Trade Centers" (1925); G. A. Lundberg, "Poor Relief Legislation"

(1925); H. A. Phelps, "Comparative Study of Unionism" (1925); C. C. Zimmerman, "Farmers' Marketing Attitudes" (1925); J. F. Markey, "The Symbolic Process in Children" (1927); and R. W. Murchie, "Unused Lands of Manitoba" (1927). Chapin's colleagues and former students, in fact, tended later to romanticize the open and "democratic" years before the austerity of the man and of his sociology became legendary.[30]

By 1925, however, there were already signs that things were not going well, despite Bernard's departure that spring. Sorokin was aggrieved because his $2000 salary was half that of most professors; a strong personality, he also disliked Chapin's increasingly autocratic ways. "Sorokin says that the little details are brought before the faculty, and the real policies are decided outside," a graduate student reported to Bernard in the spring of 1926.[31] Chapin's strained relations with Ross Finney and one or two other more "practical" sociologists was an open secret. In the spring of 1926, or so Elmer reported to another graduate student, Finney and two others went to the dean to complain of Chapin's high-handed methods. The dean then reportedly called Chapin to his office for some stern words. He seemed "to be more of a gentleman" after that, this informant continued.[32]

By this time, the Minnesota department was in fact a microcosm of the forces and tensions transforming the discipline, with social concern and vestigial reformism battling an increasingly austere scientism in the person of Chapin. As a result, the department served as something of a nursery for the leading dissidents who later battled within the A.S.S. A look at the careers of three Minnesotans provides a clearer idea of the dynamics of this process.

The first was George Lundberg (1895–1966), the most prominent professionally although only a sideline kibitzer during the battles of the thirties. Born in South Dakota of Swedish immigrant parents, Lundberg spent most of his youth working on his parents' farm. His mother, the orphaned daughter of peasants, had been a servant from childhood. "This influence," Lundberg later observed, "gave me a deep-seated emotional leaning toward the problems of social classes and social injustice."[33] Before his arrival at Minnesota, Lundberg's hard-won education, which introduced him to a range of sociological theory, had included a course with Ross at Wisconsin (M.A. 1922), where his youthful reformism clashed directly with the new scientific spirit. Lundberg later recalled that he had "quite an argument" with the economist John Commons over a statistics requirement, which he insisted had "no relevance" for sociology. Bested in that exchange (he finally took a C− for the course), he determined to have nothing more to do with the "dismal science."[34]

At Minnesota, Lundberg accordingly sought what he termed "the larger implications of science and sociology": in Chapin's course in Statistics, Elmer's in Methods of Social Investigation, and Bernard's in Theory. In the end, he abandoned reform of "the militant type" for "scientific method," proclaiming that he owed his greatest debt to Bernard. In 1929, he served as chief editor for *Trends in American Sociology*, a celebration of Bernard-style scientific sociology.

A second young Turk was Harold A. Phelps (b. 1898), a native New Englander who had made his way to the plains through the sedate corridors of Brown University (B.A. 1920), Harvard, and George Washington University (M.A. 1922). Introduced to sociology by Ward's successor J. Q. Dealey, Phelps soon tired of memorizing "the theories of social philosophers," while paying no attention to practical problems. At Minnesota he enjoyed the courses of Chapin and the others, but unlike Lundberg he remained essentially eclectic in his work, which finally centered on social problems and social work. Looking back on the Minnesota years, he later judged the craze for statistics to have been the first of many such fads that drew sociology from its true mission.[35]

Manuel Elmer (b. 1886), although a faculty member rather than a graduate student, was in his way the most disaffected. Born near Monroe, Wisconsin, of Swiss immigrant parents, he had lived on a farm until 1907 when he graduated from high school at the age of twenty-one. After four years at Northwestern (B.S. 1911), he studied at Wisconsin (summer 1910), Illinois (M.A. 1913), and the University of Chicago (Ph.D. 1914). Active in the local evangelical church, he had found much to dislike in Ward's sociology, and spent most of the summer at Wisconsin reading "furiously . . . to get facts to prove he was wrong and that I was right." At Chicago he wrote a dissertation on *Social Surveys of Urban Communities* (1914), but only after considerable resistance from Henderson. The experience left him especially sensitive to the charge that the social survey was not *really* sociology, a criticism, he once remarked, that "sounded like a novice telling a store keeper . . . that *making an inventory was not selling goods*."[36]

Elmer's appointment at Minnesota required that he coordinate all survey work as a "definite phase of sociology." His strong point, on the social-work side, was his many community contacts. As president of a local tuberculosis association, he served *ex officio* on the directorates of a number of local welfare agencies, which gave him access to research data and assistance in using them. When in 1926 Chapin made him resign this position, so the story went, he left for the University of Pittsburgh.[37]

Others at Minnesota meanwhile nursed their own complaints. John Markey, later a professor at Maryland, suspected that there was a set policy to get rid of anyone "who wishes to say something about Dept. and U. affairs." Many reportedly complained about Chapin's classes and his skills as a statistician (shades of Giddings!). One student said that Chapin had confined comments on his qualifying examination to spelling errors. Sorokin's use of "figures and facts" was also suspect, while his anti-Soviet tirades were interpreted as the sort of "conservatism" that pleased the administration.[38]

5

Chapin's transformation from an open, friendly, and concerned chairman to the austere autocrat of later legend was the other half of the story of his conversion to a rigid scientism. Although local speculation on the matter has become part of university folklore, no single factor explains the change. One probable factor was Chapin's increasing involvement in foundation work, where rigorous definitions of social science were clearly in favor. Chapin apparently sensed as much when, applying for funds for his pet project, the *Social Science Abstracts*, he wrote to the Rockefeller Memorial: "If a plan of systematic study of social investigations could be put into operation, we would be in a position to discard ineffective methods and to concentrate on the methods which get us the facts."[39]

Another factor was a personal crisis that occurred in 1925, when Chapin's wife died suddenly of peritonitis at age thirty-six—a chilling replay of his earlier loss of his mother. Their fourteen-year marriage had produced three children, and was by all accounts uncommonly happy; their relations with the world were outgoing, informal, even "democratic." His remarriage two years later—so colleagues reported—was another matter. Socially ambitious, his second wife was extremely protective of her husband's reputation. Reporting local opinion, a junior colleague wrote that the new Mrs. Chapin had "a mind like a steel trap, a tongue like a rapier and the instincts of a tigress protecting her cub." Chapin, on being saddled with the sole care of his three children, had begun to show his autocratic instincts even before his remarriage; but his new wife certainly did not improve the situation.[40]

The collapse of the *Abstracts* after three years, and his return to Minnesota from New York, put the finishing touches on the new Chapin. Despite his enthusiasm, the *Abstracts* project had been shaky from the start. A close colleague later claimed that neither he nor the staff had had a clear idea as to its objective. Leaving aside the question of reviewer objectivity, many social scientists felt that scholars should do their own reviewing of the literature. By the summer of 1933, the S.S.R.C. concluded that the project was not worth the expenditure of increasingly scarce funds.[41] To add to his disappointment, Chapin's department had virtually collapsed in his absence: Sorokin and then Zimmerman had left for Harvard; Sutherland had accepted a new chair in criminology at the University of Chicago, created with S.S.R.C funds.

Whatever the precise cause, Chapin in this period became the formal, austere, and intensely private person that colleagues remembered in his later years. As one associate put it: ". . . he was not the sort of person whom you would stop off to see on a Sunday morning, and even see some morning and say it was a fine spring day for a walk to the river. . . . There just was no really personal association or even worse, any desire for it."[42]

At the level of theory, Chapin's austerity translated into a methodological asceticism that increased in severity as the years went on. In *Cultural Change* (1928) he abandoned the unilinear evolutionism of his earlier work. Also during 1927–28 he devised the first of several social scales, while announcing the behaviorist assumptions that underlay them. In *Contemporary American Institutions* (1935) he used these measurements to examine social structures. In *Experimental Designs* (1947) he outlined a program of "social experiments." Although the details of each are unimportant, these later works together trace his path to objectivism, and to a particularly uncompromising version of the value-neutral ideal that finally molded his personal no less than his professional life.

A variation of Ogburn's theory of "cultural lag," *Cultural Change* rested on a cyclical theory that Chapin had adopted a year earlier. Now labeled "synchronous cultural change," it combined the work of Ogburn and Bernard on technology, the diffusionist anthropology of Franz Boas and his disciples, and a touch of Spenglerian *Weltschmerz* (Spengler had "beautiful theories of social change," Chapin later noted, "but nothing to put your fingers on"). With this theory, Chapin attempted to reconcile two hypotheses that seemed initially at odds: the theory of selective, cumulative change; and the cyclical view of history.[43]

Stripped of technicalities, the new theory rested on two assumptions that reflected Chapin's postwar experiences. First, just as unilinear evolutionism meant progress, so the cyclical view seemed to deny its possibility. Behind the charts and graphs of *Cultural Change* lurked the unmistakable message that the triumphs of human intelligence, whether in material or social invention, were subject to an unending cycle of growth and decay. Second, confirming the lesson drawn from Karl Pearson, it was the business of sociology to measure differential rates of change rather than to explain the principles underlying them. This conclusion, in turn, led directly to the formulation of new and more sophisticated scales of social measurement.[44]

The immediate results were the "living-room scales" that Chapin first developed for his graduate classes during the academic year 1927–28. He was not the first to examine material possessions as clues to class,[45] but Chapin outdid his predecessors in the humorless rigor of his analysis. After demonstrating to his own satisfaction that the contents of an individual's living room correlated with other indices of socioeconomic status (income, community participation, and the like), he devised schemes for quantifying household items, from books to floor coverings. Thus, an electric light or a fireplace with three utensils was worth eight points, and hardwood floors ten. A kerosene heater in the living room *cost* two points, as did a sewing machine or an alarm clock. Unlike alternative scales that measured social class in terms of social- or self-perception, this test of status proceeded on the assumption that behavior rather than attitude was the crucial issue.[46]

In 1928, Chapin made these behaviorist assumptions explicit. Citing an analysis of political institutions by the psychologist Floyd Allport, he argued that social institutions could also be "reduced to a form of behavior." Institutions consisted of four "type-parts": attitudes, symbols, utilitarian traits, and oral or written "specifications." The family, for example, could be analyzed into (a) attitudes of love, loyalty, and respect; (b) symbols such as the wedding ring or coats-of-arms; (c) home equipment and property; and (d) wills and marriage licenses. Each of these elements could be quantified, and Chapin proceeded to dissect institutions such as the church in a similar manner. In *Contemporary American Institutions* (1935), he applied such tests in his one major contribution to structural analysis.[47]

During the Depression, Chapin at times outdid Ogburn in restricting the sociologist's sphere of action. In a 1934 symposium he drew a sharp distinction between the "political-economic" and the "social" realms, effectively limiting sociology to the family, schools, churches, and welfare organizations—quite different from the "political" sociology that Bernard and his allies hoped to foster. Moreover, even within this limited sphere, sociologists must recognize the important difference between the "active" leader and the "research scientist," who "serves in an expert advisory capacity and refuses to accept the responsibility of executive action."[48]

Embellishing the argument in his presidential address to the American Sociological Society in 1935, Chapin further distinguished "goal directed" action from its "unintended consequences" (the latter a Weberian phrase soon to be popularized by Robert Merton): the first was the business of leaders; the second, of social scientists. Among theorists there existed a similar division between what he called "normative" and "non-normative" sociologists. Between the two, however, Chapin refused to take sides, thus preserving neutrality even where neutrality was at issue.[49]

Chapin by this time was also sympathetic to the operationalism of George Lundberg, his former student. By "operationally," Chapin told colleagues at the A.S.S., he meant that "social concepts" must be defined "in terms of the operations and processes used in attempts to measure them or test them by experiment." An unstated corollary was that concepts not so testable were meaningless. What were such concepts? It would be difficult, Chapin answered, to provide operational definitions for such terms as "social class, wage slaves, proletariat, bourgeoisie, socialite, aristocrat, plutocrat"—in short, the rhetorical and conceptual arsenal that had sustained the American left for a century![50]

True to his theory, Chapin kept his views of the New Deal largely to himself. But the indications are that, among the quantifiers, he was less sympathetic than even Ogburn, and certainly less than Read Bain and others. Social security he termed a "patchwork" that had been created by a fusion of the "unexpressed wish fantasies" of the aged with modern communications. "Unplanned results" were bound to occur. By tracing these results, "non-normative theory" could provide the necessary check.[51]

Chapin meanwhile decided that statistics, even in combination with social indices, could not give a truly "scientific" result without the "controls" that were an integral part of the laboratory experiment. "Experimental designs," as he described them, required "experiment" and "control" groups, to be determined by frequency distributions of designated traits. In a study of 102 former Boy Scouts, for example, he divided them into two groups: the first, the short-term scouts, who had dropped out of scouting after an average of 1.3 years; the second, the more committed, whose tenure had averaged four years. The first ("control") and the second ("experimental") groups were then paired by equating frequency distributions on place of birth, father's occupation, health rating, and mental ability. Finally, to equalize the two groups, 22 subjects were eliminated, and the two groups of 40 were compared for performance in later life as measured by Chapin's "Social Participation Scale" and an awesome selection of similar yardsticks.[52]

While the methodology grew ever more complex, the issue, in one study after another, remained social adjustment, the hearty perennial of behavior-ism. Which groups in society show greater "social intelligence" and "social insight"? What is the effect of "good housing" on former slum-dwellers? Do active Boy Scouts show "better adjustment" in later life than "drop-out scouts"? Is work relief better than direct relief? The answers were accordingly predictable, especially in view of the questionable assumptions and sampling techniques: people who join more organizations have higher "social intelli-gence"; persons affiliated with political, professional, social, and civic groups rank highest in "social insight"; good housing and regular scout attendance foster adjustment; work relief is better than the dole.[53] As with Giddings at Columbia three decades before, Chapin's new interest gradually left an imprint on Minnesota's doctoral dissertations, which became less concerned with agencies of social change, and more with mobility, achievement, and family patterns.[54]

Although Chapin's reputation endured, his final decades were not entirely trouble-free. While some contemporaries applauded these new departures, he found himself caught in something of a cross-fire by the time *Experimental Designs* appeared (1947): between those who wanted better statistics, and those who had begun to question the entire enterprise. Among the former were biometricians and mathematicians who took his "designs" to task for statistical inadequacies. Closer to home, one colleague faulted his mechanical attempt to quantify the cognitive aspects of experience, while another thought the whole notion of a "random sample" to be the ultimate absurdity of pluralist behavior-ism. A third wondered whether the world *really* knew more about housing or college student behavior as a result of Chapin's studies.[55]

Criticisms of Chapin's administration of the department also mounted, and in the late 1940s produced an unsuccessful revolt against what one young member called his "benevolent dictatorship." The principals were men who had joined the department in a second wave of appointments during the thirties: Raymond Sletto (1930); Clifford Kirkpatrick (1930), a specialist on family psychology; Joseph Schneider (1937), a social theorist; Lowry Nelson (1937); and Elio Monachesi (1929). At a supposedly "secret meeting" at Sletto's home (as Nelson later told it), Kirkpatrick and Sletto tried to persuade Nelson to take the chairmanship if Chapin could be forced to give it up. Chapin soon learned of the meeting, allegedly thanks to Monachesi, who eventually succeeded him as chairman. The plot was foiled when Chapin gave up social work but stayed on in sociology. Sletto and Schneider left the department shortly thereafter.[56]

These criticisms of his statistical work bothered Chapin (who insisted that he had never intended his studies for mathematicians),[57] but he remained the quantifier until the end. While Ogburn agonized over the role of the neutral observer, and Bernard virtually despaired over realizing his objective standard, Chapin became his own best subject. "He had a passion for order," an associate later reminisced. "When we were graduate students under him at Minnesota we used to say, when Chapin goes to bed at night he files himself under 'C'." As he grew older, his life was an extended social experiment. Constructing birdhouses, he made meticulous measurements to ensure that larger birds could not raid the food intended for smaller ones. When reading detective stories for pleasure or as an editor, he based his judgment solely on the internal consistency of the plot. A file drawer bulged with jokes classified for appropriate occasions. On his frequent fishing trips, he invariably carried a notebook in which he recorded the date, time, place, size, and even weather conditions attending each catch. No leisure activity was off limits. Even in his oil painting he experimented systematically with various techniques.[58]

And so he remained in retirement. At a luncheon in Omaha in 1953 honoring Chapin and Ogburn, both men spoke of their future plans. "Ogburn had to admit that he hadn't made any," one guest later recalled. "Chapin was able to spell out just exactly what where and when he would spend the rest of his life." The "where" was Asheville, North Carolina, chosen from other possibilities after he had collected weather data and compared distances to the homes of his several children. Within Asheville, he chose his new neighborhood for its balance of different religious denominations, homes, and shops, and its proximity to a well-stocked bass pond. To confound the critics of behaviorism and the well-ordered life, he then proceeded to have a doubt-free and, by all reports, happy retirement.[59]

11

A BETTER CODE

[In my youth] I rebelled against sham, against pretense,
against conventional morality. Very strong surely must
have been a rebellion against the restraints on sex. Yet it
was not "wilderness" in sex I wanted. But a better code.

William F. Ogburn, 1946

1

With his presidential address to the American Sociological Society in 1929, William Fielding Ogburn became the high priest of "scientific sociology." Sociology, he told his colleagues, was "not interested" in improving the world. "Science is interested directly in one thing only, to wit, discovering new knowledge," he continued. This goal required a "wholly colorless literary style" and a rigorous method, preferably statistical. A service-intellectual, the truly scientific sociologist would not pretend to "guide the course of evolution," but rather would generate the "information necessary for such supreme direction to some sterling executive who will appear to do the actual guiding."[1]

Among the interwar objectivists, Ogburn was the most eminent professionally. Born and educated in the South, he did his graduate work under Giddings at Columbia, and in 1911 earned his Ph.D. for a statistical study of child labor legislation. In *Social Change* (1922) he introduced the phrase "cultural lag" to the sociologists' lexicon. During the 1920s, he represented sociology at the Social Science Research Council. In 1927 he joined the faculty at the University of Chicago, where he later chaired the sociology department. During his tenure, the department produced more than one hundred Ph.D.s, including some of the leading quantifiers of the next generation.[2]

In a pioneering study of the 1928 election Ogburn demonstrated the new possibilities of sophisticated multivariate analysis, for which he has won a minor footnote in histories of quantitative social science.[3] From 1920 to 1926 he served as editor of the *Journal of the American Statistical Association*, and in 1931 he was elected president of the association. As research director of President Herbert Hoover's Committee on Social Trends, he played a pivotal role in producing the pathbreaking *Recent Social Trends* (1933). During the Depression years he served on several New Deal agencies. After World War II, he became one of the nation's best-known analysts of the impact of technology on society. In *Future Shock* (1970) Alvin Toffler cited Ogburn's "cultural lag" as a source of his own futurology.[4]

Although he himself shunned controversy, Ogburn became a favorite target for critics: for humanists, who pictured him as an uncritical apologist for technology;[5] for fellow sociologists, usually to the left politically, who questioned the analytic utility and value-neutrality of the "cultural lag" concept;[6] and for New Left critics of the sixties, who saw him as the archetypal "corporate liberal."[7] At best, he appeared in the guise of a "transitional" figure, representing the discipline's move from a biological to a more genuinely cultural analysis; from general theory to quantitative research; and from social evolutionism to a nonteleological positivism.[8]

While each of these portraits contains an element of truth, they ignore both the complexity of the man, and the personal and professional pressures that made him a leading proponent of scientism in sociology. Ogburn's immediate associates, in fact, saw a sympathetic figure, in his way no less complicated than Luther Bernard. His pretended neutrality, they believed, masked a deeply emotional nature. As one former student put it: "Dedicated to the scientific and, where possible, the quantitative statement of human behavior, he continually yielded, as though in spite of himself, to the lure of the artistic and creative." An associate remembered his "deep sensitivity to art and artistic methods." Late in life, Ogburn himself pondered his reputation as a "*mere* technician and a person without ideas." To his diary he confided: "One thing I do know, is that my love for ideas amounts to a passion. It seems to me I love ideas much more than facts, and much more, I am sorry to say, than I love people."[9]

Ogburn's career, accordingly, was studded with paradox. Although he attacked emotionalism, he was fascinated by Freud, underwent analysis himself, and helped found the Chicago Institute of Psychotherapy. Scorning "speculation," he was as much social philosopher as statistician. Like Bernard (and Giddings before him), he turned to fancy as an antidote to fact, and poured his soul into fiction written under a pseudonym—"for fun," he told a friend. "My desire springs from a yearning for freedom," he again confided to his diary; "freedom from reputation, freedom from standards, particularly the standards of science."[10]

What distinguished Ogburn's version of objectivism—more obviously than it did Bernard's, and certainly Chapin's—was not the denial of feeling, but the radical divorce of intellect and emotion, and ultimately of the public and private person. He insisted that sociologists as human beings have a full fund of emotional and spiritual commitment. Scientific investigation itself begins with feeling, imagination, or a "hunch." He believed that modern Americans needed more emotional outlets—in sports, leisure, and even sexual expression. But the public man (and for Ogburn the creed was a distinctly masculine one) required a "better code." Ogburn did not wish to deny feeling so much as to banish it to a private sphere. In so doing, he provided a blueprint for the separation of public and private, professional and citizen, work and leisure that was fast becoming a distinctive feature of American life in the twenties.

Statistics served this end admirably. On public issues, the calculation and correlation of rates of change promised a standard of value formerly given by "natural law" or "evolution." On a personal level, the sheer arduousness of the activity satisfied the compulsive demands of a still-nagging work ethic. Within academia, the cult of measurement promised sociology new legitimacy, not to mention easier access to the grants now available through the foundations.

Despite the gulf that separated Ogburn and Bernard, in personality no less than in belief, the factors that shaped their views of the discipline and of the world were, on the surface, remarkably similar: the insecurities and disappointments of a provincial background; youthful hopes for a radical reconstruction of society, followed by disillusionment; the quest for power and prestige in a profession that was rapidly changing. If men must be alike truly to differ, Ogburn and Bernard were natural rivals.

2

William F. Ogburn, born in Butler, Georgia, on June 29, 1886, was heir to a tradition of family life that he loved but never quite understood. Simon Ogburne, the first American ancestor, had arrived in Virginia in 1651. Ogburn's mother was also descended from an old and distinguished family, the Wynns, and was distinctly proud of the fact. Both of Ogburn's parents remained close to their brothers and sisters throughout their lives. Yet to Ogburn it seemed like another world. "They lived in a face-to-face community," he wrote, using the phrase Charles H. Cooley had coined. "I have known the point intellectually, but I never quite got the feel of it. It is still something of a mystery."[11]

Ogburn was alternately fascinated and embarrassed by his lineage. When at the faculty table at the University of Chicago someone casually asked him if a Miss Jane Ogburn were his sister, he answered, somewhat to his own surprise: "No, my original ancestor came over in 1658 [sic] and her original ancestor did not get here until 1684." Repeating the incident to Read Bain, he confided: "There were two or three men around the table whose fathers were born in Europe, and it did not take long for someone to crack down upon me with a remark about my blue blood, which increased my confusion." One day toward the end of his life, he spent an afternoon tracing the genealogy of the original Simon, only to recognize the absurdity of the enterprise; had not "modern studies" shown that one's personality was the product of the "social environment," he wondered? Had not the same studies "taken all—or nearly all meaning—from a study of ancestry?"[12]

Ogburn's youth diverged sharply from this family tradition. His father died while he was quite young, and he then lived with his mother and an aunt in circumstances that required taking in boarders to make ends meet. "As a boy I carried a good deal of responsibility [and had] little money which I had to stretch for the family," he recalled. Under these circumstances, family pride took the form of extreme sensitivity to reputation, and a compulsion to conform. On the streets of small-town Georgia, gossip was a deadly weapon, and a good name was "the most valued of possessions."[13]

In later years, Ogburn's concern for normality and his distrust of eccentricity amounted to an obsession. "The truth is I love (I think) to be ordinary, to be like my fellow man, not to be an extreme deviate," he once wrote in his diary. This view shaped his attitudes toward matters great and small. Of success in one's career, he wrote: ". . . all 'big shots' do things appropriately. But a sense of appropriateness is a distinct asset. . . . I have known a few people who might have been 'big shots' if they had not been awkward, inept, and given to saying the wrong thing at the wrong time." After an evening in the company of Edward Ross and his new wife, he commented: "Nothing queer or eccentric about either." And of a Christmas card from a friend: "less eccentric than any they have sent." In a self-critical mood, he speculated that this same attitude probably explained his penchant for research that earned prestige rather than money, when more profitable opportunities beckoned. "The big idea is that we do the things that are highly socially valued. And research is the goal we must all strive for."[14]

As with Bernard, Ogburn's concern for reputation generated his view that human behavior was a "response to stimulus," rather than the organization of habits around a preexisting or socially-created self. "All members of the human species do not respond exactly to the same material stimulus," he noted, but all actions are nonetheless "responses to stimuli." So persuaded, he sometimes spoke of himself and his professional activities as objects over which he had little control. Despite sometimes frenetic professional activity, he frequently commented on his lack of "ambition." Rather, he was "driven on by a sense of duty, or in response to the general idea, inculcated in youth, to do the immediate job ahead, rather well. . . . But no great ego, no great desire to leave my mark on the world."[15]

Ogburn inherited other traditions that seemed somehow archaic in the New Era, "regarding women, chivalry, honor, money, courage, etc." Like many of his generation, he absorbed these virtues from reading the Victorians—Thackeray, Dickens, and especially Sir Walter Scott. "One ideal I recall was that it was not good for a strong man to talk much," he added. "A brave, courageous man was a man of few words. Too much talk was feminine. To be garrulous was to be a sissy." Remembering this wisdom, Ogburn years later urged fellow sociologists to cultivate a no-frills literary style and to eschew the conventional graces.[16]

For all of his adult years, Ogburn's life was a battle between illusion and reality, between youthful ideals and a world that seemed to render them meaningless. Nowhere was this more pronounced than in his view of women. His southern upbringing reinforced his exposure to the Victorian cult of true womanhood. "I started off in my youth with a strong sense of chivalry," he remembered. "I never had any sisters and I reverenced my mother." Converted to feminism, he supported total sexual equality, but an equality premised on the belief that women were "unselfish angels." Reality again checked this fantasy: many modern women were "narcissistic, self-centered—interested only in themselves," he decided. Although they demanded equality, most women wanted men "to dominate them, to take responsibility, even to bully them." The result of this realization was a frank lament: "Here I have been treating them as superior beings who want freedom and rights! But so many of them do not." In face of the erosion of traditional sex roles, "facts" were sternly masculine, and "speculation" a dangerous feminine allurement.[17]

During the Progressive Era, Ogburn, in his way, was something of a rebel. He left home in 1901 to study at nearby Mercer College, where he developed a fascination for "wilderness"—whether embodied in wild animals, primitive men, or even the wanderings of gypsies and hoboes. As with Luther Bernard, although with less dramatic effect, his rebellion focused on "restrictions on sex." He later recalled: "Freedom of speech or thought never bothered me. I think I rebelled against sham, against pretense, against conventional morality."

Yet wilderness, and the freedom it promised, was as frightening as it was fascinating. He finally decided that it was not the "wilderness of sex" he wanted, but a "better code." A brush with some real-life hoboes years later had a similar effect. "A most crude, unattractive, eccentric lot," he mused after an afternoon spent at McSorley's bar. "Thus facts and realities cracked my fantasy."[18]

A trip to Paris in 1906, Ogburn's first outside Georgia, brought him face to face with the perils of liberation. "I was young, naive, modest, not self-assertive, well-mannered and reasonably normal," he recalled. "I met many queer characters who were egotistical, self-centered or loved power who bullied me with their views, the like of which I had never heard, because I was a listener, not self-assertive and had good manners. . . . There were Russians, poets, artists, Jews, anarchists, socialists, social workers, English, French, etc. But nearly all queer." During his stay he was drawn irresistibly to art and spent thirty successive days in the Louvre. But the beauty there also frightened him. "It was an unreal, a dream world, the world of beautiful pictures," he later wrote. "Afterward when I began my long fight for reality, I was always a bit afraid to visit the Louvre again, afraid that I might become intoxicated, and take a long flight from reality again."[19]

Whether this reference was to a real or a metaphoric breakdown, Ogburn gradually began to structure a rigid separation between his public and private selves. For the sociologist, exact measurement was an antidote to illusion, statistics the basis of a "better code." Professionalism provided rules for the office, but not for the home. "Very definitely, I would like to confine my peculiarities which are due to my occupation, to my hours of duty on the job," he resolved upon his retirement. Like many Americans in the twenties, the private Ogburn developed an enthusiasm for sports. He loved boxing and baseball, and had a passion for tennis, which he played regularly until his death. However, he never let himself go completely. Although he greatly enjoyed sporting events, he once commented, "I hardly ever go. I have the technique of denial down pretty well."[20]

3

At Columbia, where he entered graduate school in the fall of 1909, Ogburn was unabashedly a "Giddings man." Despite his low regard for his mentor's computational skills, he recalled fondly that Giddings had "praised and preached statistics to his students." Ogburn's dedication to Giddings in his doctoral thesis was lavish even by the conventions that govern this ritual.

Although some complained that Giddings ran a one-man show, Ogburn liked the fact that he "never tried to dominate me."[21]

Others who influenced Ogburn during the Columbia years were Henry L. Moore, in statistics; and Wesley Mitchell, the institutional economist. Among sociologists, the single greatest influence after Giddings was Sumner. *Folkways*, Ogburn wrote, convinced him that what usually pass for personal "values" are in fact "mores" derived from the surrounding culture. "Most of our thinking, so called, is merely taking over what someone else has said."[22]

In his thesis, *Progress and Uniformity in Child Labor Legislation* (1912), Ogburn tested the theory that evolution through natural selection converges on the average—the premise of Giddings's then-current interest in measuring social pressure. In society this process produces "l'homme moyen," neither reactionary nor radical (thus adducing Spencer's altruism without the benefit of discredited Lamarckian mechanisms); in the development of child labor legislation, it would likewise reveal a "type" to serve as a model for future laws.[23]

Nature was Ogburn's starting point. After a heavy rainstorm, he gathered a number of sparrows washed from their nests, and revived those he could. He then made statistical charts of the measurements for survivors and nonsurvivors. "The curve representing the birds which survived was a narrower curve showing that the birds killed were much more largely the unusual, the extreme, those widely deviating from the average," he concluded. Nature, that is, was as normal as Ogburn wished himself to be![24]

Applying a similar test to child labor laws, Ogburn measured the frequency of seven basic provisions (occupations, hours, etc.) in every state for five-year intervals between 1879 and 1909. Given these data, uniformity could then be defined as (a) the amount of likeness among all laws with respect to the various traits; (b) the resemblance of all laws to a single norm, which "may be an imaginary one"; or (c) the percentage of identical laws in the total number for any given time or place. He rejected the first because of the impossibility of reducing findings to a single scale. The third was useful but limited in value. Reluctantly, he thus adopted the second approach, despite the perils of using an "imaginary" law as a norm to which others were to be compared.[25]

Ogburn claimed success because child labor laws displayed an overall tendency toward uniformity for each of the different characteristics. Certain provisions, that is, tended to show up with increasing frequency while others were eliminated. The initial theory concerning the elimination of "extreme deviations" was thus "supported by fact." But was the end product an "ideal"? Could one speak of "progress" in child labor legislation?

Ogburn conceded that the "type" was more difficult to define than many had assumed. When a single trait such as age was at issue, a type could be easily described in terms of an age limit of greatest frequency; legislation could thus be said to be tending toward making age sixteen the lower limit for work in the mines. But most legislation had several provisions—for example, setting educational requirements, demanding working papers, or establishing penalty and suspension provisions. If equal weight were assigned to each of these provisions, no clearly defined type would emerge because each recurred with roughly equal frequency in the body of legislation as a whole. The question of "progress" was impossible to prove, *unless* one made an arbitrary "valuation"—for example, that safety regulations in a dangerous industry were more important than educational requirements. Interestingly, this was precisely the issue that Bernard's friend Sutherland raised several years later when he noted that there was no "scientific" way to determine whether health or wage regulations were more important for women workers. Bernard finally concluded that the sociologist must himself provide the norm (through "projective logic"); Ogburn, in effect, left the establishment of ends to others.[26]

Although child labor reformers welcomed the study as a unique attempt to quantify an important subject,[27] the issue of establishing standards of value would not go away. So long as Ogburn shared his contemporaries' uncritical faith in progress, and their enthusiasm for expertise, so long would he leave unexplored the implications of his brief remark about arbitrary "valuations." As this faith ebbed, he would realize that statistics measured, not unilinear progress, but only relative rates of change among social values, a further implication being that someone other than scientists must determine the direction of change.

After graduate school, Ogburn taught at Reed in Portland (1912–17) and at the University of Washington (1917–19). He had previously resisted the pat formulations of self-proclaimed reformers,[28] but the world on the West Coast looked different. For more than a decade the Pacific Northwest had been in the vanguard of Progressivism. When Ogburn arrived, it was a center of Wobbly activity, and a three-volume edition of Marx given to him by the Portland branch of the I.W.W. became one of his "prized possessions." The opportunity for public participation in government through the initiative, referendum, and recall procedures made Oregon state politics among the most exciting in the nation. "In government changes, Oregon is the leader," Ogburn boasted in one of several articles praising the "Oregon system" of direct democracy.[29]

Another strand in Ogburn's romance with radicalism was the economic interpretation of history. At Columbia he was doubtless exposed to the theory in Seligman's *Economic Interpretation of History* (1902) and later in Charles Beard's *Economic Interpretation of the Constitution* (1913). At the University of Washington, he taught with Vernon Louis Parrington, a leading progressive intellectual and literary historian, and with J. Allen Smith, author of *The Spirit of American Government* (1907), an influential study often cited as a forerunner of Beard's work. By 1915 Ogburn was entertaining his own classes with economic analyses of the Crusades and the Reformation, and he soon found further ammunition in such works as Louis B. Boudin's *Socialism and the War* (1916).[30]

One by one, however, the elements of this would-be radicalism dissolved. The first to go was Ogburn's faith in "democracy." In Oregon, the 1915 election provided the first real test of the initiative and referendum in a time of economic depression and the European war. Of various measures on the ballot, only four passed; of these, one favored prohibition, and another the disfranchisement of immigrants, both signs of growing reaction. Ogburn tried to dismiss these disquieting results, and criticized "shortsighted" gloom in the Progressive camp. But he was clearly disheartened.[31]

Radical predictions of imminent class warfare also proved hollow. Analyzing the opinions of different social classes on various issues, Ogburn found some differences but nowhere near enough to support the Wobbly dictum that workers and employers had "nothing in common."[32] Meanwhile, the passions of war undermined the assumption of the rationality implicit in the economic interpretation of history. Depressed by growing manifestations of the irrationality of public opinion, Ogburn by 1919 shared the popular postwar cynicism. Wartime propaganda blinded the public to the "facts," whether on the right or left. "We are not only ignorant of the Kaiser and the I.W.W., but we hate them," he lamented. Different visitors returning from the Soviet Union seemed to describe entirely different countries. Strike reports were equally unreliable: employers reported four hundred men on strike, while the workers claimed ten thousand.[33]

This disillusion set the stage for *Social Change*. Ogburn's starting point was the apparent contradiction between the model of human rationality implicit in the economic interpretation *and* the mounting evidence of irrationality. Instructed by Freud, he now saw the many ways in which unconscious drives disguise motives and shape behavior. The insight was important for his own discipline. Just as the sexual impulses were hidden or disguised, so were economic motives, an example being the wartime use of the I.W.W. as a scapegoat. Echoing Beard, Ogburn argued in a 1919 article that national symbols such as the Constitution masked economic motives, but unlike Beard he stressed that reverence for such symbols was innocent of the "real" (i.e., economic) motives that had created them.[34]

In *Social Change* (1922), Ogburn took this analysis one step further. "As I thought about it, the disguise factor in causation seemed less important than the time factor," he later recalled. That is to say, the conflict between economic interests and the announced motives of individuals was the result, not of self-deception based on unconscious drives, but of different rates of change among the several elements that constitute "culture." Many Americans, to take the example that dramatized the issue for him, believed that a "woman's place was in the home," despite the fact that former household activities such as weaving and soapmaking had long ago been moved to the factory. This gap between belief and reality Ogburn termed "cultural lag."[35]

"Culture," as Ogburn defined it, went beyond social psychology, for it embraced "material culture" as well as "knowledge, belief, morals, laws and custom," or what he termed "non-material culture."[36] This definition distanced him from Giddings, whom he now criticized for overemphasizing the psychological dimension of group activity, as well as for ignoring the cumulative, historical dimension of culture. Historically, cultural lag had not always been a gap between methods of production and values. But it tended to be so in the modern age.[37]

Ogburn intended his theory to be an antidote to the excessive biologizing of social phenomena that persisted despite the numerous attacks upon it. Too often cultural traits were wrongly attributed to heredity, he wrote, echoing Bernard's simultaneous assault on "instinct" theory. The "traits of original nature" were far fewer than popularly supposed, and they were subject to immense variability through cultural conditioning. The relation between the sexes again illustrated the point.[38]

This attack on biological sociology, however, was less thorough-going than at first appeared—one of several contradictions in the book. The theory of "lag" was actually two theories in one: the first a cultural one, in which aspects of culture changed differentially; the second a biological one, in which the "original nature" of man was unadjusted to modern life. Despite appearances, the latter was closer to prewar theories than Ogburn admitted.[39]

A second confusion derived from Ogburn's imprecise use of the term "technology" as related to "science." Although he built his reputation on his study of the impact of technology on society, the term appeared infrequently in *Social Change*.[40] More importantly, he failed to explain the relation between the material component in invention and the rules and procedures that govern new discoveries. Because such rules, strictly speaking, belong to "non-material" rather than "material" culture, he was left with the curious conclusion that a major source of change in the modern world occurs in the nonmaterial realm, a conclusion directly opposed to the one he ostensibly drew. His empirical observations compounded the confusion, for he found that discoveries in the nonmaterial realm were not only massive, but occurred at an exponential rate—a fact that he elsewhere argued was the defining characteristic of material culture. As Pitirim Sorokin, later one of his severest critics, put the matter: "If science is a part of non-material culture, and if as a rule scientific study and thought precedes a materialization of this thought in almost all inventions, it is hard to agree with the contention that changes in the material culture precede those in the non-material one."[41]

Both contradictions revealed Ogburn in one sense to be simply a man of his time. Biological determinism remained a powerful force in the twenties; the distinction between "material" and "non-material" culture was a staple of the anthropological literature upon which he drew; and his earlier interest in the economic interpretation translated easily into an emphasis on the "material" realm.[42] But the contradictions also reflected a deep personal ambivalence toward the changes described. Ogburn was convinced that extreme hereditarianism and economic determinism were untenable; but he could not accept the naive faith in human potential that sustained prewar reformism. Vestiges of biological hereditarianism in *Social Change* effectively forestalled the conclusion that society would be perfect if only the lag between outmoded values and modern methods of production were eliminated—a conclusion that his argument otherwise appeared to support. These vestiges reflected not only his postwar pessimism, but a commitment to values embedded in instinct theory, whether "maternal" feelings or "warlike" propensities.

These ambiguities invited quite different readings of *Social Change*. At one extreme, a prewar reformer such as Edward Ross saw "cultural lag" as the work of "selfish, special interests," and hence welcomed the theory as a call for much-needed "reform and regulation." At the other extreme, the social psychologist Floyd Allport found a technological fatalism because Ogburn's "culture" seemed a thing unaffected by individual behavior and beyond human control.[43] Of the two, Allport was closer to the truth: Ogburn's reform ardor had definitely cooled, as some closing remarks about socialism made quite clear.[44]

But *Social Change* was really neither pro- nor anti-"reform," as the term was conventionally understood. Ogburn's proposals, although "fragmentary" by his own admission, looked not to social justice or governmental controls, on the one hand, nor to "rugged individualism" and laissez-faire, on the other, but rather to the good life in a consumer-oriented, leisured society. More enlightened attitudes toward sex, perhaps earlier sex education, might relieve "psychoses and neuroses," he speculated. The sublimation of sexual drives into creative activities, and an increase in sports and recreation, would also help. Whereas Progressives from Lester Ward to William James urged the channeling of private passion into public projects, Ogburn argued, in effect, that Americans should frankly accept the separation of the public and private spheres. In the modern world, recreation and sexual fulfillment would foster adjustment to a situation one could not or would not change.[45]

Others meanwhile fleshed out the details of this New American Way. In one textbook after another, "cultural lag" was invoked against outmoded behavior: from clinging to one's native language (if a recent immigrant), to baking bread at home. Fundamentalism was a favorite target. "Religion for some is a refuge from social responsibilities," wrote Ogburn's onetime collaborator Ernest Groves, who likened this lag to a "neurotic reaction." The alleged "backwardness" of blacks illustrated lag, as did the failure of highway departments to keep pace with the automobile. But above all, the gap manifested itself in archaic assumptions concerning women's domestic duties, and the "traditional domination of the husband and father." In fact, as a critic noted wryly, the concept generally served less as description than as an "opprobrious epithet of an enthusiastic missionizing for a new cause."[46] The irony, of course, was that this blueprint for the New Era was the work of a displaced Southerner suspended between traditions he loved but could not accept, and an order he accepted but could not love.

In sociology, and in Ogburn's own career, *Social Change* was significant less for its prescriptions than for the implication that sociologists should devote their energies to measuring rates of change in different areas of human activity, rather than to constructing grand theories of evolution or the ideal society. In moving the statistician to center stage, that is to say, Ogburn's imaginative theory paved the way for a sociology that ostensibly eschewed both imagination and theory.

12

A PILE OF KNOWLEDGE

*I rather like the term a pile of knowledge, since
an important characterization of science is that
it accumulates.*

William F. Ogburn

1

While *Social Change* established Ogburn's reputation as a theorist, his professional activities pushed him toward statistics and quantification. The years on
the West Coast honed his statistical skills. The very existence of the initiative
and referendum procedures, whatever the outcome of the elections, provided
data on an unprecedented scale. For his study of the "Political Thought of
Social Classes" (1916), he generated statistics on voting in more than twenty
Oregon counties on 103 issues over a four-year period. Prior to his appointment at Columbia in 1919, he spent a year working for the Cost of Living
Section of the National War Labor Board and the Bureau of Statistics, travel-
ing up and down the coast making surveys of industry, labor, and social
conditions. "The usefulness of statistics," he later reflected, "was very apparent during the war."[1]

The appointment at Columbia was a milestone. "I had been in the minor
leagues, now I was in the Big League, in the upper division, if not a pennant
winner," Ogburn later wrote. He owed the position in part to the efforts of
Elizabeth F. Baker, an economist who joined the Barnard department the same
year, but he attributed the appointment to the impersonal working of "social
forces" whose time had come. "The fact that I was offered a professorship at
Yale on the same day that I received the offer from Columbia should be
considered evidence on this point."[2]

Ogburn likewise credited his professional success less to his own efforts
than to the good fortune of being in the "right group" at the right time. ("In
their passion for democracy, for egalitarianism, and for race equality," sociolo-

gists too often overlook the fortuitous, he once commented.) His Columbia associate, the economist Wesley Mitchell, offered him an entrée to the community of statisticians, the Social Science Research Council, and later to President Hoover's Committee on Recent Social Trends. During his years at Columbia, Ogburn was apparently a successful teacher, and by one report "the idol of the girls at Barnard." Within a few years, some saw him as Giddings's heir apparent.[3]

For reasons that are unclear, however, Ogburn was soon dissatisfied—perhaps because Giddings hung on longer than expected; perhaps because Ogburn reportedly did not enjoy the support of Columbia's President Nicholas Murray Butler; perhaps because currents were already in motion that finally resulted in the surprise appointment of Robert MacIver as Giddings's successor. At any rate, Ogburn in 1927 accepted an invitation to join the department at Chicago, where he remained for the rest of his career.[4]

2

Chicago's appointment of a Giddings man was a bold stroke. But the situation was not exactly promising. Department chairman Ellsworth Faris disliked Freudianism, cared little for statistics, and suspected anything that smacked of behaviorism. Robert Park was outspoken in his contempt for statistics and probably opposed the appointment. Louis Wirth and Herbert Blumer, although only assistants, reportedly shared Park's opinion, yet Blumer later insisted that the appointment had general support within the department. Ernest Burgess, best known for his work on the family, and later the closest thing to an ally Ogburn would have, was at best eclectic in his methodological preferences. With characteristic understatement, Ogburn later summed up the situation: "On coming to the U. of C., I found a more hostile attitude toward statistics than I ever had at Columbia."[5]

Ogburn's personal relations with his new colleagues were cordial but uneasy. "Ogburn was a Southern gentleman and he generally didn't make remarks about anybody," one graduate student of the time later recalled. But the fact that he commanded a larger salary than anyone in the department, including chairman Faris, did little to endear him. Nor did the attitude of Ogburn's wife. She presented herself "as a southern aristocrat [and] felt she was making a big sacrifice to come out to the prairies," the same graduate student remembered. These attitudes "made her unpopular with the Chicago people." Mrs. Ogburn in turn reportedly disliked Robert Park's wife especially and, unlike her taciturn and gentlemanly husband, did not hide these feelings.[6]

The competition between Ogburn and Park, although known at the time, went deeper than many supposed. Their relationship began on a sour note when the Parks failed to invite the newcomers to a large party given shortly after the Ogburns' arrival. Several attempts at conversation in the early months foundered when Ogburn suspected that the senior man was "trying to tell me what was what." On one occasion Park brought Ogburn a "handful" of books to review for the *AJS* and then allegedly proceeded to tell him how to review them. To make things worse, Park scoffed openly at statistics in class, reports of which quickly filtered back to the sensitive Southerner. "I never forgave Park, which is a trait in me, not to forgive or forget a slight," Ogburn recalled, adding regretfully: "I wish I were different and had not been so sensitive in regard to Park."[7]

A tinge of envy colored these feelings. Despite Ogburn's professional success, and his influence on some key graduate students, his teaching lost the appeal it had had at Columbia. His course on "social change" was a dull repetition of his book, one graduate student remembered, and actually contained less than the printed version. Another remembered Ogburn as a "very tall austere man" and "not an exciting speaker at all." Many sociology students continued to study statistics with L. L. Thurstone in the psychology department. Park, in fact, also had his student critics, some of whom thought his teaching "atrocious." But Ogburn remembered the situation differently: "Sometimes it seemed to me that Park's popularity was vastly greater with students than with colleagues who had not been his students."[8]

The differences that separated the two were finally more than personal, however. Both were "conservative" by the standards of prewar humanitarians, and of younger liberals such as Blumer and Wirth. While Ogburn discreetly attacked socialism, Park sometimes reduced students to tears with his attacks on "damned do-gooders." Both voted Republican. But these apparent similarities obscured the fact that the two represented different sides of the Progressive legacy: Ogburn, the technocrat's love of efficiency and planning-without-politics; Park, the journalist's thirst for "real life" combined with a moral commitment to the reestablishment of genuine community.

Both men wanted sociology to be more "scientific," but they defined the term differently. On the spectrum from nominalism to realism, Ogburn was closer to the first, Park to the second. To Ogburn, scientific method was a rigorous set of procedures, the more complex and statistical the better. To Park, it was observation and classification, in the spirit of nineteenth-century Baconianism; "science," as he once put it in a remark that could be interpreted as a dig at Ogburn, "is not a ceremonial matter, as some reverent souls seem to think."[9]

Although Ogburn eventually became chairman, he was often at odds with others in the department. As research director of the Social Trends project (1929–33), he drew heavily on Columbia sociologists rather than on his Chicago colleagues, most of whom had little sense of the project as it progressed. The completion of a social science building at Chicago in 1929 brought tensions to the surface in a heated debate over an appropriate motto to be inscribed on the new building, which had been financed in part by the Social Science Research Council. Ogburn won with the same quotation from Lord Kelvin that he had first used in his doctoral thesis, to the effect that knowledge of things that cannot be measured precisely is "meagre and unsatisfactory."[10]

In apparent response, Herbert Blumer in the summer of 1930 launched a scathing attack on "Science Without Concepts," first at a meeting of an Interdepartmental Society for Social Research, and then in a lead article in the *AJS*. Warning against sociologists who "urge us to cling closely to facts and confine ourselves to separate, specific problems," he charged them with being "mere artisans" rather than "scientists" as claimed. Lest the reference be lost, Blumer singled out the work of statisticians.[11]

As it happened, Ogburn already had a less than favorable impression of his junior colleague. When his friend Howard Odum had written Ogburn in the spring of 1930 to complain about Blumer's review in the *AJS* of the textbook by Odum and Jocher, *Introduction to Social Research*, Ogburn adopted an avuncular tone that only slightly masked his feelings. Blumer was "a very young man and perhaps compensates for his youth and ambition by being ultra-critical." Moreover, he was "a football player and . . . not a bridge whist or tennis player," and his reviews were thus "more likely to be after the football pattern than the bridge whist pattern." Faris and Park "are very fond of Blumer," Ogburn added. But he himself was less so. "Blumer has on one or two occasions launched out and attacked me as vigorously as he has you and even more so. This was not in print, however, but before an audience."[12]

Ogburn's relations with Louis Wirth were apparently less contentious but not much closer. A theorist with a special interest in the city, Wirth had begun his work under Park and Burgess and had little sympathy for quantification. "We should try to carry our findings to as precise a point of mensuration as the data and our techniques allow," he later wrote Odum. "I do not, however, agree with those who believe that measurement is the sole criterion of science."[13]

Ogburn admired Wirth, but the fact that he was a Jew complicated their relations. "Another possibility is Louie Wirth at Tulane," Ogburn wrote concerning an opening at Smith in 1930, shortly before Wirth returned to Chicago as an associate professor. "He has a very keen mind. He is a Jew, however."[14] In later years, Ogburn confessed that his relations with Jews within the profession combined idealism and frustration, not unlike his dealings with women. Seeing discrimination during his Columbia years, he spent "great gobs of time" helping Jews obtain jobs and fellowships. But their "aggression, ego, contempt, etc." soon got under his skin. Invited to dinner parties, he would wonder "if Mr. ———, a Jew, would be there, or Prof. ———, a Jew was invited. If so, I braced myself for a bad time." Finally, he asked himself "why I have to be so damned nice to the Jews if I do not enjoy them." At the same time, he realized how unjust it was to endow "the individual with the traits of the race."[15]

Faced with this dilemma, a nineteenth-century liberal might have reread John Locke on "natural rights," or quoted the Declaration of Independence. Ogburn instead made a chart. Listing thirty-five Jews he had known at Columbia and at Chicago, and a random list of thirty-five non-Jews, he compared the two for ten to fifteen objectional traits often attributed to Jews. The result showed that 85 percent of the Jews had the traits, but only 15 percent of the non-Jews. "So I declared my independence of my conscience about the Jews," he concluded this tortured diary entry. "And I am not 'nice,' to those I don't like, no matter how much I sympathize, or how well I understand how they got that way."[16]

From the "scientific" perspective, as Ogburn defined it in the early thirties, social prejudice was a matter of faulty prediction rather than of being "immoral" in some absolute sense: traits observed in a small sample of a population were simply generalized wrongly to the group as a whole. "The differences as measured are not nearly so marked as appears from opinion," he concluded one such analysis of prejudice. But the unanswered question remained whether prejudice, and presumably discrimination, were justified if certain traits recurred with sufficient frequency within a group. Ogburn's survey of Jewish traits appeared to answer "yes."[17]

Looking back on these troubled relations within the department, chairman Ellsworth Faris recalled his own efforts as peacemaker. "Men of the Park school were scornful of statistics," he confided to Odum two decades later, "and the statisticians seemed at times to have a superior air because they got the answers in exact figures though whether exactness always corresponded with accuracy was sometimes a question." Although it was his pleasant duty to "keep the peace," he was able to do it "only after a fashion."[18]

The stuff of academic gossip everywhere, these minor differences and petty feuds do not *explain* Ogburn's increasing enthusiasm for quantitative analysis.

But the departmental situation at Chicago, as the context for Ogburn's meta-morphosis, sheds light on its timing and the intensity of his public statements on the issue at the A.S.S. and elsewhere. If Ogburn were to establish a niche at Chicago, it would have to be as an outspoken apostle of quantification.

The years 1929–33 marked the high tide of Ogburn's professional success and of his belief in the potential of statistics. In 1929 he published a path-breaking analysis of the Hoover-Smith presidential election, possibly the most important piece of research on American attitudes toward Prohibition at the time. In it, he also calculated partial correlation coefficients to prove that the urban vote, when other factors were accounted for, was actually against Smith.[19] The same year, he startled many colleagues at the A.S.S. with his presidential address "The Folkways of a Scientific Sociology."

His work as a quantitative sociologist also accounted for his growing suc-cess at Chicago. Within the department, he competed with his colleagues for the best graduate students. One of the first to be attracted was Robert Faris, son of the department chairman, who began his graduate work in the fall of 1929. Young Faris took several courses with Ogburn, served as his grader in statis-tics, and fell in love with the new methodology. Unfortunately, this infatuation quickly landed him in the middle of the Park-Ogburn rivalry. He had already discussed the possibility of an M.A. thesis with Park, and now had the awkward task of confessing his new passion. "I didn't realize I was hurting his feelings," Faris recalled of the interview with Park, "but he didn't approach me any more and he didn't notice me in the corridors." The incident "destroyed" their relationship for several years, although it was ultimately Park and the senior Faris who had the greatest influence on young Faris's career.[20]

A more permanent convert was Samuel Stouffer. "Sam Stouffer was tre-mendously ambitious," a fellow graduate student later remembered. But the route to preferment in the department was already blocked by Herbert Blumer, who at the time had a firm place in the affections of department chairman Faris. The problem was how to push aside the not-easily-pushable Blumer. Ogburn's arrival offered a solution. "Stouffer left Faris and went to Ogburn," this same informant recalled. "They became great buddies. You see what he did was to bypass the prestige advantage that Blumer already had." Ironically, though, these academic competitors were very much alike: pipe-smoking, nonchalant. "Very often," the informant concluded this reminiscence, "we tend to go like our competitors, you know."[21]

The dedication of Ogburn's graduate students soon paid off in a series of dissertations that bore his imprint: Samuel Stouffer's *Experimental Compari-*

son of Statistical and Case History Methods (1930); Ellen Black Winston's *Statistical Study of Mental Disease* (1930); and John Dollard's *Changing Functions of The American Family* (1930). Others who were considered to be among Ogburn's growing coterie of students were Clark Tibbetts, who collaborated with Ernest Burgess on a study of parole violators; Frederick Stephan, later an expert on sampling methods; and Thomas C. McCormick, who wrote a thesis on *Rural Unrest* (1930). Ogburn's influence was not exclusive, as the historian Martin Bulmer has suggested, nor should it be exaggerated; both Stephan and Tibbetts owed at least as much to Burgess, Dollard soon went off in new directions, and even Stouffer's work bore the marks of Thurstone's influence more than of Ogburn's. But the collective impact of these students on later quantitative work was considerable, from Stouffer's monumental study of *The American Soldier* (1941) to McCormick's more pedestrian contributions to the teaching of quantitative methodology.[22]

3

The educational foundations provided Ogburn a larger stage, and eventually a national reputation as research director of *Recent Social Trends* (1933). By the 1920s, three agencies were especially active in support of the social sciences. The first was the Russell Sage Foundation, which funded the massive "Pittsburgh Survey" before the war, and continued to favor social surveys. The second was the Carnegie Corporation of New York, which supported a major study of immigration after the war, including studies by Thomas and Park. The third was the Laura Spelman Rockefeller Memorial, established in 1918, and revitalized five years later with the appointment of Beardsley Ruml, a twenty-seven-year-old Chicago Ph.D., as director.[23]

For sociologists, the chief vehicle of this support was the Social Science Research Council, which, in addition to receiving more than $2.7 million for individual grants between 1923 and 1928, also controlled the Memorial's fellowship program.[24] From the start, the S.S.R.C. had two basic objectives: to foster more empirical, inductive, "scientific" research; and to break down the barriers that divided the separate disciplines. In theory, the two appeared contradictory—the first looking to narrow and more specialized studies, the second premised on an ideal of the unity of knowledge worthy of Albion Small. In practice, however, the two converged in a nominalistic definition of science: the unity of the social sciences lay in their methods, not in their material. There *was* integration, a political scientist later explained, but it was an "integration along new scientific and methodological lines."[25] In the S.S.R.C., that is to say, Pearson's *Grammar of Science* was institutionalized.

Whether intended or not, the staff and the academics on the S.S.R.C. soon constituted a new elite in the world of scholarship. During Ogburn's tenure, the Council was chaired by Charles Merriam, Wesley C. Mitchell, Arthur Schlesinger, and finally by Ogburn (1937–39). In 1927, a central office was established in New York under Robert S. Lynd (permanent secretary 1927–31) whose *Middletown* (1929) would soon appear. Other representatives of sociology were Chapin (1923–27), Howard Odum (1925–29), and W. I. Thomas (1928–32). In 1931–32 Stuart Rice served on the staff for "social statistics." From the start, the sociologists played a prominent part. During 1925, Odum chaired and Ogburn served on a key committee on Problems and Policy, which reported to the prestigious "Hanover Conference" that year, one of a series that met annually during the decade. During his term, Chapin served on the grants committee.[26]

By the late 1920s, the work of the S.S.R.C., so far as it affected sociology, consisted of (a) establishment of "advisory councils" dealing with major research topics such as Crime and Population; (b) support of a methodological study, eventually published as *Scope and Methods in Sociology*, edited by Rice; (c) individual grants; and (d) the creation of *Social Science Abstracts*. Within a few years, however, most of these projects were victims of hard times. The publication of the Rice volume was in fact a move to cut losses, and in 1933 *Social Science Abstracts* folded after three years.[27]

The grants program of the Memorial and the S.S.R.C. inevitably pleased some more than others. Among those institutions receiving grants between 1923 and 1928, the totals tell the story: Chicago, $3,398,000, including one-half million for additional staff in the social sciences; Columbia, $1,416,000; Harvard, $1,195,000; and Minnesota, $965,000. The University of North Carolina in 1924 received almost half a million dollars to establish the Institute for Research in Social Science under Odum, the first such in the country, in part thanks to Ogburn. Chicagoans also dominated the individual grants: one historian has estimated that the S.S.R.C. financed the so-called Chicago School almost single-handedly.[28]

Although Chicago's lingering reputation as Rockefeller's university made it a natural target, no direct evidence supports the charge that these bequests were consciously designed to strengthen capitalism. Ruml and his closest advisors were self-styled reformers who outdid many sociologists in their faith that social science would create a better society. The S.S.R.C.'s policy of denying grants to explicitly political or reformist organizations was virtually a necessity if it were to survive; beyond that, however, it left things entirely to the universities. Howard Odum spoke genuinely when he later wrote the North Carolina journalist Gerald Johnson that the Council was "about as far from propaganda as anything in the country," adding: "I have just about made an iron-clad rule not to join anything else."[29]

Yet the S.S.R.C.'s more subtle impact on the making of public policy was through its influence on the nature of the disciplines, and the resulting definition of "social science." At its worst, the stress on methodology, research design, and the like was an inevitable by-product of bureaucracy; at its best, it was a necessary compromise between the reality of academic fragmentation and the perennial ideal of the unity of knowledge. The fact that American society, quite apart from the foundations, had produced men such as Ogburn who were amenable to this vision, completed the picture.

Until 1930, sociologists rarely discussed the foundations publicly, despite some private grumbling.[30] In that year, however, an exchange between Luther Bernard and Lynd promised trouble for the future. After attending a spring Council meeting as a guest, Bernard reported that he was disturbed by Lynd's narrow conception of sociology, and by his belief that most theorizing belonged to "social philosophy." "Perhaps your institution might help the poor sociologists a little by bringing them within the range of their more civilized brothers," he wrote, tongue-in-cheek, at the close of a long discussion of their differences. Indeed, Bernard wondered if sociologists were adequately represented in the deliberations of the Council. Lynd repeated his concerns over sociology's imperial tendencies, but he assured Bernard that the discipline was well represented, citing Ogburn and the others. Bernard replied that he well knew who the official representatives were, but knew little about the actual deliberations of the "investigative committees." He added that he looked forward to seeing Lynd at the annual meetings in December.[31] At the 1930 meeting, as it turned out, Ogburn presented an invitation from the Council offering to fund a committee of the A.S.S. to look into social research. With this proposal, the question of foundation influence suddenly assumed new urgency.[32]

The appointment of the President's Committee on Recent Social Trends in the fall of 1929 brought Ogburn national prominence. Originating with Hoover, the plans for the committee and its three-year study were worked out by French Strother, a special assistant to the president, and guided by Edward Eyre Hunt, a relief worker and former member of the Economic Trends group, who served as executive secretary. Other participants included Secretary of the Interior Ray L. Wilbur; Shelby Harrison, of the Russell Sage Fund; and the social scientists Wesley Mitchell (chair), Charles Merriam, Howard Odum, and Ogburn, who was named "director of research." The committee had its first meeting in December—appropriately, the month of Ogburn's defense of "scientific sociology" before the A.S.S.[33]

Of twenty-nine principal contributors to the final report, eleven were Ph.D.s in sociology, all of them university professors and predominantly Columbia-trained. Because Ogburn and Odum, apparently, had a relatively free hand in the choice, the group quite reasonably contained men whose work they especially admired. As it happened, all except one also had some connection with the S.S.R.C., then or later, either as committee members or grant recipients. However innocuous this fact, the composition of the Trends panel did little to dispel a growing sense that a "research funds group" was in the making.[34]

The committee stood in a long tradition of similar investigations in American history: from urban surveys by sanitary engineers in the 1830s and 1840s, to the philanthropic studies of the Progressive Era, and the activities of such bodies as the War Industries Board and the more recent National Bureau of Economic Research. Despite, or perhaps because of, this rich and varied tradition, however, a basic question remained unanswered: What was a "social survey," exactly?

To this question, the principals in the Hoover study offered three quite different answers. For Hoover, the model was earlier engineering surveys, in which mechanical and technological factors were seen as the key to social problems. For Shelby Harrison of the Russell Sage Foundation, it was the reform survey, stressing problems such as labor and child welfare. But for the social scientists, it was the definition and measurement of social phenomena, and even a rejection of the "survey" concept to the extent that experts were to make no assumptions concerning conclusions.[35]

Compounding these differences were fundamental questions concerning the nature and role of social science, and of "objectivity." At the policy level, the president and his aides assumed from the start that the "experts" would provide information, but no recommendations. The White House alone would make recommendations and take action. Among the experts, Ogburn and Odum were closest to this view; Mitchell and Merriam found it most difficult to accept. This difference, in fact, influenced their willingness to serve. "Odum and Ogburn were more deeply committed to the absolute objectivity of social research, yet far more willing to move directly to the service of the President as a non-partisan representative of the nation as a whole," the historian Barry Karl has noted. "Mitchell and Merriam . . . respected political involvement as part of social research, yet shied away from making the social science community an instrument of presidential policy-making."[36]

At the start, these awkward questions concerning the committee's relation to the government were avoided or papered over. The question of whether procedures and assumptions developed at the National Board of Economic Research or the S.S.R.C. could be brought directly into government without being compromised was obscured by the committee's simple assertion that data were available. A White House proposal to divide the budget into funds for research, conferences, and publicity (the latter implying some "political" use, and violating foundation procedure in which outside sources normally funded publicity) was side-stepped when a lump sum was requested for the single goal of social research. Although Hoover initially wanted to request funding from the Rockefeller Foundation under his own name, the committee incorporated itself as the President's Research Committee on Social Trends, and requested funds on its own. [37]

Ogburn apparently agreed that Hoover would have an entirely free hand in the use of the report, but the issue of when, and in what form, became a continuing source of disagreement. When, in the search for a woman to add to the committee, the White House proposed the secretary of the American Federation of Labor, the committee chose an M.D. from the Harvard Medical School, a less obviously "political" candidate. When Hoover asked that the chapter on crime include material on immigration, Ogburn replied: "This may be difficult, but I think it can be done"; the contributors in question balked because of the paucity of data, but something was finally included, even though no evidence confirmed the popular view that second-generation immigrants were disproportionately responsible for crime, or even that a "crime wave" existed. An eleventh-hour tiff over a chapter on race relations was narrowly avoided without rewriting, thanks to Odum's diplomacy. [38]

Because the committee had begun its investigation in quite a different political and economic climate from that of the Depression, the 1932 election posed a real challenge. The failure of Ogburn and others to anticipate that politics might arise in an election year was a measure of their naiveté, or, at the least, the strength of their belief in a world-without-politics. During the summer, Ogburn busily multiplied excuses why the report was not ready, while attempting to stay above the swirling storm. [39]

After the election, the issue was whether the committee should officially present their findings to the incoming president. Still devoted to Hoover, and reluctant to see three years' work swept away in a tide of politics, Ogburn retreated again to Olympus. "The data prepared are useful to either conservative or radical, to Republican or Democrat," he wrote to Raymond Moley, requesting that his former Columbia associate help get the material to F.D.R.

Others more realistically believed that for Hoover to present the report to Roosevelt would truly politicize it. In the end, Ogburn lost on this issue, as on others, when Hoover decided not to "present" to his successor the fruits of their effort.[40]

Procedurally, the objectivity issue arose over "fact-gathering" versus something more—typically formulated as "facts" versus "opinion"—and over how "technical" the report should be. The treatment of "facts," moreover, was itself subject to two different interpretations: classification, in the spirit of Baconianism, and in line with most older surveys; or statistical correlations to describe and analyze rates of change, and perhaps to project trends into the future.

Although Ogburn never faced the issue systematically, his training under Giddings, his work in statistics, and the logic of *Social Change* pointed in the latter direction. "Fact-finding," moreover, was getting a bad name. Writing in *Harper's* in February 1932 a journalist lambasted "The Great Fact-Finding Farce" in a piece that Odum brought to Ogburn's attention. Odum tried to make the best of it, but Ogburn took the diatribe almost personally. "I don't believe 'fact-finding' is as popular a word as it was in 1922 or 1923, and I am inclined to avoid the word as much as possible and substitute for it words such as, perhaps, science, evidence, conclusions, or data," he wrote to Wesley Mitchell two weeks later. "For after all we are not just finding facts. We are organizing them, drawing conclusions, and interpreting them in the scientific sense of the word."[41] But what was this "sense"? As the report took shape, it appeared that Ogburn would not or could not say.

The issue of the shape of the final report quickly eclipsed the debate over methodology. Worried about readability, the White House suggested that a Mark Sullivan or Ray Stannard Baker be engaged to lighten the prose, and during 1932 it escalated criticism along these lines. Wesley Mitchell, sympathizing with Ogburn, while at the same time justifying the interpretive character of the graceful introduction he himself had written, wrote Ogburn in May: "My guess is that you will go down in history as the editor of a good national inventory of value to future historians"—cold comfort, given Ogburn's expectations. Nevertheless, Ogburn fought against Mitchell's interpretive summary, as well as against a "political" essay by Merriam. Both were finally included, while in his own foreword, the president split the difference: the committee statement "sets forth matters of opinion as well as strict scientific determination."[42]

Ogburn knew there were two issues at stake, as he had already written to Odum: one was measurement itself, to answer the question "How do you know it?"; the second was presentation of this measurement. In one meeting he felt he had stressed the latter to the exclusion of the former; but having said as much, he retreated to the position that the presentation must be in such a form as to answer the first question. In the heat of debate, there was neither time nor incentive to discuss the finer points of methodology. Ogburn perforce fell back on a simple prescription: "more facts."[43]

At the level of metaphysics and epistemology, a third aspect of the objectivity issue, a crude realism affected everyone's view of the project. Hunt, for example, thought of the study in terms of a photo, while Odum thought "fact-finding" was fine. Ogburn was uneasy with the term, but could not shake the assumptions behind it. After listening to a lecture on "What is Science" in 1930, he had frankly admitted his impatience with the entire issue. "I shall waive all the admirable searchings and doubts," he wrote in one of his few attempts to formulate a philosophy of science, "[and] state simply that science is the discovery of new knowledge." Years later, he retreated to the even simpler formulation that it was a "pile of knowledge."[44]

Political pressures, time constraints, and the paucity of data in many areas all played a part in making *Recent Social Trends* less than a methodological breakthrough, whatever its other merits. Furthermore, the prevailing realism, and the old suspicion of speculation, were factors in Ogburn's case. To be more than counting or even "trend lines," statistics finally demanded extrapolation, an act of imagination that Ogburn feared. His own contributions to *Recent Social Trends*, one on technology and another on the family, were two of the least statistical in the volume. The result, as critics were soon to point out, was that the rhetoric of "scientific" sociology seemed to promise much more than was delivered. For this reason, publication of the report set off a new round in the debate as to what sociology could or should be. Although the experience by no means altered Ogburn's willingness to serve government on committees or agencies,[45] events within the next few years revealed that his service on the Hoover Committee had put the first dent in his faith in a totally objective sociology based on statistical analysis.

The critics went straight to these conceptual and methodological shortcomings. One of the severest critics was Pitirim A. Sorokin, now chairman of Harvard's new sociology department. Sorokin knew Ogburn's work well, and had discussed it extensively in his *Contemporary Sociological Theories* (1928), where he had faulted him only for overemphasizing economic and material determinants. But thereafter Sorokin's relations with Chicago sociologists had gradually soured. In 1930 he confided to Odum his dissatisfaction

with *AJS* reviewing policy, and he was soon an active participant within the
A.S.S. against the dominance of a group he termed "the Chicago Mutual
Back-Padding [sic] Co.," a group that presumably included Ogburn. Despite
alleged attempts by some to eliminate his "pernicious influence" within the
society, Sorokin took comfort in the fact that "nobody can fool many people
for a long time and, if so-called scientific work of any faction is mediocre as is
the case with the 'Co.,' it will be understood so sooner or later."[46]

In his review of *Recent Social Trends* Sorokin accordingly made Ogburn the
villain of the piece. He charged that the "methodology, epistemology, and
'philosophy' " of the project were derived directly from Ogburn's speech to the
A.S.S. in 1929. In biting, often sarcastic prose he damned the work on all
three counts. The use of statistics and quantitative method was excessive, and
even absurd when applied to the arts, religion, and intellectual life. Its epistemology ruled out any view of American life "as a whole," despite its claims to
the contrary. Ogburn's theory of cultural change was merely "a diluted variety
of Marxian philosophy." Talk of "units" of social change was an empty pretense, for there was not and could not be any way to measure and to compare
changes in such diverse areas as mechanics, religion, or art.[47]

Ogburn's conclusion that inventions had and would set the pace in modern
society was based, not on "facts," as claimed, but on sheer speculation because, in Sorokin's view, recent patent statistics showed a decline such as had
occurred several times in history. In reality, the committee's "facts" were
commonplace. Who doubted that divorce and energy consumption were increasing, or that the birth rate and rural population were decreasing? Little
wonder that the public preferred the work of Spengler, the technocrats, or even
"the flat philistinism of H. G. Wells."[48]

Seconding Sorokin's point, the historian Charles Beard charged that, despite the value of its "details," *Recent Social Trends* reflected "the coming
crisis in the empirical method to which American social science has long been
in bondage"—namely, the illusion that "data" in sufficient amount would yield
their own conclusions. The committee's "Review of Findings" was not confined to the "facts," but was actually "an interesting, suggestive, and valuable
declaration of opinion by a competent and intelligent group of American
citizens. It expresses hopes, aspirations, and values as well as facts." But
where did these values come from? In his presidential address to the American
Historical Association in 1934—entitled "History as an Act of Faith"—Beard
argued that the definition of "fact" was a highly subjective affair.[49]

Ogburn replied to the several points in turn. First, *Recent Social Trends* was
not predominantly quantitative; ironically, however, he attempted to prove this

point by measuring the space given to charts and statistics, and by counting the critics who had reviewed certain chapters ("Be respectful," Sorokin rejoined, "60 artists read the manuscript!"). Second, a genuine "synthesis" demanded "correlations" which were impossible to obtain given the current state of statistical science. Sorokin's insistence that velocities of change should be calculated precisely was a curious turnabout given his distaste for quantification—"one might say a 'complex' judging by his rush of words and the nature of his colorful and exaggerated adjectives." Finally, the charge that the "facts" contained so little that was new rested on a misunderstanding of the immense effort required to obtain the smallest advance in knowledge.[50]

But Ogburn evaded (if he understood it) the essence of the Sorokin-Beard attack on the limits of empiricism. Were the discoveries of science to be in the nature of "correlations" based on a probabilistic conception of natural law, and on nominalist assumptions about the nature of reality? Were they to be "classifications" based on the naive Baconian premise that reality is accessible to the careful observer? Could "facts," however defined, be politically neutral?

These questions notwithstanding, Ogburn claimed to be pleased by the reception of his work. "I think the almost universal acceptance of the social trends study was a tribute to a measure of success in making it reliable," he wrote fifteen years later to Odum. "The idea was that as a multiplication table should be reliable both for the Tory and the Communist, so the conclusions of social trends should be valid alike for the radical and the conservative."[51] Whether he would push for "scientific" sociology in quite the old way, however, or continue to celebrate "statistics" with quite the same ardor, remained to be seen.

13

REHEARSAL FOR REBELLION

I think [my Methods] *will prove demolishing to extreme
"objectivism" and "quantitativism" in sociology and will
serve to reestablish sociology upon the sane basis of
Lester F. Ward.*

Charles Ellwood to E. A. Ross, 1932

*As you know, my primary object has been to make the
Society a strictly scientific organization.*

Maurice Parmelee to Luther Bernard, 1932

1

For sociology, a still-fragile discipline, the decade of the 1930s was a time of trial. Economically, the Depression meant salary cuts and a shrinking job market.[1] Money put an edge on discussions of the A.S.S. and its annual programs; Bernard himself noted that having an official function was essential in getting one's expenses paid.[2] With the alphabet agencies offering new opportunities for prestige and influence, the public role of sociology became a hotly debated issue.[3] Academic freedom cases multiplied, two of the messiest involving sociologists. The American Sociological Society meanwhile underwent its own version of hard times: first in declining membership,[4] and then in a threat that regional societies and special groups would destroy the organization entirely.[5]

The training of graduate students also caused tension among the leading graduate centers. Starting in March 1932, the *AJS* ran a "personnel exchange"—juxtaposed with ever-lengthening lists of "student dissertations." Noting the unintended irony, Chapin in January 1934 warned colleagues of an impending crisis. While few qualified sociologists were retiring and many were unemployed, some 258 doctoral candidates were in the pipeline; by

Chapin's calculation, however, there were at most 130 bona fide positions in sociology in all American universities combined. Chicago, with fifty-one candidates, and Columbia, with forty-nine, were especially responsible for the glut. Sensitive to the attack on his institution, Ellsworth Faris of Chicago responded with his own analysis of the facts and figures, and a high-minded lecture on alternative sources of employment.[6]

During the decade, these problems served as backdrop to a series of battles within the American Sociological Society. Often technical, sometimes tedious, the battles ostensibly concerned the structure and role of the society. Should its constitution be revised to make the society more "democratic," more "scientific," or both? Should the long-standing tie with the *AJS* be dissolved? Should a permanent, paid position of executive secretary be established? But behind these questions lay more important ones concerning the nature and control of the discipline. Was "research" to supplant "theory," and, if so, what sort of research? Should any group, whether at Chicago or elsewhere, dominate or even define the field? What responsibility had sociology to American society during the Depression years?

The struggle over these issues developed in several stages. At the December meetings in 1930 the executive committee, acting on a proposal from the S.S.R.C., created a "Special Committee on the Scope of Research," chaired eventually by Stuart Rice of Penn—which immediately raised suspicion that a "Rice-Ogburn group" (as it came to be called) sought control of the society. During 1931 opposition to the committee took shape under the leadership first of Charles Ellwood, and then of Maurice Parmelee. As president in 1932, Bernard first moved to clip the wings of the Rice Committee, and then appointed an entirely new Committee on the Constitution whose recommendations were accepted at the 1933 annual meeting.

By this time, demands for a new publication to replace the *AJS* as the official organ of the society had gained momentum with the appointment of a Publications Committee, the final result being the appearance of the *American Sociological Review* in January 1936. The establishment in the spring of 1936 of the Sociological Research Association, an attempt to create an elite group within the discipline and to achieve the goals of the earlier Rice Report, kept the dispute simmering for the remainder of the decade.

The causes of this A.S.S. rebellion have been the subject of considerable debate. To the sociologist Robert Faris, the central issue was social activism: the Chicago sociological establishment feared that the rebels planned to abandon the discipline's hard-won focus on "research." The Minnesota sociologist Don Martindale recalled that the battle pitted "scientific positivism and grass-roots empiricism" (as represented by Chapin, among others) against the humanistic emphasis of earlier Chicago sociology. A recent observer has argued, in contrast, that institutional loyalties, rather than theoretical orientation or politics, shaped the struggle. Still another has concluded that a generalized antielitism fused private grievances, career-related anxieties, the shock of the Depression, and dissatisfaction with structure of the profession into an "organizational ideology" that facilitated the reorientation of theory without marking the triumph of one or another theory group.[7]

Although a multicausal approach best captures the complexity of the situation, it leaves unexplored the role of "scientific positivism and grass-roots empiricism" in these battles. The struggles within the A.S.S. not only pitted positivists against humanists, and value-free professionals against social activists, but brought into the open the split between the two versions of objectivism, represented by Ogburn and Chapin on the one hand and by Bernard on the other. Neither side won, in the sense of converting a significant proportion of the discipline to their version of positivism, but the former were relatively more influential in the long run. The elitist S.R.A. folded by the early 1940s, by which time Ogburn himself had lost his early enthusiasm for statistics. Bernard, after a series of humiliations (as he saw them), resigned bitterly from the A.S.S in 1938 and subsequently waged a private war against virtually the entire profession.

In this sequence of events, Ellwood's protest deserves initial attention despite his final lack of influence. Speaking self-consciously for the "fathers," he hoped for nothing less than a return to the tradition of Ward and the prewar founders. His inspiration and much of his support came from individuals such as Sorokin, MacIver, and Blumer, who represented an antipositivist tradition that would soon find a far more authoritative and influential voice in Talcott Parsons's *Structure of Social Action* (1937). Had they succeeded in uniting behind Ellwood, antipositivism might have become an organized presence within American sociology considerably earlier than it did. As it was, given an opposition led by Parmelee, and later by Bernard, the battles of the thirties largely pitted one style of "scientific" sociology against another.

2

The Rice Committee originated innocuously enough in a motion before the executive committee at the Cleveland meeting of December 1930. William F. Ogburn, so the minutes of the meeting state, "presented the invitation from the

Social Science Research Council that the American Sociological Society un-
dertake the preparation of a plan for the promotion of sociological research."
Moved by Stuart Chapin, the proposal resulted in the creation of a seven-
person committee, chaired initially by Howard Odum, and eventually by
Stuart Rice. The Committee was charged to spend no more than was allocated
to it by the S.S.R.C.[8]

Although no evidence supports the later rumors of a plot, the funding and
composition of the committee fueled fears that a coup was in the making. The
generous grants of the S.S.R.C. and the Spelman Fund to the universities of
Chicago and North Carolina were matters of record, as were the close ties of
Ogburn, Chapin, and Odum to the foundations. The committee's membership
was weighted heavily toward quantification and a rather narrow definition of
"research."[9] A set of questions that the committee posed before an invited
audience at the 1931 meetings did little to calm fears: should the society
maintain a "research clearing house"? should a trimmed-down board of directors manage the day-to-day affairs of the A.S.S? should membership qualifications be tightened? should an Honor Society be created? Although presented
only for debate, these and other questions pointed toward more centralized
control, restricted access, and more honorifics for the elite that survived the
winnowing process.[10]

Charles Ellwood, now a professor at Duke, launched the opposition. Con-
demning "emasculated sociologies," he warned that sociology was "again in
danger of becoming a dead science." When he had first leveled this charge a
decade before, his list of offenders had included Sumner, Durkheim, and some
lesser European theorists. The list now embraced Ogburn (especially in view
of his 1929 presidential address before the A.S.S.); Howard Becker of Smith
College, a proponent of the "value-free" approach of Leopold von Wiese; and
the contributors to Bernard's *Trends in American Sociology* (1929). A particular villain was the Social Science Research Council, whose motto, Ellwood
alleged, was "Millions for concrete research, but not one cent for philosophy."[11]

At first glance, Ellwood's vehemence is somewhat puzzling. Trained as a
social psychologist in the Dewey tradition, with a bias against Albion Small's
"social realism," he underwent something of a conversion to a more "realistic"
and "scientific" sociology during a year studying with R. R. Marrett of Oxford
and Leonard Hobhouse of the University of London on the eve of the war.[12]
"All modern science is essentially inductive in spirit," he wrote in *Social
Forces* in 1924, "that is, it proceeds from the facts to the theory rather than

from the theory to the facts." He insisted only that scientific method be defined so as to include the methods of anthropology and history.[13]

Why, then, at an age when many scholars fall back on their laurels, did Ellwood decide to take on the objectivists with such vigor? One factor was a genuine and life-long religious commitment, expressed in such works as *The Reconstruction of Religion* (1922), and *Man's Destiny in the Light of Science* (1929). A second factor was a sense that he was now one of the few surviving "founders." A chief victim of "the behaviorists, the statisticians, and the experimentalists," he wrote to a colleague, was Lester Ward.[14] A third, and more immediate, was his sense that the antiobjectivist opposition was growing and now included Sorokin of Harvard, MacIver of Columbia, and young Herbert Blumer at Chicago.[15]

By the late twenties, Ellwood also had reason to suspect the hopelessness of political causes to which he had devoted his career. Since the war he had fought, and lost, battles against military conscription, immigration restriction, and the racism that was endemic in his adopted state of Missouri. "After the lynching here last spring," he wrote Ross in 1923, "I do not find myself very happy in this environment."[16] The popular reaction even hit his pocketbook when the antievolution crusade cut into the sales of his textbook *Sociology and Modern Social Problems*.[17] Three months in Mussolini's Italy in 1927–28 brought these concerns to a head. "They caused me to revise my estimate of human social evolution," he wrote; "I now see that the Democratic Movement is not certain of victory in our culture, unless strong efforts are made in the direction of political and social education."[18]

An additional factor in Ellwood's crusade was the perennial one of professional power and prestige. Since his earliest days at Missouri, scientism in one form or another had clouded his reputation and blighted his prospects for advancement. Other faculty members ridiculed what they saw as his "hypocritical religious professions"—or so Bernard later reported. Bernard, in fact, was a special nemesis. When Ellwood went abroad in 1914–15, he asked the president to appoint Bernard chairman in his absence, only to find on his return that the administration wished to make the appointment permanent. Ellwood was later returned to the position, but he was forced for a year to work under his junior colleague.[19]

Although Bernard left Missouri a year later, the slights and indignities, as Ellwood saw them, did not abate. In 1917 he was deeply disappointed not to be elected president of the A.S.S. (he was eventually chosen six years later). At issue was his reported intolerance, and a fear that he might use the office to punish enemies as well as to reward friends. When asked for his opinion on the

Ellwood candidacy, Bernard equivocated, in part because he privately suspected that Ellwood had attempted to discredit him with Small so as to remove any suspicion that Ellwood was responsible for Bernard's leaving Missouri. When Bernard told Ellwood of this discussion, the older man was remarkably contrite, and, again as Bernard told it, ate a portion of humble pie that could not have been easy to digest.[20]

During the 1920s Ellwood continued an on-again, off-again relation with Bernard, in part because he wanted very much to leave Missouri and felt that his former student was in a position to help him, first for the chairmanship at Minnesota, and then for a post at Cornell. If Bernard would help him get a position in the East, he wrote at one point, he would see to it that his former student succeeded him at Missouri.[21] Because Ellwood was only one of many names mentioned for the Minnesota job, which finally went to Sorokin, he could not reasonably blame either Bernard or the rising tide of behaviorism for the outcome. However, the fact was that (unknown to Ellwood) Chapin dismissed him, with most of the prewar generation, as a purveyor of "opinions about opinions." Small, for his part, did not seriously push Ellwood for the Minnesota post because he knew how Bernard felt about his former teacher.[22] In the case of Cornell, Ellwood explicitly asked help from Bernard, who was there on a temporary appointment during 1925–26. Bernard later claimed that he had no more influence with department chairman Walter F. Willcox than had Ellwood, which in this instance was probably correct—whether or not Ellwood thought otherwise.[23]

The appearance of Henshaw Ward's *Thobbing* (1926), a humorous send-up of sentimentalism in religion, education, and the social sciences, pushed Ellwood to the brink of open war with the objectivists. A Yale graduate (M.A. 1899), an associate of A. G. Keller, and an avowed partisan of Sumnerology, Ward was a satirist of wit and penetration. "When a person thinks without curiosity, has an opinion because he likes it, believes what is handy—then he thobs," he explained. The term derived from the initial letters of thought, opinion, and belief. As example, he cited Ellwood's sociology, which he pronounced "bunk." Not amused, Ellwood worried that most readers would take it as "simply a humorous book," not realizing that Ward's aim was to popularize "behaviorism" and the Sumner-Keller brand of sociology.[24]

The incident over Ogburn's election as president of the A.S.S. for 1929[25]— in the course of which Bernard won a reputation as the leader of the move to oust Ellwood's candidate, Emory Bogardus—brought an open break between Ellwood and Bernard in letters that are among the most bitter in the annals of the discipline. "The whole procedure of the younger crowd was stupid," Ellwood wrote in February 1929, "and if anyone was guilty of any wrongdoing at our annual meeting they alone were." Pronouncing their relation over, he demanded that Bernard return an autobiographical sketch and departmental history he had prepared for a history of sociology that Bernard was planning. Although Bernard believed that Ellwood himself had been "the chief plotter" at Chicago, he attempted to smooth his feathers, but with little success. "I do not think that you could be fair to me if you tried," Ellwood shot back.[26]

Ellwood's appointment at Duke in 1929 offered some consolation, but it did not mean the end of incidents that the increasingly sensitive Ellwood saw as evidence that his status within the profession was at peril. One such incident occurred sometime in 1930 when Ellsworth Faris, in the hearing of one of Ellwood's students, distinguished "ethical" from "scientific" sociologists, adding that the former were not really sociologists at all.[27] When the new *Encyclopedia of the Social Sciences* appeared, Ellwood was further distressed to see how little space was given to his work, and he wrote the editor, Alvin Johnson, to complain. In *Systematic Sociology* (1932), young Howard Becker seemed equally ready to exclude Ellwood from the profession. "Naturally, I object to being read out of scientific ranks," Ellwood wrote Becker, recalling that Faris's earlier comment had drawn him into "this war." To Hornell Hart, whom he hoped to attract to Duke, he put the matter more plaintively: "I am not trying to fight the pure scientists in sociology. I simply want them to stop fighting me."[28]

The Duke appointment, although not a cause of Ellwood's crusade, nonetheless probably helped to determine its timing. The offer allowed the escape from Missouri that he had long sought. After the Cornell job failed to come through, an apparently certain call to teach Christian Ethics at Yale had collapsed, allegedly because of a monumental gaffe on Ellwood's part: rumor had it that Dean Weigle of Yale went personally to Columbia to offer the position, to be greeted at Ellwood's door with the remark, "Mohammed has finally come to the mountain." No offer followed.[29]

Duke fortunately provided an even better setting for Ellwood's brand of sociology. A southern Yale that had not yet outgrown the religious commitments of its founders, the university was soon known (and sometimes criticized) as a bastion of Christian orthodoxy. When faced with this charge—as by Hornell Hart, who was reluctant to teach there for this reason—Ellwood denied that anyone was subject to "denominational or sectarian constraints." But he freely admitted that "we should not hire anyone here who is not an avowed Christian, in the sense of accepting the ideals of Jesus."[30]

The fact that Sorokin was called to Harvard, and MacIver to Columbia, at roughly the same time, may further have convinced Ellwood that the behaviorist tide was turning. Sorokin, whose relationship with Ogburn was then souring, wrote Ellwood after the 1929 meeting (where Ogburn had delivered his blistering defense of scientific sociology) that he would be "very glad if our contact would be closer" because he too was organizing a new department. He proposed the creation of an eastern regional association, quite separate from the A.S.S., "which besides its own tasks can correct also the policies of the Chicago group." After receiving an offprint of one of Ellwood's attacks on objectivism, Sorokin replied that he "fully agreed" with the argument.[31] MacIver, in response to one of Ellwood's papers in *Social Forces*, wrote that he was in "hearty sympathy . . . with your protest against the narrowing and, in fact, crippling view of scientific method which prevails with certain of our colleagues."[32]

Ellwood struck a sympathetic note among sociologists who felt themselves or their fields to be threatened by the increasing popularity of scientism. Ernest R. Groves, a rural sociologist at nearby Chapel Hill, applauded Ellwood's battle against the "extrovertive tyranny" that attempted to turn people into "mere mathematical units." Arthur J. Todd, whom Chapin had replaced at Minnesota a decade earlier under less than happy circumstances, and whom Ellwood had already defended against charges that he was not adequately "scientific," thanked him for exposing the "danger of tying ourselves up in statistics, behaviorism, or mere counting and numbering and measuring." Jerome Dowd, who had studied briefly under Small in 1906–7 before accepting a lifelong appointment at the University of Oklahoma, regretted the "unfortunate drift of sociology from . . . social values."[33]

The targets of Ellwood's attacks were naturally less receptive. Probably the testiest was Stuart Rice, who demanded to know, if "philosophy" and "thinking" were properly "research," how organizations such as the S.S.R.C. could assess proposals for funding.[34] Robert Treat Crane, the executive director of the S.S.R.C., was more conciliatory, confiding to Ellwood that he too believed that "simple fact gathering" had contributed little to progress in the natural sciences. ("On the other hand," he added, "I see no reason to despair at this stage of discovering actual uniformities in human behavior.") Ogburn was diplomacy itself: their differences were largely "a matter of emphasis," he wrote, speculating that they both had been "euchred into positions of having attitudes attributed to us which were not ours."[35]

3

Ellwood had hoped to revive the tradition of the founders, but his campaign produced no coherent theory group, Wardian or otherwise. For this failure there were several reasons. One was the fact that Ellwood himself, for all his references to Tyndall or Gestalt psychology, added little to current debates over scientific method. Behaviorists ignored the fact that human personality was a "functional whole" within a "total situation," he charged, citing Blumer's "Science without Concepts." Scientific method must perforce be "synthetic." Against narrow inductionism, he defended hypothesis; and against positivism, the role of "imagination," a position he traced to Tyndall's "Belfast Address." To this he added only a plea that practitioners remain tolerant in the face of competing methodologies.[36]

Nor did the antipositivists who supported Ellwood add much in their turn. Sorokin had raised a powerful voice against scientism in his *Contemporary Sociological Theories* (1928), but his monumental *Social and Cultural Dynamics* (1937–40) lay in the future. Robert MacIver had published several books—including *Society: Its Structures and Changes* (1931), which contained some early American references to Max Weber—but his reputation as an outsider lingered, despite his appointment at Columbia.[37] Howard Becker, who also early appreciated Weber, published an American version of Leopold von Wiese's *Systematic Sociology* in 1932, but would earn his reputation only gradually through the decade. Blumer's mature theory of symbolic interaction was not yet developed.

Another important factor was that Ellwood's allies had quite different reasons for offering comfort. Regional loyalties, particularly East versus Midwest, cut across ideological and philosophical lines. Potential allies sneered at his brand of reform almost as often as did his leading opponents. The case of Pitirim Sorokin (1889–1968) is illuminating in this regard. A revolutionary in the Czarist days, and Kerensky's secretary in the first post-Czarist government, the Russian émigré was ostensibly a liberal, for which reason he earned the support of E. A. Ross on his rapid rise from Minnesota (1923) to chairman of the new department at Harvard. As with other anti-Bolshevik émigrés, however, the ascent of Stalinism drove him steadily to the right. In the same letter in which he had written Ellwood concerning their mutual interests in 1930, he had warned him that one job candidate's major weakness was a "reform complex."[38] From the start he distrusted the New Deal faith in "officials, bureaucrats, and scholar governors," as he told Ross in 1933. Although he thought Communism and Fascism were alike in being the "grave worms" in the decaying corpse of Western culture, he wrote Read Bain in 1935 that, between the two, he would "vote for Mussolini and even Hitler as against Stalin."[39] Sorokin supported Ellwood for several reasons: his growing differences with Ogburn; his distrust of Chicago; and his interest in a new regional association and/or a new journal. But for Ellwood's brand of prewar reformism he had little use. By the time Bernard and his allies assumed control of the rebellion, Sorokin, not surprisingly, was on the other side.

Finally, Ellwood's scatter-shot attack on "behaviorism," by placing Bernard among the enemy, deprived him of an ally who at least shared his view that sociology should be more politically active. Conflating "behaviorism" and "analytical investigation," Ellwood implied that the former had no interest in either intellectual synthesis or the fundamental reordering of society. Bernard was willing to concede the charge for quantifiers such as Ogburn, but he was unwilling to do so for himself. In a churlish review of Ellwood's *Methods of Sociology*, he charged that Ellwood's typical behaviorist was a straw man composed in equal part of Pavlov, Watson, and "a man named Zeliony (some believe his name was Seliony)." The review, needless to say, did little to patch up their relationship.[40]

While advancing age, and his wife's serious illness, kept Ellwood's role in later battles to a minimum, Bernard continued to cultivate the older man's support, whether for a new journal, a favored presidential candidate, or an A.S.S. free of Chicago control. Ellwood was sometimes sympathetic, but he increasingly viewed the squabbles and intrigue with despair. When in 1935 Stuart Chapin was elected president of the A.S.S. over Henry Pratt Fairchild, the choice of the nominating committee upon which Ellwood had served, he vowed never to accept the assignment again. Reports of Chicago chicanery (provided by Bernard or his allies) were equally distressing. "There is no chance that I will cooperate with any university that uses methods of this sort to control a scientific organization," he assured Bernard after one such report. But he also hinted that his trust of his former student was less than perfect. "[There] is always danger when we wrest control from one faction that it will fall into the control of another faction," he continued in the same letter. "I feel very strongly that we should try to free the American Sociological Society *from all factional control.*"[41]

Ellwood continued to celebrate the tradition of the fathers in less dramatic ways for the remainder of the decade. At the annual meeting of the A.S.S. in 1936 he joined others in an old-timers' dinner in honor of E. A. Ross—and, by extension, of the entire prewar generation. In *The Story of Social Philosophy* (1938) he presented the soon-to-be-conventional "liberal" account of Ward's role in American sociology. After protracted correspondence with a young Ward disciple named Samuel Chugerman, he helped arrange for Duke University Press to publish *Lester Frank Ward: The American Aristotle* (1939).[42]

4

While Ellwood campaigned for a return to basics, protest specifically against the Rice-Ogburn proposals took shape within the A.S.S., initially under the leadership of Maurice Parmelee (1882–1969), a sometime sociologist and government economist.[43] During the summer and fall of 1931, Parmelee circulated his counterproposals to key members for consideration at the December meetings. Unlike Ellwood, he wanted sociology to be more "scientific," but at the same time more "liberal." His proposals accordingly ranged from the exclusion from the A.S.S. of "religious, civic, and reform groups," to the democratization of nomination and election procedures.[44] Even more than was the case with Ellwood, Parmelee's allies and favorite sociologists formed a widely disparate group: from Sorokin and MacIver (whom he touted as future presidents of the society), to an assortment of old-timers, and to such prominent academic radicals as Harry Elmer Barnes, Scott Nearing, and Jerome Davis.[45]

Although Bernard was at odds with Ellwood, an alliance with Parmelee seemed natural. The two had taught briefly together at Missouri; both opposed instinct theory; both were hostile toward organized religion and ultimately defended behaviorism; and both found Ellwood ridiculous ("As a sociologist as well as a man," Parmelee later wrote Bernard, "he is almost beneath contempt").[46]

But Bernard finally could not accept Parmelee's attempt to divorce science from social concern. Parmelee had his "strong points," but was not interested "in improving the present order," he had written Ellwood in 1913, when all three were together at Missouri. In 1931, he wrote to Bain that he "did not think very much of Parmelee's pronouncement" because he thought that sociology had to "say much more in addition to reporting the actual movements of the day." The situation was not helped when Parmelee later made some caustic comments on Bernard's *Scope and Methods of Sociology*, the substance of which was that many of the papers were not sufficiently "scientific."[47]

Other members of the A.S.S. shared Bernard's objections to the Parmelee proposals, including some who would later support Bernard in his own attempt to reform the organization. Ross flatly rejected the idea of limiting membership ("Shall we withdraw to a monastery?" he scrawled across the top of a letter to Parmelee), and he thought the cost of supporting the *AJS* an unnecessary expense. Susan Kingsbury, a professor at Bryn Mawr and a disciple of Bernard and Chapin (among others), was reportedly "indignant." Floyd House of Virginia later remembered the Parmelee revolt mostly for its opposition to "meliorism." To yet another observer, the differences between Parmelee and his opponents blurred into a single "Parmelee-Rice" movement.[48] Rural sociologists, perennially sensitive, felt that Parmelee's call for science and centralization threatened their status in the profession.[49]

At the annual meetings in December 1931, the A.S.S. considered proposals from the Special Committee on the Scope of Research (the "Rice Committee") and the unofficial Parmelee committee. Of these only two were enacted, both from the Parmelee group: committees were established to look into the matter of nominations, and to consider the publications issue. Other Parmelee proposals were put off, including a resolution to divide members into voting and nonvoting, and another to take control of the program away from the sections. The membership passed a recommendation from a committee chaired by Ellsworth Faris that the Rural Sociology section be given a permanent position on the executive committee, a concession that in spirit went against both the Parmelee and Rice-Ogburn proposals.

Equally important for the future, the 1931 meeting elected Luther Bernard president for the following year. Bernard thus acquired the task of carrying forward the agitation already under way. Although he was convinced that those behind the Rice Committee "eventually aimed at the control of the Society through a small executive Research council," the protests of Ellwood and Parmelee had presented unacceptable alternatives: the one, mush-headed and mystical, despite its claims to be "scientific"; the other, undemocratic and elitist, despite a pretense of "liberalism." Whether he would succeed where they had faltered, remained to be seen.[50]

14

DEMOCRACY

*I saved [the American Sociological Society] from piracy in
1932, and I have saved the correspondence.*

Luther Bernard to Read Bain, 1940

1

A victory for a new generation, Bernard's election was apparently not even
close. His most formidable opponents were James E. Hagerty of Ohio State,
and Frank Hankins of Smith. Read Bain of Miami reported that he and others
from Ohio had deserted Hagerty for Bernard. George Lundberg wondered if
Hagerty got "*any* votes" and denounced those who had the cheek to put him
forward. "The younger crowd seems not to have been entirely fooled even after
a couple of years of incubation by the Fathers," Lundberg continued, predicting that in "five or ten years they should control."[1]

Bernard knew that the 1931 Washington meetings had healed few wounds.
Bain reported that they were "sitting on a mine" that threatened to tear the
A.S.S. "into four or five regional bodies and two or three or four 'Schools'
who will be continually at each other's throats—the statistics group, the
MacIver-like mystics, the case-study-attitude-boys, the reformatarians–community 'organizer,' social work–'applied' sociology fellows." Sociology's
still-marginal status made the situation worse. "A disruptive fight at this time
would be a sweet morsel to the other disciplines that are just beginning to give
sociology some consideration as a science," he cautioned.[2]

The Rice Committee remained the problem. In one of many postmortems on
the convention, one Bernard ally confided that the "Chicago group," in push-
ing their proposals, "acted as if they were handling a car of dynamite." Manuel
Elmer of Pittsburgh observed that there was "a rumbling everywhere, especially from the *large number* of 'inarticulate' members of the group that the
society was being dominated too much by the relatively small group interested
primarily in research." Floyd House of Virginia agreed that the growing
emphasis on research was "excessive." So also did Frank Hankins, who,

despite his many differences with Bernard, saw eye-to-eye on this issue: "I am not sure that fruitful research can be promoted like the sales of tooth-paste; in fact, I seriously doubt it and think the general failure of the Soc. Sc. Res. Council to provide anything of note is strongly indicative."[3]

2

As president, Bernard was determined to make the society more "democratic," while at the same time not abandoning his goal of a more "scientific" discipline. He therefore proposed a number of sweeping changes, from open committee meetings to a new constitution and unrestricted membership (contra the elitist restrictions of the Parmelee plan). He attempted to increase the number of women on committees and on the program, although with mixed success.[4] In one of his first acts as president, he moved to enlarge the Rice Committee and to redefine its scope so as to include the "teaching" and "public functions" of the society.[5]

By "democratic" Bernard also meant that the A.S.S. should provide more guidance to society in a time of crisis. As he later outlined his plan, it included (a) the establishment of a broad-based Social Science Commission to report to the president, Congress, and other authorities; (b) a reorientation within the discipline toward economic relations (as with Hobson, Tawney, and G. D. H. Cole in Great Britain), collective psychology, and social control; and (c) a restructuring of training for social workers to emphasize reform, rather than amelioration. He also made it clear that he had in mind something other than the current service of some sociologists to various New Deal agencies. The Social Science Commission, he warned, "should not . . . be picked either by politicians or by 'trusted' representatives of the social science groups [Ogburn and Odum?]."[6]

Although Bernard's commitment to democracy was nothing new, his interpretation of the term wavered between calls for fuller representation for all factions and his own brand of elitism. As a young instructor in the prewar years he had complained to Ross that the A.S.S. appeared to exist "primarily, if not wholly for the benefit of a score or so of gentlemen who hold good positions."[7] But even then his definition of "democracy" was colored by a preference for "efficiency" in public policy, and by the distrust of the two major parties that he had developed in the Bull Moose years. During the 1930s, Bernard's politics remained almost as difficult to decipher as they had been for Small to understand two decades earlier. In 1932, he urged former Progressives Gifford Pinchot and Harold Ickes to run on a third-party platform of "constitutionalism, agrarian defense, and the welfare of the workers and the unemployed."[8] In one scathing attack on F.D.R. and the New Deal (apparently unpublished) he charged that the New Deal's chief beneficiaries were "speculative business," "speculative overcapitalized railroads," "credit speculators and professional stock waterers." Its leader was "the face debonair and the ingratiating radio voice," the "hero of the Hudson," and "ninety percent Eleanor and ten percent mush."[9] Then and later, however, the politics of his own utopia of perfect adjustment remained regrettably vague.

Like many proponents of efficiency, Bernard could on occasion also show resentment toward the less fortunate. "The fact is," he wrote in reply to an appeal for funds, "that I have been giving too much of my income to practically useless purposes, such as keeping alive people who should be dead and perpetuating the influence of people so demoralized by their environment that it would be better if the cancer were cut out entirely and thus make it possible to purify the social environment." Half apologetically he added: "I mean, I have been making too large contributions to traditional charity."[10]

The fact that Bernard's program was not quite what many meant by reform complicated his relations with some potential allies. Among these was the social worker Susan Kingsbury of Bryn Mawr, who in the spring of 1932 sent Bernard a clipping from The New York Times praising the contributions of sociologists in the current crisis. Bernard replied that he had no intention of offering "any temporary aid to a rather discredited political organization." Far better to "orient ourselves with regard to our problems of research," he concluded, than to attempt to persuade "a group of men who are dominated by a viewpoint that is almost wholly unsociological."[11]

One of Bernard's most controversial proposals for a new Constitution for the A.S.S. suggested that "democracy" could also serve self-interest—namely, the idea that ex-presidents should be permanent members of the executive committee. The proposal undercut the representation argument in that ex-presidents, as some younger members feared, could hold back progress within the discipline. Also, as eventually happened, a ruling clique could in effect negate annual elections to the executive committee simply by controlling the presidency over a number of years. Although Bernard finally pushed this proposal through, it was the most fiercely debated of the constitutional changes, and the first to be rescinded.[12]

Just as Bernard defined "democracy" in his own way, so also his conception of research was unclear. During and after his presidency, he was in fact increasingly at odds with the research faction within the A.S.S. Two incidents, in particular, fed his resentment on this score. The first was Howard Odum's rejection of his planned contribution to *Recent Social Trends* on sociological method, a rejection that compounded the damage done several years earlier by Odum's remarks concerning "research." In his presidential address in December, Bernard cited the Odum exchange (without names) in the course of a vituperative, and often sarcastic attack on the pretensions of the research mandarins.[13]

A second incident involved Bernard's own attempt at quantitative research in the form of a questionnaire on nationality traits that he distributed to the membership midway through his presidency. By any standard, the questionnaire was appallingly crude: on one axis were listed twenty "Races and Peoples," ranging from Native Americans (by whom he meant WASPS) to Bohemians; on the other, twenty-seven "Imputed Attitudes," including such traits as "dirty," "grasping," "tricky," "crude," and their opposites. Respondents were asked spontaneous reactions, with the results to be tabulated by occupation, sex, birthplace, and the like.[14]

A few loyalists duly complied, and even distributed the form to their students, but the majority mounted a firestorm of protest. The anthropologist Melville Herskovits noted that all traits could be found among all peoples, and refused to participate. Robert Lynd, now at Columbia, declared himself "unable to think of whole peoples in these terms." Keller of Yale grumbled that all such questionnaires were attempts to get others to do one's work. "Moreover, I see little use in collecting 'opinions' that are mostly prejudices," he added. Bernard replied that crude prejudice was precisely what he wanted to measure. But given his thin skin, the episode must have been acutely embarrassing. In any case, with so many respondents refusing to participate, he dropped the project.[15]

At the 1932 meetings Bernard gave the quantifiers a minor role. He limited statistics to a single session, and counseled Chapin not to make his paper too technical. Not a single Chicagoan chaired a session, while the Parmelee-Bernard group dominated the program.[16]

3

Bernard's allies fell roughly into three groups: rank-and-file supporters, numbering about thirty, who offered intermittent advice and support; half a dozen "fellow travellers," including Read Bain and Howard Becker, who gave substantial support early on, but drew back after their objectives had been realized; and Bernard's chief lieutenants, Jerome Davis of Yale, who chaired the committee for a new constitution (1932–33), Newell Sims of Oberlin, who directed the first stage of the battle over publications (1933–34), and William Meroney of Baylor, who spearheaded the final drive for the *American Sociological Review* (1935–36).[17]

Although generalizations are difficult, given the shifting and informal nature of the dissident group, the five individuals mentioned above may be said to represent the mosaic of rebel concerns as a whole: Bain and Becker, the desire to create a sociology at once humanistic, socially concerned, and value-free; Davis and Sims, a less complicated "radicalism" combined with a fear that rigorous definitions of research would put theorists out of business; and Meroney, the resentments of the many who taught at "second"- or "third"-rank institutions, and felt permanently excluded from the society's "inner circle."

A former student of Bernard, Read Bain (1892–1980) was among his earliest and most enthusiastic supporters. Like Bernard, he was a self-avowed "positivist" who had definite if sometimes ambiguous ideas concerning "science" and "democracy." Like Bernard also, he was an avid academic politician, who supported the rebellion wholeheartedly until it became clear that it had run its course.

Bain was born in Woods, Oregon, and grew up in what he later described as "a backwoods region where children never wore shoes." His youth was the stuff of which behaviorists are made. "Never went to school until age 12; never saw a train till 14. Have never seen a circus yet," he wrote matter-of-factly of himself at age thirty-five. "Divorce at age 12. I went with my mother and her paramour—whom I liked much better than I did my own father. I finally came to hate him—still do—but never did care much for my father." Following the death of his mother in 1911, and a "psychological" adoption by another woman whom he later considered a mother, Bain was "converted" to Methodism, but had "completely backslidden" by the time he graduated from Willamette University (Methodist) in Salem, Oregon, in 1916.[18]

Self-aware, and refreshingly self-analytical, Bain knew that these experiences were a crucial influence on his later sociology. "I am slightly cynical, perhaps," he wrote Bernard in 1927; "possibly my interest in 'finding out the facts' and my lack of interest in 'doing something about it,' is a reflection of this scepticism or semi-cynicism." His first interest was in the law, but he then turned to sociology, which he hoped to make a "real science."[19] After teaching school, and serving as a flight instructor during the war, he resumed his graduate education under some of the nation's leading sociologists.[20] By the late 1920s he considered himself "strictly behavioristic," with little sympathy for "any subjectivistic type of sociology."[21]

Bain's career, however, did not fulfill its early promise. After publishing *The Socialized State* (1921), a 200-page study suppressed by Oregon authorities for its alleged radicalism, he edited and contributed to numerous books but never again published one of his own. Although his publications included almost two hundred articles, some seventy-five book reviews, and even half a dozen poems, they were not sufficiently distinguished to take him to the top. Following a junior appointment at the University of Washington (1925–27) he came to Miami University (Ohio) in the fall of 1927, and there he remained for the rest of his career (but not without trying, for a time at least, to find another position).[22]

An appealing personality, Bain was possibly the most entertaining correspondent in the profession. No reputation intimidated him: his correspondents included John Dewey, Sigmund Freud, and Thomas Mann, as well as most of the leading sociologists of his day. But a sparkling personality is not always an asset, and perhaps particularly not in academia, where awkwardness is sometimes confused with profundity. At Harvard, where he hoped for an appointment in the late thirties, his personality probably hurt him: Sorokin later included Bain among the "popular guys," the "Sinatras" of scientism, who were "driving out real singers."[23]

When Bain joined Bernard in 1932, he still flaunted his behaviorism. Three years earlier, he had praised the "scientific" character of Stuart Rice's *Quantitative Methods in Politics* (1928). "[Social] phenomena *per se*," he argued in another piece the same year, "are no more or less 'ordered' than any other type of natural phenomena."[24] With the onset of the Depression, however, he shifted ground to argue that "scientists" were not just value-free but the "true prophets" of the new age, urging his colleagues to "come out of the laboratory and do battle for the good life that may result from the truth they have discovered." Any scientist who made a fetish of "research" or "scientific method" as an end in itself was "a moral eunuch or a civic hermit."[25]

Howard Becker (1899–1960), Bain's friend and confidant, also offered support early in Bernard's presidency. In January 1932 he wrote that a proposed survey of annual research was too important to be left to "hobby riders" such as the didactic Hornell Hart of Duke, or to those "whose interest is fixed upon statistical techniques." In October, he applauded the attack on the Rice Committee, convinced that "the linkage of Ogburn and Rice" boded ill for the A.S.S. The following December, he supported efforts to cut the society loose from the University of Chicago Press.[26]

Like Bain, Becker was an outsider. Born in New York City, he began working as an unskilled laborer at age fourteen, and was sufficiently proud of the fact to report it in *Who's Who*.[27] At the late age of twenty-three he entered Northwestern. He was subsequently an exchange fellow at the University of Cologne (1926–27), where he developed an appetite for Germanic ideas and *Wissensociologie*. As a graduate student at Chicago (Ph.D. 1930) he became interested in "ideal types," a Weberian concept that he imbibed in Park's classroom.[28] By 1930, his support of the ideas of Leopold von Wiese had won Becker a place on Ellwood's list of "objectivists." After a three-year stay at the University of Pennsylvania, he joined Hankins at Smith, where he remained until appointed Ross's successor at Wisconsin in 1937.

Although opposites intellectually ("big word boys," Bain once called devotees of *Wissensociologie*),[29] Becker and Bain developed a spirited rapport composed in equal part of earthy humor and irreverence toward colleagues and profession. "Lissen, mister—I've taken several socks at you . . . but it's all in good clean fun," Becker wrote Bain after criticizing one of his articles. "Serves you right for being such a shining light. After all, you've delivered a few socks in your times, and the man that slingeth a stockingfull of shit, the same shall have it entwined about his own brow." In the same letter, Becker continued: "Did you ever hear the story of the whorehouse proprietor who ran a 'high-class' establishment? Some of the girls were one day so indiscreet as to cavort around the front yard with little or no clothing on, zealously squirting each other with vichy and bottled beer. He called them in the parlor, and sez he: 'Ladies, always remember that you're ladies, you goddammed bitches!' And even so," Becker concluded, "must we, as sociologists, uphold the honor of the profession."[30]

On the issue of science and values, Becker was at odds with both the "purists" (as he dubbed objectivists of the Ogburn variety) and their "meliorist" opponents. Science *was* value-laden, because the scientist starts with a belief in the value of "prediction" and "control," just as surely as the religious mystic has his own preconceptions. To the goal of "no value-judgments in science" must be added the clause "other than *the supreme value-judgment that control is ultimately desirable*." But science also was (or should be) value-free in that no other basic commitment must shape inquiry. Sociologists must cultivate a "sane" schizophrenia, Becker wrote in the first issue of the *ASR*. "Let the program of action as a sociology society be the promotion of bigger and better schizophrenics."[31]

Bain was a less sophisticated thinker than Becker, but he followed his lead. By the end of the decade he had emended his earlier idea—that the scientist was a "prophet," in that his findings looked to a better life—to the Beckerian one that science was a priesthood *within itself*. The rituals and methods of science must be kept sacred, he explained in an *AJS* editorial screened by Becker. The scientist "must conduct himself *as if* there were no values other than that of amoral, objective, nonutilitarian research."[32] Because Bain was fond of saying that *as a scientist* he could work in Hitler's Germany as well as anywhere, his critics might well have judged this a distinction without a difference. By this time, in any case, both Bain and Becker had essentially deserted Bernard.

4

Bernard's three chief lieutenants, although outsiders in their own ways, were reformers of more conventional stripe. The first to move to center stage in the fight for the new constitution in 1932 was Jerome Davis (1891–1979). Born in Kyoto, Japan, the son of missionary parents, Davis throughout his life viewed the native land of his parents with priggish bemusement. He came to the United States at age thirteen. As a child, he later wrote, he had "rather assumed that the ideological pattern of our parents was reasonably typical of the United States as a whole. Consequently, I thought our country would be more ethically and socially intelligent than I later found it to be."[33]

A born disapprover, young Davis quickly found things to dislike. At a posh private school (owned by his uncle) in Washington, D.C., it was "sexual smut and profanity [and] . . . the ostentatious display of wealth." At Oberlin, where he took a B.A. in 1913, it was America's corporations. When he served as secretary for the industrial committee of the Minnesota Civic and Commercial Association, it was the fact that payment by check drove workers into the city's gin mills. When he volunteered for a summer tour aboard the hospital ship *Strathcona* at the start of the war, it was the "stubbornness" of Eskimos who insisted "we are not cattle, we can't eat grass," and who thus refused to eat local foliage to cure their beriberi. At Columbia graduate school (Ph.D. 1922), where he worked with Edward Devine, it was the "social ignorance and stupidity" that produced the three Ds (dependents, defectives, and delinquents).[34]

In 1917, interrupting his graduate studies, Davis made the first of several trips to Russia. There he observed the Revolution at first hand, an experience that gave him both a model of the good society and a topic for his doctoral dissertation and several books. During the twenties Davis's radicalism was a source of unending academic difficulties. In 1922 several New Hampshire manufacturers demanded that he be fired from Dartmouth (where he had just started teaching) because of a study of a strike in a Manchester factory. At Yale, where Davis was appointed assistant professor in Practical Philanthropy in the Divinity School in 1923, Albert Keller refused to have "such a radical" in his department, citing particularly Davis's support of United States recognition of the Soviet Union. Each year brought new troubles. In 1925, Davis's sympathy for the revisionism of Harry Elmer Barnes and Sidney B. Fay brought a warning from Yale President James R. Angell, and possibly cost him a Guggenheim Fellowship. In 1926 a public speech in favor of organized labor and against the open shop brought press cries of "wild-eyed ranting." In 1927, following a trip to the Soviet Union, the charge was that Davis had taken "Moscow Gold" in connection with a series of books he was editing for Vanguard Press. In 1928, he was included in a "D.A.R. Blacklist" (with the Yale economist Irving Fisher). And so it went.[35]

In this period, Davis increasingly wrapped his social concerns in a rhetorical mantle of science and quantification. Giddings, he later wrote, taught him that it was "possible scientifically to chart the social influences which play upon the life of society." Increasingly, he was "convinced that sociology must rely on the statistical method to a greater extent than before." His best-known work, *An Introduction to Sociology* (1927), was subtitled "A Behavioristic Study of American Society."[36]

Davis's publications, although numerous, were the sort that the new professionals increasingly dismissed: studies of labor, the church, immigration, and related social problems; readers and textbooks. By 1932, he had published almost a dozen books, but as Dean Weigle of Yale was unkind enough to point out, many were written with other authors or were filled with source material.[37] The reviews were lukewarm at best: an especially critical one by Sorokin in 1930 even prompted Davis to demand that the journal print a second.[38]

Davis's ascent at Yale was correspondingly slow. After declining an offer at Wisconsin, he was promoted to associate professor in 1927. When six years later he was denied an expected elevation to professor for the second or third time, Yale offered him a six-month sabbatical to tone up his scholarly credentials. Although the resulting study of *The Jail Population of Connecticut* (1935) was a solid piece of work, he followed it almost immediately with the highly controversial *Capitalism and Its Culture* (1935) which, he later alleged, finally did him in.

Meanwhile, the social crisis of the decade brought to the surface the potential conflict between Davis's commitments to science and to reform. Like Bernard, he feared that sociology, in becoming more "scientific," was losing interest in "social action." Never one to worry over the intellectual fine points, however, he concluded that in practice no conflict existed. Survey research, he admitted of one of his own polls, served to "stimulate" informants to think about radical solutions, as well as to gather information. There was also no reason why sociologists as citizens would not automatically put their findings into action. Indeed, a survey that Davis took of 170 members of the A.S.S. suggested that the majority of American sociologists acted precisely in this manner.[39]

So convinced, Davis joined the battle to democratize the A.S.S. as chair of a committee on the constitution created at the 1932 meetings. Stacked with Bernard loyalists,[40] the Davis Committee carried the day at the 1933 meetings for a new constitution that Bernard claimed to have written almost single-handedly. Among its provisions for greater democracy were regional representation at every level, the election of all officers at the annual meetings with nominations allowed from the floor, and the submission of most actions to a vote of the members. Less obviously democratic (but in line with Bernard's definition of the term) was the selection of the nominations committee by the president, and the inclusion of past presidents on the executive committee, the provision that would allow Bernard to keep his hand in.[41]

At the 1934 meetings, it appeared that the Bernard forces might have difficulty recapturing the presidency despite the new constitution. In November Bernard wrote John Gillin, chairman of the nominations committee, his detailed recommendations for the leading offices, including, for president, the perennial Fairchild (rather than Sorokin, MacIver, or Hankins, also easterners, but men who "do not seem to be favorites with members of the society"). At the meetings, however, Chapin was nominated from the floor and defeated Fairchild and MacIver, the final choices of the nominations committee.[42]

Davis attempted to put the best face on things ("I do not see why Chapin should not make a reasonably good president"). But Bernard was clearly upset. The Chicago group (by whom he meant Faris, Blumer, et al.) had combined with the "research funds group" (Ogburn, Rice, and W. I. Thomas) to defeat Fairchild. He was convinced that Chapin would also be on their side. Meroney agreed: "the machine was well organized and greased and we did not have a chance in the face of a packed meeting." Meroney also charged that some of "our own men" had deserted to Chapin.[43]

In early 1935, Bernard floated the idea of a Davis candidacy. Given Davis's growing problems at Yale, and his reputation among sociologists, the suggestion was a measure of desperation, poor judgment, or both. In any case, it met a predictable torrent of negatives.[44] Bain and George Lundberg worked meanwhile for Fairchild (who in December finally won, over Rice), only soon to be disappointed with his policies as president.[45]

The election of Ellsworth Faris at the 1936 meetings marked the end of rebel attempts to control the organization. Despite their apparent victories, Meroney was convinced that every president since Bernard had been in Chicago's pocket: Edward Reuter of Iowa State, who had switched to the Chicago side early in his presidency; Burgess and Chapin, from the start; and finally Fairchild, who had done "some double-crossing" during his administration.[46] By this time, Jerome Davis himself was deeply embroiled in the battle with the Yale administration that finally led to his dismissal a year later. His role in the A.S.S. rebellion had come to an end.

5

With the new constitution in place, the Bernard group in 1934 focused on the issue of a new journal, a battle led initially by Newell Sims of Oberlin, and then by William Meroney of Baylor. At the time, there were three professional journals in the field: *The American Journal of Sociology* (founded by Albion Small in 1895), *Sociology and Social Research* (founded by Emory Bogardus in 1916), and *Social Forces* (founded by Howard Odum in 1922). The *AJS* early became the "official" journal of the A.S.S., sent automatically to all dues-paying members. The University of Chicago Press also published the society's *Publications*, for which the university provided an annual subsidy.

Complaints over this arrangement had come from several quarters. Some society members wanted a journal that, in Ogburn's words, would publish "scientific results for a scientific audience." Others were simply annoyed at the reviewing of their own books in the *AJS*—a list that by 1932 included Odum, Sorokin, and Hankins (who on one occasion complained to Odum that the review of his latest book was "more or less contemptible").[47]

Because the existing journals were based at different institutions, factors other than theoretical orientation or book reviewing were bound to enter. Bain, and probably Bernard, initially favored giving *Social Forces* official status, but Bain also noted that it would be difficult for Bernard to push the point when he was one of the editors. Bernard diplomatically suggested that it would be "more objective and less partisan" to offer members a choice for their dues of any one of the three journals, even though he was aware that Bogardus's poor reputation in the East might defeat the plan. The fact that the *AJS* was *the* Chicago journal, and that the A.S.S. had somehow accumulated a sizable debt to the university over the years, further complicated any discussion purely on the merits of the journals.[48]

Thus entered Newell Sims (1878–1965), a Columbia Ph.D. (1912) whom Bernard appointed chairman of a new publications committee in 1932. For Sims, the road to this position had been a bumpy one. Born on a farm in Indiana (near Fremont), the child of Disciples of Christ, he spent his first thirty years in theological seminaries and pastorates in the old Southwest. Fundamentalist and "other-worldly" to the extreme, as he later described himself, he was untainted by the Modernist and Social Gospel currents until about 1907, when some local socialists persuaded him that his attitude toward the poor was indifferent if not callous. After considerable soul-searching, and a public uproar that made its way to the pages of Upton Sinclair's *Appeal to Reason*, he resigned his pastorate to enter the Union Theological Seminary (1908), and eventually the department of sociology at Columbia. There he wrote *A Hoosier Village* (1912), one of the better community studies done under Giddings. After the war had destroyed what remained of Sims's religious beliefs, he entered academia with a sense of being freed from the "trammels of the Church," although, ironically, his first teaching job at the University of Florida ended when he came under fire from local Fundamentalists.[49]

Like Davis, Sims embraced science without abandoning his social concerns, and he was likewise a textbook academic radical: opposed to World War I (he termed Wilson a "traitor to his country"), sympathetic to the Russian Revolution, and blacklisted during the Red Scare. At the University of Massachusetts (1920–24) and then at Oberlin, (1924–44) he settled down to the more mundane concerns of rural sociology (now officially his field), but he remained proud of being "a pacifist, a reformer, a social liberal, and something of an absolutist."[50]

Also like Davis, Sims had published widely without advancing his professional standing. By 1932 he had published six books;[51] the reviews, however, although charitable, had been less than glowing. Sims was himself aware that his scholarship was a bit unfashionable in the new age of quantification. "My *Society and Its Surplus* [1924] appeared as a wholly original bit of sociological theorizing," he wrote of his best-known book. "No doubt it was mainly an armchair product rather than a statistical investigation or field research," he added, "but I have the satisfaction of knowing that it was not the mere elaboration by means of tiresome tables and formulas of the altogether obvious."[52] For whatever reason, until 1932 (at age fifty-four), he had not played much of a role in the A.S.S.

Sims headed the struggle for a new publication from late 1932 through the 1934 meetings. The battle was vintage academic politics: constitutional complaints, proceduring over procedures, and mounting hard feelings between the Bernard forces and a Chicago-cum-research group. When Bernard appointed the Sims Committee, there already existed an older publications committee consisting of Rice, Frederick Lumley, and Ulysses Weatherly.[53] Capitalizing on the confusion, A.S.S. Secretary Herbert Blumer pushed through an arrangement with the Chicago press to his own liking. Although Blumer offered Bernard a credible explanation (the constitutional issue was clouded, to say the least), their correspondence quickly grew edgy. "As I read this over, it sounds kind'a mean," Blumer apologized at one point, "but I don't intend for it to." From a sickbed, Sims wrote that Blumer's actions made him "thoroly mad."[54]

At the 1933 meetings, after a Sims Committee resolution failed (through a parliamentary foul-up, Bernard grumbled), the dissidents found themselves further outflanked when Ellsworth Faris, another Chicagoan, submitted a supposed compromise that severed A.S.S. ties with the *AJS* but did nothing else, leaving the impression that the issue was closed. During 1934 Ernest Burgess, now president, first disbanded and then reinstated the Sims Committee.[55] An informal poll of the executive committee in the fall convinced Sims that the Chicagoans were now in the minority.[56] At the December meetings the Sims resolution sailed through the executive committee and the General Meeting: as of January 1936, all connections between the society and the University of Chicago would be ended, and a new journal was a strong possibility. With Sims headed for a year-long sabbatical in Europe, the final struggle passed to another Bernard ally, Meroney—who, as it turned out, had his own axe to grind.[57]

If not the most prominent of the rebels, William Meroney (1881–1938) was probably the angriest, although also the one best able to see his own situation realistically. Born in Plano, Texas, the same year as Bernard, he spent most of his youth in a series of obscure Baptist institutions, the best known being Baylor, where he earned a B.A in 1907. Originally destined for the ministry, he collected several advanced degrees in theology before entering sociology at the University of Chicago in the early 1920s;[58] there he studied with Bernard, Small, and Faris, among others. In 1922 Meroney received his doctorate for a study of "The Town Church and the Modern Family," which he never published. Five years later, he put at the top of the list of his sociological interests "the introductory course upon which I have expended most of my study and thought."[59]

At Baylor, where Meroney taught for the remainder of his career, he was ostensibly the model Chicago loyalist: praising the school at every chance, sending graduate students, and even fighting for the freedom to use his mentors' textbooks in his classes. At the annual meeting in 1928, he joined gleefully with the group that elected Ogburn from the floor over Emory Bogardus, recalling years later "how the Chicago delegation chuckled over putting it over."[60]

But inwardly, Meroney was a bundle of discontents. It rankled that he had not been invited to give a paper at the annual meeting. A glimpse of Bogardus after the 1928 election debacle—"stricken, crushed, and disappointed"—nagged at his conscience. At the 1930 meetings he sat with a group prepared to undo the official nominee, who was again Bogardus. This time, he blocked any action from the floor.[61] Invited at last to give a paper at this same meeting of 1930, he got even, after a fashion, by documenting how midwestern and eastern interests had thoroughly dominated the offices and programs of the A.S.S. through most of its history, quite out of proportion to their numbers.[62]

Although Meroney's paper brought no public reaction at the time, he later heard, from two sources, that the Chicago sociologists never forgave him. Ellsworth Faris certainly did not: at the 1934 meeting, with the publications issue bubbling in the background, he cornered Meroney to accuse him of trying to "weaken the department that gave [him] his degree."[63] Meroney, in response, wrote Faris an extraordinary five-page indictment of alleged Chicago chicanery, which he then circulated to selected members of the society. Airing a decade of grievances, he charged that such tactics were responsible for the decline of A.S.S. membership, no less than the spread of regional organizations. Should the same clique insist on control—for example, in the forthcoming appointment of a new executive secretary—"it will be the beginning of the end." Even if he was only a "two-by-four sociologist" at a "jerkwater" institution, Meroney concluded with a self-deprecating humor rare among the rebels, the Chicago group should know their sociology well enough to know that he was telling the truth.[64]

During the first half of 1935 the "Meroney letter" threatened to eclipse the battle for a new journal. Bernard applauded Meroney's effort, but said he thought it "too humble rather than too aggressive." Others in the Bernard circle were generally pleased. Cecil North of Ohio State, affecting naiveté, thought it "illuminating." James Bossard of Penn termed its author "courageous." Maurice Davie of Yale had to "admire his guts."[65]

If Bernard hoped that the new journal would be a vehicle for his own brand of radicalism (and his aims in this regard remain unclear), the growing splits in the rebel ranks should have persuaded him otherwise. In May, the Eastern Sociological Conference (whose members Bernard generally counted on in his battles) voted down a motion supporting the establishment of a new journal by the A.S.S. Although Fairchild, the leader of the opposition, claimed the reason was simply that the E.S.C. should not be giving advice to the larger body, Jerome Davis wrote Bernard that Fairchild was "playing up to the Chicago group. He is ambitious to be president."[66]

The issue of possible editors also caused trouble. During the spring, Bernard sounded out Chapin, Ellwood, and Bossard, although whether he did so seriously or merely to garner their support for the journal is a matter of speculation. As the meetings approached, suspicion mounted that Bernard and/or Meroney were angling to control the new publication themselves. Sorokin wrote Bain that he supported the idea of a journal on the single condition that Bernard *not* be editor. Bernard denied any interest (while leaving the door open), but Bain diplomatically suggested in mid-December that all members of the publications committee rule themselves out "for the time being."[67]

At the December meetings, the executive committee was seriously split. Rice and Ogburn spoke against the new journal; Ross, Davis, and now Fairchild for it. Although the antis obtained a negative vote in the executive committee (by a margin of one), the projournal forces nonetheless carried the day at the business meeting. Parmelee later reported that Lundberg and Hankins were nominated as editor, but that Lundberg refused to run. The special interests meanwhile fought for positions on the editorial board: the social workers for Neva Deardorff, a Penn Ph.D. who was director of the Research Bureau of the Welfare Council of New York; and the feminists for Susan Kingsbury of Bryn Mawr (an issue "dragged in," according to Parmelee, "in a most belligerent fashion"). Meroney was a candidate for managing editor, but Harold Phelps was finally voted to this post as well as that of secretary of the Society. Meroney considered the outcome to be a victory for the Bernard forces, and later recalled that Chapin as chairman of the meeting was "exceedingly fair" when he might "have given us considerable trouble." How permanent a victory this was, the next few years would reveal.[68]

15

DEFEAT

I have a feeling that the [A.S.S.] is on the verge of
disorganization. It is certainly disgraceful for such a spirit
to exist in a supposedly learned society composed of men
who pose as being devoted to science and [who]
presumably are more rational than people in general.

Read Bain to Bernard, January 1937

What price detachment! What price thinking!

William F. Ogburn, May 1947

1

Despite their apparent victory over the journal issue, things quickly soured for
Bernard and his allies. In the spring of 1936, the formation of the by-invitation-only Sociological Research Association (S.R.A.) signaled another round
in the battle to create a truly "professional" organization. By 1937 the society's
new journal, the *American Sociological Review*, was also proving a disappointment. "My feeling," Sims wrote to Bernard in January, "is that the
Review has not fallen into good hands."[1] The presidency of Ellsworth Faris the
same year began a string that can hardly have pleased Bernard: Frank Hankins
(1938), a perennial antagonist; Edwin Sutherland (1939), a graduate-school
friend with whom relations had somehow cooled; Robert MacIver (1940),
whom the rebels had blocked four years earlier; and Stuart A. Queen (1941),
Bernard's chief foe at Washington University.

Ogburn, in contrast, apparently thrived. During the thirties he served on
various New Deal agencies, including the Consumer's Advisory Board of the
N.R.A., the Resettlement Administration, and the National Resources Commission. Meanwhile, he saw his best graduate students carrying the cause of
scientific sociology into the postwar era. But the Chicagoan, too, had doubts

and disappointments in his final years—first concerning the place of statistics, and then the personal and political implications of the "objectivity" he had so assiduously cultivated.

The rise of fascism added yet another twist to the debates over "science." Was fascism the latest incarnation of the mystical, metaphysical spirit that had warred against science since the Reformation? Or was it the ultimate attenuation of positivism itself, as the philosopher Herbert Marcuse would soon argue?[2] To these questions, Luther Bernard had an unequivocal answer: both interpretations were correct. The cosy alliance of "mystical sociologists" and "statisticians" within the S.R.A. constituted a sort of intellectual "fascism"—a charge he hurled with increasing abandon as the war approached. At the same time, although apparently from sources other than Bernard, the same charge led Ogburn into a new round of soul-searching.

Taken literally, the charge was, of course, unfounded: few if any American sociologists openly supported fascism, and certainly not the leading members of the S.R.A. But, despite a hysteria bordering on paranoia, Bernard had raised an important point. Had the quantifiers and researchers, in their concern with means, any basis for defending the values of democracy other than personal whim? Were the philosophical idealists (the "mystics") fundamentally soft on the sort of authority and order the fascists promised? In Ogburn's case, the answer to the first question is at best a qualified "maybe"—qualified in the sense that the issue continued to trouble him into the postwar years. A further question was whether Bernard, intellectually, had anything more to offer, a challenge he took up in *War and Its Causes* (1944), his last book. In the end, fascism and war cast a pall over objectivism just as the First World War had blighted the reformist evolutionism of the founders.

2

The S.R.A. went back to the Rice Committee plan for selective membership, a more "professional" society, and the centralization of scholarly activity. "While there is no direct cause-and-effect relationship between [the Rice Report] and the new organization, I think the motivation is a common one," explained Malcolm Willey of Minnesota two years after its founding. Surprised to be elected, Read Bain later recalled much bold talk in the association's early days about "professional" and "real" sociology. Bossard understood that the S.R.A.'s formation was "an aftermath" of the rejection of the Rice Report.[3]

More specifically, it had direct roots in the Research Planning Committee (R.P.C.) of the A.S.S., established under the new constitution, presumably as part of a compromise. Composed of the society's president, its secretary (Herbert Blumer), and three members chosen by the president, this committee during 1934 included Burgess (chair), Rice, Ogburn, and W. I. Thomas (the "T-O-R forces," as Bernard now called them). From the start, the rebels viewed the R.P.C. with suspicion. In the spring of 1934, Parmelee wrote Bernard that he had heard a rumor to the effect that Burgess and Blumer were in New York at the same time that the S.S.R.C. was meeting. Although the A.S.S. membership in 1934 accepted an R.P.C. recommendation for a permanent secretary for the society, it also endorsed a Bernard-Davis resolution that required the approval of the executive committee for any expenditure of funds.[4]

In the wings was the hope that the A.S.S. would soon receive considerable funds from the foundations for a publication series. The year 1935 was to be a "momentous one," President Chapin reported in February, because the R.P.C. had "well-developed plans to secure a subsidy from foundations. . . ." Later that spring, Bain reported that Chapin was especially keen on a monograph series to be financed through the R.P.C., a move Bain also supported.[5]

This prospect frightened many dissidents. In February, Davis wrote Ross that there was "some feeling" that the R.P.C. "may be inclined to foster research of a particular sort which they will control," and to "look askance" at investigation of the current scene such as Ross himself undertook. Meroney shared the concern. "When a man is nominated for this place on the basis of funds having been provided, " he wrote of the permanent secretary, "and that he is acceptable to the Foundation providing the funds, it will be too late to protest his election, and it will be too late to protest selling out to some Foundation."[6]

Bernard saw the appointment of a full-time secretary as being at the heart of the plot, describing the post as "located in Washington and financed by a foundation that works hand-in-glove with the Thomas-Ogburn-Rice combination." Despite Davis's counsel of caution, Bernard during 1935 used the Meroney letter as ammunition. When in March he learned that the still-unemployed Parmelee was interested in the permanent secretaryship, however, he shifted gears to lobby on Parmelee's behalf. In the end, the position went to Harold A. Phelps of the University of Pittsburgh, a sometime rebel whose ardor was already cooling.[7]

Established the following spring, the S.R.A. provided for a maximum membership of one hundred sociologists, Ph.D.s or the equivalent, "who have made a significant contribution to sociological research other than in the doctoral dissertation."[8] A moving force in its founding was Donald Young, a Penn sociologist (Ph.D. 1922), professor at the Wharton School, and now also research secretary of the S.S.R.C. The author of a well-regarded quantitative study of racial attitudes, Young was particularly interested in research design. Chapin was also a founder, but Ogburn apparently was not, although he later served on the executive committee. Initially this central body consisted of five men, each to serve successively as president: Chapin, Young, MacIver, Rice, and Reuter. By 1938, additions included Ogburn and E. H. Sutherland. Using a preliminary membership list of forty-nine, Parmelee calculated that eight were at the University of Chicago, and that ten of the fourteen members of the A.S.S. executive committee belonged, as well as five of the nine members of the editorial board of the new *ASR*.[9]

Rather than comprising a coherent "theory group," the more prominent members of the S.R.A. represented two extremes. At one extreme were the leading quantifiers and other scientific sociologists. Malcolm Willey, himself a quantifier, later claimed that the association represented "a desire to get away somewhat from speculation to something approximating scientific thinking"; although he was quick to add that the latter meant more than statistics, he conceded that, on a scale between the extremes of Charles Ellwood and George Lundberg, it was probably closer to the latter. The social psychologist Kimball Young also remembered that the group aimed to "break down the long-lasting philosophical tradition of the . . . A.S.S." Lundberg himself was in favor of the group from the start. At the other extreme, however, were some of the profession's best-known theorists—MacIver of Columbia, House of Virginia, and the vehemently antipositivistic Sorokin.[10]

By 1938, Bain claimed that the group had lost any coherence its founders might have intended, for it combined "some who think research is solely quantitative, some who think sociology is repetitive mouthing of Wissensoci-ologie and other Germanic maunderings, some who think sociology is social work, social surveys, case studies, and god knows what." He predicted that in a few years it "will be dead."[11] But Bain was only partially correct. Although the S.R.A. did not outlast the war years, the alliance represented by MacIver and Sorokin, on the one hand, and Ogburn and Rice, on the other, anticipated the so-called Harvard-Columbia connection of the 1950s.

However diverse the membership, it was clear that Bernard was not welcome. Bain and Lundberg nominated him for membership, but his name failed to get beyond the nomination committee. "I think its the shits," Lundberg wrote Bain, wondering whether Bain had actually seconded the nomination: "All I want to know is whether Bernard was left out for want of a second or whether they threw him out. . . . If so, I'll raise hell. If not, I have nothing to say, except that the S.R.A. will be in a funny role with some of the bastards now on its roll and LLB out." Bain also termed his exclusion "a damned shame and scandal." But when Bernard attempted to find out who exactly had kept him out, Bain claimed that he did not know.[12]

3

During its first two years, the *ASR* disappointed the rebels—especially Bernard and Sims, who soon joined the editorial board. Confounding the hopes of some, and the fears of a few, editor Frank Hankins tried to make sure no one group dominated. Articles ranged from narrowly technical discussions of sampling procedure to a defense of "Imagination in Social Science." Gradually, the *ASR* even made space for the structural-functionalism of Robert Merton and Talcott Parsons (even though the *Structure of Social Action* was not reviewed for more than two years, while Louis Wirth sat on the review copy). Most of the contributors were academics, but some held positions in government, and a few were social workers. Sensitive to the regional issue, Hankins strove for sectional balance (or so he claimed), although another Meroney survey would doubtless have shown a tilt toward eastern contributors. Howard Becker's hand was evident in the relatively large number of European, and especially German, books reviewed.

Trouble first appeared in late 1936 when Bernard refused to sign a joint editorial concerning the S.R.A.'s relation to the A.S.S. The issue was resolved,[13] but other grievances soon followed. The imbalance of eastern contributors, even though less than Bernard charged, sparked a running debate during 1937—nor was Bernard placated when Hankins speculated that that region perhaps contained more "young and promising scholars," in part because eastern institutions paid better.[14] A Bernard proposal to devote a special issue to papers of the "political sociology" section of the 1936 meetings was finally squelched in favor of one on "marriage and the family," the excuse being that the latter promised to sell better. When his own contribution to the same session was refused, Bernard speculated that it was "because it did not express fascistic sympathies." Soon after this dispute, Hankins turned down a study of "Neighborhoods" by Bernard's wife Jessie, which, when published elsewhere, won praise from many in the profession, including Chapin; and he refused to allow space for a review of Bernard's *Methods and Scope* on the grounds that it had been published before 1936, although other earlier works were reviewed.[15]

Sims, in turn, criticized Hankins's apparent determination "to run anything and everything of German origin," which he attributed to the influence of "that Nazi Becker." He saw the refusal to run the "political sociology" issue as part of a pattern. Probably only Stouffer (who joined the board in 1937) or Folsom or Deardorff had reviewed the manuscripts, he wrote to Bernard. "If the majority of the editorial board says my article and your article are 'the bunk' then, presumably they are. Until then I am not convinced."[16]

By mid-1937 Bernard and Sims had launched a two-pronged attack: Bernard to get rid of Hankins as editor, and Sims to install Bernard in his place. During the late spring, Bernard undertook another of his now-famous mail blitzes ("dandruff correspondence," Becker called it) to gather opinions of the *ASR*. In June he tactfully suggested to Hankins that a two-year term was the ideal. In August, Meroney shrewdly noted that it might be impossible to get rid of Hankins so long as the vote on a two-year renewal coincided, as it now did, with the biennial eastern meeting.[17] Changing strategy, Bernard in October wrote the chairman of the nominating committee to suggest Hankins for president, presumably a convenient way to elevate him from the editorship. In December Hankins announced that he would step down. Sims suspected a trick, but recommended to Bernard that they treat the announcement *as though* it were genuine, and hence make it so. Meanwhile, he lobbied for Bernard. Hankins was indeed elected president for 1938, but the scheme backfired when Read Bain was elected editor to replace him.[18]

Looking back on the election, Sims took a dim view of the future. "I am persuaded that our effort to rescue the Society from the hands of the Chicago group . . . has been in vain for this new group has risen and seized control and will run it as they see fit. It looks like a hopeless case," he wrote to Bernard. Bain's choice of Becker to continue as book review editor sealed the case. "It is politics throughout."[19] Bernard soon had new reason to agree when Bain inexplicably delayed judgment on a manuscript Bernard had submitted, the excuse being that an assistant editor (who turned out to be Stouffer) failed to provide the requested assessment. After demanding that Stouffer be relieved of the post, Bernard finally backed off when Stouffer apologized and in fact offered to resign. Bernard was already addressing Bain coolly as "Editor Bain" or "Professor Bain," and this incident did little to ease their strained relations.[20]

Although Bain never broke publicly with Bernard, and indeed continued to flatter him, patience with the rebels was growing thin in the editorial offices of the *ASR*. "It seems to be my luck (and yours) to get mixed up with paranoiacs and other psychopathetic gents to a greater degree than seems our just desserts [sic]," Bain wrote to his friend Becker in March 1937, mentioning Bernard among others. When Bernard again complained about a paper he had written, Becker confided to his editor: "Apparently he is trying to discover whether or not you are being 'democratic' by letting the editorial board see all the horrible examples that come over the desk. I will tell the old buzzard anything you want me to, for I know how obnoxious he can be." In other exchanges, the two made it clear they held hardly less flattering views of Sims.[21]

For Bernard, the breaking point came at the 1938 meetings. As agitation to rescind the "past presidents" clause of the constitution mounted during the year, he saw former allies deserting him on the issue. When the A.S.S. decided to restrict past presidents to a five-year term, he was, as he later put it, "turned . . . out of the Executive Committee," and on top of this he was not allowed to speak from the floor of the business meeting to a motion he had made.[22] Although his battles with the management of the *ASR* did not cease, he resigned from the society soon after.

Had the battle been in vain? Bernard's answer was characteristically immodest. "I'll say that I've done more for the organization than all my critics together," he wrote Bain two years later, defending his decision to resign. He had "put over" the *ASR* when even the committee wished to withdraw; he had written the new constitution, and was now "preventing it from getting into the hands of the pirates." The plot, he had earlier explained to another critic, began even before he became president, and could be dated roughly to the moves that put Ogburn in office in 1928. It had been his "unwished-for task." "I didn't like the job, for I shrink . . . from . . . politics," he added, apparently straight-faced.[23]

Because little evidence exists concerning the motives of Rice, Ogburn, or Thomas, a more balanced judgment is difficult to make. In Ogburn's case, as will appear, "piracy" was unlikely, for he was immersed in *Recent Social Trends* and already was becoming more modest concerning the claims of scientific sociology. When the S.R.A. was formed, he in fact urged that it not be too exclusive. At one point, he even counseled Blumer to drop the name "research" from the title, because it seemed "too smug."[24] Nor is there evidence that the S.R.A., at its worst, was anything more than a mutual admiration society.

Bernard and his allies probably opened up the A.S.S. and its publication to groups previously underrepresented—although less extensively, and less permanently, than their manifestos suggested. Insofar as the *ASR* became the arena in which developed the postwar alliance of the Harvard-Columbia theory-technicians, the rebels' role in creating the journal must rank high among what Robert Merton in 1936 called "The Unanticipated Consequences of Purposive Social Action."

The failure of the dissidents, if so it should be judged, was in large part an intellectual one. One need only compare the writings of a Bernard, Sims, or Davis with those of the "radical" sociologists of the generation of C. Wright Mills and after, to realize how impoverished was the positivist tradition within which they wrote. The Bernard rebels of 1932, in fact, had a bewildering assortment of viewpoints: as theorists, they included radical behaviorists, philosophical idealists, and at least one champion of *Wissensociologie*; as professors, they came largely from marginal universities or "good" small colleges outside the orbit of the major universities; as political activists, they ranged from pro-Soviet radicals to anti-Bolshevist conservatives. While the demand for "democracy" provided a rallying cry within the A.S.S., it stood for little in the way of sociological theory or even political conviction on national or world issues.

The prickly personalities of the leaders, and the half-suppressed animosities that are a perennial feature of academic life, placed a constant strain on effective cooperation. Fearing conspiracy elsewhere, they distrusted each other. Davis early warned Bernard that Manuel Elmer was "not to be trusted" (because of reports from the University of Pittsburgh that he was a "yes" man), while Elmer was permanently aggrieved at being excluded, whether intentionally or not, from a caucus of the "Sims Committee" at the 1934 meetings.[25] Sims in turn thought Davis a "good chap but a little too aggressive on his own behalf," and Meroney, he alleged, was sometimes a victim of his own Gaelic exuberance. Add to this Bernard's many quarrels with Hankins, Ellwood, and countless others, the irreverence of Bain and Becker (not to mention Lundberg, who stayed out of things but kibitzed from the sidelines), and the notorious sensitivities of Sorokin, and it is little wonder that the initial Bernard coalition barely survived his presidency. By 1938 his allies had been driven to the pages of Bernard's own publication, *The American Sociologist*.[26]

4

And what of Ogburn during the troubled 1930s? He enjoyed a happier fate professionally, and never formally repudiated the extreme scientism of his 1929 presidential address; nevertheless, he backed away from it perceptibly from 1933 onwards. One factor was the deepening economic crisis. Speaking to the American Association for the Advancement of Science in December

1933, he observed that "the reality of present issues" now gave primacy to "applied" over "pure" sociology, reversing their previous positions. Earlier that same year the S.S.R.C., with Ogburn chairing, not coincidentally had voted "to give recognition to the immediacy of important public and social problems." Theorizing and "fact-finding," speculation and verification, were not eternal opposites, Ogburn insisted, but simply different stages in the development of all science.[27]

A second factor was probably the heated battle that raged at the University of Chicago during 1933–34 between "humanists" and "scientists." In the spring of 1933, Chicago's President Robert Hutchins fired the first shot. In a talk otherwise defending the service of professors to government, he cited Ogburn, Charles Merriam, and Wesley Mitchell as a new breed of academic realists whose work "rested on the study of observed phenomena." If their work could be criticized, he continued, "it is only from the standpoint that rigorous theoretical analysis plays too small a role in it." At a University of Chicago convocation in December, Hutchins continued the attack, although without naming Ogburn. "Hell broke loose shortly thereafter," the philosopher Mortimer Adler remembered. " 'Facts *vs.* ideas' became fighting words."[28]

Chicago sociologists left little record of their reactions, but Ellsworth Faris suggested that the attack stung some members of the department. "There is a small group of men here who are making an unblushing effort to restore again the methods and terminology of medieval scholasticism," he wrote to Ellwood. "It would also interest you to know that these same men with whom the president in the [convocation] address cast in his lot regard sociology as an absolutely impossible attempt to make a science." Hoping to soften Ellwood's attack on the quantifiers, Faris added: "Let us not get excited about statistics. Fortunately, the best of them know that many things cannot be measured yet."[29]

As if to underline the point, Ogburn twice during 1934 cautioned that too much must not be expected of science, statistics in particular. The first warning was in a speech on "The Limitations of Statistics" before the American Statistical Association. "The vast number of discoveries in any science are quite minor," he observed. "Science grows by small increments to the store of knowledge." He also conceded that statistics served primarily to make more exact "something that is already known," the central point in Sorokin's earlier attack on *Recent Social Trends*.[30]

A similar caution sounded in an article on "The Prediction and Distortion of Reality." The subject this time was of the sort that increasingly opened quantifiers to the charge of triviality: a comparison of football score predictions by sportswriters with estimates of grades made by students in courses at Reed and Barnard. In both instances, advance estimates tended to ignore the unusual, whether the stunning victory or the exceptional grade. If this finding was hardly earthshaking, a deeper lesson was more significant: "Optimists tend as a group to be less intelligent than 'pessimists' when measured by other tests."[31]

About 1935 Ogburn effectively abandoned statistics for what would later be called futurology. While some of his articles continued to have the now-mandatory tables and charts, he undertook no new work in the field, and he eventually gave up his courses in statistics altogether. Echoes of his 1929 presidential address sounded in his published work and in his diary, but his tone was increasingly defensive. In an important sense, "The Limitations of Statistics" was a valedictory.

Many years later, Ogburn reflected on this stage of his career. The reflection was occasioned by an incident at the University of Chicago Quadrangle Club. At dinner with his wife and some friends, he observed three prominent statisticians at a nearby table: R. A. Fisher of Cambridge, and Allan Wallis and L. L. Thurstone of Chicago. Two days later he again spotted Fisher, this time at lunch in a private dining room surrounded by twenty or so distinguished guests. Fisher had apparently been awarded an honorary degree, Ogburn mused, although he himself had not been "invited or consulted." He *was* emeritus, and had been away for a year, Ogburn consoled himself. "But this does not explain my not being in on this statistical gathering."[32]

Once it had been different, when he was editor of the *Journal of the American Statistical Association*, and then president of the organization. "The feeling of devotion and loyalty was very strong," he reminisced. Although his ambition sustained him during his early years at Chicago, the Depression and later the war had changed things until he gave up teaching statistics altogether. "But I envy those who stayed by statistics," he added, "and sometimes I think I wish I had."

As this confession concluded, Ogburn reflected that this envy was itself evidence that his earlier interest was not quite the unemotional, scientific commitment he had imagined: "My worship of statistics has a somewhat religious nature." Statistics was his God. "But God only meets an emotional need, which has little to do with reason." Still, the regret lingered. "There was a vacant place at R. A. Fisher's table."[33]

The rise of fascism was a further blow to Ogburn's vision of a value-free social science. The subject needs much more investigation, but it would appear that Bernard and Sims were not alone in suspecting scientific sociologists of being soft on fascism. "I have already been run out of 2 or 3 households almost for saying that I believe I could get along in Nazi Germany *as a scientist*, about as well as here—some better," Bain wrote Lundberg in early 1938. "If I got into trouble it wd be because I stuck my neck out, i.e. tried to play a part in policy making, and value promoting—instead of doing my stuff—*find out what is*."[34]

Although in Ogburn's case the evidence is less direct, it is clear that some colleagues felt he *was* soft on fascism. "The consensus expressed about you was that your professional career . . . has been seriously marred and your reputation injured by your non-belief in democracy and your obsession with [and] your fondness and admiration for totalitarian dictatorships," one former student wrote him after the war, shocked to hear him being so criticized during a Princeton conference. "Your friends cited the fact that you seemed to be pro-Nazi in the late thirties, even up to Pearl Harbor. They now say you are just as strongly in favor of the Soviets, and that you evidently adhere to a totalitarian form of government." Nor was she comforted when another friend defended Ogburn, saying he was reported as pro-Nazi "merely because of the absurd notion you had that you could view objectively a war in which the world was involved, and remain neutral."[35]

The letter shocked Ogburn ("jerked me up quick"), but his explanations in his diary left the cloud hanging. He *did* admire organization and efficiency; he *did* despise hatred, even when directed against Hitler. At a meeting in June 1942 to hear the impressions of a former head of the Associated Press in Berlin, for example, he found himself marveling at the skill of the Nazi propaganda machine ("not admiration of course for the end, but for the means"). While others listened "with contempt, disgust, and horror," he reflected to himself that the propaganda minister was only doing what every family, fraternity, and college does in indoctrinating its members.[36] Was he "psychotic"? Was he "in any way abnormal"? No, he decided. But he disliked seeing his colleagues "so emotional and so hating. And then there was that lonely feeling."[37]

On V-E day, Ogburn looked back over the troubled years. "Now that the war is over, I may say that I have felt lonely during the war with no person that I knew with whom I could talk." His position, as he now reviewed it, was probably not unlike that of many isolationists and "America Firsters." He had "always wanted us to win." But the price of victory had included hatred and passion. The root of his difficulty was merely "(a) a certain detachment and (b) an ability to see the other fellow's side." From this Olympian perspective, even Hitler was but "a symbol to stimulate and arouse the masses." In yet another entry he complained that it was impossible to say any "kind words" about

Hitler without being ostracized. What "kind words" he had in mind, he did not specify.[38]

Between 1945 and his sudden death in 1959 from a heart attack, Ogburn remained professionally active, while enjoying the travel and leisure unknown to his sociological predecessors, most of whom died in harness. In the late 1930s, he had become a "recognized authority" on technology and social change. During the 1940s he published studies of the impact of war babies, and of the airplane. In 1947 he joined project RAND, for which he produced a study of the evacuation of American cities in case of nuclear attack. Three years later he participated in a UNESCO conference on technology and education.[39] After retiring from the University of Chicago in 1952, he was visiting professor at various universities in the United States and abroad.

Even after the war was over, Ogburn continued to wrestle with the issues that had caused him such grief: organization and freedom, reason and emotion, scientist and citizen, public man and private self. Unfortunately, the wisdom of age did not dissolve these dualities. The public Ogburn met hated "deadlines" (for example, in revising the widely-used Ogburn-Nimkoff textbook), gave speeches, and attended conferences. The private Ogburn meanwhile traveled to ever more primitive and exotic places, rediscovered favorite poems, and gloried in his tennis, which he played avidly to the end of his life ("To play tennis when the temperature is 5 degrees and there is snow on the ground is like a miracle," he wrote at age sixty, after jogging a block from the Quadrangle club to the field house in shorts).[40]

If he achieved a resolution of sorts, it was in the frank acceptance of the separation of the public and private spheres. In his diary he returned repeatedly to the theme of the artificiality of the "professional" life, and his desire to break out of the mold. Some lines from the poet Dorothy Parker perfectly expressed his mood:

> In youth, it was a way I had
> To do my best to please,
> And change, with every passing lad,
> To suit his theories.

> But now I know the things I know,
> And do the things I do;
> And if you do not like me so,
> To hell, my love, with you!

Behind this sentiment was a deepening conviction that quite different roles should govern the public and private spheres.[41]

In the summer of 1959, in his last published article, Ogburn translated a personal "to hell with you" to a more dignified "it doesn't matter." In his travels he had discovered that this phrase had an equivalent in most non-Western cultures: from Bangkok to Syria, men and women used it to meet disaster and disappointment. By reducing tension, it served sociologically to preserve "kindliness, manners, and cooperation." In the West, with its "time pieces, scales, record keeping, statistics, progress charts, and schedule making," the sphere for the application of this attitude was sharply reduced. But just as the language of the church was not that of the cocktail lounge, or the dress of the factory that of the home, so he urged Americans to "taboo ['it doesn't matter'] in our business, but use it extensively outside." Thus was completed the blueprint for the separation of spheres in a corporate, technological society that Ogburn had sketched four decades earlier.[42]

5

Bernard's resignation from the A.S.S. did not end his personal or professional trials. By the late 1930s his personal life was a shambles, his marriage to Jessie Bernard strained almost to the breaking point. While their bitter exchanges drove him to near-desperation, they also dramatized the old conflicts between his personal behavior, his conventional, even puritanical, view of women, and his incredible insecurity and compulsive need to dominate and control. In the war years his energies and attention were further absorbed by a protracted quarrel that led finally to his departure from Washington University in 1946.[43]

During 1939 he was again at odds with the editors of the *ASR*. At issue this time was a review of his *Social Control*, in which, as he explained to Ross, he continued his crusade on behalf of an objective standard for social policy.[44] The reviewer, a recent Harvard Ph.D., charged that his demand that "the theorist of social control recognize the operation of the social control process" confused the "objective" and the "subjective," because such recognition was precisely the sort of subjective act that the method was designed to avoid. Bernard's book was also shot through with metaphysics. "A miraculously evolutionary trend" sustained the argument that science would replace force and fraud in human affairs. "Bernard seems to think that social scientists will enlighten mankind, and will effect the complete triumph of ethical control," the critic continued, repeating the point that Hankins earlier had made in his review of *Instinct*. Then, sarcastically: "perhaps it is refreshing to find a positivistic and evolutionary optimist in times such as these." The issue was the old one of value and fact; the charge, that Bernard arbitrarily imported those values that suited him, and called it "science."[45]

When Bernard protested, the editors were ostensibly sympathetic, but urged him to tone down a projected reply. Bain said that he seemed to be engaged in the same sort of name-calling of which he accused the reviewer. "I think myself that [he] deserves a spanking," Becker added, "but one of the maxims of child training is that one should never spank in anger."[46]

Bernard complied in toning down the personal side, making his reply instead an attack on his old nemesis, the S.R.A., whose members he now described as "particularistic mystical sociologists." One wing denied any regularity in human affairs, and hence the possibility of social control through science. "Many, perhaps most of the sociological mystics are Fascists at heart, and, when they can overcome their repugnance to the espousal of a cause, are so in fact," he continued. In their view, sociology was "a mere esthetic exercise," the universities "a natural product of human stupidity, made to serve the function of providing them with incomes and intellectual amusement." A second type of mystic inhabited the house of science itself: "he often regards himself as a statistical methodologist (and indeed does frequently play with numbers and equations and with fact gathering)." Such sociologists confined their work to "finding out how many Arunta tribesmen are left alive" or constructing methods of predicting presidential votes (Ogburn had once analyzed election statistics, but it is not clear whether he was Bernard's target).[47]

In a draft editorial for *The American Sociologist*—initially entitled "Little Sociologist, What Now?"—Bernard sharpened the attack. The S.R.A., having "drawn ridicule" for the "poverty" of its research and the "mediocrity" of its candidates for election, now proposed to secure its grip on the A.S.S. by creating different categories of members (a proposal at the 1941 meetings). This report would be accepted "by the 'Heil Hitlers' of the Society." So bitter were his feelings that he temporarily succumbed to an adolescent temptation to jibe at the society's initials—A.S.S. The result would be the domination of the society by the S.R.A.'s "Fascistic machine."[48]

Although Bernard's friends persuaded him to delete the reference to the "Heil Hitlers," the charge contained a serious point: idealism and empiricism, despite being philosophically opposed, amounted at the extreme to the same thing. Denying a natural order, the "sociological mystics" despaired of reintroducing order in "this world of chaos" other than through the imposition of an external "dictator," just as the "theologically minded" had earlier turned to "priestly hierarchies." The worship of "fact" led down the same path. Coming from a positivist, the charge against idealism was nothing new. What distinguished it now was the related allegation that the trouble was with positivism itself. "Strange bedfellows indeed!" Bernard commented, thinking again of the cosy alliances within the S.R.A.[49]

In *The Origins of American Sociology* (1942), Bernard made the same point in a more scholarly context, summoning sociological positivism to the radical mission that it had failed to fulfill. "I have watched the decline of Positivism in several countries before the new political and social escape policy," he wrote in a 1942 article in commemoration of Comte's *Positive Philosophy*. "My conclusion is that the Religion of Humanity died because it sacrificed humanity to mere formalism." The positivism of the present had likewise "become a ritual of method and has forgotten the human welfare end it sought to serve."[50]

But did Bernard have anything better to offer? His most direct answer came in *War and Its Causes* (1944). An encyclopedic survey in three sections, the book considered social institutions, the causes of war, and the future of war. By any standard the work was a curious one, especially so from someone who for half a dozen years had been railing against "fascists" in his own profession. Although reviewers differed as to its merits, the critical ones converged on a single point: Bernard's detachment, even pedantry, in face of the monstrous war then raging. "If this book were readable, it would be dangerous," a Harvard historian wrote in the *New York Times*. By blaming "social systems" for war, he put aggressor and defenders on the same level. As a result, "no war appears profitable and no cause good": not the Civil War, not the war against the Axis. Ultimately, he concluded, the fault lay not with Bernard, but with the thrust of modern "objective" scholarship.[51]

In a broader sense, the work dramatized the flaws of Bernard's lifelong quest for an objective standard: his inadequate psychology, his deep antipathy to history, his dismissal of ideals as instruments of something called interpersonal manipulation. The tragedy of his career, if his final bitterness and alienation can be so described, was compounded by the fact that for all his foibles and eccentricities, there was something immensely appealing about the man and his vision. To the many students, colleagues, and friends who loved him, "L.L.B." was an attractive and fascinating human being. However much a product of particular times and circumstances, or however flawed intellectually, his vision of a world attuned to an "objective standard" promised an appealing alternative to the politics of self-gratification and unprincipled pragmatism that was fast becoming a permanent feature of American life.

When Bernard died in 1951 after months of refusing drugs that would diminish the pain of his cancer, his wife Jessie found among his belongings numerous uncashed checks, unspent cash, and more than a dozen dress shirts still in their wrappers. "Money," his friend Read Bain eulogized, "was merely a symbol of an economic system for which he did not have too high a regard." But these possessions were not mere symbols. In his quest for financial security, better clothes, and younger women, Bernard, like some hero of a Dreiser novel, expressed longings that even his poetry could not fully express. So also his vision for society, his "objective standard," meant more than social engineering or a neutral technocracy. "It is the passion and need of the age to see things whole," he once wrote, sounding more like Albion Small than he would have cared to admit. "Sociology is in large measure a response to this demand for effective and functional unity in the world under the guidance of science."[52]

CONCLUSION

Those who cultivate the sciences among a democratic peo-
ple are always afraid of losing their way in visionary
speculation. They mistrust systems; they adhere closely to
facts and study facts with their own senses. . . . Scientific
pursuits then follow a freer and safer course, but a less
lofty one.

Alexis de Tocqueville, 1840

Objectivity is not neutrality, but alienation from self
and society. . . . Objectivity is the way one comes to terms
and makes peace with a world one does not like but will
not oppose.

Alvin Gouldner, 1970

Whatever the personal trials and triumphs of Bernard or of Ogburn, empiricism, quantification, and value-neutrality continued to find defenders and
practitioners in the postwar years. During the 1940s and into the 1950s, the
operationalism of George Lundberg's *Foundations of Sociology* (1939) and his
propagandistic *Can Science Save Us?* (1947) kept alive the issue of science,
values, and reform.[1] While Samuel Stouffer and others built on Ogburn's
work, Paul Lazarsfeld and his associates introduced European traditions of
quantitative work largely unknown or ignored by the interwar objectivists,[2]
although Lazarsfeld himself suggested that Americans mistakenly thought of
such work as characteristically "American."[3] Periodic surveys of the discipline
attested that, whatever the source, it remained a vital force in American
sociology.[4] With a new generation of "radical" sociologists preferring Marx to
Comte, the radical aspect of Bernard's objectivism proved to be a dead end,
although it had an echo of sorts within psychology in B. F. Skinner's *Walden
Two* (1948).

By the late 1940s, there were signs, in any case, that the profession was tiring of the old issues. Robert Merton of Columbia conceded that "empirical" research was valuable not only in testing theory, but in refining it, citing Chapin and Ogburn as examples.[5] The authors of a popular text on "methods" seconded the motion. "At the present writing the conflict has died down," they wrote in 1952 of the battle between "intuitionists" and "neo-positivists." Both the MacIvers and the Ogburns had "contributed greatly to the present level of sociological achievement."[6] Although Sorokin and others kept the humanist tradition alive, and critics of Merton's "middle range" soon emerged, the battles of the thirties, for better or worse, were history.

If interwar objectivism was not entirely a unique episode in American sociology, it was nonetheless a distinct one. Resisting any single explanation, this study has argued that it was a product of the convergence of various factors that shaped the nation's academic culture generally from the 1910s through the 1930s. Socially, it was nourished by the fluidity, and the resulting absence of tradition and community, that increasingly marked American life toward the end of the nineteenth century. To characterize that life in terms of "status" and "nostalgia" is to ignore a more basic element in the lives of many Americans—the lack of the institutional density that in more stable societies defines rules, mediates meanings, and induces the comfortable feeling that society and shared values are a natural and enduring aspect of the human condition. For rootless westerners like Ward (and Ross), or for Sumner, the offspring of recently arrived immigrants, this absence was a daily reality, only partially offset by the cult of "rugged individualism" that was already crumbling by the 1880s. For Small and the early Giddings, it was obscured by the comfortable associations of their youth. For the later objectivists, it assumed new urgency.

Whereas the democracy of nineteenth-century American life sustained a rough empiricism that preferred "facts" over "theory," as Tocqueville observed, it also produced a vision of the irreconcilable opposition of man and nature, self and society, that surfaced in Ward's *Dynamic Sociology*. How are the needs and wants of individuals related to social customs and institutions? Ought a science of society to study motives or outcomes? Answering these questions, Ward's "social forces," Small's "interests," Giddings's "imitation," and even Sumner's "mores" posited some connection between existing values and the social order. For prewar functionalism, social institutions arose to satisfy needs in ways compatible with the well-being of the individual *and* the survival of the group. Hence, for example, monogamy serves to satisfy the sexual instinct *and* to provide care for the young and preservation of the race. Whether called "interests" or "instincts," these social building blocks were typically defined so as to honor traditional assumptions, and were set in the warm embrace of progressive evolutionism. Ostensibly scientific, prewar sociology, in this sense, was also historical and humanist.

The emergence of objectivism, in turn, registered a growing sense of social fragmentation and the absence of common values and standards in the late Progressive Era. This issue was obviously more pressing for some than for others. Among the founders, Sumner—and Giddings, after his breakdown and wartime traumas—sensed its urgency (as did Veblen and Ross, socially the most marginal of the first generation). So even more did the leading objectivists, who not coincidentally came from backgrounds that differed significantly from the comfortable middle-class ones of most eastern and midwestern Progressives half a generation older: Ogburn, the small-town Georgian raised by a widowed mother; Bernard, the son of a ne'er-do-well, mean-spirited Texas farmer; and Chapin, the scion of New York patricians whose fortunes were temporarily in decline. Whereas the celebration of "community" and "social cohesion," one of the several languages of Progressivism, incorporated a nostalgic longing for a past social order, the language of efficiency, rationalization, and social engineering judged the past irredeemably irrelevant.[7]

Objectivism also represented both a rejection and a secularization of nineteenth-century American Protestantism. From Giddings onward, battles over scientific sociology pitted individuals who in one fashion or another had rejected their childhood religion against those who remained faithful to it—the running controversy between Bernard and Ellwood being a dramatic example. By extension, the rejection of the Christian conception of "soul" translated to the behaviorists' repudiation of the "self." But in this very opposition, objectivism was in several ways a secular manifestation of the Protestant spirit. Its vision of an "efficient" social order contained more than a little missionary zeal. So also, the celebration of "hard facts" and the "rigors" of research brought the Protestant Ethic into the era of modern professionalism. Finally, by reifying experience in the manner of behaviorism, the objectivist gained control over self and others, in effect having the exquisite pleasure of playing God while denying His existence.

Protestant denominationalism shaped different readings of Darwin, and finally different definitions of "science" and conceptions of sociology. Roughly speaking, the Baptists, Small and Bernard,[8] the Anglican, Sumner, and even the Calvinist-turned-Unitarian, Ward, never entirely escaped the Baconian belief that the direct observation and classification of experience is the essence of scientific method. The stricter Calvinism of Giddings, Chapin, and Ogburn, in contrast, disposed them to accept the idea that there was an order in nature and society despite the fact that its "causes" cannot be known. Thus the latter three took Darwinian selectionism more seriously, and from it proceeded to a nominalist and statistical conception of natural and social law.

Objectivism was also a byproduct of the professionalization of scholarship, although neither the only nor the inevitable one. Among the many impulses that shaped nineteenth-century professionalism, a prominent one, as Burton Bledstein has argued, was the desire to consolidate and control. From their fascination with "words" (the jargon of the different specialties) to their claims of "autonomy," professionals embodied the Victorian effort "to set apart, regulate, and contain" the different elements of an increasingly chaotic experience, and to transcend the partisan strife that threatened to destroy society and to undermine the recently-won power of the WASP middle class. Offering more than psychic comfort (although this too), the all-embracing standard of science, in Bledstein's words, "provided the *raison d'être* of the middle class . . . and justified its standard of living."[9]

Viewed in this light, objectivism appears, in one sense, to have been an extreme of professionalism, indeed almost a caricature of its open-ended demand for work, its organized procedures for obtaining credentials, and its claim of disinterested service. But the fact that the objectivists in their private lives were less than the model of professional rationality suggests that this regimen exacted its own price. At its most benign, the professionals' bifurcation of self into public and private, scientist and citizen led to escapes in poetry, painting, sports, or travel. At its worst, the jargon of objectivity and disinterested activity masked chaotic inner lives that led Ogburn at one point to psychoanalysis and Bernard to compulsive philandering. For the profession as a whole, the pretense of superior rationality, as Read Bain finally observed, did not rule out often-vicious squabbling and backbiting.

The institutionalization and specialization of sociological scholarship, first within the university and later within foundation-sponsored institutes, also played a part. Within the universities, several factors together narrowed the scope of the discipline, including: the need to defend and define the newcomer against the other social sciences (a circumstance that differed from one university to another); the need to devise easily reproducible "methods" for the training of graduate students, as was early evident in the case of Giddings; and perhaps even the practical realization that grand theory in the style of Spencer or Ward assumed more knowledge than the average undergraduate commanded in the age of free electives. In addition to these pressures, the First World War gave the still-marginal sociologists new incentive to prove their professionalism and public worth, as illustrated particularly in the careers of Ogburn and Chapin.[10]

Political pressures as filtered through university administrators put a premium on "objectivity" in some form, although again objectivism was only one possible strategy. Sumner's run-in with Noah Porter over Spencer's *Study of Sociology* in the early 1880s, for example, was a factor in his drift toward the narrowly inductive approach of *Folkways* (1906). At Chicago, institutional pressures led Small to find some middle way between the promiscuous empiricism of a Bemis, and the potentially socialistic "organic analogies" of his early work. The rise of the foundations and related institutes produced even more restrictive definitions of "research," as again evidenced in the careers of Ogburn and Chapin, not to mention Small's own eleventh-hour celebration of "technique."

The emergence of objectivism, however, also underlines the danger of a too-exclusive emphasis on the professionalization-institutionalization model, particularly in unilinear versions that typically overestimate the strength and success of the process.[11] For the 1880s, evidence of this weakness may be seen in the dream of economists and others of professional associations modeled on the German *Verein für Sozialpolitik*, which would impose strict definitions of science on their disciplines. In the case of economics, and in such departments as Small's at Johns Hopkins, the dream quickly gave way to decentralized and diverse organization. Future sociologists coexisted with historians, and remained yoked to economists, however uneasily, for almost two decades. As a result, sociology remained imperfectly professionalized through the interwar period: uncertain of its boundaries, sensitive to attack, and a tempting target for any group that wished to promote a new paradigm.

Objectivism, rather than being the end product of a unilinear professionalization, was a symptom of this vulnerability. American sociology began as a discipline with no agreed-upon theory or coherent research area; it never dropped the appeal to utility; and it altered its initial boundaries in dramatic ways, first in the triumph of the "group" concept in the 1910s, later with the ascendancy of structural-functionalism in the 1950s, and most recently with the near-anarchy that has obtained since the 1960s. Ward's definition of "pure" sociology, Giddings's emphasis on statistics, and Small's definition of "interests" were episodes in the initial reorientation. Although never a majority position, objectivism was yet another bid to redefine the discipline's boundaries. But the attempt to impose restrictive definitions of sociology within the A.S.S. during the 1930s finally came up against the same centrifugal forces that had earlier kept American scholarship from developing along European lines.

Ideologically, the emergence of objectivism coincided with a growing interest in efficiency, adjustment, and social control. These slogans, in turn, reflected a growing concern with order over freedom, and with how society shapes the individual rather than vice versa. This process began with Ward's concessions concerning the restraining role of religion in the late nineties, and found full expression in the behaviorism of Ogburn, Chapin, and Bernard. Convinced that the tradition of natural law and natural rights was bankrupt, the prewar founders sought various bases for social order, from Charles Horton Cooley's interactionist "social self" to Sumner's "mores" and to Ross's "social control." What distinguished the objectivists was not their concern for order, or even for a basis of authority in science, but their implicit conviction that this order must be imposed from outside, ideally with the help of experts of one sort or another.

Did sociology thus contribute to the "corporatism" that took shape during the twenties?[12] For the founders, the answer is clearly no, despite some pervasive assumptions concerning the benefits of "organization." Ward's radical subjectivism remained closer to the sexual radicalism of Herbert Marcuse than to the corporatism of Adolph Berle or other post-New Deal theorists, despite his later qualifications of this position. Small's blueprint for an ongoing struggle of interest groups pictured the "wealth" interest as one of many. Giddings and Sumner, in their lingering sympathy for laissez-faire, were troubled by precisely the proto-corporatist elements of Progressivism.

For the objectivists themselves the situation is more complicated. If one may distinguish theories of corporatism (whether "liberal" or otherwise) from its emergence in practice, none of the three leading objectivists deserves the label, in the sense of advocating that decisions on social policy be left to a coalition of government and corporate leaders, or that the corporation be the model for governmental organization or policy making. Bernard certainly does not, however vague his notion of a policy-making body of social scientists. And Chapin and Ogburn also do not, in that their position was precisely that the sociologist *as scientist* should not prescribe in the first place. After a year with the N.R.A., Ogburn reported that government-business cooperation was a leading feature of New Deal policy, speculating that it might be the wave of the future. But he also reported that it raised the perennial question of the balance between freedom and order, an issue upon which he would venture no opinion.[13]

As to the emergence of corporatism in practice, however, the case is different. The entire conception of the world as a possible object of prediction and control presupposes that someone will use knowledge to this end, making politics an exercise in finding the most effective means to given ends.[14] In assuming that someone other than the scientist will determine these ends, Ogburn's objectivism appeared to put sociology at the service of the highest bidder, thus setting the stage for a service-intellectual conception of the discipline, which, in the eyes of its critics, had unfortunate consequences in later years.[15]

This creed of value-neutrality reflected neither a reasoned corporatist ideology, nor an uncritical fondness for New Era capitalism. Rather, as Alvin Gouldner has written of the cult of objectivity more generally, it betrayed a distrust of self and alienation from society—"the way one comes to terms and makes peace with a world one does not like but will not oppose."[16] The result was an important difference between the "fact-gathering" of naive empiricism and a consensualist quest for "hard data," however much the two blurred in the sociologists' own discussions of the issue. In the first, the test of truth was the perception of the individual; in the second, it was the agreement of experts. Naive empiricism never entirely disappeared from American sociology (witness Park and his students)—but for the would-be professional it threatened not only to bring in its wake the reckless or undisciplined reformism of the academic radical or social worker, but also to undermine the professional's own authority, resting as it did on the discovery of patterns of which the layperson is unaware.[17] For the objectivists, as the sociologist Michael Schudsen has written of journalism in the same period, a "person's statements about the world can be trusted [only] if they are submitted to established rules and values deemed legitimate by a professional community." Implicit in this view was a distrust of individual judgment, whether exercised in the voting booth or in the market place.[18] From Sumner to Bernard, Giddings to Ogburn, the celebration of objectivity, not coincidentally, was the other side of disillusionment over the workings of American democracy, often compounded by the huckstering excesses of the advertising age. The result was profound doubt in the ability of the average person to know what is good for the individual, let alone for society.

It is easy, in conclusion, to criticize the objectivists: for ignoring the realities of power, exploitation, and class conflict; for narrowing the focus of their discipline to parochial and often trivial concerns; for failing to see the cultural, class, and gender biases of their conception of scientific neutrality; and perhaps even for promoting an apolitical and amoral vision of the role of the sociologist. If Bernard may be exonerated on the last count, he revealed by example the inadequacies of positivism for the creation of a truly radical sociology, virtually admitting as much in his later years. But the spirit behind their program also obviously had a strong appeal, particularly in the United States in the interwar years: perhaps because it proposed to eliminate the arbitrary and the subjective from public life and policy; perhaps because the future for many Americans seemed an improvement on the past; or perhaps because, whatever its own class or cultural biases, "science" seemed the only possible standard in an increasingly pluralistic and fragmented America.

NOTES

ABBREVIATIONS

AGK   Albert G. Keller Papers, Yale
AJS   *American Journal of Sociology*
APS   Anson P. Stokes Papers, Yale
AS   Ward, *Applied Sociology*
ASR   *American Sociological Review*
ATH   Arthur T. Hadley Papers, Yale
AWS   Albion W. Small Papers, Chicago
BPPS   Luther L. Bernard Papers, Penn State
BPUC   Luther L. Bernard Papers, Chicago
CAE   Charles A. Ellwood Papers, Duke
COP   Columbia Official Papers, Columbia
DS   Ward, *Dynamic Sociology*
EAR   Edward A. Ross Papers, Wisconsin Historical Society
FG   Frank Goodnow Papers, Columbia
FSC   F. Stuart Chapin Papers, Minnesota
GS   Small, *General Sociology*
HBA   Herbert Baxter Adams Papers, Johns Hopkins
HWO   Howard W. Odum Papers, Chapel Hill
JBC   John B. Clark Papers, Columbia
LFW   Lester F. Ward Papers, Brown
PASS   *Publication of the American Sociological Society*
PF   Ward, *Psychic Factors in Civilization*
PP   Presidential Papers, Chicago
PS   Ward, *Pure Sociology*
PSQ   *Political Science Quarterly*
RB   Read Bain Papers, Michigan Historical Collections
RP   Robert Park Papers, Chicago
RTE   Richard T. Ely Papers, Wisconsin Historical Society
SDI   Sociology Department Interviews, Chicago
SF   *Social Forces*
WFO   William F. Ogburn Papers, Chicago
WGS   William G. Sumner Papers, Yale
WRH   William R. Harper Papers, Chicago

INTRODUCTION

1. For elaboration of this point see Giddens, *Positivism and Sociology*, pp. 3–4; Bryant, *Positivism*, pp. 1–10.

2. For example, see Bain, "Trends in American Sociology," quoted in Bryant, *Positivism*, pp. 4–5.

3. Eubank, "Errors of Sociology," p. 181, quoted in Hart, "Value-Judgements in Sociology," p. 862.

4. Bryant, *Positivism*, pp. 141–45.

5. See Purcell, *Crisis of Democratic Theory*.

6. For discussion of confusion between "bias" and "psychological" in definitions of "subjectivity" see Rudner, *Philosophy of Social Science*, pp. 73–83.

7. For example, see Schoeck and Wiggins, *Scientism and Values*; Riley, *Values, Objectivity, and the Social Sciences*.

8. MacIver, "Is Sociology a Natural Science?"; Bendix, *Distrust of Reason*.

9. On this point see Rodgers, "In Search of Progressivism," pp. 127–32.

10. For this formulation I am indebted to Rossides, *Sociological Theory*, p. 53. On antiformalism see M. White, *Social Thought in America*.

11. For discussions of the persistence of positivism within sociology see M. J. Vincent, "Trends and Emphases"; Warshay, "Current State."

12. For Gilfillan's debt to Ogburn see Gilfillan, "A Sociologist Looks at Prediction," pp. 5, 24–25; Gilfillan, "An Ugly Duckling's Swan Song." On Duncan, see Mullins and Mullins, *Theories and Theory Groups*, chaps. 7, 9; Wiley, "Recent Journal Sociology." Tracing the roots of "new causal theory," Wiley refers to a "Giddings-Ogburn-Duncan" line of "quantitative positivism." For a critical view of Ogburn's legacy in this regard see Miles and Irvine, "Social Forecasting," p. 311.

13. For "realism" and "nominalism" in sociology see Park and Burgess, *Science of Society*, pp. 36–44; Lewis and Smith, *American Sociology and Pragmatism*, chap. 6; Bryant, *Positivism*, pp. 4–5.

14. For example, see Ogburn, "Folkways."

15. See, for example, Small: "Era of Sociology"; "Scholarship and Social Agitation," p. 581. See also Ross, *Principles of Sociology*, quoted in Hart, "Science and Sociology," p. 366.

16. On this point see H. Kuklick: "Boundary Maintenance in American Sociology," p. 208; "Scientific Revolution."

17. See Giddens, *Positivism and Sociology*; Halfpenny, *Positivism and Sociology*.

18. Hayek, *Counterrevolution of Science*.

19. For example, see Small, *Origins of Sociology*.

20. For example, see Mills, "Professional Ideology."

21. For example, see Oberschall, "Institutionalization"; Haskell, *Professional Social Science*. For discussion of these approaches see Janowitz, "Professionalizing of Sociology"; H. Kuklick, "Restructuring the Past."

22. For example, see Smith, "Rise of Corporate Capitalism"; Schwendinger and Schwendinger, *Sociologists of the Chair*.

23. Matthews, *Quest for an American Sociology*; Bulmer, *Chicago School*.

CHAPTER 1

1. Ward, *DS*, 1:702, 2:203, 1:60.

2. Ward: *DS*, 700; "The Province of Statistics," in *Glimpses*, 2:165, 169–70; *PS*, p. 4.

3. See Ellwood, *Story of Social Philosophy*; Chugerman, *Ward*; Hofstadter, *Social Darwinism*; Burnham, *Ward in American Thought*, and "Ward as a Natural Scientist"; Nelson, *Ward's World View*; E. Becker, *Structure of Evil*, p. 71; Schwendinger and Schwendinger, *Sociologists of the Chair*.

4. Ward: *DS*, 2:100; *Glimpses*, 1:lxxxi.

5. Ward to Emily Cape, October 3, 1910, in Cape, *Ward*, p. 98.

6. Ward, *Glimpses*, 1:lxvi. On Ward's career see Ward, "Personal Remarks," ibid., pp. lviii–lxxxix; Ward, "Autobiography," LFW; Chugerman, *Ward*; Scott, *Ward*.

7. Church, *Education*, p. 57; Fishlow, "The American Common School Revival"; Katz, *Irony*, pp. 213–18.

8. Ward, "Our Aim" [academic essay #30], LFW.

9. Ward: "The Popular Idea" [essay #34], LFW; *Young Ward's Diary*, pp. 82–83. See also "Teacher's Examination" [essay #43], LFW.

10. Ward: *Young Ward's Diary*, p. 10; "Kant's Antinomies."

11. Ward, *Young Ward's Diary*, p. 45.

12. For Ward on Hamilton see Ward, *DS*, 1:3, 404, and 2:93.

13. Ward, "The Human Race" [essay #17]; see also "The Mind" [essay #26], LFW.

14. Ward, "The Day of Miracles" [essay #7]; "The Human Race," LFW.

15. Ward, *Glimpses*, 1:411–12; Scott, *Ward*, pp. 135–42.

16. For this analysis I am indebted to B. Kuklick, *American Philosophy*, pp. 16–21.

17. Ward, *Young Ward's Diary*, pp. 274–76. On Ward's view of women's rights, see Scott, "Women's Reform."

18. Ward, *DS*, 2:93.

19. On the appeal of Kant during the 1870s see B. Kuklick, *American Philosophy*, pp. 105–14, 43, 144–47.

20. Ward: *DS*, 1:404; "Kant's Antinomies"; *DS*, 1:3.

21. Ward, *DS*, 1:144. See also Cashdollar, "European Positivism."

22. Ward, *DS*, 1:159, 89.

23. Ibid., 1:160.

24. Ward, *Young Ward's Diary*, p. 278. On Amasa Walker and Alexander Delmar see Dorfman, *Economic Mind*, 3:98–110.

25. Ward, *Glimpses*, 1:182, 165–67.

26. See especially Ward, *PS*, p. 170.

27. Ward to George M. Beard, ca. September 1879, LFW; Ward, *PS*, p. 47. The exchange with Beard referred to Beard's two articles: "Remarkable Coincidence," and "Experiments."

28. Ward, *DS*, 1:2. Bernard ("Sociological Research," p. 207) attributed Ward's failure to develop a statistical approach to the habits of induction acquired in his work at the Smithsonian.

29. Ward, *Young Ward's Diary*, p. 318.

30. Ward, *Glimpses*, 2:71.

31. Parsons, *The Structure of Social Action*, pp. 113–17: "Behaviorism draws the logical consequence [of Darwinism] in its method. The subjective approach . . . is not only superfluous but illegitimate; it is contrary to the canons of 'objective science.' " On Darwin's implications for nineteenth-century philosophies of science see Hull, "Darwin," and Herbert, "Place of Man."

32. Ward, *DS*, 1:76, 2:260. For a probabilistic reading of Darwin see Winchell, *Science and Religion*, pp. 231–63; Peirce, "Fixation of Belief."

33. Ward, *Glimpses*, 2:81.

34. Ward, *DS*, 1:177–81. On Spencer's formulation see Bannister, *Social Darwinism*, pp. 41–47.

35. Gasman, *Scientific Origins*, pp. xviii–xx.

36. Ward: *Glimpses*, 2:84.

37. Ward, *PF*, p. vi. On the academic and popular aspects of psychology see Lowry, *Psychological Theory*; Meyer, *Positive Thinkers*.

38. Lowry, *Psychological Theory*, chap. 6.

39. James, *Psychology*. For a useful discussion of James's position, see Conkin, *Puritans and Pragmatists*, pp. 280–95.

40. Dewey, "Reflex Arc."

41. Patten, "Biologic Sociology." On Patten see D. M. Fox, *Discovery of Abundance*.

42. Dewey, review of Ward, *PF*.

43. Ibid.

44. Ross to Ward, April 8; Ward to Ross, April 14, 1894, January 1, 1895, in Stern, "Ward-Ross," *ASR* 3:384–85, 388.

45. Ward to Ross, March 4, 1892, ibid., p. 369; James, *Psychology*, marginal notes in 1:181–82, copy in LFW. For Ward's reaction to Dewey's review see Ward, *Glimpses*, 5:24. For his own sources Ward preferred articles such as Nichols, "Origin of Pleasure," and Stanley, "Primitive Consciousness."

46. For a discussion of the impact of Weismann's theories see Bannister, *Social Darwinism*, chap. 7.

47. For examples of his correspondence with leading neo-Lamarckians see letters by the following to Ward: Baker, April 7; John H. Comstock, November 17; Edward Cope, February 2; David Hutcheson, January 11; Henry F. Osborn, January 22, August 17; A. S. Packard, December 10; and John A. Ryder, June 12, 1891, LFW.

48. For this reaction see Ward: "Neo-Darwinism," "Transmission of Culture," "Weismann's New Essays," "Weismann's Theory of Heredity," and "Weismann's Concessions." See also Ward, *PS*, p. 114.

49. On the Romanes address cf. Bannister, *Social Darwinism*, pp. 142–50; Helfand, "Huxley's Evolution and Ethics."

50. On Kidd see Bannister, *Social Darwinism*, pp. 150–63; Crook, *Kidd*.

51. Ward, "The Gospel of Action." See also Ward: *PS*, p. 123, and *AS*, p. 18.

52. Small to Ward, March 12 and July 14, 1894, and March 12, 1895, "Letters," *SF* 12:168–70; Kidd to Ward, August 18, 1894, LFW; Ward, *Outlines*, pp. 28, 131, 186.

53. Kidd, *Social Evolution*, pp. 5, 11.

54. Small to Ward, March 28, 1894, *SF* 12:168.

55. Ward, "Essential Nature of Religion."

56. For the roots of this attitude in Ward's earlier thought see Ward, "Organization." On a shift in Ward's attitude at this time see Foskett, "Ward's *Dynamic Sociology*."

57. Ward, *PS*, p. 135.

58. For this criticism see Gillette, "Critical Points," p. 35.

59. Ward, *PS*, p. xx.

60. Ward, *PS*, pp. 4–7.

61. For examples see Newcomb, "Exact Science" and "Abstract Science"; Rowland, "Pure Science." For discussion of the idea in physical science see Kevles, *Physicists*, chap. 4.

62. Ward, *PS*, pp. 5, 144, 6, 38.

63. Ward, *Glimpses*, 3:232–40, 244–45. On the emergence of applied sociology see Shenton, *Practical Applications*, chap. 4.

64. Gillette, "Critical Points," p. 35.

65. Small, "Notes," p. 570; Ross to Ward, June 25, 1904, in Stern, "Ward-Ross," *ASR* 13:85.

66. Gillette, "Critical Points," pp. 31–67.

67. Bawden, review of Ward, *PS*.

68. Ward to Ross, November 29, 1903, in Stern, "Ward-Ross," *ASR* 12:717–18.

69. Small to Ward, November 24, 1903, in Stern, "Letters," *SF* 15:311–12; Small, "Notes," p. 405.

70. Ross to Ward, July 7, 1904, and Ward to Ross, July 11, 1904, in Stern, "Ward-Ross," *ASR* 13:86–88.

71. Small to Ward, in Stern, "Letters," *SF* 15:315–18; Small, review of Ward, *PS*; Ward, *Glimpses*, 6:145–46; Small to Ross, June 6, 1912, EAR.

72. Odin, *Génèse*. See Ward, *AS*, pp. 147–54.

73. Ward, *AS*, pp. 299–300.

74. Ward, *AS*, pp. 288–90.

75. Ward, *Glimpses*, 6:230.

76. Howard, review of Ward, *AS*; Thorndike, two reviews of *AS*.

77. Hayes, " 'Social Forces' Error," p. 622.

78. Dealey et al., "Ward," p. 66.

CHAPTER 2

1. For this formulation and the examples I am indebted to Dibble, *Small*, pp. 40–46. Although Dibble notes that Small had "less grandiose visions of sociology in his old age" (p. 46), he is concerned with the interrelation of his different views of objectivity with comparison to later sociological theory, rather than the reasons why he increasingly emphasized "technique" and "research" in his later years.

2. Dibble, *Small*, pp. 45, 141–42; Small, "Church," p. 482.

3. Krout, "Small's Sociological Theory," p. 231.

4. For the opinions of Keller and Bernard, see chaps. 8–10 below. Barnes, "Small," in Barnes, *History of Sociology*, pp. 766–92; E. Becker, *Lost Science*, pp. 3–70; Schwendinger and Schwendinger, *Sociologists of the Chair*, pp. 247–54.

5. Becker, *Lost Science*, p. 26; Dibble, *Small*, p. 152.

6. On Small's career see Dibble, *Small*; Hayes, "Albion W. Small."

7. Small to W. R. Harper, March 28, 1891, WRH.

8. Dibble, *Small*, pp. 60–63.

9. Small, review of Dealey and Ward, *Textbook of Sociology*, p. 268.

10. Small and Vincent, *Study of Society*, p. 10.

11. On the American interpretation of Ranke see Iggers, "Image of Ranke."

12. Small: *GS*, p. 19; review of Schmoller, *Grundriss*; "Fifty Years," pp. 807–8. For evidence of how later sociologists viewed the Schmoller-Menger controversy, see Johnson, *Encylopedia*, 10:311, 13:577–78.

13. Small, *Beginnings of American Nationality*, p. 12; review of Small, *Beginnings of American Nationality*; Small, "Von Holst."

14. Small, *Beginnings of American Nationality*, pp. 8, 9.

15. On Johns Hopkins see Hawkins, *Pioneer*.

16. Small to Ely, May 27, 1901, RTE; Small to H. B. Adams, February 26, 1901, HBA.

17. Harper to Small, January 31, 1892, PP. On the University of Chicago see Storr, *Harper's University*; Diner, "Department and Discipline"; Graham, "Preparation for an Event."

18. On Harper see Storr, *Harper's University*, pp. 18ff.

19. Small to H. B. Adams, November 5, 1891, and Adams to Harper, February 15, 1891, HBA; Harper to Ely, March 16, 1891, RTE; Small, "Course of Study," HBA; Small to Harper, February 2, 1892, PP.

20. Small to Harper, October 30, 1891, WRH.

21. University of Chicago, *Catalogue*, p. 187; Storr, *Harper's University*, chap. 11.

22. On these points see Bulmer, *Chicago School*, chap. 2.

23. Small and Vincent, *Study of Society*, pp. 15–20.

24. Ibid., pp. 92, 271, 94.

25. G. Stanley Hall, quoted in Hofstadter and Smith, *American Higher Education*, 2:759; W.B. Smith to C. A. Ellwood, January 13, 1930, CAE. For Small's sensitivity to the charge see "Fifty Years," p. 764.

26. Small and Vincent, *Study of Society*, pp. 320, 32, 77.

27. Bemis to Henry C. Adams, April 4, 1894, quoted in Furner, *Advocacy and Objectivity*, p. 178.

28. Small and Vincent, *Study of Society*, pp. 87, 90. For Small's later assessment of the biological analogy see Small, *Meaning of Social Science*, p. 80.

29. Patten, "Organic Concept"; Patten, review of Small and Vincent, *Study of Society*; Giddings, review of Small and Vincent, *Study of Society*; Review of Small and Vincent, *Study of Society*, p. 351.

30. On the Bemis case see Hofstadter and Metzger, *Academic Freedom*, pp. 153–62; Berquist, "Bemis Controversy," and a longer MS version in PP; Storr, *Harper's University*, pp. 83–85, 96–98, 136, 205, 341; and Furner, *Advocacy and Objectivity*, pp. 163–98.

31. Hofstadter and Metzger, *Academic Freedom*, p. 154; Bemis to Ely, August 13, 1894, RTE; University of Chicago, "A Statement by Professors Small and Butler" [1896], PP.

32. Bemis to Ely, September 29, 1886, RTE. For Laughlin on Bemis see Laughlin to

Harper, August 31, 1893, PP, and August 10, 17, 1894, WRH.

33. Laughlin to Harper, September, 1895, quoted in Furner, *Advocacy and Objectivity*, p. 175.

34. Bemis to Harper, February 26, 1892, WRH; Storr, *Harper's University*, p. 136.

35. Small to Bemis, March 31, and to Harper, May 16, 1892, WRH; Bemis to Ely, January 12, 1895, RTE.

36. Bemis to Ely, January 12, 1895, RTE; Small to Harper, August 27, 1895, PP; University of Chicago, "A Statement By Professors Small and Butler" [1896], PP.

37. Bemis to Ely, March 8, 1895, RTE; Furner, *Advocacy and Objectivity*, p. 181. The effect of the Bemis case was apparent in several book reviews Small wrote soon after; see his review of Crafts, *Practical Christian Sociology*, and review of Bascom, *Social Theory*.

38. Bemis to Ely, January 12, 1895, RTE.

39. Small: "Civic Federation," p. 102; "Era of Sociology," p. 15.

40. Small, "Scholarship and Social Agitation," p. 582.

41. Small, "Academic Freedom," pp. 466, 471.

42. The concept of class-above-class is developed in Watkins, review of Furner, *Advocacy and Objectivity*.

43. Small to Ward, July 25, 1891, in Stern, "Letters," *SF* 12:166.

44. Small, *Some Undeveloped Social Resources*, p. 15. For Small on Kidd see Stern, "Letters," *SF* 12:168–70; Small, review of MacIntosh, *Comte to Benjamin Kidd*.

45. Stern, "Letters," *SF* 15:309; Small, "Category 'Human Process,' " p. 225.

46. Small, "Technique," p. 646.

47. Small, review of Spencer, *Principles of Sociology*, p. 742; Small to Ely, May 21, 1901, RTE.

48. Small: *GS*, p. ix; "Fifty Years," p. 773.

49. Haskell, *Professional Social Science*, pp. 209–10.

CHAPTER 3

1. For useful discussions of *General Sociology* see Aho, *German Realpolitik*; Kress, *Social Science*; Dibble, *Small*.

2. Small, *GS*, chap. 31. See also Dibble, *Small*, pp. 116–17.

3. Small, *GS*, pts. 4–5.

4. On Simmel in the United States see Abel, "Simmel"; Levine, "Simmel's Influence," pp. 1112–32.

5. On the history of "process" theory see Arendt, "Concept of History."

6. On this point see R. Adams, "Social Unity."

7. Small, *GS*, pp. 461–64, 39.

8. Ibid., p. 303.

9. Ibid., p. 535. On the reaction of one older disciple of Ward see Frank Blackmar, review of Small, *GS*, p. 148.

10. Small to Ross, April 22, 1903, EAR; Small, *GS*, p. 88.

11. Ellwood, "Prolegomena to Social Psychology"; R. Adams, "Social Unity"; Small to Ross, December 19, 1901, EAR.

12. Small: *GS*, p. 433; "Points of Agreement."

13. Ward, "Contemporary Sociology."

14. Small, *GS*, p. 184; review of Small, *General Sociology*.

15. Small, "Relation between Sociology and Other Social Sciences," pp. 11–13.

16. American Historical Association, "Meeting at New Orleans," pp. 448–50; Small to Ross, November 23, 1905, EAR; and G. B. Adams, "History and the Philosophy of History."

17. Robert Hoxie, "Sociology," p. 753.

18. Ibid.

19. Sutherland to Bernard, November 24, 1912, BPPS.

20. On Bentley see Kress, *Social Science*; Hale, "Bentley"; Dowling, "Pressure Group Theory"; James F. Ward, "Bentley."

21. Bentley, *Process of Government*, pp. 26–37.

22. Small, review of Bentley, *Process of Government*.

23. Ibid.

24. Small, "Relations of the Social Sciences."

25. For Small's support of T.R. see Small to John Burgess, September 8, 1904, AWS; Small to Ross, October 15, 1912, EAR.

26. Small, "Evolution," p. 14.

27. Small, "Some Structural Material," p. 270.

28. Small: "Vision of Social Efficiency," p. 433; "Shall Science be Sterilized?"

29. Small, *Between Eras*, p. 427.

30. On Chicago sociology in this period see R. Faris, *Chicago Sociology*, chap. 1; Diner: "Department and Discipline," and *A City and Its Universities*. On the economics department see Coats, "Origins of the 'Chicago School(s).'"

31. Bogardus, *Much Have I Learned*, p. 4.

32. Bogardus, "Autobiography," p. 4, BPPS; Sutherland to Bernard, January 31, 1913, BPPS.

33. E. H. Sutherland, "Autobiography," BPPS.

34. Sutherland to Bernard, November 24, 1912, BPPS.

35. Sutherland to Bernard, May 27, 1912, BPPS.

36. Sutherland to Bernard, October 23, November 24, 1912, BPPS.

37. Sutherland to Bernard, January 31, 1913, BPPS.

38. Sutherland to Bernard, May 11, 1913, BPPS.

39. Sutherland to Bernard, May 11, 1913, BPPS.

40. Sutherland to Bernard, April 26, 1915, BPPS.

41. Sutherland to Bernard, November 24, 1912, BPPS.

42. Small to Bernard, April 12, 1915, BPPS. See also Small, "Fifty Years," pp. 804–6.

43. Small, "Americans and the World Crisis," p. 148. On Small's role in the St. Louis Exposition see Coats, "American Scholarship."

44. Small: "Americans and the World Crisis," pp. 169, 158; "Germany and American Opinion," p. 110.

45. Small, *Origins of Sociology*, p. 32.

46. On the Thomas case, and Small's reaction, see Bulmer, *Chicago School*, pp. 59–60.

47. Thomas and Znaniecki, *Polish Peasant*; Park and Burgess, *Science of Society*, p. 45.

48. Sutherland to Bernard, April 26, 1915, BPPS.
49. Small, "Technique."
50. Small, "Category 'Human Process.' "
51. Ibid., pp. 207–9.
52. Small, "Category 'Progress.' "
53. Small: "Fifty Years," pp. 860–61; *Origins of Sociology*, pp. 349–51.
54. On the formation of the L.C.R.C. see Bulmer, *Chicago School*, chap. 8; Small, "What Should be the Idea of Our Own Graduate School of Social Science," paper read February 28, 1923, quoted in ibid., pp. 132–33. Small referred to a "federated search after knowledge" in "Technique," p. 650.
55. Small, "Some Researches into Research."

CHAPTER 4

1. Small to Ward, March 3, 1896, in Stern, "Giddings," p. 308.
2. [Giddings?], "Sociology in the Universities"; Small to Ward, April 10, 1895, in Stern, "Letters," *SF* 12:171; Giddings, review of Small and Vincent, *Science of Society*; Giddings to Ward, April 15, 1896, in Stern, "Giddings," p. 310.
3. Small, review of Giddings, *Elements of Sociology*; Martindale, *Nature and Types*, pp. 305–38.
4. Hofstadter, *Social Darwinism*, p. 134; Oberschall, "Institutionalization," pp. 225–32; Northcott, "Giddings," p. 764. For the literature on Small see chapter 2 above.
5. On Giddings's career see Tenney, "Giddings"; Hankins, "Giddings"; Gillin, "Giddings"; Page, *Class and American Sociology*, chap. 5; and Davids, "Giddings: Forgotten Pioneer"; Northcott, "Sociological Theories."
6. On this point see Moore, *Post-Darwinian Controversies*, pp. 346–51.
7. On Springfield in this period see Frisch, *Town into City*. For Giddings's view of the labor question see Giddings, "Three Phases." On the Cooperative movement see Rodgers, *Work Ethic*, pp. 40–45. On Giddings's position see Giddings: "Cooperation," p. 531; "Cost Production of Capital"; and review of Ely et al., *History of the Cooperative Movement*.
8. Giddings, "Theory of Profit Sharing," p. 367.
9. Giddings to Ely, November 2, 1886, March 22, 1889, October 6, 1888, RTE.
10. Giddings to J. B. Clark, October 24, 1886, JBC; Giddings, "Ethics of Socialism," p. 239.
11. Giddings, "Natural Rate of Wages," pp. 620–21.
12. Giddings, "Sociological Character."
13. On Jevons see Jevons, *Theory*; Giddings, "Sociological Character," p. 35. For the increasing popularity of deduction among economists in these years see Furner, *Advocacy and Objectivity*, pp. 185–90.
14. Black, "Introduction," in Jevons, *Theory*, p. 20.
15. Giddings's earlier publications included "Theory of Sociology," "Province of Sociology," and "Sociology as a University Study."
16. Giddings, *Principles*, pp. 16–20.
17. Ibid., pp. vxi, 12.
18. Ibid., pp. 64–67, 417. On Lewes see Tjoa, *Lewes*.

19. On Giddings's use of the Method of Difference see Martindale, *Nature and Types*, p. 320. For its later influence see Easthope, *History of Social Research Methods*, pp. 24–47.

20. On Columbia see Ralph G. Hoxie et al., *History*; Tenney, "Columbia," BPUC; Oberschall,"Institutionalization," pp. 225–32. Furner (*Advocacy and Objectivity*, pp. 282–91) has suggested that Columbia's tradition of public administration fostered an emphasis on the procedures required to implement established policies, rather than to set policy goals.

21. "Doctorates Conferred by American Universities."

22. On social work see Robert Divine, "Autobiography," BPUC; "Samuel Lindsay," in J. T. White, *National Cyclopedia*, 12:374.

23. Giddings, "Sociology as a University Study," p. 635. For the resulting conceptions of the discipline see Giddings: "Relation of Sociology to other Scientific Studies," "Province of Sociology," and "Concepts and Methods."

24. Small, review of Giddings, *Principles*.

25. Giddings, "Sociological Character," p. 31.

26. Giddings, *Principles*, pp. 412, 414.

27. For explicit discussion of the concept of natural selection see especially Giddings, review of Pearson, *Chances of Death*.

28. Giddings, *Democracy and Empire*, p. 45.

29. See for example Small to Ward, June 4, 1896, in Stern, "Giddings," p. 313; Ward, review of Giddings, *Principles*.

30. Ross to Ward, July 1, 1896, in Stern, "Ward-Ross," *ASR* 3:397; Small, review of Giddings, *Elements of Sociology*, p. 552; Small to Ward, November 12, 1900, in Stern, "Letters," *SF* 14:105.

31. Means, review of Giddings, *Principles*, p. 92; Small to Ward, March 3, 1896, in Stern, "Letters," *SF* 13:325; Small, review of Giddings, *Principles*. See also Small to Giddings, May 5, 1896, in Stern, "Giddings," p. 311. For the later exchange see Giddings, *Principles*, pp. xvi–xvii; Small to Ward, May 22, 1896, in Stern, "Letters," *SF* 13:338.

32. Ward, review of Giddings, *Principles*; Ross, review of Giddings, *Principles*. See also Ross to Ward, March 29, 1896, in Stern, "Ward-Ross," *ASR* 3:392–93.

33. Giddings to Small, May 10, 1896, in Stern, "Ward-Ross," *ASR* 3:312.

CHAPTER 5

1. For example, see Giddings, "Sociology as a University Study," p. 652; Small to Harper, December 29, 1894, PP.

2. B. J. Norton, "Pearson and Statistics," p. 10.

3. Giddings, *Inductive Sociology*, p. 22.

4. Ellwood, review of Giddings, *Inductive Sociology*; Peirce: "Fixation of Belief," and review of *Inductive Sociology*.

5. On Tenney see Taft, "Tenney."

6. Tenney, "Columbia," BPUC; Chapin quoted in Althouse, *Chapin*, p. 275; Malcolm Willey, interview with Ronald Althouse, April 3, 1963, FSC.

7. Others included Hobart (James M. Williams, 1906), Kenyon (Arthur C. Hall, 1901), Oberlin (Newell Sims, 1913), and Western Reserve (Charles E. Gehlke, 1914).

8. Lichtenberger, "Giddings."

9. Giddings: "Political Program"; "American Idea," p. 1702; "Social and Legal Aspects of Compulsory Education"; "Laws of Evolution"; and "Mr. Bryan and the Complex Social Order"; Giddings to F. P. Keppel, July 31, 1906, COP. See also Giddings to Ellwood, May 22, 1909, CAE.

10. Giddings, *Theory of Socialization*, p. 44.

11. Soule, *American Village Community*, pp. 86–88; Gillin, *Dunkers*, p. 199; Todd, *Sociological Study*, p. 106.

12. Todd, *Sociological Study*, p. 110; Jones, *Sociology of a New York City Block*, p. 133.

13. Giddings, "Social Marking System." See also Giddings, "Measurement of Social Pressure."

14. Giddings, "Social Pressure and Moral Weather."

15. Arner, *Consanguineous Marriages*, p. 88; Parmelee, *Inebriety in Boston*, p. 7. Woofter, *Negro Migration*, was the first Columbia sociology thesis to employ the correlation coefficient. See Easthope, *History of Social Research Methods*.

16. Giddings to N. M. Butler, March 7, 1911, and April 22, 1912, COP.

17. Giddings to Frank Goodnow, March 20, 1914, FG.

18. Giddings, *Pagan Poems*, pp. 77, vii.

19. Giddings: "Failure of *Sittlichkeit*"; "Mannerless Age"; "Will Puritanism Remain?"

20. Giddings: "Trusts," "Future of the Railroads," and "Industrial Commission Reports"; Giddings to Paul Kellogg, January 16, 1915, Wald Papers, Columbia University.

21. Giddings, "Moral Reactions of the War"; Gruber, *Mars and Minerva*, p. 205; Review of Giddings, *Responsible State*; Giddings, "Bolsheviki Must Go."

22. Giddings: "Ohio Idea," "Camouflanguage," "Price," and "Women, Clothes, and Race Salvation." For a similar analysis of Mencken see Cowing, "Mencken."

23. Giddings: *Scientific Study*, pp. 256, 191; *Mighty Medicine*, p. 59.

24. Hankins, "Giddings," p. 359; Giddings, *Scientific Study*, p. 26.

25. Giddings, *Studies*, pp. 226, 228; cf. *Democracy and Empire*, pp. 71, 73. On Spencer's revisions see Bannister, *Social Darwinism*, pp. 50–56.

26. Giddings, *Scientific Study*, p. 167.

27. Ibid., pp. 142, 190, 91; Giddings, "Intensive Sociology."

28. *Springfield Republican*, April 24, 1925, p. 3; *Boston Transcript*, May 16, 1925, p. 3, quoted in *Book Review Digest*, 21 (1925): 256–57.

29. Bernard, review of Giddings, *Studies*; Lundberg, review of Giddings, *Studies*.

30. F. S. Chapin, review of Giddings, *Scientific Study*; Willey and Willey, "Conditioned Reflex"; Hankins, "Giddings," p. 367.

31. On these studies see Easthope, *History of Social Research Methods*, pp. 133–34; Tenney, "Columbia," BPUC.

32. Martindale, *Nature and Types*, p. 321.

CHAPTER 6

1. Sumner: "Sociology as a College Subject," in *Challenge*, pp. 408, 410; "The Scientific Attitude of Mind" [1905], in *Earth-Hunger*, p. 20; "Purposes and Consequences" [ca. 1900–06], in *Earth-Hunger*, p. 67.

2. Sumner, *Earth-Hunger*, p. 18.

3. Chapin, *Education*, p. 5 ; Bernard, "Toward an Objective Standard," p. 530.

4. See Hofstadter, *Social Darwinism*, chap. 3; Bannister, *Social Darwinism*, chap. 5. The persistence of the conventional view can be seen in Garson and Maidnet, "Social Darwinism."

5. See Starr, *Sumner*, p. 147.

6. Sumner, "The Application of the Notions of Evolution and Progress on the Superorganic Domain" (n.d.), quoted in Hinkle, *Founding Theory*, p. 215, and discussed in n. 1, pp. 345–46. I am indebted to Hinkle for clarifying the relation of Sumner and Keller. See also Hinkle and Smith, "Sumner versus Keller."

7. On Sumner's career see Starr, *Sumner*; Curtis, *Sumner*.

8. Sumner's letters to Jennie Elliott are in WGS; Starr (*Sumner*, pp. 535–36) describes his affection for children.

9. Sumner, "Tradition and Progress," January 14, 1872, quoted in Starr, *Sumner*, p. 147. Although I have examined all these sermons in the Sumner Papers, I cite Starr for more convenient reference.

10. On Yale see Pierson, *Yale College*; Kelley, *Yale*.

11. Martineau, *Illustrations*, 1:ix; William C. Whitney to Sumner, ca. 1872, quoted in Starr, *Sumner*, pp. 155–57; Henry Holt to Sumner, May 19, 1885, WGS.

12. On the difficulty of Sumner's decision to study in Germany see Thomas Sumner to Sumner, ca. November, 1863, and E. R. Beadle to Sumner, October 31, 1863, quoted in Starr, *Sumner*, p. 56.

13. "Sketch of William Graham Sumner," in Sumner, *Challenge*, p. 7.

14. Buckle, *History of Civilization in England*, 1:3, 23.

15. Ibid., 1:16, 455, 459.

16. Sumner, "Sketch," p. 8 (see above, n. 13).

17. For the clerical stage of Sumner's career see Sheketoff, "Sumner."

18. Sumner, "Truth," February 21, 1869, quoted in Starr, *Sumner*, p. 151; Sumner to Jennie Elliott, 1870, WGS; Sumner, "Memorial Day Address" [1872] in Sumner, *Challenge*, pp. 347–62.

19. Sumner: "Rationalism," 1871 [sermon #72], and "Church's Law," April 3, 1872, WGS. See also Bannister, *Social Darwinism*, pp. 101–2.

20. Sumner, "Crisis of the Protestant Episcopal Church."

21. Sumner, "Introductory Lecture," in Sumner, *Challenge*, pp. 391–403.

22. Sumner, "American Finance."

23. Sumner: *Forgotten Man*, pp. 213, 225; "Roscher's Political Economy."

24. Sumner, "Sociology" [1881], in Sumner, *War*, p. 180. See also Bellomy, *Sumner*, pp. 284–91.

25. For example, Sumner, "Socialism." See also Bellomy, *Sumner*, pp. 588–90; Sumner, review of Spencer, *Descriptive Sociology*.

26. Starr, *Sumner*, chap. 15; Hofstadter and Metzger, *Academic Freedom*, pp. 335–

38; Heyl and Heyl, "Sumner-Porter Controversy."

27. Porter, *American Colleges*, p. 226; Heyl and Heyl, "Sumner-Porter Controversy," pp. 43–45; Porter to Sumner, December 6, 1879, quoted in Starr, Sumner, p. 346.

28. Sumner to the Yale Corporation, June 1881, quoted in Starr, *Sumner*, pp. 357–66; Sumner, "Sociology" (see above, n. 24), pp. 167–92. See also Sumner, "Professor Sumner's Speech."

29. Sumner, "Sociology" (see above, n. 24), p. 191. Sumner almost immediately was drawn into controversy over the legitimate use of Darwinian metaphors applied to society, an episode that again warned him of the perils of "speculation" in science.

30. Bellomy, "Sumner," pp. 649–51. Other assigned readings in these courses included August Rauber's *Urgeschichte des Menschens* (1884), Friedrich Ratzel's *Volkerkunde* (3 vols., 1885–88), and Julius Lippert's *Kulturgeschichte der Menschheit* (2 vols., 1886–87), the last a major influence on *Folkways*.

31. Sumner, *What Social Classes Owe*, pp. 11–12, 23.

32. Ibid., pp. 14, 113, 127. Marginalia in copy in my possession.

33. For example, see Sumner, "Some Natural Rights," in Sumner, *Earth-Hunger*, pp. 222–27. For a similar view of Sumner see McCloskey, *American Conservatism*, chaps. 2–3.

34. Sumner, "Doctrine of Survival Again." For a detailed account see Bannister, *Social Darwinism*, chap. 5.

35. Sumner, *What Social Classes Owe*, p. 156.

36. For example, see Sumner: "Industrial War," in Sumner, *Challenge*, p. 93; and "An Old Trust" [1889], in Sumner, *Forgotten Man*, pp. 265–69.

37. See especially a series of articles in the *Independent* reprinted in Sumner, *Earth-Hunger*, pp. 131–206.

38. Sumner: "The Challenge of Facts," in Sumner, *Challenge*, pp. 17–52; *Folkways*, p. 18.

39. Sumner, "The Absurd Effort to Make Over the World," in Sumner, *War*, pp. 195–210.

40. Donald C. Bellomy, "Relativism and Modernism in Sumner's *Folkways*," unpublished manuscript, n.d. [ca. 1979]. I am indebted to Professor Bellomy for providing me a copy of this essay and of his dissertation.

CHAPTER 7

1. Curtis, *Sumner*, pp. 56–57.

2. Keller, *Reminiscences*, pp. 6–7, 60.

3. Curtis, *Sumner*, p. 52.

4. Ibid., pp. 55, 113–20; Sumner, "The Conquest of the United States by Spain" [1898], in Sumner, *War*, p. 734.

5. Sumner, "Mores of the Present and Future" [1909], in Sumner, *War*, p. 162

6. Sumner: "Conquest" (see above, n. 4), p. 299; "War" [1903], in Sumner, *War*, p. 40; "Purposes and Consequences" [1900–06], in Sumner, *Earth-Hunger*, p. 68.

7. Sumner, *Earth-Hunger*, p. 73.

8. Keller to Ross, November 3, 1915, EAR; J. P. Norton, "Talks with a Great Teacher"; Keller, *Reminiscences*, p. 84; Sumner to Keller, July 7, 1906, quoted in Curtis, *Sumner*, pp. 55–56.

9. Sumner: "Autobiographical Sketch" [1903], in Sumner, *Earth-Hunger*, pp. 4–5; "Mores of the Present" (see above, n. 5), pp. 160–61. For further discussion of Sumner's *fin de siècle* pessimism see Curtis, "Sumner and the Problem of Progress."

10. Keller, *Reminiscences*, pp. 2–3; Hadley to Keller, December 13, 1910, AGK; Keller to Ross, October 17, 1916, EAR. The following interpretation of Keller's relationship with Sumner is indebted to Hinkle and Smith, "Sumner versus Keller."

11. Keller to Sumner, April 21, 1897, WGS. See also Keller to Julius C. Peter, April 15, 1912, AGK.

12. Keller to Sumner, August 29, 1901; January 2 [1902], WGS.

13. Keller to Sumner, July 3, August 3, 27, 1903; July 21, 1907, WGS.

14. Keller, "Sociology and Science"; and see letter commenting by Irving Babbitt in same volume, p. 620.

15. Keller, *Societal Evolution*, p. 329.

16. Sumner and Keller, *Science of Society*, chap. 61.

17. Irving Fisher to Sumner, n.d. [ca. August 1903], and August 31, 1903, WGS; Sumner, *Folkways*, p. 54.

18. Sumner, "Mores and Statistics and Mathematics" [ca. 1900–06], WGS. Keller shared this view of statistics: see Keller, "Luck Element"; Sumner and Keller, *Science of Society*, p. 2172.

19. Sumner, "Application of the Notions of Evolution," WGS; Sumner to Keller, March 20, 1908, WGS.

20. Keller, *Societal Evolution*, pp. 328–30; Keller to Lohmann, August 16, 1928, APS.

21. Sumner, "The Scientific Attitude of Mind" [1905], in *Earth-Hunger*, p. 20. For an illuminating discussion of Sumner's relation to the "New Haven" scholars of the nineteenth century in this regard see Stevenson, *Scholarly Means*, pp. 85–86.

22. Henry Farnam to Ely, February 8, 1910, RTE.

23. Kelley, *Yale*, p. 343.

24. For Keller's reactions to "publish or perish" see Keller to Anson Phelps Stokes, April 9, 1908, February 12, 1914, APS.

25. Sumner to Keller, July 13, 1904, WGS; Keller to Julius C. Peter, November 18, 1922, April 28, May 10, 1921, AGK. See also Keller to E. G. Bourne, February 27, 1907, AGK; Keller to Julius C. Peter, May 10, November 3, 1919, AGK; Keller to Hadley, May 13, 1907, ATH.

26. For a discussion of the "liberal culture" ideal see Veysey, *Emergence of the American University*, chap. 4.

27. Keller to Sumner: August 27, 1903; and n.d. [ca. March 1908], WGS.

28. Keller to Sumner, n.d. [ca. March 1908], and Sumner to Keller, March 20, 1908, WGS. For this reason, Keller objected to the label "social Darwinism" as applied to Sumner. See Keller, "What Did Darwin Really Say?" p. 8.

29. Keller to Sumner, August 27 [1903], WGS; Keller, "Sociology and Science," p. 475.

30. Keller to Ross, October 17, 1916, EAR; Keller, *Reminiscences*, p. 55.

31. Keller to Sumner, July 3, 1901, WGS; Keller to Julius C. Peter, March 8, 1915, AGK; Keller to Sumner, July 3, 1901, August 1, 1908, WGS. See also Keller to Sumner, n.d. [ca. 1908], WGS, for a softening of Keller's attitude toward Ross.

32. Sumner, *Folkways*, chap. 1.

33. Ibid., p. 81. On Sumner's research techniques see Keller, *Reminiscences*, pp. 16, 33–38.

34. Sumner, *Folkways*, p. 80; Ellwood to Harry E. Barnes, April 15, 1926, CAE.

35. Sumner, *Folkways*, pp. 65–66.

36. Sumner, *Folkways*, pp. 50–56. For this analysis I am indebted to Donald C. Bellomy, "Relativism and Modernism in Sumner's *Folkways*," unpublished MS., n.d. [ca. 1979]. For fuller discussion of Sumner's distinction between the "anterior" and "posterior" assessment of mores, see Bannister, *Social Darwinism*, pp. 111–13. The fact that this distinction effectively applied an evolutionary test to the mores without acknowledging so, simply underlines how strong were the pressures that led Sumner to reject evolutionism.

37. Sumner, *Folkways*, pp. 173–74.

38. Sumner: *Folkways*, pp. 55, 114; "Purposes and Consequences," WGS, quoted in Bellomy, "Relativism and Modernism" (see above, n. 36), p. 17.

39. For criticism of Sumner along these lines see Lemert, "Folkways and Social Control."

40. Bellomy, "Relativism and Modernism" (see above, n. 36).

41. G. Vincent, review of Sumner, *Folkways*. See also Berkowitz, review of Sumner, *Folkways*; C. H. Hawes, review of Sumner, *Folkways*; C. S. Day to Keller, n.d. [ca. 1909], AGK.

42. Hinkle, *Founding Theory*, pp. 282–83. "Incipient" because, as Hinkle correctly notes, Sumner waffled between a "realist" and a "nominalist" definition of science.

43. List of doctoral candidates compiled from Lunday, *Sociology Dissertations*.

44. Keller to Anson Phelps Stokes, May 8, 1917, APS. For Fairchild's career at Yale see also J. E. Cutler to Keller, December 24, 1915, and M. R. Davie to Keller, June 26, 29, 1918, AGK.

45. See Lumley, "Autobiography," in BBPS and in BPUC.

46. G. Vincent, review of Sumner, *Folkways*; Small, "Fifty Years," p. 732.

47. Cooley, "Sumner and Methodology"; Park, "Social Methods." See also Park, "Sumner's Conception of Society."

48. Park, "Social Methods." For a similar evaluation see Murdock, "Science of Culture," p. 305.

49. Bernard, "Transition to an Objective Standard," p. 530.

CHAPTER 8

1. Odum, *American Sociology*, p. 161.

2. Small to Frank D. Fackenthal, February 4, 1914, BPPS.

3. Bernard, "Invention," p. 21.

4. On Bernard's career see Bain, "Bernard"; Brooks, "Bernard"; Odum, "Obituary." A recent scholarly treatment, which appeared after the present study was substan-

tially completed, is Vidich and Lyman, *American Sociology*, chap. 11. The best source of biographical information, however, is the Bernard Papers, Pennsylvania State University (BPPS).

5. Bernard to Hiram H. Bernard, February 5, 1919, February 27, 1922; and to Helen Bernard, August 9, 10, 1919, BPPS.

6. Bernard, "Theory of Rural Attitudes," p. 631.

7. Frances Bernard to Bernard, August 4, 1914; Helen Bernard to Bernard, August 20, 1923, April 5, 1934; Bernard to Helen Bernard, February 5, 1919; and Bernard to H. H. Bernard, February 6, 1919, BPPS.

8. Helen Bernard to Bernard, April 5, 1934, BPPS.

9. Bernard, "Edmondson and Hale" [faculty sketch], BPPS.

10. Ibid.

11. Bernard, untitled MS [ca. 1936], BPPS.

12. Bernard to Helen Bernard, August 9, 1919, BPPS.

13. On Ellwood see Barnes, "Ellwood"; Whitaker, "Ellwood." Ellwood's later career is discussed in chapter 14 below.

14. Bernard, "Charles A. Ellwood" [faculty sketch], BPPS.

15. Bernard to Ellwood, October 10, 1941, August 17, 1946, CAE.

16. Bernard: "Max Sylvius Handman" [faculty sketch], and "William I. Thomas," BPPS.

17. Bernard, "The Pragmatic Significance of Small's Classification of Interests" [n.d.: attached to Bernard to Small, October 12, 1910], BPPS.

18. Bernard, "Social Psychology Studies Adjustment Behavior."

19. For a similar analysis of the more extreme behaviorism of John B. Watson see Bakun, "Behaviorism"; Creelan, "Watsonian Behaviorism."

20. Bernard, "My Wild Heart," 1905, BPPS; Bernard to Frances Bernard, October 24, 1921, BPPS.

21. Bernard, "George Vincent" [faculty sketch], BPUC.

22. Small to Charles Richmond (president of Union College), February 6, 1913, and Bernard to Small, April 6, 1914, BPPS.

23. Bernard, "Vincent" (above, n. 21).

24. Bernard, "Thomas" (above, n. 16).

25. Bernard, "Charles Horton Cooley" [faculty sketch], BPUC.

26. Bernard, "Charles R. Henderson" [faculty sketch], BPPS.

27. Bernard, "Albion W. Small" [faculty sketch], BPPS.

28. Bernard to Small, October 12, 1910, BPPS.

29. Ibid.

30. Bernard, "Thomas" (above, n. 16), pp. 13–14.

31. Bernard, "Transition to an Objective Standard," pp. 171, 174, 341.

32. Ibid., pp. 177, 326; Bernard, "Small" (above, n. 27), p. 7.

33. Bernard, "Transition to an Objective Standard," pp. 521, 532, 340.

34. Ibid., p. 197.

35. Ibid., pp. 531–34.

36. Bernard, "Henderson" (above, n. 26), pp. 11–12.

37. Small to Bernard, April 4, 1916, BPPS.

38. Hayes, review of Bernard, "Transition." On Hayes's "realism" see Lewis and Smith, *American Sociology and Pragmatism*, pp. 180–84.

39. Hayes, "Some Social Relations Restated," pp. 344–45. See also his "'Social Forces' Error," and *Introduction to the Study of Sociology*, chaps. 1–2.

40. Sutherland to Bernard, April 26, August 13, 1915, BPPS.

41. Sutherland to Bernard, August 13, 1915, BPPS.

42. Sutherland to Bernard, February 2, 1916, BPPS.

43. Sutherland to Bernard, April 20, 1916, BPPS; Bernard, review of Moody, *Social Adaptation*; Bernard to Small, April 2, 1916, BPPS.

44. Bernard to Small, May 4, 1920, BPPS; Bernard, "Ellwood" (above, n. 14).

45. Bernard, "Handman" (above, n. 16), pp. 6–8.

46. Bernard to Frances Bernard, August 21, 1921, BPPS.

47. Bernard, "Family," pp. 436–41.

48. Bernard to Frances Bernard, August 21, 1921, BPPS.

49. Bernard to Frances Bernard, September 10, 1919, BPPS.

CHAPTER 9

1. Martindale, *Romance*, chaps. 1–2; Gray, *University of Minnesota*, p. 182. For Todd's negative reaction to these developments see Arthur Todd to A. G. Keller, January 25, 1917, AGK.

2. Bernard to Ross, July 2, 1919, EAR.

3. Bernard to Small, May 4, 1920, BPPS.

4. Small to Bernard, May 27, and Ross to Bernard, May 28, 1921, BPPS.

5. Bernard to Small, June 20, 1922, BPPS.

6. Bernard to Ross, November 29, 1926, EAR; Chapin to Bernard, August 1, 1924, and Bernard to Chapin, August 19, 1924, BPPS.

7. Chapin to Bernard, August 11, 1924; Bernard to Chapin, August 19, 1924, BPPS.

8. Bernard to Frances Bernard [n.d.; ca. autumn 1921], BPPS. See also letter of August 8, 1921, BPPS.

9. Student to Bernard, November 24, 1922, BPPS.

10. Jessie Ravage [Bernard] to Bruce Melvin, ca. May 1925, and Bernard to Melvin, May 4, 1925, BPPS.

11. Bernard, "The Journal of an Intimate Affair," BPPS.

12. Bernard to Miss X, August 20, 1921, BPPS. Bernard continued: "but what I fear most is that if you deny yourself its expression you will grow away from me."

13. Bernard, "Attitudes," pp. 47, 48, 52, 57.

14. Ibid., pp. 48, 52, 57.

15. Bernard to Mary Marjorie Bernard, January 15, 1939, BPPS.

16. Chapin to L. D. Coffman, January 17, 1925; Chapin to Bernard, January 17, 1925, BPPS. Bernard (to Moore C. Tussey, November 29, 1926, BPPS) denied that he had been fired from Minnesota. Bernard (to Robert Park, November 26, 1926, BPPS) also gave a detailed account of his career at Minnesota, perhaps in connection with his still-hoped-for appointment at Chicago.

17. Bernard to Ross, December 26, 1926, BPPS. Among the many other letters on this issue in the Bernard Papers see Bruce Melvin to Bernard, April 29; Bernard to Melvin, May 4; Melvin to Dwight Sanderson, May 4; Bernard to Melvin, May 6;

Manuel Elmer to Melvin, May 6; and Bernard to Melvin, May 7, 1925; Bernard to Hankins, December 25, 1926; and Bernard to Ross, November 29, 1929, BPPS.

18. John F. Markey to Bernard, April 10; Edward Reuter to Bernard, January 11, 1926; and Bernard to Sanderson, September 6, 1926, BPPS; Jesse Steiner to Howard Odum, June 13, 1927, HWO.

19. Cecil North to Bernard, November 7, 1925, BPPS; Todd to Ross, January 5, 1926, EAR; Ellwood to Bernard, July 20, 1926, BPPS.

20. Ross to Todd, January 7, 1927, EAR.

21. Bernard, "Objective Viewpoint."

22. Bernard: "Function of Generalization," and "Method of Generalization," p. 345.

23. Bernard, "Method of Generalization," pp. 348–50.

24. Cooley, "Moderate Behaviorism."

25. Bernard to the *Nation*, September 18, 1925, BPPS; Bernard, *Instinct*, p. 524.

26. Bernard, *Instinct*, pp. 73, 515.

27. Bernard, "Invention," p. 32.

28. Cooley, "Moderate Behaviorism"; Hankins, review of Bernard, *Instinct*.

29. Bernard to the *Nation*, September 18, 1925; Hankins to Bernard, November 3, 1925; and Bernard to Harry E. Barnes, January 16, 1929, BPPS. The fact that Hankins reportedly gossiped that Bernard was "fired" from Minnesota and "had some relations with a coed" fueled this antagonism the following year. See Bernard to Hankins, October 18, December 25, 1926, BPPS.

30. Bernard to Kimball Young, November 1, 1926, BPPS. Bernard gave a veiled account of this episode in "Albion W. Small" [faculty sketch], BPPS. Bruce Melvin (to Bernard, April 24, 1927, BPPS) wrote: "I have been told that the man who prevented you being there some time ago was Small and no one else." See also Jessie Bernard to Fred Matthews, December 8, 1964, RP.

31. Blumer to Ellwood, September 15, 1926, CAE; Faris to Robert Park, July 9, 1924, RP; Faris, review of Bernard, *Introduction to Social Psychology*.

32. Bernard to Kimball Young, November 1, 1926, and Bernard to Harry E. Barnes, October 17, 1929, BPPS. Steiner (to Odum, June 17, 1927, HWO) said that Faris attributed the nonappointment to "unexpected administrative problems."

33. Dwight Sanderson to Bernard, February 11, 1927; Bernard to Odum, April 25, 1927; Odum to Bernard, June 15, 1927; and Jesse Steiner to Odum, February 18, 1928, BPPS.

34. Bernard to Odum, August 11, 1930, BPPS.

35. Bernard, "Interpretation," p. 211.

36. Bernard, "Sociological Research."

37. Bernard: "Standards of Living"; "Invention"; "Family."

38. Ogburn to Odum, August 24, 1927, HWO; Ogburn to Hankins, April 18, 1930, WFO.

39. Bernard to Bain, March 28, 1929, RB; Ellwood to Bernard, February 2, 1929, BPPS; Bernard to E. H. Sutherland, February 4, 1929, BPPS; Bernard to Bain, February 12, March 28, 1929, RB.

40. Sutherland to Bernard, February 1, 1928; Bernard to Sutherland, February 4, 1929; and Bain to Bernard, January 22, 1929, BPPS; Bernard to Bain, March 28, 1929, RB.

41. Bernard to Sutherland, February 4, 1929, BPPS; Bernard to Bain, March 28, 1929, RB.

42. Cooley to Bernard, November 27, 1925, BPPS.

43. Cooley to Bain, September 11, 1927, RB. See also Hornell Hart to Bain, November 30, 1928, RB. Lundberg to Bernard, January 19, 1932, BPPS.

44. C. J. Bittner to Bernard, November 11, 1931, BPPS; Bernard, "Social Psychology Studies Adjustment Behavior," p. 8; Bernard to E. Faris, February 13, 1932, BPPS.

CHAPTER 10

1. "Chapin in Retirement," pp. 1, 4. The Chapin Papers (FSC) contain a copy of this article, and a list of the books in the series.

2. This judgment was in fact that of Ogburn, who felt that Chapin built a reputation by riding the latest wave, and who for this reason among others had a rather low opinion of him as a sociologist; see Ogburn, "Journal," November 30, 1942, WFO.

3. On Chapin's career see Althouse, *Chapin*; Martindale: *Nature and Types*, pp. 330–36, and *Romance*, chaps. 3–4; Chapin, "Autobiography" [dated October 18, 1928], BPUC. I am especially indebted to Professor Althouse's study, which also contains the transcript of extensive personal interviews with Chapin.

4. Chapin, quoted in Althouse, *Chapin*, p. 16.

5. Ibid., pp. 17, 28, 256.

6. Ibid., p. 20; R. Althouse, "Partial Interview with George Vold," April 3, 1963, FSC.

7. Althouse, *Chapin*, pp. 23–24.

8. H. D. Chapin, "Social and Physiological Inequality," p. 762.

9. H. D. Chapin: ibid.; "Struggle for Subsistence"; "Problem of a Pure Milk Supply"; "Preventive Medicine and Natural Selection"; "Survival of the Unfit."

10. H. D. Chapin, "Survival of the Unfit," p. 182.

11. H. D. Chapin, "Christian Science and the Child"; (F. S.) Chapin, "Moral Progress."

12. Althouse, *Chapin*, p. 269.

13. Chapin, *Education*, p. 18.

14. Ibid., pp. 7, 8.

15. Ibid., p. 104.

16. Chapin: "Variability"; *Introduction to Social Evolution*, p. 296; "How We Waste Our Coal"; "Our Submerged Forbears"; "Organizing the Labor Market"; *Historical Introduction to Social Economy*. The quotation is from "Ounce of Prevention."

17. Chapin praised Keller's *Societal Evolution* for this reason. See Chapin to Keller, August 29, 1915, AGK.

18. Chapin, "Moral Progress," p. 467.

19. Chapin, *Introduction to Social Evolution*, pp. 297–310, originally published as "Primitive Social Ascendency."

20. Chapin, "Moral Progress." For the omission of the reference to eugenics cf. Chapin, *Cultural Change*, pp. 387–401, with the original version in note 19 above.

21. Althouse, *Chapin*, p. 326.

22. Chapin, "Business System"; Chapin to Ross, December 12, 1919, EAR.

23. Althouse, *Chapin*, p. 133.

24. See, for example, Chapin, *Education*, p. 70.

25. Chapin, "Relations of Sociology."

26. Chapin: "Elements of Scientific Method"; "Relations of Sociology," pp. 360–61.

27. Chapin, "Experimental Method and Sociology."

28. Martindale, *Romance*, chap. 3.

29. Martindale, *Romance*, p. 55.

30. See Martindale, *Romance*, pp. 75–76; University Microfilms, *Comprehensive Dissertation Index*. Martindale also lists Dorothy P. Gary (Ph.D. 1928), later of Wheaton College, as one of Chapin's students, although no thesis is listed in the *Comprehensive Index*.

31. John Markey to Bernard, April 10, 1926, BPPS.

32. Bouzet to Bernard, May 30, 1926, BPPS.

33. Lundberg, "Autobiography," BPPS.

34. Grazia, *The Behavioral Sciences*, p. 8, quoted in Martindale, *Romance*, p. 51.

35. Phelps, two autobiographies, BPPS, BPUC.

36. Elmer, "Autobiography," BPPS.

37. [Unidentified Minnesota faculty member] to Read Bain, February 20, 1927, RB.

38. Markey to Bernard, April 10, 1926, and Bouzet to Bernard, May 30, 1926, BPPS. Markey conceded that he was "not sure" that there was "a definite policy," but thought that "there could easily be . . . from what is happening."

39. Chapin to Beardsley Ruml, September 29, 1922, quoted in Althouse, *Chapin*, p. 38.

40. Martindale, *Romance*, pp. 71–72.

41. Althouse, interview with Malcolm Willey, April 3, 1963; Conrad Taeuber to Althouse, July 24, 1963; and Donald Young to Althouse, July 10, 1963, FSC.

42. Althouse, Willey interview, p. 13, FSC.

43. Chapin, *Cultural Change*, passim; Althouse, *Chapin*, p. 296.

44. Althouse, *Chapin*, p. 265.

45. See Easthope, *History of Social Research Methods*, p. 126.

46. By the same token, Chapin's approach differed from later "operationalist" definitions of class wherein a term like "success" was defined as a prediction of the probability that an individual will get the most of whatever is going; see Alpert, "Operational Definitions." Chapin's "living-room scale" has recently had a satiric revival in Fussell, *Class*, pp. 194–97 ("Identifiable Naugahyde aping anything customarily made of leather—subtract 3").

47. See especially Chapin, "Some Results," and "Observability."

48. Chapin, "What Has Sociology to Contribute?" pp. 473–75.

49. Chapin, "Social Theory and Social Action."

50. Ibid., p. 6.

51. Ibid.

52. Chapin, *Experimental Designs*, pp. 36–37.

53. Chapin: "Social Participation"; "Preliminary Standardization"; "An Experiment"; *Experimental Designs*, pp. 35–40.

54. Dissertations done under Chapin in this period were as follows: C. E. Lively, "Family Living on Ohio Farms" (1931); C. Taeuber, "Migration to and from German Cities" (1931); C. A. Anderson, "Assortative Mating with Reference to Age" (1932); P. H. Landis, "Cultural Change in a Mining Town" (1933); R. F. Sletto, "Personality Scales" (1936); M. J. Walker, "Social Interaction of Children" (1937); B. O. Williams, "Mobility among Farmers" (1938); M. Conway, "Prediction of Achievement" (1939); and W. H. Sewell, "A Scale of Measurement . . ." (1939).

55. Chapin, "Notes on Experimental Designs," April 23, 1963, FSC, discusses the critics. Althouse: Willey interview; interview with George Vold, April 3, 1963; and interview with Monachesi et al., June 23, 1964, FSC.

56. Martindale, *Romance*, p. 79.

57. Chapin to Sol Haberman, April 4, 1957, FSC.

58. Althouse, *Chapin*, pp. 2–3.

59. Michael H. Harper to Althouse, June 25, 1963, FSC.

CHAPTER 11

1. Ogburn, "Folkways" [presidential address to the A.S.S.], pp. 300–306.

2. On Ogburn's career see Ogburn, *On Cultural and Social Change*, pp. vii–xxii; Huff, "Theoretical Innovation"; Martindale, *Nature and Types*, pp. 324–30; and the obituaries cited below (note 9).

3. Ogburn, "Measurement of Factors"; Easthope, *History of Social Research Methods*, pp. 114–19, 133–34, 145–46; Maus, *Short History of Sociology*, pp. 136–38.

4. Toffler, *Future Shock*, p. 3.

5. Mumford, *Technics and Civilization*, pp. 316–17.

6. Choukas, "Concept of Cultural Lag"; Frost, "Functionalism"; Herman, "Answer to Criticism"; Mueller, "Present Status"; Standing, "Critique"; Schneider, "Cultural Lag"; Woodward: "Critical Notes," and "New Classification of Culture."

7. Schwendinger and Schwendinger, *Sociologists of the Chair*, pp. 460–62; Lasch, *Haven*, pp. 37–38. See also Ewen, *Captains of Consciousness*, pp. 120, 135, 164, 178.

8. Martindale, *Nature and Types*, p. 326.

9. H. M. Hughes, "Ogburn," p. 2; Everett Stonequist, interview, April 15, 1972, p. 9, SDI; Ogburn, "Journal," September 19, 1946, WFO. See also obituaries by Nimkoff and Hauser.

10. Ogburn, "Journal," October 19, 1948, WFO.

11. Ibid., November 27, 1952, November 30, 1942.

12. Ogburn to Bain, January 9, 1934, RB; Ogburn, "Journal," November 3, 1946, November 30, 1942, WFO.

13. Ogburn, "Journal," November 30, 1942, WFO.

14. Ibid., July 4, 1946, July 27, 1943, January 17, 1949, December 26, 1946, March 11, 1948.

15. Ibid., August 2, 1952, July 4, 1946.

16. Ibid., March 24, 1944. E. T. Thompson, a graduate student of Ogburn's, spoke frankly of his own experience in this regard: "I sort of turned against everything Southern I could think of. . . . That was part of my excess zeal to be objective" (Thompson, interview, March 27, 1972, p. 9, SDI).

17. Ogburn, "Journal," March 12, 1948, WFO.

18. Ibid., August 13, 1946, July 13, 1946, September 3, 1946.

19. Ibid., July 15, 1950.

20. Ibid., March 22, 1947, August 4, 1946.

21. Ogburn: *Progress*, p. 6; "Journal," April 5, 1955, WFO.

22. Ogburn: *On Cultural and Social Change*, p. 9; "Journal," December 11, 1948, April 8, 1947, August 14, 1955, WFO.

23. Ogburn, *Progress*, pp. 20–25.

24. Ibid., pp. 21–22.

25. Ibid., pp. 201–2.

26. Ibid., p. 202. On the Sutherland-Bernard exchange see above, chapter 8.

27. Reviews of Ogburn, *Progress*, in *Survey* and *Dial*.

28. Ogburn ("Journal," April 5, 1955, WFO) discusses his relation at Mercer with William Heard Kilpatrick, the educational reformer.

29. Ogburn: *On Cultural and Social Change*, p.ix; "Methods of Direct Legislation," and "Social Legislation."

30. Ogburn, "Psychological Basis," p. 302.

31. Ogburn, "Initiative and Referendum." See also his "How Women Vote."

32. Ogburn, "Political Thought."

33. Ogburn, "Bias, Psychoanalysis," p. 290.

34. Ogburn, "Psychological Basis."

35. Ogburn, "Cultural Lag as Theory."

36. On the culture concept in the social sciences see Cravens, *Triumph*, chaps. 3–4.

37. Ogburn: *Social Change*, p. 4; *On Cultural and Social Change*, p. xvi.

38. Ogburn, *Social Change*, pp. 7–11, 31–32.

39. Martindale, *Nature and Types*, pp. 325–26.

40. Huff, "Theoretical Innovation," p. 266.

41. Sorokin, *Contemporary Sociological Theories*, p. 745; see also MacIver, *Society*, pp. 469–73.

42. Orton, review of Ogburn, *Social Change*.

43. Ross, *Principles of Sociology*, p. 113; Allport, "Social Change."

44. Ogburn, *Social Change*, p. 363.

45. Ogburn, *Social Change*, pp. 346–63.

46. Groves, *Introduction*, pp. 162, 438, 659; Eubank, *Concepts*, pp. 369–70; Cooley et al., *Introductory Sociology*, p. 420. See also Mueller, "Present Status," p. 320.

CHAPTER 12

1. Ogburn, "Political Thought."

2. Ogburn, "Journal," August 14, 1955, WFO.

3. Ibid.; H. M. Hughes, "Ogburn," p. 1; Kimball Young to Bain, November 22, 1922, RB.

4. Robert Faris, interview, May 24, 1972, p. 7, SDI.

5. Herbert Blumer, interview, May 22, 1972, pp. 10–12; Leonard Cottrell, interview, March 28, 1972, p. 1; and E. T. Thompson, interview, March 27, 1972, p. 8,

SDI; Ogburn, "Journal," June 14, 1952, WFO.

6. Faris, interview, pp. 5, 8 (see above, n. 4).

7. Ogburn, "Journal," April 4, 5, 1955, WFO; Blumer, interview, p. 12 (above, n. 5). Leonard Cottrell, for example, remembered that Park "would rumble about those stupid statisticians and stupid Freudians" (Cottrell, interview, p. 11).

8. Robert Faris, interview, p. 3; Everett Stonequist, interview, May 15, 1972, p. 8, SDI; Ogburn, "Journal," April 4, 5, 1955, WFO. See also Thompson, interview, p. 1 (see above, n. 5).

9. Park and Burgess, *Science of Society*, p. 42; Park quoted in Matthews, *Quest for an American Sociology*, p. 179.

10. Ogburn, *Progress*, p. 23. E. T. Thompson (interview, p. 12) recalled that there "was a whale of a debate between Blumer and Ogburn [that evening] . . . [and] there was a certain amount of acrimony." He added: ". . . but I don't recall what the debate was all about. Isn't that terrible?"

11. Blumer, "Science."

12. Ogburn to Odum, May 23, 1930, HWO.

13. Wirth to Odum, April 17, 1948, HWO.

14. Ogburn to Hankins, April 18, 1930, WFO.

15. Ogburn, "Journal," March 15, 1948, WFO. (This ambivalence continued to color their relationship; see Ogburn, "Journal," August 3, 1945: "Yesterday we had a meeting of the Department of Sociology. I note that Wirth can be managed and kept happy if he is allowed to strut and to take some leadership."

16. Ibid.

17. Ogburn, "Studies in Prediction," p. 224. At Chicago the issue was an especially sensitive one, given the open anti-Semitism within academia. In 1936 Read Bain wrote Samuel Stouffer concerning an appointment at Miami University: "So I want a bright young non-Jewish, non-Negro male under thirty. . . ." After Burgess, as acting chairman, read the letter aloud to the department, Stouffer begged Bain for a personal disclaimer to soothe hurt feelings; see Bain to Stouffer, October 3, 1936; and Stouffer to Bain, October 17, 1936, RB.

18. Faris to Odum, August 9, 1948, HWO.

19. Ogburn, "Measurement of Factors," p. 175. On the importance of Ogburn's contribution, see R. Faris, *Chicago Sociology*, p. 118.

20. Robert Faris, interview, pp. 2–4 (above, n. 4).

21. Thompson, interview, p. 9 (above, n. 5).

22. The preceding is taken entirely from Bulmer, "Quantification."

23. Bulmer, "Support for Sociology."

24. Kuhlman, "Social Science Research Council"; Bulmer, "Support for Sociology."

25. Ronald Althouse, "Interview with William Anderson," April 4, 1963, FSC.

26. Kuhlman, "Social Science Research Council"; S.S.R.C., *Decennial Report*, pp. 19–23, 25.

27. S.S.R.C., *Decennial Report*, p. 67; Donald Young to Ronald Althouse, July 10, 1963, FSC.

28. Bulmer, "Support for Sociology," pp. 190–91; Ogburn to Odum, January 18, 1924, HWO. For a complete list of research fellows and "Grants in Aid" see S.S.R.C., *Decennial Report*, pp. 77–102.

29. Odum to Gerald Johnson, June 22, 1937, HWO.

30. For Bernard's growing dissatisfaction see Bernard to Maurice Price, February 29, 1928, BPPS.

31. Bernard to Lynd, June 16; Lynd to Bernard, November 24; and Bernard to Lynd, December 21, 1930, BPPS.

32. American Sociological Society, "Minutes . . . December 29, 1930," p. 22.

33. The following is derived largely from Karl, "Presidential Planning," supplemented by my own work in the Ogburn Papers. Whereas Karl was primarily interested in planning and the structure of the executive, my focus is on the impact of the experience on Ogburn and his view of sociology.

34. President's Research Committee, *Recent Social Trends*, 1:vi–ix; S.S.R.C., *Decennial Report*, passim.

35. Karl, "Presidential Planning," p. 368.

36. Ibid., p. 369.

37. Ibid., pp. 372–76.

38. Ibid., pp. 382–83, 373, 393; President's Research Committee, *Recent Social Trends*, chap. 22; Ogburn to Odum, April 8, 1930, quoted in Karl, "Presidential Planning," p. 373.

39. Karl, "Presidential Planning," p. 391.

40. Ibid., p. 399.

41. Odum to Ogburn, January 25, 1932, HWO; Lillian Symnes, "Great Fact-Finding Farce," p. 356; Ogburn to Mitchell, February 10, 1932, WFO.

42. Hunt to unidentified correspondent, May 21, 1930, WFO; Mitchell to Ogburn, May 8, 1932, quoted in Karl, "Presidential Planning," p. 391. President's Research Committee, *Recent Social Trends*, 1:v.

43. Ogburn to Odum, January 15, 1932, HWO; Ogburn to Mitchell, September 8, 1932, WFO.

44. E. E. Hunt to Ogburn, March 25, 1930, WFO; Ogburn, "Science and Society," p. 197. The talk was probably Blumer's "Science without Concepts," given at the University of Chicago Institute of Social Research, August 1930.

45. During the New Deal years these included the Consumer Advisory Board of the N.R.A. (director 1933), the Resettlement Administration (advisor 1936), and the National Resources Committee (consultant and committee member 1935–43).

46. Sorokin to Bain, January 6, 1931, RB.

47. Sorokin, "Recent Social Trends." pp. 194–204.

48. Ibid.

49. C. A. Beard: review of *Recent Social Trends*, and "Written History." See also Dewey, "Social Stresses."

50. Ogburn, "Reply."

51. Ogburn to Odum, October 7, 1948, WHO.

CHAPTER 13

1. For complaints over salary cuts see Meroney to Bernard, February 24, 1932, BPPS; Charles E. Lively to Bernard, September 28, 1933, BPPS; Bernard to Ross, January 5, 1937, EAR.

2. Bernard to Ross, January 5, 1937, EAR. See also Meroney to Ellsworth Faris, January 23, 1935, BPPS; Ross to Bernard, June 7, and Hankins to Bernard, June 1, 1937, BPPS.

3. For example, see Bernard et al., "Questions."

4. Membership totals were as follows:

Year	Total	Number Resigned	Number Unpaid
1930	1558	36	178
1931	1567	69	267
1932	1340	95	363
1933	1149	63	311
1934	1202	35	166
1935	1164	29	291
1936	1002	18	223
1937	1006	16	136

(See American Sociological Society, "Official Reports.")

5. By the late 1930s six regional societies had been established: the Ohio Valley Sociological Society (1925); the Pacific Sociological Society (1930); the Eastern Sociological Conference [later Society] (1931); the Southern Sociological Society (1936); the MidWest Sociological Society (1937); and the Southwest Sociological Society (1937). To these should be added the Southwestern Social Science Association (1931), in which Bernard and others were active; the Sociological Research Association (1936); the Rural Sociological Society (1937); and the American Catholic Sociological Society (1938). See Odum, *American Sociology*, chaps. 21–23. Discussion of this issue increased after 1935; see correspondence in BPPS.

6. F. S. Chapin, "Present State"; E. Faris, "Too Many PhDs?"

7. R. Faris, *Chicago Sociology*, p. 121; Martindale, *Romance*, p. 72; H. Kuklick, "Scientific Revolution"; Lengerman, "Founding."

8. American Sociological Society, "Minutes . . . December 29, 1930."

9. In addition to Odum and Rice, it included Hornell Hart, an Iowa Ph.D. (1921) then teaching at Bryn Mawr; Malcolm Willey, a Columbia Ph.D. (1926) and colleague of Chapin at Minnesota; Neva R. Deardorff, a Penn Ph.D. (1911) with a distinguished career in social work, and currently director of research at the Welfare Council of New York; J. H. Kolb, a rural sociologist at Wisconsin, who in 1932 took a year's leave to work with Ogburn on the Committee on Recent Social Trends; and Ernest Burgess, who, although not a quantifier, was a colleague of Ogburn at Chicago. See A.S.S., "Organization for Research."

10. Ibid., pp. 37–38.

11. Ellwood: "Objectivism," p. 289; "Emasculated Sociologies"; "Scientific Method," pp. 44–50.

12. On Ellwood's later career see Barnes, "Ellwood"; Whitaker, "Ellwood"; Bernard, "Charles A. Ellwood" [faculty sketch], BPPS; Ellwood, "Autobiography," BPUC.

13. Ellwood, "Scientific Methods of Studying Human Society," p. 329.

14. Ellwood to R. O. Rivera, January 26, 1937, CAE.

15. MacIver, "Is Sociology a Natural Science?"; Sorokin, "Sociology as a Science"; Blumer, "Science."

16. Ellwood to Senator Selden P. Spencer, February 7, 1920; to Calvin Coolidge, April 19, 1924; to editor, *Chicago Defender*, September 17, 1924; and to Ross, September 24, 1923, CAE.

17. Ellwood to Ross, September 15, 1923, EAR.

18. Ellwood, "Autobiography," BPPS.

19. Bernard, "Ellwood," BPPS.

20. Ibid.

21. Small to Bernard, March 21, 1921; Bernard, "Ellwood"; and Ellwood to Bernard, November 7, 1927, BPPS.

22. Chapin to Robert Park, February 8, 1922, FSC; Small to Bernard, March 21, 1921, BPPS. On Chapin's later attitude toward Ellwood see Chapin to Harold R. Hosea, May 20, 1931, FSC. Sutherland (to Bernard, April 13, 1921, BPPS) reported that the Chicagoans were afraid to admit Ellwood to their conferences "for fear he would rush away and publish their stuff before they got to it."

23. Bernard, "Ellwood," p. 12, BPPS. For other issues that divided them, see Ellwood to Bernard, March 14, 1929, BPPS; Bernard, *Instinct*, p. 340; Ellwood to Bernard, November 1, 1928, CAE.

24. C. H. Ward, *Thobbing*; Ellwood to Harry E. Barnes, April 15, 1926, CAE.

25. Bernard to E. H. Sutherland, February 4, 1929; and to Ellwood, March 12, 1929, BPPS.

26. Ellwood to Bernard, January 14, February 2, 26, March 14, 1929; and Bernard to Ellwood, March 1, 1929, BPPS.

27. Ellwood to Howard Becker, April 25, 1933, CAE. For Ellwood's worsening relations with Faris over the next few years see Ellwood to Faris, January 11, and Faris to Ellwood, January 13, 1934, CAE; Faris, review of Ellwood, *Methods*; Ellwood, letter to editor of *AJS*.

28. Ellwood to Alvin Johnson, June 1, 1933; to Howard Becker, April 25, 1933; and to Hornell Hart, November 12, 1931, CAE.

29. Bernard, "Ellwood," BPPS.

30. Hart to Ellwood, October 22, November 10, 1931, April 5, 1932; and Ellwood to Hart, November 12, 1931, CAE. See also Ellwood to William H. Glasson, October 24, 1934, CAE.

31. Sorokin to Ellwood, January 11, 1930, HWO; Sorokin to Ellwood, February 9, 1932, CAE. See also Ellwood to Sorokin, February 23, 1933, CAE.

32. MacIver to Ellwood, November 10, 1931, January 15, 1934, CAE.

33. Ernest Groves to Ellwood, December 30, 1933; Todd to Ellwood, November 5, 1933; and Jerome Dowd to Ellwood, December 12, 1931, CAE. See also Fairchild to Ellwood, June 9 1933; Joseph Mayer to Ellwood, March 19, 1934; and Leroy Allen to Ellwood, March 29, 1934, CAE.

34. Rice to Ellwood, October 22, 1931, CAE.

35. Crane to Ellwood, March 14, 1933; Ogburn to Ellwood, November 13, 1931, CAE. See also Park to Ellwood, December 10, 1931, CAE.

36. Ellwood, "Scientific Method."

37. On MacIver see Bramson, *MacIver*, "Introduction."

38. Sorokin to Ellwood, January 11, 1930, HWO.

39. Sorokin to Ross, August 15, 1933, EAR; and to Bain, April 6, 1934, May 21, 1935, RB.

40. Bernard, "Great Controversy," p. 64.

41. Ellwood to Bernard, March 14, 1935, BPPS.

42. A.S.S., "News and Notes," *AJS* 42 (1936): 723; "Program—Founders Banquet," April 16, 1936, CAE. The Chugerman-Ellwood correspondence is in CAE.

43. On Parmelee see Parmelee, "Autobiography," BPPS; Gibbons, "Parmelee."

44. Parmelee to Bernard, March 14, 1938, August 14, 1932, March 24, 1935, October 1, 1931, BPPS; A.S.S., "Minutes . . . December 12, 1931," pp. 24–27. For evidence of Parmelee's earlier political views see Parmelee to Richard Ely, November 13, 1907, RTE.

45. Parmelee to Bernard, March 24, 1935, BPPS. An exception was Ross, who expressed his "total dissent." See Ross to Parmelee, October 12, 1931, and Parmelee to Ross, November 10, 1931, EAR.

46. Parmelee to Bernard, June 28, 1937, BPPS.

47. Bernard to Ellwood, May 6, 1913; to Bain, April 27, 1931; and to Parmelee, October 1, 1931, BPPS.

48. Ross to Parmelee, October 12, 1931, EAR; Parmelee to Bernard, March 4, 1935, BPPS; House, *Development*, p. 332, quoted in Gibbons, "Parmelee," p. 407.

49. H. D. Duncan to Bernard, April 10, 1934, BPPS.

50. Bernard to Davis, [1935], BPPS.

CHAPTER 14

1. Bain to Bernard, January 5, 1932 [misdated 1931]; and Lundberg to Bernard, January 19, 1932, BPPS.

2. Bain to Bernard, March 23, 1932, BPPS.

3. William Meroney to Bernard, January 21, 1932; Elmer to Bernard, March 3, 1932; House to Bernard, March 10, 1932; and Hankins to Bernard, March 11, 1932, BPPS.

4. Bernard, "Some Problems Confronting the American Sociological Society" [1932?]; and Bernard to Susan Kingsbury, May 4, 1932, BPPS.

5. The new committee consisted of those who, for one reason or another, had opposed the Rice-Ogburn strategy: Manuel Elmer, Robert MacIver, and Arthur J. Todd. See A.S.S., "News and Notes," *AJS* 38 (1932): 450.

6. Bernard et al., "Questions," p. 166.

7. Bernard to Ross, March 30, 1914, EAR.

8. Bernard to Pinchot, June 1932; and to Ickes, August 1932, BPPS.

9. Bernard, "Shall It Be 'Goodbye Mr. Roosevelt'" [1935], BPPS.

10. Bernard to [?] Matthews, February 6, 1930, BPPS.

11. Bernard to Kingsbury, May 4, 1932, BPPS. See also Bernard to Kingsbury, January 26, 1932, BPPS.

12. Among the many letters in which this issue is discussed see Bernard to Ross, June 17, 1934; Davis to Bernard, January 16, 1935; Miller to Bernard, April 27, 1935;

Bernard to Ross, January 5, 1937; and Meroney to Bernard, March 4, 1937, BPPS.

13. Odum to Bernard, August 9, 1932, BPPS; Bernard, "Sociological Research." To make matters worse, Ogburn (*Recent Social Trends*, 1, 162) used Bernard's phrase "social inventions" without attribution, although Bernard did not discover this slight until later; see R. L. Duffus to Bernard, May 22, 1935, BPPS.

14. Copies in BPPS for 1932.

15. Melville Herskovits to Bernard, September 15; Robert Lynd to Bernard, September 30; and Albert Keller to Bernard, August 14, 1932, BPPS. See also Henry P. Fairchild to Bernard, September 15, 1932, BPPS.

16. Chapin to Bernard, April 12, and Bernard to Chapin, April 14, 1932, BPPS; A.S.S., "News and Notes," *AJS* 38 (1932): 113–14.

17. Cf. Lengerman, "Founding." Although I have modified and somewhat simplified Lengerman's classifications, I am indebted to her article for the basic categories and terminology.

18. Bain to Bernard, June 1, 1927 [autobiography], BPPS.

19. Ibid.

20. University of Oregon (M.A. 1921); a summer quarter at the University of Chicago (1922); University of Michigan (Ph.D. 1926) under Charles Horton Cooley.

21. Bain to Bernard, June 1, 1927 [autobiography], BPPS.

22. In 1930, Bain asked Bernard if Ellwood's appointment at Duke would mean a "good job" at Missouri. During 1935, he visited at Minnesota, where an offer was apparently a prospect, but none came. The next year he was negotiating with Syracuse, and in 1937–38 he spent a year at Harvard—but again to no avail. See Bain to Ross, December 2, 1936, EAR; to Bernard, March 26, 1930, to Sims, May 4, 1935, and to Lundberg, March 2, 1937, BPPS.

23. Sorokin to Ross, April 6, 1945, EAR. Bain's correspondence with Freud and others is in the Bain Papers (RB).

24. Bain: "Measurement"; "Concept of Complexity," pp. 222–31. For Bain's debt to Watson see Bain to John B. Watson, July 14, 1930, RB.

25. Bain, "Scientist as Citizen."

26. Becker to Bernard, January 21, October 5, 1932; December 13, 1933, BPPS.

27. On Becker see Becker, "Autobiography," BPPS.

28. Faris, *Chicago Sociology*, pp. 101, 110. See Becker, "Culture Case Study."

29. Bain to Becker, February 3, 1939, RB.

30. Becker to Bain, November 11, 1932, RB.

31. Becker: "Supreme Values," p. 167; "Discussion" [of Woodward], p. 104. For Becker's opposition to positivism see Becker, "Limits of Sociological Positivism."

32. Bain, "Editorial Notes," p. 552. See also Becker to Bain, June 15, 1939, RB.

33. Davis, "Autobiography," BPUC.

34. Ibid.

35. "Some Aspects of the Jerome Davis Case," EAR; Davis to Ross, April, 22, 1936, EAR.

36. Davis: "Testing"; "Autobiography," BPPS; *Introduction to Sociology*. Other contributors to the *Introduction* were Harry E. Barnes; Ellsworth Huntington, the Yale anthropologist; Frank Hankins; Bernard; Malcolm Willey; and Seba Eldridge, a Columbia Ph.D. (1925) then teaching at Kansas.

37. Davis to Dean Weigle, October 19, 1936, EAR.

38. Ogburn to Yale, November–December 1929, quoted in "Some Aspects of the Jerome Davis Case"; Davis to Ross, April 2, 1931, EAR.

39. Davis: "Social Action Pattern"; "Sociologist and Social Action."

40. The committee consisted of Herbert A. Miller, fresh from an academic-freedom battle at Ohio State; Charles E. Lively, a recent Minnesota Ph.D. (1931); Warren E. Gettys, chairman at the University of Texas; and Manuel Elmer of Pitt. An apparent exception was Ernest Burgess, although Bernard assured Davis he had appointed Burgess simply to represent the view of the now-disbanded Rice Committee: his was thus "a minority representation and should be treated as such." See Bernard to Davis, February 18, 1933, BPPS.

41. A.S.S., "Constitution." Cf. A.S.S., "Proposed Constitution."

42. Bernard to Gillin, November 17, 1934, BPPS.

43. Davis to Bernard, December 31, 1934; Bernard to Davis, n.d. [January 1935]; Davis to Bernard, January 30, 1935; Meroney to Bernard, January 24; and Ellwood to Bernard, February 12, 1935, BPPS.

44. Sims to Bernard, February 27; Bernard to Ellwood, February 29; Sims to Bernard, March 16; Bernard to Ellwood, March 21; Sims to Bernard, April 8; Davis to Bernard, April 14; Bossard to Bernard, April 16; Elmer to Bernard, April 30; Davis to Bernard, May 6, 7; Bain to Bernard, May 23; and Davis to Bernard, December 31, 1935, BPPS.

45. Davis to Bernard, December 31, 1935, BPPS.

46. Meroney to Bernard, January 24, 1935, and March 4, 1937; Parmelee to Bernard, August 12, 1937, BPPS.

47. Ogburn, "Folkways"; Odum to Hornell Hart, April 21, 1930, Sorokin to Odum, May 23, 1930, and Hankins to Odum, May 28, 1930, HWO. See also Lundberg to Bain, February 24, 1927, RB.

48. Bain to Bernard, March 26, April 17, 1930; Bernard to Bain, April 4, 1930, BPPS.

49. Newell Sims, "Autobiography," BPPS.

50. Ibid.

51. Sims: *A Hoosier Village* (1912), *Ultimate Democracy and Its Making* (1917), *The Rural Community* (1920), *Society and Its Surplus* (1924), *Elements of Rural Sociology* (1928), and *The New Russia* (1932), the latter edited by Davis.

52. Sims, "Autobiography," BPPS.

53. A.S.S., "Minutes of the First Meeting."

54. Bernard to Blumer, April 8; Blumer to Bernard, April 10, 14; and Sims to Bernard, May 16, 1933, BPPS.

55. Meroney to Burgess, July 27, 1934; and Bernard to Davis, May 3, 1934, BPPS.

56. In favor of the Sims Committee resolution: Ross, Weatherly, Ellwood, Miller, Dealey, Fairchild, Queen, Elmer, Gillette, Bogardus, Davis, Meroney, Sims, and Bernard. Opposed: Park, Gillin, Thomas, Reuter, and Odum (although the latter was "on both sides of the issue at the same time," Sims noted). See Sims to Bernard, June 21 and August 31, 1934, BPPS.

57. A.S.S., "Report of the Committee on Publications."

58. Th.B. (1912), Southwestern Baptist Theological Seminary; Th.M. (1917), Th.D. (1919), Southern Baptist Theological Seminary.

59. The following account of Meroney's career and the quotations are taken from

Meroney, "Autobiography," and Meroney to Ellsworth Faris, January 23, 1935, both in BPPS.

60. Meroney to Faris, January 23, 1935, BPPS.

61. Ibid.

62. Meroney, "Membership and Program."

63. Meroney to Faris, January 23, 1935, BPPS.

64. Ibid. Meroney's reference, in fact, masked a deep pride in his institution. Following a Baylor football victory in 1937, he wrote Bernard that the win would show that the university was "not merely a little jerkwater denominational school" (Meroney to Bernard, November 1, 1937, BPPS).

65. Bernard to Meroney, February 7; North to Bernard, May 24; Bossard to Bernard, March 13; and Davie to Bernard, June 18, 1935, BPPS.

66. Fairchild to Davis, April 29, and Davis to Bernard, May 14, 1935, BPPS. See also Bossard to Davis, May 1, and Elmer to Bernard, April 30, 1935, BPPS.

67. Bernard to Chapin, March 7; to Ellwood, February 29, mentioned in Ellwood to Bernard, March 14; and to Bossard, March 28; Sorokin to Bain, November 12; Bernard to Bain, December 19; and Bain to Bernard, December 20, 1935, BPPS.

68. Davis to Bernard, December 31, 1935; Parmelee to Bernard, March 15, 1937; and Meroney to Bernard, November 1, 1937, BPPS. The editorial board finally consisted of Davis, Deardorff, Gehkle, Gillin, Folsom, and Bernard.

CHAPTER 15

1. Sims to Bernard, March 9, 1937, BPPS.

2. Marcuse, *Reason and Revolution*, p. 342.

3. Willey to Bain, May 14, 1938, RB; Bain to Bernard, January 11, 1938, and Bossard to Bernard, December 14, 1938, BPPS.

4. Parmelee to Bernard, May 13, 1934, BPPS; Blumer, "Minutes."

5. Chapin, "Letter," p. 3; Bain to Sims, September 4, 1935, BPPS.

6. Davis to Ross, February 13, and Meroney to Bernard, February 18, 1935, BPPS.

7. Bernard to Davis, n.d. [January 1935]; Davis to Bernard, January 30; Davis to Bernard, May 18; Hertzler to Bernard, January 30; and Bain to Bernard, May 23, 1935, BPPS.

8. A.S.S, "News and Notes," *AJS* 42 (1936): 259.

9. Ibid.; Young, "Note on Procedure"; Parmelee to Bernard, March 7, 1938, BPPS.

10. Willey to Bain, May 14, 1938, RB; Jessie Bernard to Bernard, January 23, 1936, and Bain to Bernard, January 11, 1938, BPPS; Kimball Young to Ronald Althouse, June 27, 1963, FSC.

11. Bain to Bernard, January 11, 1938, BPPS.

12. Lundberg to Bain, November 30, 1936, RB; Bain to Bernard, January 13, 1937, January 11, 1938, BPPS.

13. Hankins to Bernard, October 27, December 26, 1936, BPPS; Hankins, "Editorial."

14. Hankins to Bernard, January 9, and Sims to Bernard, January 25, 1937, BPPS.

15. Sims to Bernard, March 9, 1937, and Bernard to Bain, [May–June] 1938, BPPS.

16. Sims to Bernard, January 1937, BPPS.

17. Meroney to Bernard, August 12, 1937, BPPS.

18. Bernard to Willey, October 19, 1937, and Sims to Bernard, October 9, November 29, 1937, BPPS; Becker to Bain, July 18, 1938, RB. Bernard believed and later charged openly that Bain was elected editor over him by a "political group," a charge Bain vigorously denied; see Bernard to Bain, December 4, and Bain to Bernard, December 15, 1941, RB.

19. Sims to Bernard, January 31, 1938, BPPS.

20. Bernard to Bain, n.d. [ca. May–June 1938], RB; Bain to Bernard, August 4, 1938, BPPS; Stouffer to Bain, August 28, 1938, RB; Stouffer to Bernard, September 14, 1938, BPPS, and August 1938, RB; Bain to Bernard, September 13 and September 28, 1938, BPPS. On Bain's sensitivity to Bernard's cool manner, see Bain to Bernard, May 10, 1940, RB.

21. Bain to Becker, March 2, 1937, and Becker to Bain, July 18, 1938, February 8, 1939, RB.

22. Bernard to Bain, May 7, 1940, RB.

23. Ibid.; Bernard to McKenzie, August 10, 1937, BPPS.

24. Ogburn to Rice, February 6, and to Blumer, February 18, 1936, WFO.

25. Davis to Bernard, April 14, and Elmer to Bernard, January 21, 1935, BPPS.

26. Sims to Bernard, February 27, 1935, BPPS. Sims (to Bernard, January 25, 1937, BPPS) reported: "Meroney seems to have soured on the situation." Meroney had severe health problems and died in December 1938.

27. Ogburn, "Trends in Social Science," pp. 260–62; S.S.R.C., *Decennial Report*, p. 14.

28. Hutchins, *No Friendly Voice*, pp. 156, 24–25; Adler,"Chicago School," p. 385.

29. Faris to Ellwood, February 2, 1934, CAE.

30. Ogburn, "Limitations of Statistics."

31. Ogburn, "Studies in Prediction."

32. Ogburn, "Journal," June 14, 1952, WFO.

33. Ibid.

34. Bain to Lundberg, December 1, 1938, RB. This issue surfaced repeatedly in their correspondence. Bain (to Lundberg, March 2, 1937, RB) wrote: "I know you are quite Fascist in speech, but I imagine you wouldn't like it if you had to live under it—because you dearly love your 'inalienable right' to shoot off your mouth." Lundberg (to Bain, March 22, 1937, RB) replied: "Whence came this idea that I 'am quite Fascist in speech'? I hate the bastards as much as any Hebrew." See also Bain to Lundberg, February 19, and Lundberg to Bain, February 23, 1941, RB.

35. Mary Sims Walker to Ogburn, quoted in Ogburn, "Journal," May 8, 1947, WFO.

36. Ibid., May 8, 1947, and June 22, 1942.

37. Ibid., June 22 and July 10, 1942.

38. Ibid., May 7, 1945, and September 16, 1944.

39. Ibid., July 15, 1950.

40. Ibid., December 19, 1946.

41. Dorothy Parker, "Indian Summer," quoted in Ogburn, "Journal," July 15, 1952, WFO.

42. Ogburn, "Social Philosophy of 'It Doesn't Matter.' "

43. Bernard to Dr. Schwab, July 24, 1936; Dr. Schwab to Jessie Bernard, May 28, 1936; Jessie Bernard to Bernard, March 30, 1938; and Bernard to M. Mehus, June 4, 1939, BPPS. Correspondence concerning the situation at Washington University is also in the BPPS.

44. Bernard to Ross, May 5, 1937, EAR.

45. Williams, review of Bernard, *Social Control*.

46. Bain to Bernard, April 17, 1940, BPPS; Becker to Bain, April 22, 1940, RB.

47. Bernard, "Method of Generalization."

48. Bernard, "Little Sociologist, What Now?" [1939], BPPS. Cf. "S.R.A. Plans to Die," p. 1.

49. Bernard, "Method of Generalization," p. 343.

50. Bernard, "Recent Discussion," p. 14.

51. E. W. Fox, review of Bernard, *War*. See also reviews by Roucek and Snyder. For the same charge three decades later when the book was reprinted see Israel Charny, "Introduction," in Bernard, *War*, pp. 5–13. Vidich and Lyman (*American Sociology*, p. 173), in contrast, argue that Bernard restated sociology's moral mission and, unlike sociologists of the S.S.R.C., would not subordinate the discipline to U.S. foreign policy. Although true, this fact does not alter the intellectual critique presented here.

52. Bain, "Bernard," p. 293; Bernard, "Scientific Method," p. 17.

CONCLUSION

1. For example, Hartung: "Operationalism as a Cultural Survival"; "Operationalism: Idealism or Realism"; and "Sociology of Positivism." Also Cicourel, *Method and Measurement*. For the view that Lundberg "won" over the following decades see Bierstedt, *American Sociological Theory*, p. 388.

2. On Lazarsfeld's work, see Barton, "Lazarsfeld."

3. Lazarsfeld: "Notes"; "Sociology of Empirical Social Research."

4. For example, Gittler, *Review*, chap. 1; Mullins and Mullins, *Theories and Theory Groups*, chap. 7; Warshay, *Current State*, chaps. 1, 4; Cohen, "Is Positivism Dead?"

5. Merton: "Bearing of Empirical Research," p. 513; and "Bearing of Sociological Theory," p. 147.

6. Goode and Hatt, *Methods*, chap. 1.

7. On the three "languages of discontent" during the Progressive Era, see Rodgers, "In Search of Progressivism," pp. 123–27.

8. Vidich and Lyman (*American Sociology*, pp. 169, 177) state without evidence that Bernard represented "midwestern Lutheranism." Although I have found no direct evidence of the family sectarian connection, his Texas background, and his attendance at the Pierce Baptist College, make a Baptist affiliation more likely. The connection suggested here, in any case, is admittedly speculative and in need of further investigation.

9. Bledstein, *Culture*, chaps. 1–3.

10. For an extended treatment of this theme see Gruber, *Mars and Minerva*.

11. For the following I am indebted to H. Kuklick, "Restructuring the Past," and Higham, "Matrix."

12. On corporatism see Hawley, "Discovery"; Lustig, *Corporate Liberalism*; Panitch, "Development of Corporatism."

13. Ogburn, "Future of the New Deal."

14. For this criticism see Keat, "Positivism and Statistics," p. 84.

15. For example, Horowitz: "Project Camelot," and *Professing Sociology*.

16. Gouldner, *Coming Crisis*, p. 103.

17. On this point, see Bledstein, *Culture*, p. 88.

18. Schudsen, *Discovering the News*, pp. 7, 121–22.

BIBLIOGRAPHY

MANUSCRIPT COLLECTIONS

ANN ARBOR, MICHIGAN
Michigan Historical Collections
Read Bain Papers

BALTIMORE, MARYLAND
The Johns Hopkins University
Herbert Baxter Adams Papers

CHAPEL HILL, NORTH CAROLINA
University of North Carolina, Southern Historical Collection
Howard W. Odum Papers

CHICAGO, ILLINOIS
University of Chicago
Luther Lee Bernard Papers
William Rainey Harper Papers
William Fielding Ogburn Papers
Robert Park Papers
Presidential Papers
Albion W. Small Papers
Sociology Department Interviews

DURHAM, NORTH CAROLINA
Duke University
Charles A. Ellwood Papers

MADISON, WISCONSIN
Wisconsin Historical Society
Richard T. Ely Papers
Edward A. Ross Papers

MINNEAPOLIS, MINNESOTA
University of Minnesota
F. Stuart Chapin Papers

NEW HAVEN, CONNECTICUT
Yale University
Arthur T. Hadley Papers
Albert G. Keller Papers
Anson P. Stokes Papers
William Graham Sumner Papers

NEW YORK, NEW YORK
Columbia University
John Bates Clark Papers
Columbia Official Papers
Frank Goodnow Papers

PROVIDENCE, RHODE ISLAND
Brown University, John Carter Brown Library
Lester Frank Ward Papers

UNIVERSITY PARK, PENNSYLVANIA
Pennsylvania State University
Luther Lee Bernard Papers

PRINTED SOURCES

Abel, T. "The Contribution of Georg Simmel." *ASR* 24 (1959): 473–81.
Adams, George B. "History and the Philosophy of History." *American Historical Review* 14 (1909): 221–36.
Adams, Romanzo. "The Nature of Social Unity." *AJS* 10 (1904): 208–27.
Adler, Mortimer. "The Chicago School." *Harper's* 183 (1941): 377–88.
Aho, James A. *German Realpolitik and American Sociology.* Lewiston, Pa., 1974.
Allport, Floyd H. "Social Change." *SF* 2 (1923–24): 671–76.
Alpert, Harry. "Operational Definitions in Sociology." *ASR* 3 (1938): 855–61.
Althouse, Ronald C. *The Intellectual Career of F. Stuart Chapin.* University Microfilms: Ann Arbor, 1964.
American Historical Association. "The Meeting of the AHA at New Orleans." *American Historical Review* 9 (1904): 437–55.
American Sociological Society. "Constitution of the American Sociological Society." *PASS* 28 (February 1934): 30–35.
―――. "Minutes of the Executive Committee Meeting December 29, 1930." *PASS* 25, no. 1 (1931): 21–22.
―――. "Minutes of the Executive Committee Meeting December 12, 1931." *PASS* 26 (1932): 20–27.

_____. "Minutes of the First Meeting of the Executive Committee . . . December 28, 1932." *PASS* 27 (1933): 20–23.

_____. "News and Notes." *AJS* 38 (1932): 109–27.

_____. "News and Notes." *AJS* 38 (1932): 445–52.

_____. "News and Notes." *AJS* 42 (1936): 256–77.

_____. "News and Notes." *AJS* 42 (1936): 723–42.

_____. "Official Reports." *ASR* 3 (1938): 79–80.

_____. "Organization for Research in the American Sociological Society." *PASS* 26 (1932): 1–39.

_____. "Proposed Constitution." *PASS* 27 (November 1933): 1–8.

_____. "Report of the Committee on Publications." *PASS* 29 (1935): 3–10.

Arendt, Hannah. "The Concept of History." In Hannah Arendt, *Between Past and Future*, pp. 41–90. New York, 1961.

Arner, George B. L. *Consanguineous Marriages in the American Population*. New York, 1908.

Babbitt, Irving. Letter. *Nation* 102 (1916): 620.

Bain, Read. "Concept of Complexity." *SF* 8 (1929): 222–31, 369–78.

_____. "Editorial Notes." *ASR* 4 (1939): 560–67.

_____. "Luther Lee Bernard." *ASR* 16 (1951): 285–97.

_____. "The Measurement of Political Attitudes." *SF* 7 (1929): 461–63.

_____. "Scientist as Citizen." *SF* 11 (1933): 412–15.

_____. "Trends in American Sociology." *SF* 5 (1926–27): 413–22.

Bakun, David. "Behaviorism and American Urbanization." *Journal of the History of the Behavioral Sciences* 2 (1966): 5–25.

Bannister, Robert C. *Social Darwinism: Science and Myth*. Philadelphia, 1979.

Barnes, Harry E. "Charles A. Ellwood." In *An Introduction to the History of Sociology*, edited by Harry E. Barnes, pp. 853–68. Chicago, 1948.

_____. *An Introduction to the History of Sociology*. Chicago, 1948.

Barton, Allen H. "Paul Lazarsfeld and Applied Social Research." *Social Science History* 3 (1979): 4–44.

Bawden, H. Heath. Review of Ward, *PS*. *AJS* 9 (1903–4): 408–15.

Beard, Charles A. Review of *Recent Social Trends*. *Yale Review* 22 (1933): 595.

_____. "Written History as an Act of Faith." *American Historical Review* 39 (1934): 219–31.

Beard, George. "Experiments with Living Human Beings." *Popular Science* 14 (1879): 751–57.

_____. "A Remarkable Coincidence." *Popular Science* 15 (1879): 628–31.

Becker, Ernest. *The Lost Science of Man*. New York, 1971.

_____. *The Structure of Evil*. New York, 1968.

Becker, Howard. "Culture Case Study and Ideal-Typical Method." *SF* 12 (1934): 399–405.

_____. "Discussion" [of Woodward, "New Classification of Culture"]. *ASR* 1 (1936): 102–4.

_____. "Limits of Sociological Positivism." *Journal of Social Philosophy* 6 (1941): 362–69.

_____. "Supreme Values and the Sociologist." *ASR* 6 (1941): 155–72.

Bellomy, Donald C. "William Graham Sumner: The Molding of an Iconoclast." Ph.D. dissertation, Harvard, 1980.

Bendix, Reinhard. *Social Science and the Distrust of Reason*. Berkeley, 1951.

Bentley, Arthur. *The Process of Government*. Chicago, 1908.

Berkowitz, Henry. Review of Sumner, *Folkways*. *Ethics* 21 (1911): 340–44.

Bernard, Luther L. "Attitudes and Redirection of Behavior." In *Social Attitudes*, edited by Kimball Young, pp. 46–74. New York, 1931.

_____. "The Family in Modern Life." *Ethics* 38 (1927): 427–42.

_____. "The Function of Generalization." *Monist* 30 (1920): 623–31.

_____. "The Great Controversy." *SF* 14 (1935): 64.

_____. *Instinct*. New York, 1924.

_____. "An Interpretation of Sociological Research." *AJS* 37 (1931–32): 203–12.

_____. "Invention and Social Progress." *AJS* 29 (1923): 1–33.

_____. "The Method of Generalization for Social Control." *ASR* 5 (1940): 340–50.

_____. "The Objective Viewpoint in Sociology." *AJS* 25 (1919): 298–325.

_____. "Recent Discussion Regarding Social Psychology." *AJS* 48 (1942): 13–28.

_____. Review of Giddings, *Studies in the Theory of Human Society*. *AJS* 28 (1922): 231–32.

_____. Review of Lucius Moody, *Social Adaptation*. *AJS* 22 (1916): 119–21.

_____. "Scientific Method and Social Progress." *AJS* 31 (1925): 1–18.

_____. "Social Psychology Studies Adjustment Behavior." *AJS* 38 (1932): 1–9.

_____. "The S.R.A. Plans to Die—and to Achieve 'Immortality.'" *American Sociologist* 1 (October 1939): 1–3.

_____. "Sociological Research and the Exceptional Man." *PASS* 27 (1933): 3–19.

_____. "Standards of Living." *SF* 7 (1928): 190–202.

_____. "A Theory of Rural Attitudes." *AJS* 22 (1917): 630–49.

_____. "Toward an Objective Standard of Social Control." *AJS* 16 (1911): 530.

_____. "The Transition to an Objective Standard of Social Control." *AJS* 16 (1910–11): 171–212, 309–41, 517–37.

_____. *War and Its Causes*. Edited by Israel W. Charny. New York, 1972.

Bernard, Luther L., et al. "Questions for Sociology." *SF* 13 (1934–35): 165–223.

Berquist, Harold E. "The Edward W. Bemis Controversy." *AAUP Bulletin* 58 (1972): 384–93.

Bierstedt, Robert. *American Sociological Theory*. New York, 1981.

Blackmar, Frank. Review of Small, *General Sociology*. *Dial* 40 (1906): 146–48.

Bledstein, Burton J. *The Culture of Professionalism*. New York, 1976.

Blumer, Herbert. "Minutes," American Sociological Society. *PASS* 29 (1935): 20.

_____. "Science Without Concepts." *AJS* 36 (1931): 515–33.

Bogardus, Emory. *Much Have I Learned*. Los Angeles, 1962.

Boston Transcript. May 16, 1925, p. 3. Quoted in *Book Review Digest* 21 (1925): 256–57.

Bramson, Leon. "Introduction." In Robert M. MacIver, *On Community, Society, Power*, pp. 1–25. Chicago, 1970.

Brooks, Lee M. "Luther Lee Bernard." *Sociology and Social Research* 36 (1952): 215–19.

Bryant, Christopher G. A. *Positivism in Social Theory and Research*. London, 1985.

Buckle, Henry Thomas. *History of Civilization in England*. 2 vols. London, 1865–66.

Bulmer, Martin. *The Chicago School of Sociology*. Chicago, 1984.

————. "Quantification and Chicago Social Science in the 1920's." *Journal of the History of the Behavioral Sciences* 17 (1981): 515–33.

————. "Support for Sociology in the 1920s." *American Sociologist* 17 (1982): 185–92.

Burnham, John C. "Lester F. Ward as a Natural Scientist." *American Quarterly* 6 (1954): 259–65.

————. *Lester Frank Ward in American Thought*. Washington, D.C., 1956.

Cape, Emily P. *Lester Frank Ward: A Personal Sketch*. New York, 1922.

Cashdollar, Charles. "European Positivism and the American Unitarians." *Church History* 45 (1976): 490–506.

Chapin, F. Stuart. "The Business System in the Professor's Study." *School and Society* 2 (1915): 709.

————. *Cultural Change*. New York, 1928.

————. *Education and the Mores*. New York, 1911.

————. "The Elements of Scientific Method in Sociology." *AJS* 20 (1914): 371–91.

————. *Experimental Designs in Sociological Research*. New York, 1947.

————. "The Experimental Method and Sociology." *Scientific Monthly* 4 (1917): 133–43, 238–47.

————. "An Experiment on the Social Effects of Good Housing." *ASR* 5 (1940): 868–79.

————. *Historical Introduction to Social Economy*. New York, 1917.

————. "How We Waste Our Coal." *Independent* 74 (1913): 1102–4.

————. *An Introduction to the Study of Social Evolution*. 2d ed. New York, 1919.

————. "Letter from a President." *PASS* 19 (1935): 1–9.

————. "Moral Progress." *Popular Science* 86 (1915): 467–71.

————. "The Observability of Social Institutions." *Sociology and Social Research* 17 (1933): 230–33.

————. "Organizing the Labor Market." *Independent* 83 (1915): 330–31.

————. "An Ounce of Prevention." *Independent* 82 (1915): 540.

————. "Our Submerged Forbears." *Independent* 77 (1914): 30–31.

————. "Preliminary Standardization of a Social Insight Scale." *ASR* 7 (1942): 214–28.

————. "The Present State of the Profession." *AJS* 39 (1933–34): 506–8.

————. "Primitive Social Ascendency." *PASS* 12 (1917): 61–74.

————. "The Relations of Sociology and Social Case Work." *Proceedings of the National Conference on Social Work 1919*, pp. 358–65. Atlantic City, N.J.

————. Review of Giddings, *Scientific Study*. *Annals of the American Academy* 122 (1925): 273.

————. "Social Participation and Social Intelligence." *ASR* 4 (1939): 157–66.

————. "Social Theory and Social Action." *ASR* 1 (1936): 1–11.

————. "Some Results of a Quantitative Analysis of the Institutional Patterns of Churches." *SF* 13 (1935): 340–49.

————. "The Variability of the Popular Vote." *AJS* 18 (1912): 222–40.

_____. "What Has Sociology to Contribute to Plans for Recovery from the Depression?" *SF* 12 (1934): 473–75.

Chapin, Henry D. "Christian Science and the Child." *Independent* 70 (1911): 1409–10.

_____. "Preventive Medicine and Natural Selection." *Journal of Social Science* 41 (1903): 54–59.

_____. "Problem of a Pure Milk Supply." *Forum* 33 (1902): 293–96.

_____. "Social and Physiological Inequality." *Popular Science* 30 (1887): 757–65.

_____. "The Struggle for Subsistence." *Journal of Social Science* 25 (1888): 93–97.

_____. "The Survival of the Unfit." *Popular Science* 41 (1892): 182–87.

"Chapin in Retirement." *Harper Books and Authors* 12 (1960): 1–4.

Choukas, Michael. "The Concept of Cultural Lag Reexamined." *ASR* 1 (1936): 752–60.

Chugerman, Samuel. *Lester Frank Ward: The American Aristotle*. Durham, N.C., 1939.

Church, Robert L. *Education in the United States*. New York, 1976.

Cicourel, Aaron V. *Method and Measurement in Sociology*. Glencoe, Ill., 1964.

Coats, A. W. "American Scholarship Comes of Age." *Journal of the History of Ideas* 22 (1961): 404–17.

_____. "The Origins of the 'Chicago Schools.'" *Journal of Political Economy* 71 (1963): 487–93.

Cohen, Percy S. "Is Positivism Dead?" *Sociological Review* 28 (1980): 141–76.

Conkin, Paul K. *Puritans and Pragmatists*. New York, 1968.

Cooley, Charles H. "Moderate Behaviorism." *New Republic* 49 (1926): 85–86.

_____. "Sumner and Methodology." *Sociology and Social Research* 12 (1928): 303–6.

Cooley, Charles H., et al. *Introductory Sociology*. New York, 1933.

Cowing, Cedric. "H. L. Mencken: The Case of the Curdled Progressive." *Ethics* 69 (1959): 255–67.

Cravens, Hamilton. *The Triumph of Evolution*. Philadelphia, 1978.

Creelan, Paul. "Watsonian Behaviorism and the Calvinist Conscience." *Journal of the History of the Behavioral Sciences* 10 (1974): 95–118.

Crook, D. Paul. *Benjamin Kidd: Portrait of a Social Darwinist*. Cambridge, England, 1984.

Curtis, Bruce. *William Graham Sumner*. Boston, 1981.

_____. "William Graham Sumner and the Problem of Progress." *New England Quarterly* 51 (1978): 348–69.

Davids, Leo. "Franklin H. Giddings: Forgotten Pioneer." *Journal of the History of the Behavioral Sciences* 4 (1968): 62–73.

Davis, Jerome. "The Social Action Pattern of the Protestant Religious Leader." *ASR* 1 (1936): 105–14.

_____. "The Sociologist and Social Action." *ASR* 5 (1940): 171–76.

_____. "Testing the Social Attitudes of Children in the Government Schools in Russia." *AJS* 32 (1927): 947–52.

Davis, Jerome, et al. *An Introduction to Sociology*. Boston, 1927.

Dealey, James Q., et al. "Ward." *AJS* 19 (1913): 61–78.

Dewey, John. "The Reflex Arc Concept." *Psychological Review* 3 (1896): 357–70.

_____. Review of Ward, *Psychic Factors. Psychological Review* 1 (1894): 400–408.

_____. "Social Stresses and Strains." *Ethics* 43 (1933): 339–45.

Dibble, Vernon K. *The Legacy of Albion Small.* Chicago, 1975.

Diner, Steven J. *A City and Its Universities.* Chapel Hill, N.C., 1980.

_____. "Department and Discipline." *Minerva* 13 (1975): 514–54.

"Doctorates Conferred by American Universities." *Science*, n.s. 42 (1915): 557.

Dorfman, Joseph. *The Economic Mind in American Civilization.* 5 vols. New York, 1946–59.

Dowling, R. E. "Pressure Group Theory." *American Political Science Review* 59 (1960): 944–54.

Easthope, Gary. *A History of Social Research Methods.* London, 1974.

Ellwood, Charles A. "Emasculated Sociologies." *Social Research* (1933): 109–14, reprinted from *Sociology and Social Research* 17 (1933): 219–29.

_____. Letter to editor. *AJS* 40 (1934): 138–40.

_____. "Objectivism in Sociology." *AJS* 22 (1916): 289–305.

_____. "Prolegomena to Social Psychology." *AJS* 4 (1899): 656–65, 807–22; 5 (1900): 98–109, 220–27.

_____. Review of Giddings, *Inductive Sociology. Annals of the American Academy* 19 (1902): 134–36.

_____. "Scientific Method in Sociology." *SF* 10 (1931): 15–21; 11 (1932): 44–50.

_____. "Scientific Methods of Studying Human Society." *SF* 2 (1924): 329–32.

_____. *The Story of Social Philosophy.* New York, 1938.

Ely, Richard. "Religion as a Social Force." *Christian Quarterly* (July, 1897): 321.

Eubank, Earle E. *The Concepts of Sociology.* Boston, 1932.

_____. "Errors of Sociology." *SF* 16 (1937–38): 178–202.

Ewen, Stuart. *Captains of Consciousness.* New York, 1976.

Faris, Ellsworth. Review of Bernard, *An Introduction to Social Psychology. AJS* 32 (1926): 482–86.

_____. Review of Ellwood, *Methods in Sociology. AJS* 39 (1934): 686–89.

_____. "Too Many PhDs?" *AJS* 39 (1934–35): 509–12.

Faris, Robert. *Chicago Sociology 1920–1932.* San Francisco, 1967.

Fishlow, Albert. "The American Common School Revival." In *Industrialization in Two Systems*, edited by Henry Rosovsky, pp. 40–67. New York, 1966.

Foskett, John W. "The Frame of Reference of Ward's *Dynamic Sociology*." *State College of Washington Research Studies* 17 (1949): 35–40.

Fox, Daniel M. *The Discovery of Abundance: Simon N. Patten and the Transformation of Social Theory.* Ithaca, 1967.

Fox, Edward W. Review of Bernard, *War. New York Times.* December 31, 1944, pp. 4, 16.

Frisch, Michael H. *Town into City: Springfield, Massachusetts, and the Meaning of Community.* Cambridge, Mass., 1972.

Frost, Henry F. "Functionalism in Anthropology and Sociology." *Sociology and Social Research* 23 (1939): 373–79.

Furner, Mary. *Advocacy and Objectivity: A Crisis in the Professionalization of American Social Science 1865–1905.* Lexington, Ky., 1975.

Fussell, Paul. *Class*. New York, 1983.

Garson, Robert, and Maidnet, Richard. "Social Darwinism and the Liberal Tradition." *South Atlantic Quarterly* 80 (1981): 61–76.

Gasman, Daniel. *The Scientific Origins of National Socialism*. London, 1971.

Gibbons, Don C. "Say, Whatever Became of Maurice Parmelee Anyway?" *Sociological Quarterly* 15 (1974): 405–16.

Giddens, Anthony, ed. *Positivism and Sociology*. London, 1974.

Giddings, Franklin H. "The American Idea." *Harper's Weekly* 48 (1904): 1702, 1713.

_____. "The Bolsheviki Must Go." *Independent* 97 (1919): 88.

_____. "Camouflanguage." *Independent* 103 (1920): 148.

_____. "The Concepts and Methods of Sociology." *AJS* 10 (1904): 161–76.

_____. "Cooperation." In *The Labor Movement*, edited by George E. McNeill, pp. 508–31. New York, 1888.

_____. "The Cost Production of Capital." *Quarterly Journal of Economics* 2 (1889): 503–7.

_____. *Democracy and Empire*. New York, 1900.

_____. "The Ethics of Socialism." *Ethics* 1 (1891): 239–43.

_____. "A Failure of *Sittlichkeit*." *Independent* 76 (1913): 64.

_____. "The Future of the Railroads." *Independent* 78 (1914): 341–42.

_____. *Inductive Sociology*. New York, 1901.

_____. "The Industrial Commission Reports." *Independent* 83 (1915): 348.

_____. "An Intensive Sociology." *AJS* 36 (1930): 1–14.

_____. "The Laws of Evolution." *Science* n.s. 22 (1905): 206–8.

_____. "The Mannerless Age." *Independent* 76 (1913): 239.

_____. "The Measurement of Social Pressure." *Publications of the American Statistical Association* n.s. 11 (1908): 56–61.

_____. *The Mighty Medicine*. New York, 1929.

_____. "Moral Reactions of the War." *Independent* 84 (1915): 6.

_____. "Mr. Bryan and the Complex Social Order." *Century* 73 (1906): 154–57.

_____. "The Natural Rate of Wages." *PSQ* 2 (1887): 620–37.

_____. "The Ohio Idea." *Independent* 103 (1920): 45.

_____. *Pagan Poems*. New York, 1914.

_____. "A Political Program." *Independent* 52 (1900): 2305–7.

_____. "The Price." *Independent* 76 (1913): 63.

_____. *The Principles of Sociology*. New York, 1896.

_____. "The Province of Sociology." *Annals of the American Academy* 1 (1890): 66–77.

_____. "The Relation of Sociology to other Scientific Studies." *Journal of Social Science* 32 (1894): 144–50.

_____. Review of Richard Ely et al., *History of the Cooperative Movement*. *PSQ* 3 (1888): 529.

_____. Review of Pearson, *Chances of Death*. *PSQ* 13 (1898): 156–61.

_____. Review of Small and Vincent, *Study of Society*. *Yale Review* 3 (1894): 326–28.

_____. *The Scientific Study of Human Society*. Chapel Hill, 1924.

_____. "The Social and Legal Aspect of Compulsory Education and Child Labor." In *Journal of the 44th Annual Meeting of the N.E.A.* (1905), pp. 111–13.

_____. "A Social Marking System." *AJS* 15 (1910): 721–40.

_____. "Social Pressure and Moral Weather." *Independent* 73 (1912): 1069–70.

_____. "The Sociological Character of Political Economy." *American Economic Association Publications* 3 (1889): 29–47.

_____. "Sociology as a University Study." *PSQ* 6 (1891): 635–55.

_____. *Studies in the Theory of Human Society.* New York, 1922.

_____. "The Theory of Profit Sharing." *Quarterly Journal of Economics* 1 (1887): 367–76.

_____. *The Theory of Socialization.* New York, 1897.

_____. "Theory of Sociology." *Annals of the American Academy*, Supplement 5 (1894): 5–80.

_____. "Three Phases of the Labor Question." *Winsted Connecticut Herald*, September 7, 1877 (copy in FHG).

_____. "The Trusts." *Independent* 77 (1914): 187.

_____. "Will Puritanism Remain?" *Independent* 77 (1914): 397.

_____. "Women, Clothes, and Race Salvation." *Independent* 103 (1920): 174–77.

[Giddings?] "Sociology in the Universities." *Popular Science* 46 (1895): 698–99.

Gilfillan, S. C. "A Sociologist Looks at Prediction." In James R. Bright, *Technological Forecasting for Industry and Government.* Englewood Cliffs, N.J., 1958.

_____. "An Ugly Duckling's Swan Song." *Sociological Abstracts* 18 (1970): i–xxv, xxvi–xl.

Gillette, John M. "Critical Points in Ward's Pure Sociology." *AJS* 20 (1914): 31–67.

Gillin, John L. *The Dunkers.* New York, 1906.

_____. "Giddings." In *American Masters of Social Science*, edited by Howard Odum, pp. 191–230. New York, 1927.

Gittler, Joseph B., ed. *Review of Sociology: Analysis of a Decade.* New York, 1957.

Goode, William J., and Hatt, Paul K. *Methods in Social Research.* New York, 1952.

Gouldner, Alvin W. *The Coming Crisis of Western Sociology.* New York, 1970.

Graham, J. Morgan. "Preparation for an Event." *Minerva* 20 (1982): 25–58.

Gray, James. *The University of Minnesota: 1851–1951.* Minneapolis, 1951.

Grazia, Alfred de, ed. *The Behavioral Sciences: Essays in Honor of George A. Lundberg.* Great Barrington, Mass., 1968.

Groves, Ernest R. *An Introduction to Sociology.* Rev. ed. New York, 1933.

Gruber, Carol S. *Mars and Minerva.* Baton Rouge, La., 1975.

Hale, Myron Q. "The Cosmology of Arthur F. Bentley." *American Political Science Review* 54 (1960): 955–71.

Halfpenny, Peter. *Positivism and Sociology.* London, 1982.

Hankins, Frank. "Editorial." *ASR* 1 (1936): 967–68.

_____. "Franklin H. Giddings." *AJS* 37 (1931): 349–67.

_____. Review of Bernard, *Instinct. Nation* 121 (1926): 238.

Hart, Hornell. "Science and Sociology." *AJS* 27 (1921): 364–83.

_____. "Value-Judgements in Sociology." *ASR* 3 (1938): 862–67.

Hartung, Frank. "Operationalism: Idealism or Realism." *Philosophy of Science* 9 (1942): 350–55.

_____. "Operationalism as a Cultural Survival." *Philosophy of Science* 11 (1944): 227–32.

_____. "The Sociology of Positivism." *Science and Society* 8 (1944): 328–41.

Haskell, Thomas L. *The Emergence of Professional Social Science.* Urbana, Ill., 1977.

Hauser, Philip. Obituary of W. F. Ogburn. *AJS* 65 (1959–60): 74.

Hawes, C. H. Review of Sumner, *Folkways. Journal of Philosophy* 4 (1907): 666–67.

Hawkins, Hugh. *Pioneer: A History of the Johns Hopkins University 1874–1889.* Ithaca, 1960.

Hawley, Ellis. "The Discovery and Study of 'Corporate Liberalism.'" *Business History Review* 52 (1978): 309–20.

Hayek, Friedrich A. von. *The Counterrevolution of Science.* Glencoe, Ill., 1952.

Hayes, Edward C. "Albion W. Small." In *American Masters of Social Science*, edited by Howard Odum, pp. 149–90. New York, 1927.

―――. *Introduction to the Study of Sociology.* New York, 1915.

―――. Review of Bernard, "Transition to an Objective Standard." *AJS* 17 (1912): 852.

―――. "The 'Social Forces' Error." *AJS* 16 (1911): 613–44.

―――. "Some Social Relations Restated." *AJS* 31 (1925): 333–46.

Helfand, Michael S. "T. H. Huxley's Evolution and Ethics." *Victorian Studies* 20 (1977): 159–77.

Herbert, Sandra. "The Place of Man in the Development of Darwin's Theory of Transformation, pt. II." *Journal of the History of Biology* 10 (1977): 155–227.

Herman, Abbott. "The Answer to Criticism of the Lag Concept." *AJS* 43 (1937): 440–51.

Heyl, John D. and Barbara S. "The Sumner-Porter Controversy at Yale." *Sociological Inquiry* 46 (1976): 41–49.

Higham, John. "The Matrix of Specialization." In *The Organization of Knowledge*, edited by Alexandra Oleson and John Voss, pp. 3–18. Baltimore, 1979.

Hinkle, Roscoe. *Founding Theory of American Sociology: 1881–1915.* London, 1980.

Hinkle, Roscoe, and Smith, Norman. "Sumner versus Keller." *Sociological Inquiry* 49 (1979): 41–48.

Hofstadter, Richard. *Social Darwinism in American Thought.* Philadelphia, 1944.

Hofstadter, Richard, and Metzger, Walter. *The Development of Academic Freedom in the United States: The Age of the University.* New York, 1955.

Hofstadter, Richard, and Smith, Wilson, eds. *American Higher Education.* 2 vols. Chicago, 1961.

Horowitz, Irving. "The Life and Death of Project Camelot." *Transaction* 3 (1965–66): 3–7, 44–47.

―――. *Professing Sociology.* Chicago, 1968.

House, Floyd N. *The Development of Sociology.* New York, 1936.

Howard, George E. Review of Ward, *Applied Sociology. AJS* 12 (1906–7): 854–59.

Hoxie, Ralph G., et al. *A History of the Faculty of Political Science, Columbia University.* New York, 1955.

Hoxie, Robert F. "Sociology and the Other Social Sciences." *AJS* 12 (1907): 739–55.

Huff, Toby E. "Theoretical Innovation in Science: The Case of William F. Ogburn." *AJS* 79 (1973): 261–77.

Hughes, Helen M. Obituary of W. F. Ogburn. *SF* 38 (1959): 2.

Hull, David. "Charles Darwin and Nineteenth-Century Philosophers of Science." In *Foundations of Scientific Method*, edited by Ronald N. Giere and Richard S. Westfalls, pp. 115–32. Bloomington, Ind., 1972.

Hutchins, Robert. *No Friendly Voice*. Chicago, 1936.

Iggers, George. "The Image of Ranke in American and German Historical Scholarship." *History and Theory* 2 (1962): 17–40.

James, William. *The Principles of Psychology*. 2 vols. New York, 1890.

Janowitz, Morris. "Professionalization of Sociology." *AJS* 78 (1972): 105–35.

Jevons, William S. *The Theory of Political Economy*. Edited by R. D. Collison Black. London, 1970.

Johnson, Alvin, ed. *The Encyclopedia of the Social Sciences*. 15 vols. New York, 1930–35.

Jones, Thomas J. *The Sociology of a New York City Block*. New York, 1904.

Karl, Barry. "Presidential Planning and Social Science Research." *Perspectives in American History* 3 (1969): 347–407.

Katz, Michael. *The Irony of Early School Reform*. Cambridge, Mass., 1968.

Keat, Russell. "Positivism and Statistics." In *Demystifying Social Statistics*, edited by Ian Miles and John C. Irvine, pp. 75–86. London, 1979.

Keller, Albert G. "The Luck Element." *Scientific Monthly* 4 (1917): 145–50.

――――. *Reminiscences (Mainly Personal) of William Graham Sumner*. New Haven, 1933.

――――. *Societal Evolution*. New York, 1915.

――――. "Sociology and Science." *Nation* 102 (1916): 475–78.

――――. "What Did Darwin Really Say?" *Saturday Review of Literature* 28 (October 6, 1945): 5–8.

Kelley, Brooks M. *Yale*. New Haven, 1972.

Kevles, Daniel J. *The Physicists*. New York, 1977.

Kidd, Benjamin. *Social Evolution*. London, 1894.

Kress, Paul F. *Social Science and the Idea of Process*. Urbana, Ill., 1970.

Krout, Maurice H. "The Development of Small's Sociological Theory." *Journal of Applied Sociology* 11 (1927): 216–31.

Kuhlman, A. F. "The Social Science Research Council." *SF* 6 (1928): 583–90.

Kuklick, Bruce. *The Rise of American Philosophy*. New Haven, 1977.

Kuklick, Henrika. "Boundary Maintenance in American Sociology." *Journal of the History of the Behavioral Sciences* 16 (1980): 201–19.

――――. "Restructuring the Past." *Sociological Quarterly* 21 (1980): 5–21.

――――. "A 'Scientific Revolution': Sociological Theory in the United States 1930–45." *Sociological Inquiry* 43 (1973): 3–22.

Lasch, Christopher. *Haven in a Heartless World*. New York, 1977.

Lazarsfeld, Paul. "Notes on the History of Quantification in Sociology." *Isis* 52 (1961): 277–333.

――――. "Sociology of Empirical Social Research." *ASR* 27 (1962): 757–67.

Lemert, Edwin M. "The Folkways and Social Control." *ASR* 7 (1942): 394–99.

Lengerman, Patrica. "The Founding of the *American Sociological Review*." *ASR* 44 (1979): 185–98.

Levine, Daniel N. "Simmel's Influence on American Sociology." *AJS* 81 (1976): 813–45, 1112–32.

Lewis, J. David, and Smith, Richard L. *American Sociology and Pragmatism*. Chicago, 1980.

Lichtenberger, James P. "Franklin H. Giddings." *Sociology and Social Research* 16 (1932): 316–21.

Lowry, Richard. *The Evolution of Psychological Theory*. Chicago, 1971.

Lunday, G. Albert. *Sociology Dissertations in American Universities*. Commerce, Tex., 1969.

Lundberg, George. Review of Giddings, *Studies in the Theory of Human Society*. *SF* 1 (1922–23): 329–30.

Lustig, R. Jeffrey. *Corporate Liberalism*. Berkeley, 1982.

MacIver, Robert M. "Is Sociology a Natural Science?" *PASS* 25 (1931): 25–35.

––––––. *Society: A Textbook of Sociology*. New York, 1937.

McCloskey, Robert G. *American Conservatism*. Cambridge, Mass., 1951.

Marcuse, Herbert. *Reason and Revolution*. Boston, 1960 [original 1941].

Martindale, Don. *The Nature and Types of Sociological Theory*. London, 1961.

––––––. *The Romance of a Profession*. St. Paul, Minn., 1976.

Martineau, Harriet. *Illustrations of Political Economy*. 9 vols. London, 1834.

Matthews, Fred H. *Quest for an American Sociology: Robert E. Park and the Chicago School*. Montreal, 1977.

Maus, Heinz. *A Short History of Sociology*. English ed. London, 1962.

Means, David M. Review of Giddings, *Principles of Sociology*. *Nation* 63 (1896): 92–93.

Meroney, William P. "The Membership and Program of Twenty-Five Years of the American Sociological Society." *PASS* 25 (1931): 55–67.

Merton, Robert. "The Bearing of Empirical Research upon the Development of Sociological Theory." *ASR* 13 (1948): 505–15.

––––––. "The Bearing of Sociological Theory on Empirical Research." In Robert Merton, *On Theoretical Sociology*. New York, 1967.

Meyer, Donald. *The Positive Thinkers*. New York, 1965.

Miles, Ian, and Irvine, John. "Social Forecasting." In *Demystifying Social Statistics*, edited by Ian Miles and John C. Irvine. London, 1979.

Mills, C. Wright. "The Professional Ideology of Social Pathologists." *American Journal of Sociology* 49 (1943): 165–80.

Moore, James R. *The Post-Darwinian Controversies*. Cambridge, England, 1979.

Mueller, John H. "Present Status of the Cultural Lag Concept." *ASR* 3 (1938): 320–27.

Mullins, Nicholas C. and Carolyn J. *Theories and Theory Groups in Contemporary American Sociology*. New York, 1973.

Mumford, Lewis. *Technics and Civilization*. New York, 1934.

Murdock, George P. "The Science of Culture." *American Anthropologist* n.s. 34 (1932): 305.

Nelson, Alvin F. *The Development of Lester Ward's World View*. Fort Worth, Tex., 1955.

Newcomb, Simon. "Abstract Science in America." *North American Review* 122 (1876): 88–123.

———. "Exact Science in America." *North America Review* 119 (1874): 288–308.
Nichols, Herbert. "The Origin of Pleasure and Pain." *Philosophical Review* 1 (1892): 403–32, 518–34.
Nimkoff, M. F. Obituary of W. F. Ogburn. *ARS* 24 (1959): 564–65.
Northcott, Clarence H. "Giddings." In *An Introduction to the History of Sociology*, edited by Harry E. Barnes, pp. 744–65. Chicago, 1948.
———. "Sociological Theories of Franklin H. Giddings." *AJS* 24 (1918): 1–23.
Norton, Bernard J. "Karl Pearson and Statistics." *Social Studies of Science* 8 (1978): 5–33.
Norton, J. Pease. "Talks with a Great Teacher." *World's Work* 20 (1910): 13290–92.
Oberschall, Anthony R. "The Institutionalization of American Sociology." In *The Establishment of Empirical Sociology*, edited by Anthony R. Oberschall, pp. 187–251. New York, 1972.
Odin, Alfred. *Génèse*. Paris, 1895.
Odum, Howard. *American Sociology*. New York, 1951.
———. "Obituary [of L. L. Bernard]." *SF* 29 (1951): 480–81.
Ogburn, William F. "Bias, Psychoanalysis, and the Subjective." *PASS* 17 (1922); in Ogburn, *On Cultural and Social Change*, p. 290.
———. "Cultural Lag as Theory" [1957]; in Ogburn, *On Cultural and Social Change*, pp. 86–95.
———. "The Folkways of a Scientific Sociology." *Scientific Monthly* 30 (1930): 300–306.
———. "The Future of the New Deal." *AJS* 39 (1934): 842–48.
———. "How Women Vote." *PSQ* 34 (1919): 413–33.
———. "The Initiative and Referendum Tested in Hard Times." *Survey* 33 (1915): 693–94.
———. "Limitations of Statistics." *AJS* 40 (1934): 12–20.
———. "A Measurement of Factors in the Presidential Election of 1928." *SF* 8 (1929–30): 175–83.
———. "Methods of Direct Legislation in Oregon." *Quarterly Publication of the American Statistical Association* 14 (1914): 136–55.
———. *On Cultural and Social Change*. Edited by Otis D. Duncan. Chicago, 1964.
———. "The Political Thought of Social Classes." *Political Science Quarterly* 31 (1916): 300–17.
———. *Progress and Uniformity in Child Labor Legislation*. New York, 1912.
———. "The Psychological Basis for the Economic Interpretation of History." *American Economic Review* 9 (1919): 291–308.
———. "A Reply." *Journal of Political Economy* 41 (1933): 210–21.
———. "Science and Society." In *Science and Civilization*, edited by R. C. Stauffer, pp. 197–212. Madison, Wisc., 1949.
———. *Social Change*. New York, 1922.
———. "Social Legislation of the Pacific Coast." *Popular Science* 86 (1915): 274–89.
———. "Social Philosophy of 'It Doesn't Matter.'" *Sociology and Social Research* 43 (1959): 403–7.
———. "Studies in Prediction and the Distortion of Reality." *SF* 13 (1934): 224–37.
———. "Trends in Social Science." *Science* 79 (1934): 257–62.

Orton, William. Review of Ogburn, *Social Change*. *American Economic Review* 13 (1923): 468–71.

Page, Charles. *Class and American Sociology*. New York, 1940.

Panitch, Leo. "The Development of Corporatism in Liberal Democracies." *Comparative Political Studies* 10 (1979): 61–90.

Park, Robert E. "The Social Methods of Sumner, Thomas, and Znaniecki." In *Methods in Social Science*, edited by Stuart Rice, pp. 154–75. Chicago, 1931.

————. "Sumner's Conception of Society." *Chinese Social and Political Science Review* 17 (1933): 430–41.

Park, Robert E., and Burgess, Ernest W. *Introduction to the Science of Society*. Chicago, 1921.

Parmelee, Maurice F. *Inebriety in Boston*. New York, 1909.

Parsons, Talcott. *The Structure of Social Action*. New York, 1937.

Patten, Simon. "Failure of Biologic Sociology." *Annals of the American Academy* 4 (1894): 919–47.

————. "The Organic Concept of Society." *Annals of the American Academy* 5 (1895): 404–9.

————. Review of Small and Vincent, *Study of Society*. *Nation* 60 (1895): 351.

Peirce, Charles S. "The Fixation of Belief." *Popular Science* 12 (1877): 1–15.

————. Review of Giddings, *Inductive Sociology*. *Nation* 74 (1902): 273–74.

Pierson, George W. *Yale College*. New Haven, 1952.

Porter, Noah. *The American Colleges and the American Public*. New York: Arno Press, 1969 [first published in 1870].

President's Research Committee on Social Trends. *Recent Social Trends in the United States*. 2 vols. New York, 1933.

Purcell, Edward A. *The Crisis of Democratic Theory: Scientific Naturalism and the Crisis of Value*. Lexington, Ky., 1973.

Review of Giddings, *The Responsible State*. *Dial* 65 (1918): 572.

Review of Ogburn, *Progress and Uniformity*. *Dial* 53 (1912): 381–82.

Review of Ogburn, *Progress and Uniformity*. *Survey* 29 (1912): 205.

Review of Small, *The Beginnings of American Nationality*. *English Historical Review* 6 (1891): 787.

Review of Small, *General Sociology*. *Atlantic Monthly* 97 (1906): 852–53.

Review of Small and Vincent, *Study of Society*. *Nation* 60 (1895): 351.

Riley, Gresham, comp. *Values, Objectivity, and the Social Sciences*. Reading, Mass., 1974.

Rodgers, Daniel T. "In Search of Progressivism." *Reviews in American History* 11 (1982): 113–32.

————. *The Work Ethic in Industrial America 1850–1920*. Chicago, 1978.

Ross, Edward A. *Principles of Sociology*. 3d ed. New York, 1938.

————. Review of Giddings, *Principles of Sociology*. *Educational Review* 12 (1896): 88–92.

Rossides, Daniel W. *The History and Nature of Sociological Theory*. Boston, 1978.

Roucek, Joseph S. Review of Bernard, *War*. *Annals of the American Academy* 237 (1945): 204.

Rowland, Henry A. "A Plea for Pure Science." *Popular Science* 59 (1901): 170–88 [originally 1883].

Rudner, Richard S. *Philosophy of Social Science*. Englewood Cliffs, N.J., 1966.

Schneider, Joseph. "Cultural Lag." *ASR* 10 (1945): 786–91.

Schoeck, Helmut, and Wiggins, James W., eds. *Scientism and Values*. Princeton, 1960.

Schudsen, Michael. *Discovering the News*. New York, 1978.

Schwendinger, Herman and Julia R. *The Sociologists of the Chair*. New York, 1974.

Scott, Clifford H. *Lester Frank Ward*. Boston, 1976.

——. "A Naturalistic Rationale for Women's Reform." *Historian* 33 (1970): 54–67.

Sheketoff, Merwin A. "William Graham Sumner: Social Christian, 1869–72." Ph.D. dissertation, Harvard, 1961.

Shenton, Herbert N. *The Practical Applications of Sociology*. New York, 1927.

Sims, Newell L. *A Hoosier Village* (1912).

Small, Albion W. "Academic Freedom." *Arena* 22 (1899): 463–72.

——. "Americans and the World Crisis." *AJS* 23 (1917): 145–73.

——. *The Beginnings of American Nationality*. Baltimore, 1890.

——. *Between Eras*. Kansas City, Mo., 1913.

——. "The Category 'Human Process.'" *AJS* 28 (1922): 205–27.

——. "The Category 'Progress' as a Tool of Research in Social Science." *AJS* 28 (1923): 554–76.

——. "The Church and Class Conflicts." *AJS* 24 (1919): 481–501.

——. "The Civic Federation of Chicago." *AJS* 1 (1895–96): 79–103.

——. "The Era of Sociology." *AJS* 1 (1895–96): 1–15.

——. "The Evolution of a Social Standard." *AJS* 20 (1914): 10–17.

——. "Fifty Years of Sociology in the United States." *AJS* 21 (1916): 721–864.

——. *General Sociology*. Chicago, 1905.

——. "Germany and American Opinion." *Sociological Review* 8 (1915): 106–11.

——. *The Meaning of Social Science*. Chicago, 1910.

——. "Notes on Ward's *Pure Sociology*." *AJS* 9 (1903–4): 404–7, 567–75, 703–7.

——. *The Origins of Sociology*. Chicago, 1924.

——. "Points of Agreement." *AJS* 12 (1906): 633–55.

——. "The Relation between Sociology and the Other Social Sciences." *AJS* 12 (1906–7): 11–31.

——. "The Relations of the Social Sciences." *AJS* 13 (1908): 392–401.

——. Review of John Bascom, *Social Theory*. *AJS* 1 (1897): 492–94.

——. Review of Arthur Bentley, *The Process of Government*. *AJS* 13 (1908): 698–706.

——. Review of W. Crafts, *Practical Christian Sociology*. *AJS* 1 (1895–96): 494–96.

——. Review of James Q. Dealey and Lester F. Ward, *A Textbook of Sociology*. *AJS* 11 (1905): 266–68.

——. Review of Giddings, *Elements of Sociology*. *AJS* 4 (1899): 543–54.

——. Review of Giddings, *The Principles of Sociology*. *AJS* 2 (1896): 288–310.

——. Review of Robert Macintosh, *Comte to Benjamin Kidd*. *AJS* 5 (1899): 123–4.

——. Review of Gustav Schmoller, *Grundriss der allgemeinen Volkswirthschaftslehre*. *AJS* 6 (1900–1901): 423–24.

————. Review of Herbert Spencer, *Principles of Sociology*. *AJS* 2 (1897): 741–42.

————. Review of Ward, *Pure Sociology*. *PSQ* 19 (1904): 318–19.

————. "Scholarship and Social Agitation." *AJS* 1 (1895–96): 564–82.

————. "Shall Science Be Sterilized?" *AJS* 19 (1914): 651–53.

————. "Some Researches into Research." *Journal of Applied Sociology* 9 (1925): 101–2.

————. "Some Structural Material for the Idea 'Democracy.'" *AJS* 25 (1919): 257–97, 405–44.

————. *Some Undeveloped Resources in Christian Revelation*. Chicago, 1898.

————. "Technique as an Approach to Science." *AJS* 27 (1922): 646–51.

————. "A Vision of Social Efficiency." *AJS* 19 (1914): 433–45.

————. "Von Holst on American Politics." *Civil Service Reformer* (December 1888): 141–42.

Small, Albion W., and Vincent, George. *An Introduction to the Study of Society*. New York, 1894.

Smith, Dusky Lee. "Sociology and the Rise of Corporate Capitalism." *Science and Society* 29 (1965): 401–18.

Snyder, Louis L. Review of Bernard, *War*. *PSQ* 60 (1945): 119–21.

Social Science Research Council. *Decennial Report 1923–33*. New York, 1934.

Sorokin, Pitirim. *Contemporary Sociological Theories*. New York, 1928.

————. "Recent Social Trends." *Journal of Political Economy* 41 (1933): 194–210, 400–404.

————. "Sociology as a Science." *SF* 10 (1931): 21–27.

Soule, Frederick J. *An American Village Community*. New York, 1911.

Springfield Republican [on Giddings], April 24, 1925, p. 3.

Standing, T. G. "A Critique of the Concept of Cultural Lag." *Social Science* 14 (1959): 144–55.

Stanley, Hiram M. "On Primitive Consciousness." *Philosophical Review* 1 (1892): 433–42.

Starr, Harris. *William Graham Sumner*. New York, 1925.

Stern, Bernhard J., ed. "Giddings, Ward, and Small." *SF* 10 (1931–32): 305–18.

————. "Letters of Albion W. Small to Lester F. Ward." *SF* 12 (1933): 163–73; 13 (1935): 323–40; 14 (1936): 94–106; 15 (1937): 305–20.

————. "The Ward-Ross Correspondence." *ASR* 3 (1938): 362–401; 11 (1946): 593–605, 734–48; 12 (1947): 703–20; 13 (1948): 82–94; 14 (1949): 88–119.

Stevenson, Louise L. *Scholarly Means to Evangelical Ends*. Baltimore, 1986.

Storr, Richard J. *Harper's University: The Beginnings*. Chicago, 1966.

Sumner, William G. "American Finance." *Journal of Social Science* 6 (1874): 181–89.

————. *The Challenge of Facts*. Edited by A. G. Keller. New Haven, 1914.

————. "The Crisis of the Protestant Episcopal Church." *Nation* 13 (1871): 222–23.

————. "The Doctrine of Survival Again." *Index* n.s. 4 (1884): 603–4.

————. *Earth-Hunger*. Edited by A. G. Keller. New Haven, 1913.

————. *Folkways*. New York, 1960.

————. *The Forgotten Man*. Edited by A. G. Keller. New Haven, 1918.

————. "Professor Sumner's Speech." In *Herbert Spencer on the Americans*, ed. Edward L. Youmans, pp. 35–40. New York, 1883.

_____. Review of Herbert Spencer, *Descriptive Sociology. Independent*, May 14, 1874; quoted in Harris Starr, *William Graham Sumner*, p. 345.

_____. "Roscher's Political Economy." *Nation* 28 (1879): 53–54.

_____. "Socialism." *Scribner's* 16 (1878): 887–93.

_____. *War and other Essays*. Edited by Albert G. Keller. New Haven, 1911.

_____. *What Social Classes Owe To Each Other* [1883]. New York, 1911.

Sumner, William G., and Keller, Albert G. *The Science of Society*. 4 vols. New Haven, 1927.

Symnes, Lillian. "The Great Fact-Finding Farce." *Harper's* 164 (1932): 354–64.

Taft, Donald R. "Tenney." *ASR* 2 (1937): 67–68.

Tenney, Alvan A. "Franklin H. Giddings." *Columbia University Quarterly* 23 (1931): 319–21.

Thomas, William I., and Znaniecki, Florian. *The Polish Peasant in Europe and America*. 5 vols. Chicago, 1918–20.

Thorndike, Edward L. Review of Ward, *Applied Sociology. Bookman* 24 (1907): 291.

_____. Review of Ward, *Applied Sociology. Science* n.s. 24 (1906): 299.

Tjoa, Hock G. *George Henry Lewes*. Cambridge, Mass., 1977.

Todd, Edwin S. *A Sociological Study of Clark Co. Ohio*. Springfield, Ohio, 1904.

Toffler, Alvin. *Future Shock*. New York, 1970.

University Microfilms. *Comprehensive Dissertation Index: 1861–1972*. Vol. 17. Ann Arbor, 1973.

University of Chicago. *Catalogue, 1899–1900*.

Veysey, Laurence R. *The Emergence of the American University*. Chicago, 1965.

Vidich, Arthur J., and Lyman, Stanford W. *American Sociology: Worldly Rejections of Religion and Their Direction*. New Haven, 1985.

Vincent, George. Review of Sumner, *Folkways. AJS* 13 (1908): 414–17.

Vincent, Melvin J. "Trends and Emphases in Sociology." *Sociology and Social Research* 33 (1949): 255–62.

Ward, (Charles) Henshaw. *Thobbing*. Indianapolis, 1926.

Ward, James F. "Bentley and the Foundations of Behavioral Science." *Journal of the History of the Behavioral Sciences* 17 (1981): 222–31.

Ward, Lester Frank. *Applied Sociology*. New York, 1906.

_____. "Contemporary Sociology." *AJS* 7 (1902): 475–500, 629–58, 749–62.

_____. *Dynamic Sociology*. 2 vols. New York, 1883.

_____. "The Essential Nature of Religion." *Ethics* 8 (1898): 169–92; in Ward, *Glimpses*, 6:9–32.

_____. *Glimpses of the Cosmos*. 6 vols. New York, 1913–18.

_____. "The Gospel of Action." *Independent* 51 (1899): 1865–68; in Ward, *Glimpses*, 6:56–63.

_____. *Haeckel's Genesis of Man*. Philadelphia, 1879; in Ward, *Glimpses*, 2:64–140.

_____. "Kant's Antinomies." *Journal of Speculative Philosophy* (1881): 381–95; in Ward, *Glimpses*, 3:1–17.

_____. "Neo-Darwinism and Neo-Lamarckianism" [January 24, 1891]; in Ward, *Glimpses*, 4:253–95.

_____. "Organization." *Iconoclast* 2 (1871); in Ward, *Glimpses*, 1:167–68.

_____. *Outlines of Sociology*. New York, 1897.

_____. *Pure Sociology*. New York, 1903.

_____. Review of Giddings, *Principles of Sociology*. *Annals of the American Academy* 8 (1896): 1–31.

_____. "The Transmission of Culture." *Forum* 11 (1891): 312–19; in Ward, *Glimpses*, 4:246–52.

_____. "Weismann's Concessions." *Popular Science* 45 (1894): 175–84.

_____. "Weismann's New Essays," in Ward, *Glimpses*, 4:327–28.

_____. "Weismann's Theory of Heredity," in Ward, *Glimpses*, 4:385–88.

_____. *Young Ward's Diary*. Edited by Bernhard J. Stern. New York, 1935.

Warshay, Leon H. "The Current State of Sociological Theory." *Sociological Quarterly* 12 (1971): 23–43.

_____. *The Current State of Sociological Theory*. New York, 1975.

Watkins, Bari. Review of Mary Furner, *Advocacy and Objectivity*. *History and Theory* 15 (1976): 57–66.

Whitaker, Bruce E. "The Social Philosophy of Charles A. Ellwood." *North Carolina Historical Review* 49 (1972): 152–59.

White, James T., ed. *National Cyclopedia of American Biography*. 50 vols. Ann Arbor, Mich., 1968.

White, Morton G. *Social Thought in America*. New York, 1949.

Wiley, Norbert. "Recent Journal Sociology." *Contemporary Sociology* 8 (1979): 794–95.

Willey, Malcolm M. and Nancy B. "The Conditioned Reflex and the Consciousness of Kind." *AJS* 30 (1924): 22–28.

Williams, Richard H. Review of Bernard, *Social Control*. *ASR* 5 (1940): 131–32.

Winchell, Alexander. *Reconciliation of Science and Religion*. New York, 1877.

Woodward, James W. "Critical Notes on the Nature of Sociology." *SF* 11 (1932–33): 388–98.

_____. "A New Classification of Culture." *ASR* 1 (1936): 89–102.

Woofter, Thomas J. *Negro Migration*. New York, 1920.

Young, Donald. "A Note on Procedure in the Planning of Research." *AJS* 42 (1936–37): 95–99.

INDEX